PAUL AND THE MOSAIC LAW

Paul and the Mosaic Law

edited by

James D. G. Dunn

The Third Durham-Tübingen Research Symposium
on Earliest Christianity and Judaism
(Durham, September, 1994)

WILLIAM B. EERDMANS PUBLISHING COMPANY
GRAND RAPIDS, MICHIGAN / CAMBRIDGE, U.K.

Originally published 1996 by J. C. B. Mohr (Paul Siebeck)
P.O. Box 2040, D-7400 Tübingen, Germany
as volume 89 in the series
Wissenschaftliche Untersuchungen zum Neuen Testament

This edition, with new English translations, published 2001 by
Wm. B. Eerdmans Publishing Company
255 Jefferson Ave. S.E., Grand Rapids, Michigan 49503/
P.O. Box 163, Cambridge CB3 9PU U.K.
www.eerdmans.com

Library of Congress Cataloging-in-Publication Data

Durham-Tübingen Research Symposium on Earliest Christianity and Judaism
(3rd : 1994 : University of Durham)
Paul and the Mosaic law / edited by James D. G. Dunn ; the Third Durham-Tübingen
Research Symposium on Earliest Christianity and Judaism, Durham, September, 1994.
p.   cm.
Includes bibliographical references and indexes.
ISBN 0-8028-4499-5 (pbk. : alk. paper)
1. Paul, the Apostle, Saint — Views on Jewish law — Congresses. 2. Bible. N.T.
Epistles of Paul — Criticism, interpretation, etc. — Congresses. 3. Jewish
law — Congresses.   I. Dunn, James D. G., 1939-   II. Title.
BS2655.L35 D85 1994a
241'.2'09015 — dc21

00-050361

In Honour

of

Charles E. B. Cranfield

Emeritus Professor of Divinity
University of Durham

to celebrate his
80th birthday
13 September 1995

Contents

Preface

The third Durham-Tübingen Research Symposium on Earliest Christianity and Judaism met in St John's College, Durham, from September 19 to 23 in 1994. It followed the same pattern as the previous meetings of the Symposium: the first on 'Paulus, Missionar und Theologe, und das antike Judentum', which met at Tübingen in September 1988 and whose papers were published under the same title in 1991;[1] and the second on 'The Parting of the Ways, AD 70 to 135', which met at Durham in September 1989, and whose papers were published in 1992.[2] The pattern had been established at a previous Tübingen Symposium, organised by Peter Stuhlmacher, on 'Das Evangelium und die Evangelien' in September 1982, whose papers appeared a year later.[3]

The pattern is a simple but effective one, which has now proved itself over four Symposia. The key to success is threefold: first, to limit numbers to about 16 where all are actively engaged at a professional level with the subject of the Symposium; second, to meet for a number of days for intensive working sessions, but interspersed with opportunities for social relaxation; and third, to ensure as far as possible that papers are distributed beforehand, with introductions limited to 20–30 minutes and more than an hour allowed for discussion. In this case some of the thirteen sessions were overloaded: there was a much more positive response to initial invitations than had been anticipated! And there was the usual problem of some papers arriving late, limiting the time for preparatory reading. But as before, the blend of intensive debate (where numbers allowed all who wished to participate to do so and at sufficient length to make their point clear) and casual conversation over meals and on the outing gave the discussions a richness, including (I do not say despite) the diversity of views involved, which is often lacking in other academic exchanges. In this case, living and meeting as we did in the shadow of Durham's great Norman cathedral, the sense of collegiality and common purpose which the few days engendered among us was quite exceptional in quality and will live in our memories for a long time.

---

[1] *Paulus und das antike Judentum*, hrsg. M. Hengel & U. Heckel (WUNT 58; Tübingen: J.C.B. Mohr, 1991).

[2] *Jews and Christians: The Parting of the Ways A.D. 70 to 135*, ed. J.D.G. Dunn (WUNT 66; Tübingen: J.C.B. Mohr, 1992).

[3] *Das Evangelium und die Evangelien*, hrsg. P. Stuhlmacher (WUNT 28; Tübingen: J.C.B. Mohr, 1983).

As usual the Symposium was composed of a core of Durhamites and Tübingers with other international participants invited to take part. On this occasion, with so many engaged in the discussion on 'Paul and the Law', it was not possible to draw in the full range of those who have taken a leading part in the debate over the past fifteen to twenty years. The object was rather to achieve a representative spread of the leading New Testament scholars actively engaged in this area of contemporary debate, and in this we succeeded. Indeed, it would be hard to conceive of a more high-powered and representative gathering on this subject anywhere in the world.

This very fact may have engendered hopes and even expectations of a degree of consensus among the Symposiasts which were too high or unrealistic. One member of the postgraduate support team wrote afterwards: 'War denn in Durham nicht die Elite einer ganzen Generation von Neutestamentlern zusammengekommen? Ein jeder wußte ausgesprochen vernünftig und mit unwiderleglich durchdachten Argumenten zu debattieren, und doch war an Konvergenz in der Frage "Paul and the Law" nicht zu denken.'

Yet neither should the extent of the disagreement and diversity of opinion be exaggerated. The great bulk of disagreement was in fact contained within broad parameters of agreement. The final paper attempts to sketch out these parameters and to suggest that much of the continuing disagreement is disagreement of emphasis, or, was we might say, disagreement over the effect of perspective and the degree of light and shade appropriate in transferring such a complex subject on to our own two-dimensional canvas. Moreover, since there will always be disagreement on points of interpretation, it is equally, perhaps more important, that those who disagree learn to appreciate the strengths (as well as the weaknesses) of the others' opinions, and to frame their own views in such a way as to recognize and, if possible, incorporate these strengths (the revision of the papers following the Symposium and before publication has given opportunity for this). When the degree of complementarity is thus brought more clearly to light the extent and seriousness of the continuing disagreements can be given their proper weight.

Of those originally envisaged as taking part, Sandy Wedderburn's appointment to a Chair in München caused him to withdraw early on, though happily his newly arrived successor, Loren Stuckenbruck, was able to participate. Unfortunately Peter Stuhlmacher and Robert Jewett also had to pull out later on because of unforeseen obligations, though the presence of Paul Trebilco on research leave in Durham was an unplanned-for bonus. The members of the Symposium were delighted that Kingsley Barrett and Charles Cranfield were able to be present for some of the meetings, and still more delighted to be able to dedicate their papers to Charles in appreciation of his own work on the subject and in honour of his 80th birthday.

Thanks are especially due to the local team of postgraduates who took a mountain of work from my shoulders and left me free for the main chairing and coordinating roles in organisation – particularly Elizabeth Danna, Jey Kanagaraj, Ken Schenk and Derek Tovey. Also part of the support team were Friedrich Avemarie, Wieland Bopp, Carsten Claußen, George van Kooten, Ivar Vegge, and Arie Zwiep. Their occasional contributions to the discussion from 'the outer circle' only enhanced its value. Also featuring in the photographs of the occasion is the warum supporting presence of Marianne Hengel.

Thanks are due to the British Academy, the University of Durham Research Committee and the Durham Department of Theology and Durham Centre for Theolocial Research for their funding and sponsorship of the Symposium. Also to the Dean of Durham, John Arnold and his wife Anneliese, for offering a welcome and nightcap on the first night in the splendid Deanery, to the University of Durham and the Cathedral Chapter for delightful receptions during the course of the Symposium, to Dr. Ian Doyle and again the Chapter for much-appreciated tours of the Castle and the Cathedral, and to St John's College for providing such collegial-inducing and effective facilities. J.C.B. Mohr have done their usual efficient job in producing a volume which is a pleasure to handle and, hoffentlich, a profit to peruse.

Durham, Conversion of John Wesley,   James D.G. Dunn
May 24, 1995

Introduction

by

JAMES D.G. DUNN

For those who have spent many years studying the theology of Paul the present-day Sturm und Drang over the question of Paul and the Mosaic Law must have come as something of a surprise. Up until the last fifteen years or so there was no real debate on the subject. For the most part lectures and textbooks seemed content to rehearse lines of exposition and solutions to old exegetical problems which had been settled in previous generations. If truth be told, the subject had become boring to many students and scholars, not worth much original effort on the part of those anxious to make their name in New Testament scholarship, the results being too predictable.

As is now widely recognized among Pauline specialists, however, a new phase in Pauline studies was introduced by E.P. Sanders' *Paul and Palestinian Judaism*.[1] In English speaking scholarship my own description of Sanders' work, in the T.W. Manson Memorial Lecture of 1982, as opening up a 'new perspective on Paul',[2] seems to have caught the mood of a more widespread perception. In contrast, the initial response from within Germanspeaking scholarship was a good deal less sympathetic. As one German colleague expressed it to me, what was sound in Sanders' analysis of early Judaism was familiar to them and had already been well expressed in M. Limbeck's *Die Ordnung des Heils: Untersuchungen zum Gesetzesverständnis des Frühjudentums*.[3] However the translation of Sanders into German[4] and the hum of debate in Britain and north America occasioned by Sanders has made it impossible for the most recent wave of German-speaking scholarship to avoid addressing the challenge posed by Sanders – even if the seeming disparagement of Luther, and of some classic Lutheran scholarship, which has been a feature of Sanders' polemical style grates harshly with many German schol-

---

[1] London: SCM, 1977.

[2] 'The New Perspective on Paul', *BJRL* 65 (1983) 95–122; reprinted with slight modification and Additional Note in my *Jesus, Paul and the Law* (London: SPCK / Louisville: Westminster, 1990) 183–214. The perspective has been substantially refined in the intervening twelve years.

[3] Düsseldorf: Patmos. 1971.

[4] *Paulus und das palästinische Judentum* (SUNT 17; Göttingen, 1985).

ars.[5] The breadth and vigour of the debate to date is sufficiently indicated by the fact that in compiling a bibligraphy for the Symposium it was not difficult to amass some 150 titles (essays and monographs) on the subject, well over half of them with 'law' or 'Torah' in the title.[6]

It is probably unnecessary here to retrace the course of the renewed debate on the subject of Paul and the Law. It has been traced several times in the interim,[7] and those interested in the papers from the Symposium will probably be already familiar with it. Suffice it to say that Sanders' protest against the denigration of Second Temple Judaism as characterised by a teaching of 'works-righteousness' has been widely accepted. But the role of the law within Second Temple Judaism remains disputed. Does Sanders' alternative summary phrase, 'covenantal nomism', serve more effectively? Even if 'doing' the law was not required for 'getting in' to the covenant people, was the doing of the law, which on Sanders' formulation was necessary for 'staying in',[8] equally tantamount to making salvation dependent on 'doing' the law?

Räisänen's *Paul and the Law* heightened the crisis by postulating a Paul whose several treatments of the law in his writing, including passages within the same letter, cannot adequately be reconciled and must be left in uncomfortable juxtaposition. His work remains a standing caution to all who seek for easy syntheses, and an unavoidable challenge to all who claim to have found such a synthesis, as to whether they have given enough weight to the awkward elements and passages in Paul's letters.

My own various attempts to integrate Paul himself into Sanders' new perspective on Second Temple Judaism have focused on the social function of the law, particularly in its role of separating off Jew from Gentile.[9] That such a role is to be recognized has also gained considerable support, but the degree to which that role is focused in Paul's phrase, 'the works of the law', has been more controversial,[10] though the significance of the appearance of the phrase in the newly published 4QMMT has yet to be fully appreciated.[11]

---

[5] See now M. Hengel & R. Deines. 'E.P. Sanders' "Common Judaism", Jesus and the Pharisees. A Review Article' *JTS* 46 (1995) 1–70 (here 68–9).

[6] See the bibliography at the back, to which the following bibliographical references refer.

[7] See e.g. Barclay, 'Paul and the Law'; Bruce, 'Paul and the Law'; Klein, 'Sturmzentrum'; Laato § 2; Moo, 'Paul and the Law'; Schreiner, *Law* 13–31; Thielman, *Paul and the Law* 14–47; Wedderburn; Westerholm, *Israel's Law*; and Zeller. As well as being the most recent, Thielman's review is one of the best informed.

[8] See my 'In Search of Common Ground' below n. 5.

[9] See my *Jesus, Paul and the Law,* particularly chap. 8.

[10] See my 'Yet Once More' .

[11] See particularly M. Abegg, 'Paul, "Works of the Law" and MMT', *Biblical Archaeological Review* 20.6 (1994) 52–55, 82; and my forthcoming '4QMMT and Galatians' *NTS*.

Westerholm in particular has responded by arguing that behind the social function of the law is clearly the more fundamental issue of whether salvation depends on human activity, and it this which Paul has in mind in his key argument, Rom. 4.4–5. This passage, above all others, shows that Luther was right in understanding works of the law to denote human effort in antithesis to divine grace.

Major questions therefore remain. For example, does the phrase 'works of the law' express Jewish self-understanding (and if so what?), or simply Paul's own (possibly idiosyncratic) experience of the law? What is the focus of Paul's critique of the law? How to correlate the seemingly positive assertions he also makes (about believers fulfilling the law) with his more negative comments? Can all his statements about the law be synthesized into a single coherent view?

And within these larger questions particular questions arise. For example, Did Second Temple Judaism expect/require 'perfect' obedience to the law? What was the impact of the Damascus road event (Paul's conversion) on his view of the law? What was the issue at Antioch (Gal. 2.11–14) and to what was Paul objecting in Gal. 2.16?[12] How negative is Paul's treatment of the law in Gal. 3–4? How should the law/Torah be related to the 'old covenant' and the *gramma* in 2 Cor. 3? How does Rom. 2 function within the letter? How to translate/understand *nomos* in Rom. 3.27 and 8.2? How to understand Rom. 4.4–5 within the flow of the argument? Does Paul conceive of the law as a 'power' like sin and death in Rom. 5? Is Rom. 7.7–25 intended primarily as a defence of the law, and what does 8.3-4 say about the law and its (continuing) function for believers? How much weight should be given to Rom. 9.4 *(nomothesia* as one of Israel's blessings), and how should the train of thought from 9.30–10.8 be evaluated in reference to the law? Does 1 Cor. 7.19 indicate that Paul saw Christian paraenesis as a kind of halakah? How does Paul's own social conduct (1 Cor. 9) and the conduct he advocated for churches to which he wrote (particularly Rom. 14–15) relate to and interact upon his view of the law?

These were some of the questions posed when the Symposium was set up. They were not intended to be prescriptive and contributors were left quite free to develop their presentations as they wished. It seemed wiser to focus on the key passages in the current debate, and so passages were assigned to participants in accordance with their own preferences and suggestions so far as was possible. Given the starting point of the 'new perspective' and the ongoing character of the debate, it was obviously important to start with the understanding and function of the Torah within Second Temple Judaism. Equally

---

[12] As will be evident from my own work, I regard these last two questions and areas in Paul as of particular importance in illuminating his thought on the law.

obvious was the need to give early consideration to the impact of Paul's conversion and of his preliterary career on his view of the law. Thereafter, however, it was simply a case of working through the most important passages in sequence, without making too much depend on issues of chronological relationship.

And so the Symposium proceeded with fifteen papers in twelve sessions, two of those involved in the double sessions designed as responses to the session's main paper. As may be imagined, with participants like Hengel, Hofius, Hübner, Räisänen and Wright, the contributions were very frank and the discussion very vigorous. But always with good humour and mutual respect and never once (so far as the chairman recalls) a note of rancour.

At the end no major opinion had been radically altered or abandoned. That never was likely, nor was it to be expected. On the contrary, the participants had been invited precisely because they already had well-formed and well-informed views on the subject. Damascus road conversions we did not look for! The objective was rather to enable the strengths of these various views to be fed into the whole in the hope that the others would recognize these strengths and seek to incorporate them in some measure into their own views. Apart from anything else, where mutual respect and regard has been engendered and strengthened by such a Symposium, it becomes harder to ignore, misrepresent and dismiss the Gesprächpartner who continues to disagree. And the very effort to give and take genuine account of the other participant's view in future writing is bound to change the content and character of that writing for the better. Consequently, no 'How I changed my mind' pieces may be expected from the members of the Symposium. At the same time, however, the opportunity for each participant to revise his paper after the Symposium and in the light of the Symposium's discussions should mean that the contributions to the following volume have a roundedness and sympathetic awareness of alternative views which helps forward the continuing debate on Paul and the Law in the most positive terms.

The final session was intended as an opportunity to draw threads together into some kind of overview which would pull together as much as possible of what was agreed and integrate as much as possible of what was disagreed! In the time available that proved over-ambitious. It would probably have been impossible to draft a consensual statement which went beyond broad methodological agreement and generalised affirmations. Something could certainly have been produced, had we had sufficient time. But the Symposium was not a church body having to produce a report which could serve as basis for teaching and further study. And beyond the generalisations, the nuances which each would call for, to ensure his own view was properly represented, would soon lose the positive effect of the agreed statements in a mist of qualifications.

Instead I was charged by the Symposium to reflect on the whole sub ject as illuminated by the papers and discussion, to attempt to convey something of the scope, character and content of the discussion, including the measure of agreement and disagreement, and, in effect, to try to illustrate the success of the Symposium's objective by restating my own position in the light of and as influenced by the discussions of the Symposium. This I have attempted to do, with what success (or otherwise) I must leave others to judge.

The Understanding of the Torah
in the Judaism of Paul's Day

A Sketch*

by

HERMANN LICHTENBERGER

I. The State of the Discussion

Many determined attempts have been made to describe the calamitous story of
the way from the closing decades of the last century Christian biblical scholarship has distorted the Jewish understanding of the Torah, with devastating ramifications for our interpretation of both Judaism and early Christianity, Paul in
particular. All this may be found most clearly and extensively in the work of
E. P. Sanders,[1] and with a sense of relief, almost two decades after his *Paul and
Palestinian Judaism* appeared, we may now hope to have outlived the demonic
days when the cliché held sway that Judaism was enmired in a commercial
works righteousness, in a narrow ritualistic casuistry, and in a sterile relationship with God. Wellhausen used to speak ungraciously about post-prophetic Judaism. He failed to realize the supreme significance of Lev. 18:5 in the rabbinic
understanding of the Torah.[2] His conclusion was that after Ezekiel the laws existed in order that the people might live by them. He judged harshly the system
of Pharisaic statutes. Instead of promoting life, they hampered it. The law

* Thanks are owed to M. Hämmerle for typing the mauscript and to Dr. F. Avemarie for reviewing it and for constant aid.

1. *Paul and Palestinian Judaism*, London 1977.
2. Cf. D. R. Schwartz, *Leben durch Jesus versus Leben durch die Torah. Zur Religionspolemik
der ersten Jahrhunderte, Franz Delitzsch Vorlesung 1991*, Munich 1993, p. 5.

served only to spoil morality and to deaden religion. A veritable idolatry of the law was predominant.[3]

In the theological atmosphere of the early 20th century, which was influenced by Wellhausen, even such an undisputed scholar as P. Billerbeck, well known for his acquaintance with the Jewish literature of antiquity, could be misled into disqualifying ancient Jewish religion as one of total self-redemption.[4] Today we do not find such striking misjudgments. Only occasionally and very unexpectedly does more recent literature speak of Jewish rigidity and mummification, or refer to the Jewish God as an archaic God of the land and people, or to the fact that only scribes could fulfill the complicated law.[5]

A distinctive mark of the rethinking that has taken place in the seventies is the revised English edition of Schürer's standard work on earlier Jewish history.[6] Schürer himself, writing about life under the law,[7] had shown little sympathy for Jewish religion, and little concern to acquire a deeper understanding. He had dismissed as irrelevant some of the leading principles of Jewish theology. When considering the saying of Antigonus to Socho: "Be like those who do not serve for a reward but who serve without any reward in view," he stated that this did not correctly express the basic attitude of Pharisaic Judaism, which always had the reward as its goal (II, p. 548). Under the title "Life and Law" the English revision offers a comprehensive reformulation (II, pp. 464ff.) and does justice to the saying of Antigonus, which "foreshadows many similar counsels preserved in rabbinic literature" (II, p. 466). The reformulation that follows is a little hesitant, especially in the Introduction. This had formerly called the period that of the reign of Pharisaism, whose legal orientation had been established by Ezra, but which had carried things much further than Ezra ever did. It was not enough now to meet the demands of the biblical

---

3. *Israelitische und jüdische Geschichte,* 9th ed. 1958, pp. 283f.

4. *Kommentar zum NT aus Talmud und Midrasch,* Vol. IV, Munich 1928, p. 6.

5. Cf. K. Beyer, *Die aramäischen Texte vom Toten Meer, Ergänzungsband,* Göttingen 1994, pp. 60f. In the 1984 edition Beyer claimed that Judaism interposed the law between individuals and their neighbors and a hair-splitting casuistry developed. God was silenced and disappeared into a great distance (p. 158). This however, does not appear in the *Ergänzungsband,* and instead we find references to the work of Sanders.

6. E. Schürer, *The History of the Jewish People in the Age of Jesus Christ (175 B.C.–A.D. 135): A New English Version,* revised and edited by G. Vermes, F. Millar et al., Vol. I–III, 2. Edinburgh 1973, 1987. Cf. M. Hengel. "Der alte und der neue 'Schürer,'" JJS 35 (1990), pp. 19-72.

7. Cf. the German version of Schürer's work, Vol. II, 4th ed. Leipzig 1907, pp. 545ff. His attitude is best summed up when he says that legal piety resulted in *"an incredible externalizing of religious and moral life"* (II, p. 548), which he himself underlined.

Torah. These were divided into minute and scrupulous individual statutes, and observing these was a sacred duty, indeed, was seen as a condition of blessedness. This enhanced legalism gained unconditional control over the minds of the people and pushed all other tendencies into the background (I,2). We find a more careful formulation in the revised version: "The chief characteristic of this period was the growing importance of Pharisaism. The legalistic orientation initiated by Ezra has slowly developed into a religio-social system in which it was no longer sufficient to fulfill the commandments of the written Torah; the generalities of biblical law were resolved into an immense number of detailed precepts. The performance of which was imposed as a most sacred duty. Though never universally followed, and never completely divorced from truly spiritual and even charismatic tendencies, this concern with the punctilious observance of the minutiae of religion became the hallmark of mainstream Judaism" (I,1).

Regarding the prohibition of work on the Sabbath, Schürer tells us that this simple command was naturally not enough for the rabbis. They had to define what kinds of work were forbidden. With considerable acuteness they reached the conclusion that thirty-nine types of work come under this prohibition, though there is very little trace of these in the Pentateuch (II, 552). The new Schürer avoids the ironic tone: "The short pentateuchal ban on work on the Sabbath day . . . grew in the course of time into a lengthy Mishnah tractate. For the rabbis, feeling it necessary to be more exact, specified the following thirty-nine activities as forbidden on the Sabbath" (II, 468). In his judgment on Jewish worship, Schürer claimed that the center of religious life, namely, prayer, had become fettered in a rigid mechanism, and the result was that a vital piety was no longer possible. Judaism had already taken this fatal step in the days of Christ. The revised edition, we may thankfully note, omitted this judgment and did not try to replace it.

Jewish interest in NT scholarship cannot, of course, be content with the way in which Sanders' *Paul and Palestinian Judaism* has finally put prejudices to rest. The breach that Sanders made, by way of the problem of the Christian perspective, initiated a new and possibly stricter approach to the question of Jewish law. Of great significance is the manner in which the Jewish side takes up the issue that NT theology has posed. We can look at this from two angles. In a Franz-Delitzsch lecture at Münster in 1992, D. R. Schwartz assailed the downgrading of a religion that promises a reward for obedience to God, and put forward a revisionist exegesis that Paul never assumed that the thinking of the Jews was that the Torah promised a reward, thereby sheltering both Paul and

Judaism.[8] On good grounds the loaded term "work-righteousness" no longer appears in the vocabulary of NT scholarship, yet the question remains whether this ancient error might still find a place in the way that many scholars not only perceive but also assess traditional Jewish ideas relating to obedience to the Torah and to merit and reward.[9]

Secondly, H. J. Schoeps showed some decades ago that from the very first Christianity had a fatally perverted understanding of the Torah and that the Christian church, following the Jews of the Hellenistic diaspora, who assimilated themselves to contemporary thinking and alienated themselves from the faith of their forefathers, adopted a totally distorted picture of the Jewish law.[10] We will perhaps be disturbed by the provocative tone in which Schoeps speaks of the apostle to the Gentiles. We ought perhaps to remember that according to Acts Paul received his training in Jerusalem. Nevertheless, an explanation must be sought on why the Pauline corpus seems to take a different view of the Mosaic law at many points, both in general and in detail, from the view that Jewish studies have advanced during recent years.

Research into Judaism needs to be developed and deepened. It would be fatal if Sanders' *Paul and Palestinian Judaism,* which has been a standard work for some time, suffered the same fate as Billerbeck's *Kommentar zum NT aus Talmud und Midrasch,* which by its monumental fullness, except in a few details, released a whole generation of scholars from any independent study of the sources. Even after Sanders the question of the Jewish law is still at issue. In relation to rabbinic traditions, the Tübingen dissertation of F. Avemaria[11] has adduced a broad array of sources in a critical testing of the positions of Sanders (and his predecessors). In large part this supports Sanders' view of the way the rabbis understood the Torah, but it also revises it at certain points.[12] Above all it

---

8. Op. cit. (n. 2), pp. 10f. Schwartz appeals to the saying of Antigonus to Socho and is not satisfied with the revision of Schürer that this is an exception to the rule (n. 12).

9. He points out that this assessment results in a limited perception which largely obscures the mercy and forgiveness of God.

10. *Paulus,* Tübingen 1959, p. 278. Paul is described as a "theologian of misunderstanding" who "was also basically misunderstood by his followers." The history of the interpretation of Paul is a long chain of misunderstanding and the theology of Paul is "one of potential misunderstanding" (p. 279).

11. *Torah und Leben. Untersuchungen zur Heilsbedeutung der Tora in der frühen rabbinischen Literatur,* TSAJ, Tübingen 1996.

12. Ibid., p. 43. Avemaria admits that Sanders' work is a contribution that will set the standard for a long time to come. Sanders dealt with the debatable core issues, used a vast array of passages from the rabbinic tradition, and in spite of reservations offered a fascinating and impressively clear

shows that the many voices of the Tannaitic tradition cannot be reduced to a few clear and prominent lines, and that as regards the basis of the Torah and its claim to obedience various views may be found alongside one another.

In the sketch that follows the rabbinic literature will not be treated apart form this basis. The themes will be restricted to the period prior to the destruction of the temple. What people thought and said about the Jewish law in the lifetime of Paul was not then affected by the factual destruction of the Jewish cultus or the deporting of the rest of the people from their Jewish homeland. This gap was, of course, crossed; we find links and continuities, especially between the Tannaites and Paul.[13] The coming of A.D. 70 made a deep impression on the intellectual development of Judaism. We can see this as we detect how the theological catastrophe of the destruction of the temple affected the apocalypses of 4 Esdras and Syr. Baruch.

In what follows our focus will be only on the Qumran texts and Greek-speaking Jewish literature prior to A.D. 70 along with the writings of Josephus, which are rooted in the spirit of this age.

II. The Torah in the Qumran Texts

1. Directions for Life and Lifestyle

Reading, expounding, and following the Torah defined the life of the Qumran community and its members in every area. On entry (1QS 5,7ff.; CD 15,5ff.; 1QH 14,17ff., cf Jos. Bell. 2,139-142) the candidate pledged to observe the Torah with all its implications as seen by the community. In the formulas of blessing and cursing divine blessing is pronounced upon those who keep the Torah and cursing upon those who do not. Entry and membership signify separation between flagrant offenders (1QS 5,8-11) and those who take upon themselves the covenant pledge. The Torah governs this separation according to the interpretation that the community found for the universal will of God. The conduct

---

presentation. In opposition to the schematisms of Weber and Bousset, he adopted an unconditionally welcome counterposition in favorably interpreting rabbinic ideas of salvation. Yet even he at times let himself be obstructed by exaggerated interpretations and doubtful systematizations in relation to everything that the rabbis had to say about the Torah.

13. In the final sections of his dissertation Avemaria indicates some possible contacts (op. cit., pp. 584-89).

of the members, both inwardly and outwardly, was shaped thereby. They had to love their fellow members and hate flagrant offenders. This was in keeping with the conduct of God himself, who hates the evil and loves the good (1QS 1,3f.). Right action has been commanded by God through Moses and his servants the prophets (1QS 1,3). What the law and the prophets tells us is good and righteous in God's sight (1QS 1,2). That, however, is not enough for this Jewish community. Its profile emerges in the statement that it is to be counted against those outside the community — and the reference is not to the Gentiles — that they have not sought out and found God in his commandments in a way that enables them to know the "hidden things" in which they have culpably gone astray (1QS 5,11f.). The "hidden things" are things specifically known by the community.

We can work out historically how the Qumran community differed from the rest of Judaism as regards their exclusive observance of the Torah. The history of Israel is for them a history of nonobservance of the divine commandments, the forefathers (CD 3,2f.) and a remnant that survived the disaster of 587 B.C. (CD 3,10) being excepted. With these latter God set up an eternal covenant for Israel which would reveal to them the "hidden things" regarding which the rest of Israel was in error (CD 3,13f.). Along with the Torah the "hidden things" form the core of the divine direction whose observance gives life (CD 3,15f.). On the one side is the remnant that observes the commandments; God causes the community to develop out of them. On the other side is the rest of Israel. The community is convinced that it alone keeps the Torah. Specific doctrines distinguished it from other Jewish groups, for example, in questions of the calendar, in rules of purity and marriage. But these had been derived from the Torah, so that rejection of the community was seen as a despising of the Torah.

The covenant at Sinai also defined the identity of the community. It is true that those with whom God had set up this covenant went astray. They chose to follow their own wills. They walked in the hardness of their hearts. For this reason they were destroyed (CD 3,10-112). But out of those who kept God's commandments, a remnant, God established his eternal covenant. From this group, to whom God revealed his will (CD 3,13, 16), there developed a preliminary stage of the community (CD 3,18-20, cf. also CD 1,4ff.). Two things are important in this regard. First, the community regards itself as in continuity with Israel and God's action in relation to his people. Second, there is also discontinuity with the rest of Israel, for its history was one of apostasy from God until the day when God raised up a remnant who would keep his commandments as distinct from erring Israel. The covenant that Israel had broken has been newly set up in the community, and by conversion its members have found access to it.

The covenant pledge accepted by entrants corresponds to membership in the divinely reinstituted covenant. Those who join are to do all the things that are commanded (1QS 1,16f.). Included in the covenant are the "words of this covenant" (2,13) which the entrants must hear and confirm with their Amen (2,10 and 18). In this context reference is also made to the "curses of this covenant" (2,16) which will fall upon those who are inwardly resistant. A corresponding feature is that the candidates and members are described as these who show themselves willing.[14] Entry into the covenant involves a relationship to the Torah but it is not grounded upon divine predestination, as is often stated generally for Qumran. Instead, it involves a *voluntary* separation from sin and sinners, a turning to the Torah of Moses, and an acceptance of the community ordinances. Living according to the Torah can be depicted as a perfect walk along the ways of God (1QS 2,2), and blessing falls upon the doing of the good (1QS 2,2-4). Conversely, the parallel curse means that sinners are given up to the wrath of God and to eternal destruction. Blessing and cursing ratify the strict antithesis between the righteous and transgressors that may be seen in human actions. The possibility of observing the Torah is presupposed. So, too, is the freedom not to obey. The Torah causes a division between the righteous and sinners, between those who belong to the community and those who reject discipleship. By giving *direction* for life and lifestyle the Torah gives individuals in the community a solid anchoring their relation to God and to neighbors. It offers a framework within the community in which they can lead their lives in a way that is pleasing to God and gives the promise of salvation. The community and its members are called doers of the Torah (1QbHab 8,1; 12,4f.), while those who reject their interpretation of the Torah are called its despisers (1QpHb 1,11).

2. The Torah and the Creator

In the admonition CD 2-3 we find a very pointed linking of God as Lawgiver and God as Creator (2,21; 3,8). The kindling of wrath is the result of nonfulfill-

---

14. In the Nifal *ha-niddabim* in QS1, 7 and 11, in the Hitpael *ha-mitnaddebim* in QS 5,1 and 6 and passim.

ment of the divine will. Transgressing the law means disobedience to the Creator. Transgressors do not accept their creatureliness as constituting a divine
claim. If we ask why there is this link between the Creator and the Lawgiver,
we are self-evidently referred to the Torah, which already in Gen. 2:16f. speaks
of the of the divine will. Transgressing the law means disobedience to the Creator. Transgressors do not accept their creatureliness as constituting a divine
claim. If we ask why there is this link between the Creator and the Lawgiver,
we are self-evidently referred to the Torah, which already in Gen. 2:16f. speaks
of the command of the Creator. Authority attaches to the Torah as a whole. For
this reason those who transgressed the commandments even in the days before
Sinai will still be punished (CD 2,17ff.).

Since the fall of angels in prehistoric times (CD 2,17-19) every generation
has resisted the divine commands apart from a few individuals (CD 3,2-5) and
the remnant (CD 3,12f.) out of whom God has fashioned the Qumran community. All people have gone their own ways and walked in the hardness of their
hearts. Two constants mark this history of the world and humanity. First is the
faithfulness of God, which is unchanging. The second is the hardness of human
hearts, which is first pierced only by the Qumran community. The faithfulness
of God means that although he punishes his continually disobedient people, he
leaves himself a remnant, namely, those who hold fast to his commandments.

Relating to God as Creator and Lawgiver, human sin takes on a distinctive
twist. For Qumran sin is human self-will as a nonacceptance of human
creatureliness.[15] Sin, however, is not a destiny that we cannot evade. It rests on
the free decision of each generation. Basic here is the human responsibility of
those who are claimed as creatures and must follow the will of God, not their
own desires.

Rejection of the divine commandments is not traced back to a disposition to
sin grounded in human creatureliness, nor to temptation by demonic powers. It
rests on human choice (cf. CD 2,15; 3,2). The admonition emphasizes, of
course, that the possibilities open to us are not on the same level. We must
choose between salvation and perdition, between life and death. Yet we can
choose, and the history of Israel shows us that we must only choose that which
is pleasing to God and hate that which he hates (CD 2,15).

---

15. M. Limbeck, *Die Ordnung des Heils,* Düsseldorf 1971, p. 121 with a reference to CD 2,21;
3,8.

3. Radicalization or a Saving Order?

If we look at Judaism as a religion of law,[16] the Qumran community will seem to be an especially radical form of observance.[17] In fact the Qumran community does support a more rigorous exposition than the Pharisaic Rabbinic Halacha as concerns many details, for example, matters of cleanness, keeping the Sabbath, and the laws of marriage. Is this a particularly radical form of legalism or does it express a responsive attitude to God? This must be considered. We can adduce one text that above all others represents a very strict way of understanding the Torah. This is 4QMMT,[18] which contains the letter of a Qumranic leader (perhaps the Teacher of Righteousness) to the leader of an opposing group, most likely at the Jerusalem temple. The letter discusses questions which were at issue between the Qumran community and its (Pharisaic) opponents. Twenty controversial points show the author to be taking a stricter line of exposition than the Pharisaic Rabbinical tradition was prepared to do. The polemical character of the missive is made plainly apparent by the formulas with which the author presents his own position, for example, "We take the view" or "You well know that."[19] Examples of the strict Halachah are the forbidding of the slaying of a pregnant animal (B 36), or of giving the blind and the deaf access to the temple (B 49, 54). See, too, the insistence that the cleanness of the *t^evul yom* should come only after sunset (B 15).[20] At many points the positions of 4QMMT agree with the temple scroll, but they plainly differ from the Halachah of the Mishnah.[21]

The debate may seem to be fierce on individual matters, but the courtesy of the conclusion will surprise us. It tells us to "remember David, who did many pious acts and was rescued from many troubles, and he was granted forgiveness. We have written you about one part of the works[22] of the Torah thinking that this will be of benefit for you and your people. For we have detected your

---

16. See above, pp. 7-9.

17. Cf. H. Braun, *Spätjüdisch häretischer und frühchristlicher Radikalismus,* Vol. 2, Tübingen, 2nd ed. 1969, but for a critical response cf. M. Limbeck, op. cit., pp. 22-28.

18. Edited by E. Qimron and J. Strugnell, Qumran Cave 4 — V. Miqṣat Ma'aśe Ha-Torah, DJD 10, Oxford 1994.

19. Cf. B 29, 37, 42 or B 68, 80; C 8.

20. For the rabbinic rulings cf. Qimron and Strugnell, pp. 153, 157, 161.

21. For bibliography ibid., pp. 124-129, and cf. also the works of L. H. Schiffman and J. M. Baumgarten.

22. We could translate this by commands (Qimron and Strugnell, p. 139) or by teachings (cf. *ma'aśe bereshit* in the rabbis).

knowledge of the Torah and your cleverness in expounding it. Think of all these
things and pray to God that he will direct your counsels aright, keeping you
from wicked ways and from the plots of Belial, so that you may find joy at the
end of the age by finding some portion of what we say to be true, this being
counted to you for righteousness if you do what is true and good before God for
the salvation of yourself and of Israel" (C 25-32). This portion makes plain the
link between fulfillment of the Torah and salvation and yet it also shows that
"being counted for righteousness" is a matter only for God.

3. The Torah and the Order of Creation

In Jubilees, which is close to the Qumran texts, and also in the Qumran texts
themselves, we find that the order of life is linked to the order of creation. In
particular the order of creation is the basis of the cultic order. In Jub. 2 the
Sabbath rest and sanctification of the Sabbath underlie the election of Israel.
We read that God will fashion and elect for himself one people out of the
many peoples. They will keep his Sabbath. He will sanctify them as his people. He will also bless them. As he has sanctified the Sabbath and made it
holy, so he will bless them. They will be his people and he will be their God
(2:19). The order for women who give birth is determined by the intervals between the creation of Adam and Eve and their entry into the Garden of Eden.
This interval was one of 40 days for Adam and 80 days for Eve. "For this reason the command on the tablets of heaven for those who give birth is that if a
male child is born they should be seven days in their uncleanness (corresponding to the seven original days) and thirty and three days in the blood of their
cleanness. If a female child is born, we have twice seven and sixty-six days,
giving the total of 80 days (Jub. 3:10f.).[23] As concerns Qumran the link is particularly clear in the calendar and in the orders for times of prayer (1QS 10),
for praise should be in accord with the divine institution (1QH 1, 27-31, cf.
1QS 10,8f.). Limbeck notes that the use of חוק brings out very precisely the
connection between the divine commands and the laws underlying creation.[24]
Along such lines the Qumran community follows a Wisdom tradition which as
a theologoumenon attained considerable significance in both Greek-speaking
and rabbinic Judaism.[25]

---

23. Cf. K. Berger, JSHRZ, II,3 pp. 329, 334f, also Limbeck, op. cit., pp. 72-84.

24. Cf. Limbeck, op. cit., pp. 180f.

25. Cf. H. F. Weiss, *Untersuchungen zur Kosmologie des hellenistischen und palästinischen*

III.

1. The LXX

The beginning of Hellenistic Jewish literature came in the 3rd century B.C. First we have the great translation of the Torah into Greek. Other translations followed, producing the LXX, also pseudepigraphical texts. Torah is translated *nomos* in almost all the 270 instances. This was an important rendering. At a later time it was felt to involve a narrowing,[26] yet for all that this concept, like no other, helped to present Judaism, to establish it, and to give it an apologetic, since Jewish law was older and more vulnerable than the laws of other peoples.[27]

In expounding the Torah, and applying it to conduct, the Hellenistic-Roman diaspora faced a double problem. One part of the law related only to the land of Israel. Furthermore, the more enlightened found the meaning of some terms problematic. Thinking of their own lifestyles, and for apologetic reasons, they adopted contemporary methods which in the broad sense were allegorical. Avoiding the literal sense, they followed allegorical models, usually with an ethical or moral orientation. They could stand by the literal wording but bring out the deeper meaning and thus gain plausibility.[28]

2. The Letter of Aristeas

This letter (Ps.-Aristeas) might serve as an example. It gives an allegorical meaning to those portions of the Torah that, taken literally, do not have a religious or ethical sense.[29] Allegory here is used for ethical reasons. The Decalogue comes first and then the laws of food and ritual.

Thus we read concerning the first commandment[30] (131) that the Lawgiver

---

Judentums, TU 97, Berlin 1966, pp. 283-304; M. Hengel, *Judentum und Hellenismus,* WUNT 10, 3rd ed. Tübingen 1988, pp. 275-318.

26. This finding is disputed by, for example, E. E. Urbach, *The Sages — Their Concepts and Beliefs,* Cambridge (Mass.) and London, 2nd ed. 1979, pp. 289f.

27. Cf. P. Pilhofer, *Presbyteron Kreitton,* WUNT II, 39, Tübingen 1990, pp. 143-220 and passim.

28. Cf. M. Hengel and A. M. Schwemer (eds.), *Die Septuaginta zwischen Judentum und Christentum,* WUNT 72, Tübingen 1994, Index, p. 314 under "Allegorese."

29. N. Walter, *Jüdisch-hellenistische Literatur von Philon von Alexandrien (unter Ausschluss der Historiker)* in ANRW II, Vol. 20,2, Berlin and New York 1987, p. 84.

30. Cf. N. Meisner, JSHRZ II, pp. 62f, 65, 67.

has first given us these commandments in order to promote piety and righteousness, and he deals with each point, in terms of instruction as well as prohibition, so that we may know in advance what will be the shameful consequences and the divine judgments for those who transgress them (132). He tells us first of all that there is only one God and that his power is displayed in all things, for every place is full of his might, and nothing that may be hidden from us is not open to him, for he sees what we do and even future events are not concealed from him (133). In his basic handling of this issue, and by making it plain to us, he shows that even those who purpose to do something wrong cannot do what is concealed from him or beyond his executive power. The legislation as a whole reveals the power of God.

The interpretation of the laws of food is as follows (163). Regarding land animals, we may say that weasels and mice and the similar creatures mentioned in the law are harmful (164). Mice make everything unclean. They corrupt everything. This is not merely for their own nourishment. Whatever they have begun to harm becomes unusable by us (165). The point regarding weasels is that they, too, have a vile quality apart from what we read in the law, for they conceive through the ears and give birth through the snout (166). A human lifestyle of this kind is also unclean. What people receive with the ears they express in speech and plunge others into disaster. Themselves thoroughly stained with the spot of ungodliness, they do what is unclean beyond measure. Kings, we learn, do right when they put these people to death (167). Lying in wait to destroy others is wicked (168). Our law orders us not to do anything evil to anyone either by word or by deed. We have briefly informed you that the law regulates everything with righteousness in view, and that nothing in scripture is accidental or purely for the sake of telling, but that all our lives we must do justly by people in all our actions, mindful of God the Ruler.

The various ritual directions instruct us (158) to offer food and drink in sacrifice and then to enjoy them. Clothing is a mark of remembrance, and sayings should be put on gateposts and doors to remind us of God (159). It is also ordered that signs should be worn around wrists, the clear intention being that we must do all things in righteousness, recalling our own origin, and always in fear of God.

The sum of it is (169) that in relation to foods and to unclean serpents and animals, all that is said has righteousness and a just life with others as its aim.

3. Pseudo-Phocylides

There are innumerable references to the biblical tradition in this work.[31] Fundamentally an ethical orientation is dominant. It does not surprise us to read in sentence 228 that ritual purifications signify the sanctification of the soul, not the body.[32] N. Walter rightly observes that there is no mention of the cultic and ritual commands in the narrower sense which were typical of Judaism.[33] It displays an enlightened attitude in this regard.[34] In fact, it adopts such ethical rules as would point to the attitude of educated Jews.[35]

4. Aristobulus

As an expositor of the Torah, Aristobulus is to be viewed similarly. He presents the Jewish law as the true philosophy, whether for educated Greeks or for fellow believers touched by the Hellenistic spirit.[36] He clearly explains his allegorical method. In relation to what he wants to say, our lawgiver Moses uses words that refer to other things, I mean, things external, for he makes statements about essential matters and that which signifies the constitution of things.[37] But we are not always to allegorize. The descent of God at Sinai was a real descent in which God without mediation disclosed his all-encompassing majesty.[38] Allegorical exposition is not obligatory. It can be avoided where the literal sense serves a paraenetic or homiletical purpose.

---

31. On the Decalogue and various detailed commandments cf. P. W. van der Horst, *The Sentences of Pseudo-Phocylides,* Leiden 1978. We need not be concerned with the relation between biblical and early Judaistic elements on the one hand and Hellenistic Jewish or Greek elements on the other, though on this cf. M. Küchler, *Frühjüdische Weisheitstraditionen,* OBO 26, Freiburg and Göttingen 1979, pp. 261, 302.

32. Cf. N. Walter, JSHRZ IV,3, p. 216. For views of John the Baptist compare Josephus Ant. 18,117.

33. Walter, p. 92.

34. Loc. cit. and cf. p. 94, which says that Ps.-Phocylides wants to make it plain that the ethics of the fathers, grounded in the Mosaic law, stood at the very height of Greek ethical culture.

35. Walter, p. 92.

36. Cf. Walter JSHRZ III,2, p. 264. For a discussion of his real concerns in relation to the Eusebius quotations cf. Walter's *Der Thoraausleger Aristobulus,* TU 86, Berlin 1964, also Pilhofer, op. cit., p. 71.

37. Fr. 2 in Eusebius Praep. Ev. 10,3, Walter II,2, p. 270.

38. Fr. 2 in Eusebius Praep. Ev. 10, 12 and 17, Walter III, 2, pp. 272f.

5. Joseph and Aseneth

We catch a new coloring in this work. In an emotional and psychologizing dramatic style it proclaims that a successful life can be lived only within Judaism. The apologetic and paraenetic point is to explain why Joseph could marry the daughter of an Egyptian priest. It is stressed that Gentile marriages are possible only after the conversion of the Gentiles. Nevertheless, the divine legislation is not at the center when God is depicted.[39] This may be seen, too, in the soteriology. We acquire the divine life that we need daily, not by learning and keeping the law, not by mystical experiences, not by being called by a kerygma that has its basis in some particular event, but by eating and drinking and anointing oneself in a distinctively Jewish way and not a Gentile way. This is the message of the much debated passages about the consecrated bread of life and cup of immortality and ointment of imperishability. Gentiles court death by continually feeding at the unclean table of idols, but Jews partake of life. Thus changing over from the one to the other is a necessary and obvious part of conversion from paganism to Judaism.[40]

The Halachah focuses on dietary commands and its main feature is the confession of the one God and the rejection of idolatry, the nucleus of Judaism. This specific orientation reflects the situation of Alexandrian Judaism at the beginning of the first century A.D.

The significance of Sabbath observance for the Egyptian diaspora may be seen in a papyrus containing an account of deliveries of bricks, which for a certain period gave the daily amounts. These were usually between 1,000 and 2,000, but the seventh day simply had the clear-cut notation: Sabbath.[41]

6. Philo

Philo, at the most some twenty years older than Paul, is his nearest historical and literary contemporary. Yet that is not the only reason why he merits discussion. We must take note of him primarily because he developed a hermeneutic in his exposition of the Torah. In contrast to Paul he is a true Helleniser, yet his exposition and understanding of the law are not restricted to allegory. We may note the following principles: (1) Moses is the lawgiver but the Torah is divine;

---

39. C. Burchard, JSHRZ II, 4, p. 602.
40. Ibid., p. 604 referring to JUS An 8,5 and 9; 15,5; 16,16; 19,5; 21,135 and 21.
41. CPJ I, No. 10; Zenon Archiv, the age of Philadelphos?

(2) There is harmony between the Torah and the cosmic order; (3) Scripture has a twofold meaning and needs to be expounded both literally and allegorically; (4) Exposition has a paraenetic goal.[42]

7. Josephus

We can only sketch the multiple uses of *nomos* in Josephus; there are some 500 instances.

1. With the assurance of an apologist, Josephus affirms the antiquity of both the Jewish law and of Moses the lawgiver. Moses, he states, was born over 2,000 years ago, long before the poets could tell of the origin of the gods, let alone of the deeds and laws of mortals (Ant. 1,16). Moses was older than all the mythological or historical figures of the Greek world, and the law he gave is older than any others. The Egyptians and Phoenicians bear witness to the age of the Jews, and the Greeks were students of Moses.[43] Even in their ostensibly native sayings, the Greek philosophers followed Moses in both act and teaching (Ap. 2,281).

From Israel the law came to other peoples. The commandments, he says, were given by us to all the rest; they took them as a model. There is no people and no Greek or barbarian city into which our custom of resting on the seventh day has not found an entry (Ap. 2,280-282).

2. Disobedience to the commandments is disobedience to God (Ant. 20,44). Nothing is more righteous than obedience to the commandments (Ap. 2,293). The threatened punishments prevent transgression, but the main stress is on the advantages that keeping the commandments brings, for they are the source of blessedness.

3. The law is imperishable. Wealth and home and all good things may be snatched from us, but the law is immortal, and even far away in other countries, and fearing some embittered tyrant, Jews will still have a greater fear of the law (Ap. 2,227).

4. From early youth Jews are taught the law. Telling of himself, Josephus states that when he was not much more than a child of fourteen or so he was

---

42. Cf. Y. Amir, *Die hellenistische Gestalt des Judentums bei Philon von Alexandrien,* Neukirchen-Vluyn 1983; A. F. Segal, "Torah und *nomos* in Recent Scholarly Discussion," *Studies in Religion* 13, 1984, 19-27; A. Reinhartz, "The Meaning of *nomos* in Philo's Exposition of the Law," *Studies in Religion* 15, 1986, 337-45.

43. Cf. Pilhofer, op. cit., pp. 193-206.

lauded for his love of books, and some came from the high priests and city elders to learn more of the details of the law (Vita 9). This picture of the fourteen-year-old Josephus in Jerusalem is a bit of self-display, but Josephus repeatedly refers to the fact that as soon as they were able to understand, children were instructed in the commandments (Ap. 2,178; Bell 7,343), so that Jews knew them just as well as they knew their own names (Ap. 2,178). The commandments are impressed upon their souls, so that there are few transgressors. Indeed, they are implanted in Jews at birth, and they are even prepared to die for them.

The law commands that children, along with the whole people, must listen to the public reading of the law on the Feast of Tabernacles, first, in order to learn to read, and second to study the laws and the deeds of their ancestors with a view to imitation. Having this knowledge, they will have no excuse if they fail to keep them. Children must first learn the commandments, the best knowledge of all and the source of blessedness (Ap. 2,211). Study and knowledge of the law prevents us from sinning (Ant. 16,43).

From familiarity with the law from early youth, and its willing acceptance, Josephus derives an optimism of the law that counts not merely on its feasibility but on its factual observance.

IV. Conclusion

If we find that some of the judgments of earlier research into the Judaism of the days of Paul were erroneous,[44] the same holds good of the rabbinic tradition of the 2nd to the 5th centuries, as the work of Avemaria shows. Avemaria has demonstrated the untenability of the basic thesis of the system of Weber and Billerbeck that Israel accepted the commandments only to win merit and to achieve a share in eternal life by fulfilling them. Certainly the Torah leads to life when it is kept, but the early rabbis did not understand by "life" only participation in the world to come, nor did the way from obedience to life necessarily go by way of counting merits, reckoning up fulfillments and transgressions, and a concluding judgment. The attainment of eternal life could certainly be attributed to a judgment on human deeds, but as regards motivation the rabbis

---

44. Along with Weber, Schürer, and Billerbeck cf. also W. Bousset, *Die Religion des Judentums im späthellenistischen Zeitalter,* HNT 3.A, 3rd ed. Tübingen 1926, 4th ed. 1966.

thought not so much of the expectation of rewards but of doing things out of obedience to God and for the sake of the Torah itself.[45]

A saying from the Vita of Jeremiah in the Vitae Prophetarum 2,14 represents the Judaism of antiquity: "For the glory of God will certainly not deviate from his law."[46]

---

45. Avemaria, op. cit., pp. 581f.

46. Cf. A. M. Schwemer, *Studien zu den frühjüdischen Prophetenlegenden.* Vitae Prophetarum, Vol. I, TSAJ 49, Tübingen 1995, p. 161.

The Attitude of Paul to the Law in the Unknown Years between Damascus and Antioch*

by

MARTIN HENGEL

I. The Problem and the Sources

1. The seven undisputed epistles gives us only glimpses of what the apostle was doing during the 30 years between ca. A.D. 33 and A.D. 62-64. They cover the period between ca. A.D. 50 and 56-57, less than a quarter of the whole. If Philippians and Philemon were written in Caesarea or Rome, they range from ca. 50 to 60, or about a third. The period of 16 years between Paul's conversion before Damascus and the so-called second missionary journey (after the Apostolic Council) is relatively unknown and thus debatable. These years must have seen some development of his theology, which is complex and highly tuned in the epistles. This applies particularly to his doctrines of justification and the law.

Albert Schweitzer adopted a view which greatly influenced the History of Religions School, namely, that the doctrine of justification is a "subsidiary crater" compared to Paul's apocalyptic and mystical ideas of redemption. Many cling to this position. Paul, it is suggested, worked out his doctrine of justification only when the Judaizers caused such agitation in Galatia. At first he had a sacramentally realistic view of redemption. The issue of the law was an adiaphoron, in the words of G. Strecker. We supposedly find proof of this in

* This essay is a summary of a larger monograph entitled *Die unbekannte Jahre des Apostels Paulus,* WUNT. In that study the sources are given, so we will here dispense with the notes. I am grateful for the hints given by the co-author of the monograph, Dr. Anna Maria Schwemer, and I must also thank Marion Sieker for typing the manuscript.

1 Thessalonians, the first epistle. Neither here nor in 1 and 2 Corinthians is there any reference to either the law or justification.

Yet we should also remember 1 Cor. 9:20f. and especially 15:56. We recall, too, the problem of the strong and the weak. Again, are not all the epistles, apart from Romans, occasional writings that deal only with specific and concrete situations? Surely, too, only a poor preacher or theologian engages in endless repetition even on unsuitable occasions. In 1 Thessalonians, Paul was dealing with issues under discussion by that newly founded church, and his references to election, to saving faith, and to liberation from judgment stand in direct relationship to the doctrine of justification. We cannot otherwise understand them correctly. In Corinth Paul had to fight on various fronts, dealing with antinomian enthusiasts that were misusing his doctrine of freedom from the law. This problem also raises the question of the intermingling of the life and teaching of the apostle that he discusses in texts that treat of his pre-Christian and Jewish past and of his earlier missionary activity, for example, Gal. 1f. and Phil. 3:2-11. Indeed, in all these references there is a very plain appeal to his missionary service.

2. We must also judge whether Acts 9–15 is a trustworthy source for the disputed period. In my view the twofold work of Luke, within the framework of dramatic Hellenistic historiography, has to be taken as serious history. In no sense should we compare it to the later novelistic Acts. Acts offers a biographical description of the missionary work of the thirteenth apostle after a preliminary introduction that itself relates to Luke's first work, the life of Jesus. The "we-passages" plainly show that the author accompanied Paul when after Philippi he journeyed to Jerusalem (Acts 20:6) and also when he moved on to Rome. Luke highly honors Paul as a gifted missionary, charismatic, and church founder, though under the influence of the Jerusalem tradition relating to the apostles, and also of the Jesus tradition that led on to his Gospel, he did not wholly share his theology. Luke's aim was to mediate between the Jerusalem tradition and Paul. We can more or less date his two works. Like the Bellum of Josephus they belong to the middle Flavian period ca. A.D. 80-85. With Paul and Mark, Luke is well-oriented to relations in Palestine prior to A.D. 70.

He had probably been a God-fearer. No Greek-speaking non-Jewish author of antiquity had so exact a knowledge of Judaism as he did. We see this in relation to the question of the law. Matthew and John are perhaps to be dated during the later reign of Domitian (A.D. 90 to 100). Some non-apostolic gospels had predated the apostolic ones, and Luke investigated them historically, showing a sense and liking for "ancient" traditions (if we can use the term after only about 50 years), and seeking always to present the early Christian proclamation (cf. Paul in 1 Cor. 15:11) in all the varied theological nuances of his main characters, who are much the same as those in Paul's epistles.

His tendencies are plain to see, and from the time of F. C. Baur, especially after the Second World War, offense has been taken at his "Paulinism," which is thought to display only a limited understanding of the real Paul. He harmonizes, he simplifies, and his account of the early years is episodic and eclectic. Nevertheless, he uses great rhetorical skill in depicting individual and very important scenes such as the conversions of Paul and Cornelius. His brief biographical notes also show that he made use of many oral and written traditions (such as lists), and probably those of Paul himself. We should not be too critical if his understanding of Paul was inadequate. Students often fail to understand their teachers, as we often find in the history of theology. I very much doubt whether H. Braun or W. Marxsen really grasped the theological concerns of Bultmann. Great gaps occur and great uncertainties. These can be traced back to gaps in the tradition and to memory gaps. The harmonizing trend also played a part. Luke knew more than he could write about. Yet, I do not believe that he dealt freely with the essential facts. I have learned how hard it is to describe a person's life, on the basis of oral tradition, from the task that the Proceedings of the British Academy gave itself in writing an obituary for Günther Zuntz. Gaps occur. Casual, imprecise, contradictory, and even false information is available. And many things have to be ignored. Since engaging on my present task I have come to respect the author of the works to Theophilus as he sought to bring a new and offensive message to a member of the upper classes and his friends. The radical criticism of Luke today rests to a large degree on the historical ignorance of NT scholars, who make out that they are radically critical but are quite incapable of thinking in real historical categories. This is inevitable, for do they not spend all their time with the NT and the abundant secondary literature, and never learn to do intensive historical work with other important sources? My ten years in management made me familiar with occupational blindness!

3. Paul spent at least 15 or 16 years of his Christian career as a missionary in Arabia, Syria, and Cilicia. We thus need information about Roman Syria in the early imperial period that will give us social and religious light. At this point Josephus has a big part to play, and so, too, do historians like Diodorus,

Appian, and Cassius Dio, geographers like Strabo and Pliny the Elder, along
with inscriptions and archeological findings. New Testament scholars can speculate about the churches in Syria and their syncretism, but their work is obviously inadequate. We should not focus exclusively on Antioch, for during this
period Paul did work in Syria and Cilicia, in neighboring territories like Cyprus, Pisidia, and Lycaonia, and we must not forget Arabia. He himself mentions Antioch only once in Gal. 2:1. It is only the much despised Luke from
whom we learn how important Antioch was. Only Luke mentions Tarsus,
which was Paul's native city.

II. The Conversion of the Persecutor en route to Damascus and the Theological Consequences

1. Prior to this transformation in his life Paul had been a young and ambitious
Pharisaic student in Jerusalem. He tells us this convincingly in Gal. 1:13f.; Phil.
3:2ff., cf. 1 Cor. 15:1-11; Rom. 15:19. Before A.D. 70 there were no such individuals as diaspora Pharisees with their own Hellenistic seminaries. A strict observance of the Torah and its exact (ἀχριβής) investigation were possible only
within the Holy Land, for many of the commandments could not be followed
elsewhere. In Jerusalem Paul persecuted the Jewish Christian group of Hellenists. He made it his aim to drive them out of the city. Whether there was a persecution in Antioch, conjectured from a combination of Gal. 1:17 and 22,
seems to be highly unlikely. Only three years after the passion, it could hardly
be explained historically. Luke gives an excellent account of what took place.
Paul went to Damascus in pursuit of the adherents of the new sect, the Hellenists, who had fled there from Jerusalem. He was motivated by a "zeal for the
law" which the new sect had trodden underfoot by blasphemously invoking and
extolling a crucified seducer, who had been accursed (Deut. 21:23; 27:26, cf.
Gal. 3:13), as the Messiah and Son of God, who was now honored at the right
hand of God, and who was now awaited as the Son of Man and Judge of the
world who would come empowered of God.

The offense of such blasphemous views was aggravated by the fact that the
Hellenists were critical of some parts of the law (e.g., its rites). They also were
thought to reject the sacrificial temple cultus, for the sacrificial death of Jesus
had made the temple and its offerings obsolete. The motives all point back to
Jerusalem. At the same time the Hellenists did not engage in any basic

soteriological criticisms of the law such as those of Paul himself. Their own motives seem to have been in matters of detail. Hence we should not speak of a preaching that was free from the law, as I myself used to do. At root there never was such a thing in early Christianity in any strict sense, not even in Paul. The first commandment, the law of love, and the ten commandments all had a central role in Paul's preaching. Paul was no real antinomian, though he was perhaps misunderstood as such in Corinth. He had to contradict this view: μὴ ὢν ἄνομος θεοῦ ἀλλ᾽ ἔννομος Χριστοῦ (1 Cor. 9:21; cf. Gal. 6:2; Rom. 13:8f.; Gal. 5:13f.). The problem was that of relating saving faith to God's command, the grace of God and our own works. In what follows I shall speak only of criticism of the law, not of freedom from it.

2. Approaching Damascus Paul had a direct vision of the Risen Lord. He refers to this in 1 Cor. 9:1 and 15:8ff. In my view the three Lucan versions in chs. 9, 22, and 26 rest on the fact that Luke himself had heard the narrative on three occasions. Common to all was the vision of the heavenly δόξα of the Risen Lord that threw down and blinded the persecutor, and then the audition that made Saul into Paul, a disciple of Christ. We are reminded of the ἐχθροὶ ὄντες of Rom. 5:10, which, like the formula of the justification of the ungodly in Rom. 4:5, has universal application, yet which applied specifically to Paul, the enemy thus far of the Son of God. Paul is said in 1 Tim. 1:15 to be the πρῶτος of the sinners who have been saved by the coming of Christ into the world. The former persecutor was now a paradigm of unmerited grace.

Paul's own account of his calling in Gal. 1:16 ties together the election, the revelation of Christ, and the mission to the Gentiles. As in Luke, vision and audition are linked. The ἀποκαλύψαι τὸν υἱὸν αὐτοῦ ἐν ἐμοί, ἵνα εὐαγγελίζωμαι αὐτὸν ἐν τοῖς ἔθνεσιν does not carry with it the sense of a long development in several stages. The surprising transformation of Paul, which had all the directness of the calling of the prophets, had corresponding and equally urgent consequences. Paul did not have to wait upon other authorities that had already been given an apostolic commission. He went at once to Arabia, to the country of the Nabataeans, to proclaim the gospel there that he had received by revelation from the Risen Lord.

3. In the final account in Acts 26, Luke presents his own understanding of the Damascus encounter with Christ. He links inseparably the vision of Christ, election, and the mission to the Gentiles. In the first two accounts in chs. 9 and 22 a certain mediatorial role is given to Ananias, who is undoubtedly a historical figure. By baptism Ananias receives Paul into the early Jewish Christian

community. We can learn from the ἐβαπτίσθημεν εἰς Χριστὸν Ἰησοῦν of Rom. 6:3 that Paul was baptized. By no means was he an unbaptized preacher of the gospel to the nations, though he does say later that he seldom administered baptism himself.

It is noteworthy that Luke says nothing about the community instructing Saul/Paul in the gospel, not even when he mentions his visit to Jerusalem. There Paul told the apostles about the Damascus meeting and his open testimony to the name of Jesus. It is obvious from Luke that Paul's proclamation of the gospel was in no way dependent upon the Jerusalem authorities. Quite the contrary! The only problem is that the preaching of the converted persecutor is presented only in generally christological terms (Jesus is the "Son of God" or "Messiah" according to Acts 9:20) and that Paul preaches only to the Jews in the synagogues (9:20, 22f.) or engages in discussion with Greek-speaking Jews (9:29). Luke shows no understanding of the specificity of the Pauline gospel as the "word of the cross," of the tension between gospel and law, or of the view that fallen sinners are referred only to grace. He certainly does not express these features. This is perhaps his theological weakness. Yet in all three accounts he lays increasing stress upon the fact that Paul is a "chosen instrument" to take the gospel to the Gentiles. This is stated by Ananias in 9:15, more strongly by Ananias in 22:15 (supplemented by the temple vision of 22:21), and most strongly of all in 26:15-17 in the saying of the Risen Lord to Paul. The final depiction is the culminating point for Luke, but he still does not grasp the depth of Paul's Christology and anthropology, and might even have rejected Paul's radicalism.

It is to be noted that Luke does not tell us that at the first Paul preached to non-Jews. Perhaps he wanted to give priority to Peter (ch. 10) and the Hellenists (ch. 11), except for some preparatory moves by Philip (ch. 8). He certainly does not mention any early Gentile preaching, for example, in Tarsus.

4. We learn from Josephus that Damascus, the important oasis and metropolis in South Syria, where many trade routes from Mesopotamia and North Syria converged, was the site of a large diaspora community. He tells us that at the start of the Jewish War 10,500 or up to 18,000 Jews in the city were killed, and also that almost all the leading Gentile women there were sympathetic to the Jewish faith in God (Bell. 2,559ff.; 7,368). He probably exaggerates, but the synagogue preaching obviously had great attraction for non-Jews, and as in Alexandria, Jerusalem (6,9; 22,19), and Salamis (13,5), synagogues abounded (9,20). The Gentiles that Paul was seeking he would find among the male and

female sympathizers and the God-fearers. They would certainly have been ready to hear his new and strange message much more quickly than would the worshippers of Zeus-Hadad, of Dionysos-Dushara, of Dea Syria, or of the divine triad of Heliopolis-Baalbek. From the very outset he addressed not only the Jews (Rom. 1:16; 11:14; 1 Cor. 9:20f.), who were always within his sights, but also the Gentile sympathizers, who were already familiar with the main outlines of the Jewish scriptures. Luke is right to tell us that Paul still used this method even on his so-called second and third missionary journeys up to Ephesus. The five occasions of synagogue punishment (2 Cor. 11:24) show that already in Syria there was conflict about questions of the law. Luke does not mention this, but we learn from it that many times Paul's life was in danger at the hands of Jewish zealots.

5. Josephus tells us not only that Syria had a large diaspora population but also that the number of Gentiles favorable to Judaism was also large, especially in Antioch (Bell. 2,463; 7,45). In the cities at least the synagogue congregations were divided. On the one side was the considerable core community of Jews, which included the small number of full proselytes. On the other side was the circle of sympathizers in various stages, many of whom were women, from whom circumcision was obviously not demanded. After A.D. 70, proselyte baptism became the response to the Christian mission. The early discussion between the schools of Hillel and Shammai had considered its relation to bathing before sacrifice and to circumcision. How the sympathizers were judged was a point of controversy. A skeptical attitude was taken in the Jewish homeland; the sympathizers were still unclean Gentiles. In the synagogues of the Syrian cities the sympathizers, drawn from the Greek-speaking upper classes, helped to give social and political respect to the synagogue congregations and could be regarded as forerunners of the coming messianic kingdom, for Syria up to the Euphrates and the Taurus, which had been part of the kingdom of David, formed at least a part of the messianic kingdom as well. The same applied to the Nabataean territory south and east of Israel. The Rabbis regarded Damascus as a city on the borders of Israel. In Jerusalem the ossuary of the proselyte Ariston of Apamea, written in two languages, has only recently been discovered. Ariston had been given the Jewish name Jehuda. According to Mishnah Hallah 4,11, the priests accepted his first fruits, for in a broader sense Syria could be regarded as part of the Holy Land: "Those who dwell in Syria are like those who possess land in the suburbs of Jerusalem."

The distinctive Gentile interest in Jewish faith in God is connected with the widespread tendency in West Semitic religion toward belief in the one God of heaven, which led in late antiquity to the cult of the Sol invictus. The Arabian family and ancestral gods and the anonymous Syrian local gods (called Lord) could easily be worshipped along with the one supreme God of heaven. This explains why Judaism, Christianity, and later Islam could enjoy such successes in Syria and Arabia.

Let me give one out of many examples. In and around Palmyra toward the end of the 1st century A.D. there were around 300 inscriptions of an anonymous deity with the designation *b^{e}rīk š^{e}meh l^e'âl^{e}mâ*. This God is called the one and only merciful God and he is called upon everywhere (1 Cor. 1:2), for he hears and saves and gives life. He performs healings and others wonders *(gbwrt')*, and he is publicly confessed each day *(√ydh)*. We have here a development of Baal Shamin, but worship of him is more strongly individual. A Greek equivalent is Zeus ὕψιστος. Only a step is needed to produce the concept of God held by the sympathizers in the Jewish synagogues. As Hellenistic and Roman writers could maintain from the days of Hecataios of Abdera (ca. 300 B.C.), so, too, could the Arrian state in the 2nd century A.D. that the Arabs worshipped the Οὐρανός as their God.

Religious and legal problems still existed. A devout God-fearer, if male, could become a true Israelite only by circumcision. Only thus could he become a member of the elect people. A division was thus present in the synagogue communities, and this led to frequent discussions and tensions. We see this in Josephus in his account of the conversion of King Izates of Adiabene. The division may also be seen in the great inscription from 4th-century Aphrodisias. But we find it clearly in Luke. For strict Palestinian Jews of a Pharisaic persuasion circumcision was a precondition of salvation. At best sympathizers belonged only to the outer court of the Gentiles, which was questionable. The Gentiles were excluded.

6. The Hellenists, who came from the Greek-speaking diaspora, were already familiar with this problem. Their mission to the Greek cities of Palestine and Syria in and around the synagogues gave it a new acuteness. In the congregations they founded, they reached the conclusion that God-fearers who believed in Jesus and were baptized, thus being made certain of forgiveness of sins and redemption from the coming judgment, could be accepted without circumcision. The ten commandments were to be kept by them, and possibly, out of fear that they would be tainted by idolatry, the dietary laws also applied to them. But most of the ritual laws dropped away. As they were driven out of the

synagogues, not without some conflict, a conscious separation from Jewish customs might be seen, though this development took many years and even decades. Paul always speaks to the ἐκκλησία rather than the συναγωγή. Already perhaps in his day the Lord's Day had replaced the Sabbath as the day of assembly. The codex came to replace the roll for liturgical reading, the *nomina sacra* the tetragram, the Lord's Prayer the Prayer of Eighteen Benedictions, and the Wednesday and Friday fasts those on Monday and Thursday (Did. 8).

Only occasionally do we find any basic reflection on the relation of salvation through Christ and the law. Circumcision and the ritual laws did not basically apply to the God-fearers who had become Gentile Christians, but the dispensation was not basic. The relation between faith in Christ and the salvation he had achieved still demanded an even closer observance of the Decalogue and an obligation to do works of neighborly love. A simple life was also demanded. These things, too, were the prerequisites of salvation. We need only cite the Synoptics, especially Matthew, Hebrews, the Epistle of James, and Revelation. We must not overlook the trend toward an eschatologically motivated rigorism, at times with ascetic features. Only a few years after the original event the rich ethical Jesus tradition achieved a greater influence than it did later. As a legacy from Jewish Pharisaism, a comparatively unthinking practical "synergism" seems to have held sway, and this defined later piety in the church.

7. The situation changed with the coming of Saul/Paul, the former Pharisaic scribe and persecutor. Philippians 3:6 and Gal. 1:13-15 show us that he persecuted the church out of his own zeal for the law and his sense of faultlessness. His encounter with the Risen Lord en route to Damascus raised for him the issue of Christ as a soteriological alternative to the law. For contemporary Judaism the law in its varied forms was the epitome of salvation. It could be fundamentally equated with "life." See Hillel in Abot 2,7: *marbäh tôrah marbäh ḥajjim,* "much torah, much life." If the antithesis of Torah and Jesus of Nazareth had made him a persecutor, the relation between the two now became for him a basic question. He would now have to see the antithesis differently. The Risen Lord is now ζωή for believers (2 Cor. 4:11f., cf. 2:16). Being in or under the law is replaced by being ἐν Χριστῷ. Only on this assumption can one speak of the νόμος τοῦ πνεύματος καὶ τῆς ζωῆς ἐν Χριστῷ, the law of Christ contrasted with the death-dealing law of Sinai (Rom. 8:2; Gal. 6:2; 1 Cor. 9:21). Philemon 3:2-11 does not offer us a secondary insight. It is a basic experience that defines Paul's life after Damascus. The Crucified

One representatively bore for all of us the curse of the law and thus accomplished redemption and universal reconciliation. Exemplified by the representative atoning suffering of the Son of God, the law of God makes manifest
God's wrathful judgment (Rom. 4:15) as the letter which kills (2 Cor. 3:3), for
it gives virulence to sin and makes it fatal (Rom. 5:20; 7:9f.; 1 Cor. 15:56). It
sets sinners under the curse of God (Gal. 3:10), ruling out all human self-
righteousness (Rom. 9:31; 10:3), and making believers aware of the sin that
has been forgiven by Christ (Rom. 3:20). These were not the insights of a later
passing polemic that resulted incidentally from his irritation at Judaizing in-
roads into Galatia. From the very first they were the basic insights of his new
life under christological influence. It matters little that he formulated them
more or less incidentally in letters some 20 to 25 years after the great change
in his life. For they are not individual statements. What we find here is the astonishing wealth of the Pauline vocabulary and modes of reasoning. We do not
easily grasp this from the few fragments that we now possess. How striking it
is that Paul so seldom repeats himself. He constantly uses new metaphors and
arguments to say the same thing, the end of the law and the new salvation in
Christ. We surely misunderstand him if we apply to what he says about the
law the primitive standard of a formal logic. In these texts we have the solidi-
fied lava that flowed steadily in the apostle's life. The eruption was his transformation, the ἀποκάλυψις Ἰησοῦ Χριστοῦ described in Gal. 1:11, 16ff. Christ
is the end of the law and righteousness for those who believe (Rom. 10:4). The
outsider had now become the ἐθνῶν ἀπόστολος (Rom. 11:13) and a debtor to
the Greeks and barbarians as regards the gospel (Rom. 1:14, 16ff.). He had not
received many gospels from Christ but only the one gospel that he preached in
all the communities and that is defined in Rom. 1:16f. Luke himself shows
knowledge of this gospel (Acts 13:38-41; 20:24).

So far as I can see there were no basic changes in Paul's central message
from the days of his conversion or from the beginning of his missionary work
as an apostle. We can understand what he says in retrospect in Galatians 1 and
2 and Philippians 3 only on this assumption. The new thing in his message is
the unity of Christology and soteriology, including its anthropological ramifications. He had received the basic building blocks of his Christology at the
very start, the definitive titles Christ, Son of God, and Kyrios, and an inclusive
understanding of the atoning death of the Son of God at the cross and his resurrection and exaltation to the right hand of God. Indeed, we might even trace
back the beginning of a pre-existence Christology to the Hellenists in Jerusa-

lem. Normally the development of Paul's theology is supposed to have started at Antioch, but this is to underrate the six or seven years that came between Damascus and the end of his stay at Tarsus, where, contrary to early Christian practice, he worked alone rather than with others, and at root he always worked alone even though he was later accompanied by Barnabas and Silas/Silvanus. When we consider Gal. 1:11f., 17, we have to be careful when speaking about the influence of others on Paul. He gained his first knowledge of the earliest proclamation of the new messianic sect as a persecutor, and he must have received some basic instruction before being baptized at Damascus. The first information he acquired perhaps finds reflection in 1 Cor. 11:23-25 and 15:1-7. Nevertheless, six or seven years passed before Barnabas took him to Antioch, and during this time he made his own way and very quickly must have run into conflict.

The message of the Hellenists had been offensive, but Paul's was even more so. Regarding the law, he was not content simply to treat the ritual laws as adiaphora. They had been ready to do this in Jerusalem and Antioch so long as they did not infringe upon the confession. No, he made an implicit distinction between the ethical commandments summed up in the law of love and his presentation of new life in the Spirit, as for example, in the exhortation in 1 Cor. 10:25. He no longer viewed the law as a way of salvation alongside Christ. This was for him a fundamental decision. The new life of obedience to Christ is a gift, a fruit of the Spirit's working. God himself wills and acts (Gal. 5:22; Phil. 2:13). By nature we are wholly sinners. None is righteous before God. Perhaps we might catch an inkling here of his doctrine of predestination, and perhaps of the influence of Essene conceptions that he must have known during his Jerusalem days.

8. Regarding the Gentile Christians, mostly former God-fearers, it was no longer just a matter of their full legal and eschatological equality. He had made this plain as a self-evident truth in Gal. 3:28. If in relation to Christ the law as a whole was not an adiaphoron but a way of salvation, this would mean perdition and there would be no means of gathering believers from Gentile nations. It is a mistake to view works of the law as prerequisites of eschatological salvation. The work of Christ is the only basis, and it is wholly grace, an unmerited gift. We are not to preach the law, with circumcision as an example. Paul had not been doing that even, perhaps, in Syria (Gal. 5:11). For Gentile Christians the older debate about circumcision and observance of the ritual commandments had become, not a matter of judgment, but one of conscience,

that is, of faith. For if obedience to the commandments were thought to be a
condition of salvation, then the all-sufficiency of the work of Christ would
come into question. This problem did not arise only with the Apostolic Council or with the confrontation with Peter at Antioch. It underlies both these conflicts. Otherwise Paul would have yielded in the matter of the circumcision of
Titus and then again at Antioch, as did Barnabas and the rest of the Jewish
Christians. He could not do this. The presuppositions that were linked to his
conversion, to the ἀποκάλυψις Ἰησοῦ Χριστοῦ, and therefore to the truth of the
gospel, prevented him.

The ritual commandments were an adiaphoron for the Jewish Christians.
They could keep them out of love and for the sake of mission. But they were
freed from the "yoke of the law." Paul himself could adopt this ruling, cf. 1 Cor.
9:4, the circumcision of the Jewish (!) Timothy (Acts 16:3), which was necessary if he was to have access to the synagogue as the site of mission, the purifying of the four men under a vow in Jerusalem (Acts 21:24, 26), which Paul
probably paid for out of the collection (Acts 24:11f., 17), and the line that Paul
followed in relation to the weak. His basic denial that the ritual legislation applied to the Jews brought down upon him the charge of apostasy and frequently
led him into danger of death. His former friends and associates in the Greek-
speaking synagogues at Jerusalem no doubt regarded him as a traitor after his
unexpected conversion. In view of the acute threats to his life, he never went
back to Jerusalem in these years except for one visit to Cephas/Peter fourteen
years before the Apostolic Council.

III. Arabia and Jerusalem

1. Three years passed between his commissioning before Damascus and his
first Jerusalem visit. In Damascus he had proclaimed his new and offensive
message in the synagogues and in discussions with Jews and God-fearers, who
aroused his particular interest. Then he went to "Arabia." As noted, he showed a
special interest in Gentile sympathizers because they accepted in faith the message that he preached, namely, that salvation has its basis, not in obedience to
the Mosaic law, but only in Christ. Luke tells us nothing about the stay in Arabia. Perhaps he had little information about it. But he offers plausible reasons
for Paul's leaving Damascus. The synagogues there had expected support in re-
stricting the new and scandalous messianic sect. But their awaited champion

had been perverted, and now preached the very opposite of what they were expecting. The Damascus synagogues must have known tumultuous scenes. The ground had been cut from under Paul's feet and he therefore left the city. The incident involving the ethnarch of King Aretas IV probably took place at the end of his second stay there (2 Cor. 11:31-33). But there seems not to have been any quarrel with the comparatively small number of brethren in the city. If there had been, Paul would hardly have come back to Damascus after his stay in Arabia. These brethren helped him later in his escape over the wall. They had obviously passed on to the Judean communities news of his conversion and of his unexpected missionary activity (Gal. 1:22). Paul tells us this, and it forms the basis of the Lucan account.

Saul/Paul did not seek solitude for the short period that he spent in Arabia. Scholars often say that he did this for psychological reasons. Paul, it is stated, was seeking to find himself. Nor should we compare the stay in Arabia with the forty-day temptation of Jesus in the wilderness. Paul mentions it because he obviously spent some time there. We should link Gal. 1:16 to 1:22. Paul went to "Arabia" as a missionary to the Gentiles proclaiming the gospel he had received from Christ. The stay lasted for some two years or more. "Arabia" is the Nabataean territory south and east of Israel. It included some cities of the Decapolis on the far side of the Jordan.

But why Arabia, where Aramaic was mostly spoken, and not the cities on the Phoenician coast, or Emesa, Palmyra, and all Syria and Cilicia, which he would visit later? Well, the earliest Christian mission outside the Holy Land took place in stages, and nurtured by eschatological enthusiasm it followed the directions of the Risen Lord. The nearest neighboring territories came first. Philip went to the Samaritans, the "heretical" Israelites. Then he went to the former land of the Philistines, the coastal plain, which included the metropolis of Caesarea with a mixed Jewish and Gentile population. Other Hellenists then fled to Damascus, where Saul the persecutor took unsuccessful action against them. According to Acts 11:19ff. other Hellenists went in stages to Phoenicia, Cyprus, and finally Antioch. The parousia was expected soon and the missionary horizon did not extend very far. At this point any development did not include the center of Paul's gospel.

The response to the question: Why Arabia? is simple. As descendants of Ishmael the "Arabs" were genealogically and geographically close relatives of Israel even when viewed as "Gentiles," for Abraham was their ancestor. The descendants of Esau, the Edomites, had indeed become Jews under Hyrcanus;

they were no longer Gentiles. Did not the promised blessings apply to the physical descendants of Abraham and the closest neighbors of Israel? Among the
βάρβαροι (Rom. 1:14) Paul must have thought especially of them. Notwithstanding Rom. 1:16, they rather than the Greeks were the first to whom he
went. Since the time of the Maccabees they had been the most important political neighbors of Israel, whether as rivals or as partners. Among them there was
a considerable diaspora. God-fearers were there too. The religious situation was
very similar to that in Syria.

In Gal. 4:25, Paul says that τὸ δὲ Ἀγὰρ Σινᾶ ὄρος ἐστὶν ἐν τῇ Ἀραβίᾳ. According to H. Gese we have a word play here of both genealogical and geographical significance. Hagar denotes the trading city of Hegra (Madain Salih),
in South Nabatea, close to Petra. In the near vicinity was Sinai according to
contemporary conjectures. Paul had perhaps been there. Josephus, the Talmud,
and the Targums identify Petra as Qadesh, where Israel spent most of the time
during the wilderness journey. Ancient Jewish and pagan tradition also found a
special link between Abraham and Damascus, and particularly the Nabataeans.
In both cases newly converted scribes were immediately stimulated by this tradition to think about Abraham, the first "proselyte," and the promises that he
was given. When Paul says in Rom. 15:19 that he preached the gospel from Jerusalem ἐν κύκλῳ to Illyricum, by the ἐν κύκλῳ he probably meant the work that
he had done in Damascus and Arabia. That his stay there was short and his
work unsuccessful is a mere conjecture. He says of himself that he had worked
more, and more successfully, than all the rest, and why should we exclude his
Nabataean labors? He was probably the first Christian missionary to work
there, some three to five/six years after the resurrection (33-35/6 or so). He perhaps returned to Damascus when tensions broke out between Aretas IV and
Herod Antipas, tensions which led to military engagements in c. 35/36. A Jewish missionary who proclaimed a crucified Galilean as the divinely exalted
Messiah, as Ruler of the world and its coming Judge, an who had caused notorious unrest, must have aroused suspicion. This may help to explain why the
Nabataean governor moved against Paul when he returned to Damascus. Damascus was a Hellenistic city and a member of the Decapolis, proud of its freedom. Caligula had certainly not subjected it to the rule of Aretas IV. This
ethnarch was the governor of the Nabataean trading colony in this important
South Syrian metropolis, in the same way that the Jews, under the Ptolemies,
had had an ethnarch in Alexandria.

2. Now, after almost three years, when he had had to leave Damascus a sec-

ond time, Paul visited Jerusalem. He could not go back to Arabia and he could not stay in Damascus, and so, before he went elsewhere, he would consult the leading authorities of this young movement, only some six years old. His own account tells us that he went to see Cephas and stayed with him 15 days. Of the others he met only James, who paid sporadic visits. Of the other apostles he saw nothing. The facts here are important, and he confirms them by an oath. Reports were obviously circulating in Galatia and elsewhere that in relation to the gospel, and also his teaching on the law and circumcision, Paul was dependent on the Jerusalem authorities.

Luke might share some responsibility for this tradition. Yet at the decisive point he agrees with Paul. He never tells us that Paul's teaching came from anyone else. The idea of dependence might have come from his visit to the leading "pillars," Cephas and James. The fact that he saw so few people, and that he did not see any other apostles, was perhaps due to the secrecy of the visit. Paul was still threatened, and we learn from Rom. 15:31 and Acts 21:23 that this threat would continue. Limiting the partners in discussion was probably a cautious move. Luke tells us that Barnabas played a part relative to this dangerous visit. This sounds plausible. The fact that the former persecutor had become a leader of the new missionary sect created problems. Could he really be trusted? The later missionary companions did not count Paul as one of the Jerusalem apostles. The account in Luke finally explains why the visit was so short (15 days) after so arduous a journey. The presence of the apostate Pharisaic scribe was known to his former friends among the Jewish Hellenists, probably because Paul wished to end the secrecy, which was contrary to his temperament. Conflict thus arose. Paul was again in danger of his life. The brethren, that is, the Jewish Christians in Jerusalem, quickly sent him to Caesarea, and from there he could take ship back to his native city. This is how it might have happened. We do not have to think that Luke falsified the facts or simply invented things. Paul expresses himself with enigmatic brevity and there are many things he does not tell us. He says only enough to counteract the erroneous statements that were being made in Galatia. The apostle and the writer to Theophilus differ in tendencies but they are astonishingly agreed in their accounts.

Why did Paul visit Cephas/Peter? It was certainly not a courtesy visit. That could have been done in a single hour. Nor should we accept the modern academic solipsism that Paul was an introvert and his fears of contact caused him to subject himself to the early Christian leaders. Paul tells us himself that he wanted to know Cephas, who had been the first of the disciples and an early witness of the resurrection. And Cephas wanted to know Paul, the new (and successful?) missionary who had formerly been a Pharisaic scribe and persecutor. What was his distinctive message? The curiosity was by no means personal. It was a legitimate and unconditionally necessary theological curiosity. We are reminded of the fourth safeguard against sin in Luther's Schmalcadic Articles IV: "The mutual conversation and consolation of the brethren, as in Matthew 18. Where two or three are gathered together . . ." Here two or three really met in the name of Christ.

We must be on guard against reading into this meeting the conflict that would break out some 14 years or so later. The two talked about their preaching, their missionary experiences, and their common Lord, his work, his passion, his resurrection, and his future. They undoubtedly prayed together. From time to time James was present. There was certainly no dissension. If there had been Paul would have left sooner. On the basis of his much shorter missionary experience what took place was what Paul could 14 years later declare officially: "I explained to them the gospel that I preach among the Gentiles." And neither then nor later did he run up against any fundamental opposition. They would have to discuss Christology and the law and reminiscences of Jesus. The crucifixion and resurrection had taken place only about six years before. Nor are we to think that Paul changed his theology between this visit and the later Apostolic Council. Had there been a change his adversaries would have charged him with it and he could hardly evade this mortal objection. But we find no trace of it. Galatians 5:11 relates only to he pre-Christian activity, for from the very first, even in Damascus, Paul met with persecution as a preacher of the gospel. His life was constantly hounded by threats (2 Cor. 11). If we had an agenda of what took place on this notable visit of Paul to Peter, our NT theology and our dogmatics would be very different; we would know a great deal more!

3. Another point deserves attention. In relation to this visit, and to the unknown years that Paul spent in Antioch, there has been a good deal of speculation about what traditions Paul took over and how influential they were. We can only conjecture here. Almost nothing can be proved. Paul himself is our earliest Christian source. We must certainly reject as *fully* nonhistorical the ideas that Paul was influenced by Hellenistic syncretism, by the Mystery Religions, or by Gnosticism. A pre-Pauline Gnosticism is the imaginary product of certain advocates of the History of Religions School and the Bultmann

School, and it is connected with those in the 19th century who regarded 1 Tim. 6:20 as Pauline, or Deutero-Pauline, or at least very close to Paul. We do not have any pre-Christian Gnostic sources or references to the rise of this movement prior to that of Christianity. The earliest traceable sources date around A.D. 100.

The contrary question, whether the Pharisaically trained scribe who had also received a basic training in Greek, and who was thus intellectually superior, might not have had an essential influence on early Christian thought, has received less frequent attention. My own opinion is that the post-Pauline writings of the NT reflect many direct and indirect, positive and negative, reminiscences and influences. Did he not have an effect upon Peter?

Galatians 2:15 tells us that Paul could say to Peter: "*We* who are Jews by nature and not Gentile sinners *know,* however, that no one is justified by the works of the law but through faith in Jesus Christ . . ." Paul thinks that Peter shared this knowledge, and he takes it for granted that he sincerely accepted it. Had he not eaten (i.e., shared communion) with the Gentile Christians. Paul puts it plainly. Since Peter knew all this, he was living like a Gentile. The conclusion is that with the other pillars at Jerusalem he was accepting the gospel that Paul preached. I myself believe that he was the driving force among the three that led to this acceptance. For according to Acts 10, his later work in Corinth, and church tradition, he himself engaged in Gentile missions and did not demand circumcision. In Acts 15:8-10, Luke has him say that God who knows the hearts makes no distinction between Jew and Gentile when it comes to faith. He has purified their hearts by faith. Therefore, we should not impose the yoke of the law upon the Gentiles, which neither we nor our ancestors could bear. We ourselves as Jewish Christians believe that like the Gentiles we are saved through the grace of the Lord Jesus. In relation to the law this is not exactly what Paul assumes of Peter during the Antioch confrontation.

The question, then, is whether during the two-week visit to Jerusalem, which took place before the Apostolic Council, the scribally instructed missionary to the Gentiles influenced the leading Jerusalem disciples, the more so because his gospel corresponded to a basic trend in proclamation, namely, that God justifies sinners. And might not the impact he made have prepared the way for the later decision of the council, and especially for the freer attitude of Peter? This view finds support in the Paulinisms of Mark's Gospel, which reflects the Petrine tradition, and also offers an explanation of 1 Peter. Paul was undoubtedly nearer to Cephas/Peter theologically than were James and his circle.

At any rate the comparatively short but important visit to Jerusalem was crucial for the young messianic movement. If Paul in the issue of the law had taken
a different position during this visit from the one he took at the Apostolic Council he would have contradicted himself and could not have prevailed.

IV. The Fourteen Years in Syria and Cilicia

1. In danger of his life, Paul broke off his visit to Peter and went to a place that
the Hellenist missionaries had not yet visited, indeed, where around the year
A.D. 36 no Christian mission had been started, namely, his native city of Tarsus,
the metropolis in the Cilician part of the double province of Syria-Cilicia. According to Acts 9:30 the Christian brethren sent him there, having first brought
him to Caeasarea. Perhaps they had advised him to plant a church at the northern end of this province, as far away as possible. This is the view of R. Riesner.
Paul was still an outsider, as he had been from the very first. The attitude toward him was ambivalent. People were impressed by his argumentative powers
and by his personal and theological charisma, but they all kept him at a certain
distance, some more so, some less. Right from the outset he was a σημεῖον
ἀντιλεγόμενον.

His epistles show us that his character was by no means simple. Even then,
and not just today, it was not just theological truth that played a role but also the
personal understanding. The question of truth was, of course, at the center, as it
is not today. Paul could later stress that he never tried to work where other missionaries had been before him. This is certainly connected with his distinctive
gospel and his commissioning for Gentile missions, along with the offensively
logical position he adopted in the question of the law. Both at the first and later
he always fought alone.

At much the same period (ca. A.D. 36/37) the Jewish Christian Hellenists
began work in Antioch. During the first decade the movement of mission outside Palestine was relatively slow. This was due to the fact that imminent expectation of the second coming hampered plans for missionary journeys, and
also to the fact that outside the motherland, where the work of the Baptist and
Jesus had prepared the ground for the spread of the new messianic sect, the
singular message with its imminent eschatological expectation met considerable resistance in the Greek-speaking Syrian diaspora. That would change
later. Paul himself, after 25 years of experience, would see plainly that mis-

sionaries to the Jews were running up against a stone wall. He would find greater numbers of God-fearers, who could be more easily addressed, in the more important cities.

This would be particularly true of Antioch, the third or fourth largest city in the Empire. A famous synagogue was there that dated back to the days of the Seleucids. As in Alexandria, there were many additional synagogues. Antioch was a new and rewarding sphere of mission. Josephus tells us that there were many Jews there, and that many Greeks came regularly to the services and in some sense formed part of the congregation (Bell. 7,45). These were not just proselytes but sympathizers. According to Luke Jewish Christians from Cyrene and Cyprus, a small group, came to Antioch. These were the Hellenists who preached the Lord Jesus to the Greeks[1] and enjoyed much success. We do best to think that this group had been originally expelled from Jerusalem, where they had met with strong opposition in the synagogues. They now turned mostly to the "Greeks," to Gentile sympathizers, according to Luke. In this form of proclamation the ritual law was meaningless, and circumcision was not imposed upon the Greeks when they were baptized. This opened the door to preaching directly to Gentiles who were not sympathizers and to inviting them into gatherings in private homes, though in such cases essentially greater difficulties of understanding had to be faced. We learn from Gal. 2:13 and Acts 13:1 that Jewish Christian Hellenists had a leadership role in the community. The Roman authorities (instead of the governor of Syria) took notice of this singular messianic Jewish group who did active propaganda among non-Jews, and on the basis of the Kyrios they worshipped, gave them the name Christianoi/ Christiani (written Chrestiani). This is a sign that after thirteen years the title Christos, which was difficult for the average diaspora Jew and hard to comprehend for non-Jews, had become a proper name.

2. Hearing of these new developments, the Jerusalem community sent Barnabas to Antioch. We see here that the communities were in close touch with one another (cf. Gal. 1:22). Cohesion was needed for a young movement of "enthusiastic" outsiders. The same fact may be noted in the way that Paul writes about the churches in Judea. We must on no account agree with Haenchen that Barnabas was a displaced Hellenist and a founder of the Antioch

---

1. We should read Ἕλληνας with P74A D* Sinᶜ; Ἑλληνιστάς in B Dᶜ E Ψ Imperial Text is an assimilation to 6:1; 9:29.

community. His dependence upon Peter (Gal. 2:13) speaks decisively against this. So, too, does his close relationship with John Mark, his nephew, who was himself very close to Peter. Barnabas probably served as a mediator between the mostly Aramaic mother church in Jerusalem, on which the other Judean churches depended, and the more (but not fully) independent churches founded by the Hellenists in Syria. A constant link between the two must have existed. This occurred notwithstanding the differences that arose in how the new movement understood itself (namely, as the ἐκκλησία θεοῦ, as the eschatologically true Israel, and as the body of Christ). They still heard the *one* gospel (despite Pauline peculiarities), cf. 1 Cor. 15:11. They listened to the *one* Lord, 1 Cor. 8:6. They had received the *one* Spirit and practiced the *one* baptism, Eph. 4:5. If the first Jerusalem congregation had not recognized the Gentile mission of Paul, which was so critical of the law, the apostle would have run in vain and could not continue (Gal. 2:2). The modern view that early Christianity was wildly pluralistic is opposed by the statement of Paul himself in 1 Cor. 15:11, by his surprising attachment to Jerusalem at a later time when he sat more loosely to Antioch, and by the universal unity of the church in the 1st and 2nd centuries, attested by both the NT and the post-apostolic writings. The modern thesis finds support, not in the facts of history, but in the ideal of pluralism in a multi-cultural society. Ancient society was certainly multi-cultural, but not as we now imagine it. In questions of truth neither Jews nor Christians were pluralistic. That is why they could convince others of the truth of their faith! The fact that Barnabas remained at Antioch shows that in his view he had been used there, but also that he was in full agreement with this new development. Nevertheless, the connection with Jerusalem was never broken.

3. At this time, toward the end of the thirteen years, Paul was working in Tarsus and Cilicia. R. Riesner[2] rightly rejects Haenchen's idea that according to Luke, Paul stayed only a short time in Tarsus, his native city.[3] Haenchen consistently inclines to attribute to Luke his own critical and non-historical short-sightedness. For this reason his much lauded commentary holds no attractions. The account of Paul's preaching in the Damascus synagogues, of his free discussion with the "Hellenists" in Jerusalem, and of his vision in Jerusalem (Acts 22:18, 21), are accompanied by a schematic presentation of Peter's inaugura-

---

2. *Frühzeit*, 237.
3. *Apostelgeschichte*, 2nd ed., 1977, 321.

tion of the Gentile mission and of the work of the Hellenists in Antioch. Luke had no false ambitions to tell all that he knew or to invent where he had no knowledge. Possibly there was doubt about the first valid missionary to the Gentiles. Prior to his accompanying Barnabas, Paul was an outsider who worked alone. Luke tells us nothing about what he did at Tarsus. Riesner (loc. cit.) rightly points to Acts 15:41, where at the beginning of the second journey Paul and Silas visit and confirm the churches in Cilicia. But previously Luke had had Paul only stay there. He must have actually founded these churches. If he had lived there only in a private capacity, there would have been no reason for Barnabas to bring him to Antioch. He must have been loosely connected to the brethren in both Jerusalem and Antioch. The mention of Cilicia in Gal. 1:21 presupposes that Paul did missionary work there. If he does not refer to this work in his other epistles, this does not mean anything, for he does not refer either to his birthplace in Tarsus or to his earlier missionary successes in the eastern provinces. It is enough to refer to 1 Cor. 15:10.

We do not know how long Paul stayed at Tarsus, which had a considerable Jewish community, or how long he worked in Cilicia. The stay must have lasted for some time, in my view some two to four years. Time was needed for missionary work, especially in larger cities. Paul stayed around three years at Ephesus. The Cilician field was large, especially when we count the metropolis, Tarsus, and the thickly populated area between Tarsus and the Amanus Mountains.

The fact that Barnabas visited Paul in Tarsus and won him over for the missionary work he was doing in Antioch indicates that the two had known one another earlier, that they had had information about one another, and that Barnabas was impressed by the theological views of Paul, not least in the prickly and controversial matter of the law. We learn here how influential was Paul, the scribal scholar who had become a Christian, and also what an impact he would make upon the development of theology in Antioch. Later Ignatius, a bishop of Antioch, mentions Peter only once but refers twice to Paul, the only two figures he mentions from the primitive Christian church.[4] That Barnabas took the initiative is plausible enough. The lone fighter could not himself seek fellowship. Someone else forced him into it. He obviously did not need to stay in Tarsus or Cilicia.

---

4. Paul in Ephesians 12:2 and Romans 4:3, and Peter in Smyrn. 3:2.

Paul probably came to Antioch in 39/40 and from now on worked closely with the other Hellenist missionaries, especially Barnabas. The μετὰ Βαρναβᾶ of Gal. 2:1 and the μόνος ἐγὼ καὶ Βαρναβᾶς of 1 Cor. 9:6 point to a special personal and missionary link to this Levite from Cyprus, and Luke confirms this in his account of the missions they shared in Cyprus and then in the Roman province of Galatia in eastern Asia Minor. Though Barnabas was the elder of the two, there can be no doubt that the scribally taught Paul took the lead both in the question of the law and in the theological presentation of the message. Acts 14:12 expressly tells us that he did the speaking. We learn from Gal. 2:1 and Acts 13:1 that the two were normative authorities in Antioch. But the depiction of the controversy with Peter in Antioch, recounted only by Paul, also shows us that Paul was deeply disillusioned by Peter's conduct. He describes what took place as a chain reaction of hypocrisy. When messengers came to Antioch from the James circle at Jerusalem, Peter broke off the table fellowship that he had obviously had with the Gentile Christians, and the rest of the Jewish Christians followed his example, so that even Barnabas was involved in their hypocrisy. This incidental statement, which adds nothing to the discussion, shows both how close Paul was to Barnabas and how great his disenchantment with him was. He surely could have expected something different from this longtime missionary coworker with whom he had felt so great a theological oneness. He also mentions him because Barnabas was well-known to the South Galatian churches, which he had helped to found. The Judaizers had laid a particular charge against him: He saw that he had done wrong and drew the correct conclusions. The παροξυσμός with which Luke in Acts 15:39 describes the quarrel about John Mark, who had gone back home on the first missionary journey, was only a minor disagreement compared to the incident related in Gal. 2:1ff., which probably caused the real breach some time after the second stay in Antioch at the conclusion of the second journey (18:22). The messengers from James possibly went on to South Galatia and confused the churches there, leading to Paul's letter, sent from Ephesus. But this takes us beyond the unknown years, our present topic.

Our sole concern at this point is with the agreement between Barnabas and Paul on the question of the law. We learn from this that during the crisis at Antioch Paul demonstrated his theological and pastoral consistency, which also gave expression to his steadfast character. It cannot be proved that he had suddenly sharpened his view due to what took place in Galatia. On the contrary, he could not have reacted as sharply as he did if he had not, in founding the churches, proclaimed plainly to those in South Galatia on the first missionary journey his theology of the cross and Christ as the end of the law (cf. Gal. 3:1; 5:7 and the πάλιν in 5:1). Without a preceding proclamation of this kind the recipients could not have understood the epistle. Also the presentation of his theology in Romans, written to an unknown church in the capital city, would have been meaningless if the apostle was not here focusing upon the core of his message.

4. We need to reverse the process. In the time between the visit to Peter and the coming of the παρείσακτοι ἀδελφοί (Gal. 2:4) to Antioch that occasioned the second visit, with Barnabas, to Jerusalem (Luke says the third in Acts 15:1-3), the attitude of the younger, enthusiastic, eschatological community, at least outside Jewish Palestine, was shown by the conduct of the Hellenists, of Barnabas, and even of Peter, to be only partly subject to the authorities in Jerusalem in the matter of the law, and especially in respect of the demand for circumcision, on which it took a more generous line than would be seen in the fifties, when James apparently refused to accept the collection and Paul was almost lynched by the temple mob and finally arrested. This is connected with the persecution under Agrippa I and the "zeal for the law" that arose after his death. Today we might refer to this as political and religious fundamentalism.

We must relate all this to the nine or ten years preceding the Apostolic Council (ca. A.D. 39/40–48/49) in which, with Antioch as a base, Paul and Barnabas worked in Syria and Cilicia and neighboring territories (Cyprus, Pisidia, Lycaonia). As I have already stated, we must link the restriction to Syria (and Cilicia) to intensive eschatological expectation and to the lack of missionary direction by the Spirit. Apocalyptic geographic expectation might also have played a part. Syria as far as Taurus, the territory of Shem, would belong to the coming missionary kingdom, and therefore the earliest Christian apocalyptic hope there had to be chiliastic (Mark 14:25). The larger diaspora among the nations had to be brought home, and the Gentiles had to be collected for a pilgrimage to Zion. Riesner and Scott have shown that, among other things, geographical considerations deriving from prophecy affected the later missionary planning of Paul. But we cannot pursue this matter here.

A more important point is that in Syria and Phoenicia, according to Acts, Paul was welcomed as an old acquaintance by a whole series of churches, and accepted by them. This is perhaps because his lengthy Syrian work had caused him to visit these congregations. Luke, as an eyewitness, describes his reception at Tyre when journeying with the collection. He stayed with the disciples

there for seven days and was warned about this Jerusalem visit (Acts 21:3-6).
He also spent one day with the brethren at Ptolemais, and he spent some days in
the house of Philip at Caesarea. The warning, given greater emphasis by the
prophecy of Agabus, was repeated here.

Brethren from Caesarea accompanied Paul and Luke on the final stretch of
the journey to Jerusalem, and in the Holy City an older disciple, the Cyprian
Mnason, entertained them. On the journey to Rome friends in Sion provided for
Paul's needs (27:3). Paul must have been well-known to the churches along the
Phoenician and Syrian coasts, and also well-respected. He was probably an old
acquaintance form his many years of missionary activity in Syria. Jerusalem
was the focus of problems, and he was given warning. This would not have
been possible if these churches had made a point of rejecting his teaching on
the law. His reception by James, notwithstanding the harmonizing depiction by
Luke (courtesies were maintained and the rules were followed), makes plain the
differences between them (21:18-25). The friendly reception by the brethren
(ἀσμένως ἀπεδέξαντο ἡμᾶς οἱ ἀδελφοί, 21:17) relates only to a small group of
Hellenists who welcomed him before his meeting with James. We learn from
Romans, and perhaps from the Epistle of James, that rumors were circulating
that showed Paul to be an antinomian who promoted libertinism. Yet the time in
Syria still aroused sympathy for Paul. Typical here is what seems to be a close
relationship with Philip.

The missionary work in Syria, which had included a strengthening of the
churches already founded, had not been restricted to North Syria and Cilicia. It
also took in the South up to Caesarea, Damascus, and even perhaps the
Decapolis and Arabia. Palestine and the Decapolis east of the Jordan were
thought to be part of Syria by Greek and Roman geographers. Paul and Barnabas had time enough for these places. The ends of the earth were in the far distance. Acts 15:3 tells us that the two visited the communities of Phoenicia and
Samaria on the way to Jerusalem and that their friends there joyfully heard
about their missionary successes among the Gentiles. In these obscure eight to
ten years, Paul, with his decisive theological arguments, had spread abroad his
gospel that was critical of the law throughout Syria.

5. Jerusalem alone remained aloof, along with Judean Palestine. Paul's version of the message and its criticism of the law met with increasing resistance
there. The pogroms in Alexandria, Antioch, etc., and the attempt of Caligula to
erect a statue of Zeus/Jupiter in the temple, along with the controversy at
Jamnia and the occurrence in the synagogue at Dor, had helped to promote im-

minent apocalyptic and nationalist expectation, hatred of everything foreign, and suspicion of all apostasy. The persecution of Jewish Christians in Jerusalem under Agrippa I, and the execution of James, the son of Zebedee, and other leaders, forced Peter to leave his native land. The "other place" he went to (Acts 12:17) might have been Rome. Eusebius thought so, and perhaps, too, Clement of Alexandria. The charge now, as also twenty years later against James, the Lord's brother (A.D. 62), was that of transgression against the law. Peter and the other disciples were obviously not strict enough in keeping the law, the same accusation as was brought against James when he took over the leadership of the community at the head of the council of elders. In Gal. 2:8, James is the first of the three pillars, and this points to a change in leadership that led to a more scrupulous observance of the law.

James knew the situation well enough. He was well aware of the critical message of Paul and Barnabas, as were the other two pillars, Peter and John. Probably the crisis under Agrippa I was the reason why, twelve years after the primary event, the apostles left Jerusalem according to a well-attested report. The departure fits in well with this persecution, probably around A.D. 43.[5] This would mean not only that Peter left Judea but, also that he could no longer influence the Twelve. The death of some disciples and the departure of others had probably dissolved his influence. New members were no longer being called. One might say that under this persecution the Hebrew Christians grouped around Peter, and the Twelve suffered much the same fate as the Hellenists had done after the death of Stephen. James could hold on because he personally pursued a stricter legal piety, which was imitated by those who followed him. Things were not helped when Zelotism grew stronger after the death of Agrippa I, and the changing of Judea into a Roman province (A.D. 44). Luke offers an impressive description of this background, and like Josephus, he was an eyewitness of the events between 57 and 59 (Acts 21–26). The developing zeal for the law was what led to the sending of messengers to Antioch, the demand that the Gentile believers should be circumcised, and the ensuing controversies (ca. A.D. 48). This did not cause Paul to change his position regarding the question of the law, but the Jerusalem embassy and the conflict with Peter in Antioch after the Council gave that position a tragic sharpness when the Jewish Christians in Antioch followed the example of Peter. For the sake of compro-

---

5. Riesner, *Frühzeit,* 106ff.

mise Peter was willing to give up his "liberal" attitude. For the sake of the gospel, however, Paul would not yield but maintained unbroken his eucharistic fellowship with the Gentile Christians.

In spite of the views of Haenchen and others who are followers of Baur, the fellowship between Antioch and Jerusalem was never abandoned. We learn from Acts 13:1 that three of the five names mentioned there, Barnabas, Manaen, and Symeon, all came from Jerusalem, and the same holds good for Paul, who had been trained as a Pharisee there. Even the Cyrenian Lucius (not the same as Luke) had come to Antioch by way of Jerusalem and was one of the Hellenists who had been driven out. The collection taken to provide relief under Claudius is not a Lucan invention, nor is the visit to the Palestinian prophet, Agabus, who was favorably inclined to Paul (Acts 21:10ff.). Galatians 2:1 seems to be rather more accurate than Acts 11:30, for it tells us that for some reason Paul did not accompany Barnabas on the visit to Jerusalem. The Caligula affair had roused the emotions, and the Holy City was clearly too hot a place for Paul. Luke was perhaps simply in error. Because of this threat Jerusalem was out of bounds for Paul. Even after fourteen years he went there only on the basis of a special revelation because suddenly the validity of his Gentile proclamation of a gospel that was critical of the law was now at stake. There was all the more reason why, after the painful experiences at Antioch, Paul should maintain fellowship with Jerusalem: telling of the persecution of the Judean churches in 1 Thess. 2:14, finding here the start of the Gentile missions in Rom. 15:19, and gathering a collection for the oppressed congregation of the saints, which the people in Jerusalem would perhaps view as a substitute for the temple tax, but which Paul saw as a sign of the unity and the bond of love that encircles the church.

V. Conclusion

In no way can it be demonstrated that the doctrine of the law and of justification grew only out of the conflict in Galatia. It had its source in the conversion of the Pharisaic scribe and the ἀποκάλυψις Ἰησοῦ Χριστοῦ that was received in this connection. Its basis was the gospel that was received from the Risen Lord, that made Paul a missionary to the Gentiles, and that he had to defend consistently in various situations of conflict. We can find an approach to the critical attitude of Paul to the law in the Hellenists and then in authorities like Peter and Barnabas. Paul did not sharpen his critical attitude. A stricter observance of the law which was enforced with the external development in Judea, and which then spread outside Palestine, was responsible for the conflicts of which we read in the Epistles to Galatia, Philippi, and Rome. A separate theological question is how far Paul's attitude to the law can be based at least in part on the conduct and preaching of Jesus himself. We should certainly not rule out this possibility.

Paul's Reasoning in Galatians 2:11–21

by

JAN LAMBRECHT

This discussion paper deals with Galatians 2:11–21. In a first preliminary remark I would like to point out some delineations. This work will not address problems such as whether Galatia is the territory – my position – or the (Roman) province. The comparison between Galatians and Acts regarding historical exactitude will be omitted and thus will it not be necessary to reconstruct, e.g., the number and the dates of Paul's journeys to Jerusalem. The questions concerning the apostolic Decree of the so-called Jerusalem council which are mentioned in Acts 15 but do not appear in Gal 2 also need not detain us too long. The view that the so-called incident of Antioch occurred not before but after the Jerusalem council, as is suggested by Paul himself in Galatians, seems preferable. The letter to the Galatians may have been written not so long before Romans, about six or seven years after the Antioch incident.

My second preliminary remark concerns methodological procedure. I will try to avoid unwarranted hypotheses and reconstructions. The main question to be asked is: what does the text tell us? Perhaps the text itself does not provide us with sufficient information regarding numerous items about which we are curious.

The paper will consist of three parts. In the first part, through an initial reading, I will present my own understanding of Galatians 2:11–21, occasionally using exegetical notes taken from previous publications[1]. The second section will consider the specific characteristics of Paul's argument, again with the help of a previous study[2]. The third part will contain a presentation and discussion of positions suggested or defended in some recent studies.

---

[1] J. Lambrecht, *The Line of Thought in Galatians 2,14b–21*, in *NTS* 24 (1977–78) 484–495, *Once Again Galatians 2,17–18 and 3,21*, in *ETL* 63 (1987) 148–153, and *Transgressor by Nullifying God's Grace. A Study of Galatians 2,18–21*, in *Biblica* 72 (1991) 217–236. The three articles are republished in J. Lambrecht, *Pauline Studies* (BETL, 115), Leuven, 1994, pp. 193–204, 205–209, and 211–230.

[2] J. Lambrecht, *Unity and Diversity in Galatians 1–2*, in *Unité et diversité dans l'Eglise* (Commission Biblique Pontificale), Città del Vaticano, 1989, pp. 127–142; republished in Lambrecht, *Pauline Studies* (n. 1), pp. 177–192. – The reader is referred to the bibliography used in the four articles mentioned in notes 1 and 2.

I. Exegesis

The passage consisting of Gal 2:11–21 belongs to the first major section of the letter, Paul's autobiographical report from the days of his persecution of the church of God until the incident of Antioch (1:11–2:21). The pericope itself can be divided into two parts: the description of the incident (2:11–14a) and Paul's spoken reaction at the time, his address to Peter (2:14b–21). Although verses 15–21 cannot be considered as a literal report of the words pronounced by Paul at Antioch and partly function as a more general statement meant in the first place for the recipients of the letter, they are connected with v. 14b and together they are presented by Paul as a small but impressive discourse.

1. Verses 11–14a

Paul is interiorly convinced that he preaches God's gospel. He has not received it from a human source but through a revelation of Jesus Christ (1:11–12). After the first test case, Titus and the question of whether he must be circumcised (2:1–10) – a case which found an adequate solution agreed upon in Jerusalem – there now has arisen a second case, the incident at Antioch with regard to table fellowship, the Jewish dietary prescriptions (2:11–14a). In his address to Peter Paul intends to prove that he is right, that his missionary work is consistent with "the truth of the gospel" (v. 14a).

V. 11 provides us with the anticipatory summary of the report. In vv. 12–13 Paul explains why Peter stands self-condemned. This is taken up by the statement in v. 14a: "when I saw that they were not straightforward about the truth of the gospel". In the same verse 14a the clause "I said to Cephas before them all" repeats what is meant by "I opposed him to his face". Most probably the third person plural ἦλθον in v. 12 is the reading to be preferred. We notice that in vv. 12–13 it is Cephas who begins with the separation; he is joined by the rest of the Jewish Christians; finally even Barnabas is carried away. Peter's withdrawal is qualified by the term 'hypocrisy'; he is not only not straightforward about the truth of the gospel, but, what is worse, he knows that what he is doing is wrong. Peter and his followers are insincere. Their behavior has to do with table fellowship: first eating with the Gentile Christians, then separating themselves from them. It is not all that clear whether those meals included the Eucharist (probably not) nor is it evident that in this association with the Gentiles the prescriptions of the apostolic Decree of Acts 15 were already observed (probably not). "The people from James" are not the same as the "false brothers" of 2:4. The two cases are different: circumcision and table fellowship. Moreover, "the people from James" are not called 'false' and it would appear from 2:3–10 that the three pillars, Peter, John and also James, have not given in to "the false brothers", whereas "the people from James" seem to be to a certain degree the delegates of James. It is not plainly stated what their objections to the situation of Antioch were. Are they only scandalized because Jewish Christians eat with Gentiles, or can they also not understand how converted Gentiles do not observe the Jewish dietary laws[3]?

2. Verse 14b

Paul's address can be divided into three sections, unequal in regard to length: (1) v. 14b (second person singular, 'you'): the introductory question; (2) vv. 15–17 (first person plural, 'we'): the profound reflection in which the ultimate reason for the Christian behavior is given; for a moment the speech forgets, as it were, the incident reported in vv. 10–14a; (3) vv. 18–21 (first person singular, 'I'): Paul returns to the concrete difficulty in Antioch and begins a second train of thought.

The question of v. 14b, in fact a conditional period, contains a sharp personal reprimand. Paul says to Peter: you should not do what you are doing; how can you compel the Gentiles to live like Jews? With the verb Ἰουδαΐζω one rightly thinks of the Jewish way of life, the Jewish customs, especially circumcision, Sabbath observance, and the food laws. Yet in this specific context (cf. 2:1–10), Paul can no longer refer to circumcision; he has in mind the discriminating dietary prescriptions. In what sense does Peter compel the Gentiles? The answer to this question is not immediately obvious. The pressure on the Gentiles should presumably be explained as follows. If they want to be fully accepted by their fellow Jewish Christians, they must adopt the Jewish lifestyle and "live like Jews". It is an indirect compulsion.

In the protasis Paul says: "If you, though a Jew, live like a Gentile and not like a Jew". By these words, notwithstanding the use of the present tense ζῆς, he refers to Peter's behavior before the withdrawal; but at the same time he may implicitly appeal to what Peter is still believing. The apodosis then wants to reveal an inconsistency between Peter's supposedly persisting Christian conviction and his changed present behavior. Peter, Paul asks with probing insistence, how is this possible, how can you?[4]

---

[3] For supporting argumentation for these choices and for a more extensive study of Gal 2:11–14a, see A. Wechsler, *Geschichtsbild und Apostelstreit. Eine forschungsgeschichtliche und exegetische Studie über den antiochenischen Zwischenfall (Gal 2,11–14)* (BZNW, 62), Berlin-New York, 1991, esp. pp. 296–348 (e.g., ὅτε (δέ) in v. 11, the disputed reading in v. 12 – ἦλθεν or ἦλθον – and the implications of the choice, the meaning of ὑπόκρισις in v. 13, and the meaning of ὀρθοποδέω in v. 14a). Cf. also D.J. Verseput, *Paul's Gentile Mission and the Jewish Christian Community: A Study of the Narrative in Galatians 1 and 2*, in *NTS* 39 (1993) 36–58, esp. pp. 51–57; M. Stowasser, *Konflikte und Konfliktlösungen nach Gal 1,2*, in *TrTZ* 103 (1994) 56–79, esp. pp. 72–77.

[4] See Wechsler, *Geschichtsbild* (n. 3), pp. 349–364.

3. Verses 15–17

Vv. 15–16 together form one long repetitious sentence. The main clause
stands in the middle of v. 16 and begins with the statement "even we – you
Peter and I Paul, Jews by birth – have believed in Jesus Christ". One should
link v. 15 with v. 16a; both qualify the subject of the main clause. We may
consider the δέ at the beginning of v. 16 as authentic and also mentally add in
v. 15 ὄντες μέν so that the parallel character of both participial clauses becomes evident: on the one hand, on the other. As often in a μέν … δέ construction, the first clause (v. 15) possesses a concessive nuance: it is true, everybody knows, all agree that we are Jews by birth and not Gentile sinners. The
emphasis, however, lies on the second clause (v. 16a): yet we know, i.e., we
fully realize that a person is justified not by works of the law but through faith
in Jesus Christ.

The expression 'works of the law' means 'works done in obedience to the
law' and comprises, it would seem, all such works, not only those in obedience to the ceremonial law. In view of the main clause with πιστεύω εἰς … the
genitive in πίστις Ἰησοῦ Χριστοῦ is almost certainly objective. In v. 16 three
times the same three elements recur: the verb 'to justify', the expression 'by
the works of the law' and the noun '(Jesus) Christ'; thus three times the same
idea is put forward. First the motivation is clearly enunciated (because we
know …), then the act and its aim are indicated (we have believed … in order
that …), and finally a Scripture quotation is added (because …; cf. Ps 143:2).

The term ἁμαρτωλοί in the clause εἰ δὲ ζητοῦντες δικαιωθῆναι ἐν Χριστῷ
εὑρέθημεν καὶ αὐτοὶ ἁμαρτωλοί (v. 17a) has been interpreted in many ways.
Two important though mutually exclusive understandings may be helpful for
our further discussion. First: through and since our becoming Christians we
were found to be sinners because we started to live like the Gentiles (cf. v. 14),
not observing the law, eating with the Gentiles: sinners because of post-
conversional acts. Second: already before we believed in Jesus Christ we were
sinners, just like the Gentiles (cf. 15): sinners because of pre-conversional acts.

According to the first interpretation, we, i.e., Paul and Peter (and the Jewish
Christians in general), were found to be sinners because, having become
Christians, we no longer observe the law (or certain portions of it). We are,
therefore, on a par with the Gentiles. Our eating with them is an instance of
disobedience to the law. Since our faith in Christ, i.e., our endeavor to be justified in him, is the cause of this disobedient behavior, the question arises
whether Christ does not promote infidelity, whether he is not an agent of sin.
Paul counters this question with an indignant μὴ γένοιτο. In this interpretation, v. 17ab can easily be understood as an objection raised by the Judaizers
against the Pauline thesis of v. 16. These Judaizers are convinced that the Jewish Christians should continue to observe the law.

The second interpretation connects the phrase "we ourselves were found to be sinners" with the situation of the Jewish Christians (and particularly Paul and Peter) prior to their becoming Christians. The decision of these Jewish Christians to believe in Jesus Christ manifests their conviction that they too, like the Gentiles, are sinners and in need of redemption, and that, as sinners, they can reach justification only through faith in Christ, not through works of the law. But how, in this second interpretation, can the conclusion be drawn from the Jewish Christians' recognition of themselves as sinners and their seeking to be justified in Christ that Christ is a minister of sin? He cannot be so designated simply on the grounds that it is their faith in Christ which has brought the Jewish Christians to the recognition of their sinfulness. How then should we understand the text? By taking to himself sinners alone – and before God all are sinners – and by justifying them by grace, without works of the law, Christ promotes sin, because there has to be sin if there are to be sinners for him to justify and because the sinners know that they can obtain remission of sins in Christ apart from the works of the law. We have presumably before us then the well-known accusation that Christ (or, better, Paul's christology) furthers antinomianism, that Christ's free remission of sin removes the restraints on sin and even approves and promotes sin. And so, one understands Paul's vehement reaction: μὴ γένοιτο – Christ is not an agent of sin; that is not my christology.

Which of the two interpretations is more probably correct? Perhaps a careful consideration of vv. 18–21 can help us in our choice. But let us first analyse v. 17 in more detail. V. 17b, the apodosis of the conditional period, is best taken as a question: "Is Christ an agent of sin?" The protasis (v. 17a) is presumably not a condition contrary to fact. Our view on this point is not in the first place based on the absence of an ἄν in the apodosis – for this absence could, if necessary, be explained in terms of a transition from the 'irrealis' in the protasis to a 'realis' in the apodosis – or by the lack of a verb in the apodosis-question. It is rather the train of thought and, above all, a comparison with Paul's way of reasoning elsewhere which lead us to consider v. 17a as a simple condition, a 'realis'. In this case, just as in all other instances in Paul, the objection would contain a premise (here the conditional protasis of v. 17a) with which Paul agrees, and a question (here the apodosis of v. 17b) which draws an illegitimate, wrong conclusion from that premise. It is this conclusion, not the premise, which Paul radically rejects, here as elsewhere, by means of the μὴ γένοιτο.

In the protasis the verb εὑρέθημεν means "we were found to be". This happened (past tense) while we were seeking (present participle; possibly a causal nuance is present here: because we were seeking) to be justified in Christ. Most probably, ἁμαρτωλοί does not point to the sinful conduct of those who had become Christians (i.e., their post-conversional sins), but rather refers back to that fundamental sinfulness which in v. 15 is said to be characteristic of the Gentiles: we too, as Jews, before we believed in Christ, were sinners (i.e., by pre-conversional sins) just like the Gentiles. Precisely because we realized that nobody is justified by works of the law, even we Jews came to believe in Christ Jesus (v. 16).

The Judaizers concluded that this typically Pauline view entails that Christ promotes sin. It would appear that the ἁμαρτία in v. 17b designates the same radical idea of sinfulness as the ἁμαρτωλοί in v. 17a (and v. 15). It is Christ's promotion of sin in this sense which is dramatically negated by Paul in v. 17c. In the opponents' objection, ἁμαρτία includes, of course, actions which for Paul are no longer real 'sin', e.g., eating with the Gentiles. And, therefore, one could say that a certain ambiguity is present in the term ἁμαρτία in v. 17b. Such passages as 5:13 and Rom 3:7–8 and 6:1, 15 show, however, that in the objection about promoting sin, an objection raised more than once by Paul's opponents, 'sin' is to be taken in its most radical sense: Paul's system leads to antinomianism and immorality.

It will be noted that our understanding of v. 17 is basically in agreement with the second interpretation set out above.

4. Verses 18–21

It appears that after v. 17 there is a kind of break, a caesura. The γάρ at the beginning of v. 18 comes close to meaning "but". After his reflection on what happened at the time of the justification Paul comes back to the concrete Antioch incident which manifested Peter's behavior of restoring what was pulled down. Of course, one could argue that between v. 17 and 18 something is missing, that in his emotion Paul has omitted the necessary logical link. So one may conjecture that Paul, after v. 17 and before writing v. 18, thought: "Not Christ is an agent of sin, *but* we may become promoters of sin, *for* if I build up again …". This hypothetical intervening thought fulfills more or less the same logical function as our hypothetically slightly adversative γάρ which introduces a new idea.

The break between v. 17 and v. 18 is evident from the time references (in v. 17a: conversion; in v. 18: Antioch incident and now), and also from the sudden appearance of "I". Already in vv. 15–17 Paul, out of rhetorical skill as well as tactful concern, has associated himself with Peter. Peter must also be aimed at in v. 18, yet Paul equally reflects on what would be the consequences of his own eventual action. "But if I build up again those things which I tore down, then I prove myself a transgressor". Notwithstanding the caesura the term "transgressor" is somewhat related to "sinners" and "sin" in the preceding verse 17.

V. 19ab motivates v. 18, more specifically the idea of transgressing: we have a normal explanatory γάρ. Since through the law Paul died to the law, he transgresses by building up that law. He should not work nor live any longer for the law; he must live for Christ. Some elements of this statement remain for the moment mysterious. The general flow of thought, however, can hardly be doubted. V. 19c repeats and clarifies v. 19a. The way Paul died was the death on the cross: he has been crucified with Christ. By this complementary information we now know where, when and how Paul died. The perfect tense points to an enduring state.

In the light of v. 19c the lengthy v. 20 resumes and corrects v. 19ab as well as combining it with v. 19c; v. 20 opens with an opposing δέ. As a matter of fact Paul's actual life is no longer his own life, but that of Christ. His present bodily life is lived in faith in the Son of God. Christ loved Paul personally and delivered himself for him. The reader will note that up till now the train of thought which came to a halt at the end of v. 18 has not been further developed. What Paul adds in vv. 19 and 20 is first motivation (v. 19ab), then clarification (v. 19c) and finally concretization of that motivation (v. 20).

With its negative content v. 21a probably resumes the idea of v. 18a (here in the form of a protasis). "I do not nullify the grace of God" seems to paraphrase "I am not going to build up again those things which I tore down". If this reading is correct Paul would become a transgressor by nullifying God's grace, by building up again. In v. 21bc there is another explanatory γάρ. A verb is lacking in the protasis of this conditional period and, moreover, there is no ἄν in the apodosis. So one may wonder whether instead of an 'irrealis' (a condition contrary to fact) the grammatical form is not a 'realis', a condition of fact (a "simple condition"). The reasoning would then be: If A, then B; the form of a condition of fact is indifferent to the fulfillment or non-fulfillment of what is stated. What we have is no more than the stringent logical connection. In v. 21bc this reads literally: "if justification through law, then Christ died in vain". Thus, to the question "Why does Paul nullify God's grace?", the answer is: "Because, if justification is through the law, then Christ died to no purpose". V. 21b corresponds regarding its content to v. 18a: if the law is in force (again); if it is built up again. V. 21c draws the conclusion: then the death of Christ has been in vain. Verse 21bc explains why, in such case, Paul destroys the grace of God.

At the end of this reading of vv. 18–21 we may point to Paul's way of reasoning. The train of thought comes to a standstill, as it were, after v. 18 and is then resumed in v. 21. Vv. 19–20 motivate, explain and concretize v. 18. In v. 21a Paul denies the idea to which the hypothetical content of v. 18a leads, namely, that he is going to destroy the grace of God. Does v. 18b, therefore, not also contain that idea? V. 21bc explains the statement of v. 21a; as in v. 18 we have a conditional period. Grammatically speaking v. 21b corresponds with v. 18a (twice a protasis with εἰ γάρ), and v. 21c with v. 18b (twice an apodosis, a 'then'-clause). What about their content, more in particular that of v. 18b ("then I prove myself a transgressor")? A further analysis is needed.

V. 18. The conditional sentence of v. 18 is a 'realis', a condition of fact. In the protasis we have the opposition between καταλύω and οἰκοδομέω. Paul often uses antitheses. At first sight it does not make much difference if συνιστάνω ἐμαυτόν in the apodosis has the somewhat weaker sense "I show, I demonstrate, I prove myself" or the stronger one "I establish, I constitute myself". Pauline passages such as 2 Cor 7:11; Rom 3:5 and 5:8, however, seem to point to the weaker sense: Paul proves himself to be a transgressor. What does this mean?

The noun παραβάτης is not followed by an objective genitive, the presence of which would have indicated what Paul is actually transgressing. We shall have to look at the context to discover the implied direct object of "transgressing". The aorist tense of κατέλυσα contains a reference to the time when Paul became a Christian. The adverb πάλιν and the verb οἰκοδομῶ point the reader to the hypothetical step of Paul (and the actual step of Peter) "to live again like a Jew" (cf. 2:14). With ἅ and ταῦτα we must think in the first place of eating with the Gentiles and, further, of calendar prescriptions (4:10), and circumcision (5:2–3). All this pertains to the Jewish law. But it should be duly noted that νόμος itself is not mentioned in v. 18a. If that had been the case one would have been brought, almost inevitably, to understand the ensuing παραβάτης in v. 18b as "transgressor of the law".

Many interpreters, however, do mentally supply 'of the law' after 'transgressor'. How does Paul then show himself a transgressor of the law? There are two possibilities: either his previous pulling down of the law was a transgression of the law, or Paul, after having built up, will out of necessity sin in the future by not keeping all its commandments (see 3:10 and cf. 5:3). Because of the absence of νόμος in v. 18 and even more because of the line of thought in v. 19–21, neither of these interpretations seems satisfactory.

V. 19. The personal pronoun ἐγώ at the beginning of v. 19 is very emphatic. In view of the fact that θεῷ in v. 19b is best understood as a dative of interest and because of the correspondence between the opposing verbs ἀπέθανον and ζήσω, the dative νόμῳ in v. 19a is probably a dative of disadvantage: through the law I died "to the law" so that it has no longer any power over me. There is no qualification of either use of 'law' in v. 19a, but they must point to the same Jewish law (cf. also vv. 16 and 21). The dative νόμῳ is preceded by the genitive expression διὰ νόμου. What is the meaning of this expression?

In order to find a sense for the puzzling διὰ νόμου in v. 19a one must, it would seem, take a lead from v. 19c and, through it, from 3:13. Why has Christ been crucified? According to 3:13 Christ became a curse, i.e., cursed by the law, because he hung on the cross; and so he redeemed us from that same curse of the law which we incurred through our sins. Paul appears here to be reasoning by means of categories such as reparatory substitution and atoning sacrifice. Christ died for us, on our behalf. Paul more specifically thinks in cultic terms of salvation through death. Christ has taken over the identity of us sinners; he died the death to which the law had condemned us and so redeemed and blessed us (cf. 3:13–14). Of course, the 'cultic terms' are meant here metaphorically.

According to 2:19a Paul dies. Through the identification of Paul-sinner and Christ who on the cross became a curse, Paul was present and dying at the moment Jesus died on the cross. This death by the law was his redemption; it was at the same time a death *to* the law. Through this death Paul is no longer ὑπὸ νόμον (cf. 4:21). Henceforth he must live for God (2:19b; cf. Rom 7:4 and 6). Paul can even say in Gal 2:19c: I have been crucified with Christ. "This is a bold statement from one who was not even present at Calvary!" (G. Berényi). But Paul was present; this is his firm conviction. There and then, Paul died to the law. One realizes both the metaphorical and paradoxical qualities of the verb συσταυροῦμαι which is not found in extant literature before Paul. It is quite possible that Paul created this metaphor. The paradoxical character of v. 19c should be duly reflected upon: nothing is common between death on a cross and new life; moreover, both death and life are conceived of as through and together with Christ! The perfect tense συνεσταύρωμαι is not accidental.

V. 20. This is the longest verse of the unit (v. 18–21), much discussed because of the christological content of v. 20d which is often thought to go back a traditional *Dahingabe-Formel.* Paul continues to speak a paradoxical language: no longer his own life, Christ's life in him; Christ delivers himself up for Paul. There are, moreover, two sharp antitheses: in v. 20ab I-Christ, in v. 20cd flesh-faith. The initial δέ in v. 20a corrects what Paul has just said in v. 19b about his living for God. As a matter of fact (again a δέ in v. 20b, now opposing), it is Christ who lives in him. We note the change of subject. In v. 20a and b we have before us two short clauses of equal length, beginning respectively with ζῶ δέ and ζῇ δέ and ending antithetically – the second as it were excluding the first – with ἐγώ and Χριστός. We may refer to 1 Cor 15:10 for a similar affirmation and negation: "I worked harder than any of them, though it was not I, but the grace of God which is with me".

Yet in v. 20cd, by means of a third and opposing δέ Paul must return to the first person singular, to his own living "now". He cannot deny it completely. It is, moreover, a life in the flesh. This human life is still (νῦν) bodily, creaturely fragile; it is not yet an eschatological existence. Nonetheless, already now that life in the flesh is simultaneously a life in the faith of the Son of God who loved Paul and delivered himself for him. The clause "what I now live" (v. 20c) is the direct object of the same verb of v. 20d: "(what I now live) I live …". The relative pronoun ἅ may be limitative; it then suggests, as it were, a lesser form of life: "So far as I live now in the flesh". "I live" is qualified not only by "now" (over against the eschatological future) but also by "in the flesh" (over against a life which will be spiritual, heavenly, immortal and incorruptible – see 1 Cor 15:48–54).

In v. 20d υἱοῦ τοῦ θεοῦ is an objective genitive just as Ἰησοῦ Χριστοῦ in v. 16 which genitive is immediately explained in the same verse 16 by "even we have believed in Christ". Berényi has shown that v. 20d is not a stereo-typed and traditional formula. Both wording and content come from Paul. V. 20d is a Pauline creation. A comparison with the undoubtedly traditional formula in 1 Cor 15:3 Χριστὸς (traditional?) ἀπέθανεν ὑπὲρ τῶν ἁμαρτιῶν ἡμῶν might prove instructive. Three Pauline particularities vis-à-vis 1 Cor 15:3 must be stressed. (1) Instead of Χριστός we have in v. 20d υἱοῦ τοῦ θεοῦ. The title "Son of God" is "rarely used by Paul. With its solemnity this title underlines the contrast with 'me' and therefore contributes to the paradoxical character of the verse" (Berényi). (2) Παραδίδωμι is different from δίδωμι. Παραδίδωμι with personal object (here reflexive pronoun) possesses a nega-tive meaning; it "implies that the person is delivering himself up to a hostile treatment" (Berényi). Moreover, "... the expression ... with παραδίδωμι and the reflexive pronoun is a creation of Paul himself" (Berényi). (3) The typical and original use of ἀγαπάω by Paul is confirmed by passages such as Rom 5:6–8 and 8:32–39 which both possess a similar context. This verb "provides the motivation of and accounts for the efficacy of the Son of God's act of de-livering himself up" (Berényi). Without love Christ would not have done this; without love his action would have no result.

V. 21. "This sentence" is "abruptly introduced, without connective" (Bur-ton). In the verb ἀθετέω of v. 21a there is most probably a modal nuance: I am not going or I am not willing or I am not allowed to cancel (to render invalid, to nullify) the grace of God. In v. 20 Paul had beautifully indicated what riches are contained in the expression ἡ χάρις τοῦ θεοῦ (subjective gen.): God's grace is basically the gift of Christ, his person and all that he did, especially his dying out of love. While in v. 20d Christ himself is the active subject, here in v. 21a God has the initiative. We may refer to Rom 8:35 and 39: in v. 35 Paul writes: "Who shall separate us from the love of *Christ*?" (cf. v. 37), while in v. 39 he has: nobody and nothing "will be able to separate us from the love of *God* in Christ Jesus our Lord". Thus, without any difficulty Paul can move from Christ to God and from God to Christ. "In this expression 'the love of God in Christ Jesus' Paul makes a synthesis and shows that in reality God's love and Christ's love are the same thing" (Berényi). How could Paul nullify God's grace? The context refers us back to v. 18a: by building up again what I pulled down, i.e., the prescriptions of the law.

V. 21bc repeats that idea of clinging to the law by means of a more general formulation. The conditional period of v. 21bc is most probably in form again a "simple supposition", not an irrealis. The translation of the protasis should then be: "If justification *is* through the law". Of course, Paul is convinced of the opposite, but the grammatical form as such does not indicate this; it only stresses the logical connection between protasis and apodosis, between justification through the law and its consequence, the useless death of Christ.

The expression διὰ νόμου of v. 21b has already appeared in v. 19a. The meaning there, however, is quite different. In v. 19 Paul speaks of his death together with Christ on the cross. Why in v. 19a did he write: "through the law"? We may briefly comment on what we have already stated in our analysis of v. 19. Since Christ died on the cross, he became a curse through the law and so redeemed us from the curse of that law (see 3:13). Most probably Paul's reasoning in 3:10–14 implies that through not observing the law we are sinners and, therefore, cursed by the law (see 3:10); we cannot be justified by it. Only Christ, by becoming a curse and thus taking our place, brings redemption. In 2:19a Paul writes that the law caused his death and in 19c that he has been crucified with Christ. This seems to imply that in some sense Christ's death as well is caused by the law. This is true not because Christ violated the law, but because he had to become cursed by the law in order to redeem us from the curse of the law. Admittedly, Paul writes in a very concise way. "Through the law" in 2:19a contains, most likely, the negative connotation that Paul, like all humankind, does not keep that law.

In the protasis of 2:21b, however, the supposition is that there is justification διὰ νόμου, i.e., through observing the law, through doing the works of the law – which, of course, is impossible according to Paul. V. 21b formulates as a hypothesis something that is denied three times within v. 16, namely, that nobody is justified by works of the law. Suppose, Paul says in v. 21bc, that justification as a matter of fact occurs through the law, then Christ's death is no longer needed, Christ died in vain. The expressions "by works of the law" (v. 16) and "through the law" (v. 21b) certainly point to observation and 'doing'. Yet doing itself is not wrong. On the contrary, it is "not keeping God's law", the non-observation of that law, that makes us all sinners (see Rom 3:23) so that we are in need of justification and redemption through Christ (and no longer through the law).

V. 21c draws the conclusion from v. 21b. "The argument of the sentence is from a Christian point of view a *reductio ad absurdum*, and is adduced as proof of the preceding statement" (Burton). V. 21c can be considered as a comment upon v. 21a, its elaboration; v. 21c is therefore also connected with v. 18b.

We may thus conclude this long analysis: By building up again the prescriptions of the law (v. 18a) Paul would nullify God's grace (v. 21a). He would be acting as if there is justification through the law (v. 21b). If there is such justification, then Christ died in vain (v. 21c). In v. 18, however, Paul adds after the protasis "if I restore those prescriptions" the apodosis "I show myself a transgressor". Transgressor of what?

Leaving aside Gal 2:18, Paul five times uses παραβαίνω and παραβάτης with the meaning 'transgressing the law' (Rom 2:23, 25, 27; 4:15; Gal 3:19), and once to refer to Adam's transgression of a commandment (Rom 5:14). The conclusion cannot be avoided: Pauline usage as well as the context of Gal 2,18 impel us to postulate after παραβάτης a legal concept: the Torah or some kind of commandment or law. Can we now determine in what Paul's transgression consists? Three possibilities must be taken into account.

a) Could Paul prove himself a transgressor because by becoming a Christian he destroyed the law? We must then paraphrase as follows: "But if I build up again those things which I tore down, I recognize now that by my previous eating with the Gentiles I have violated the law and have been a transgressor of that law". These things are the food laws, calendar prescriptions, and circumcision. One could easily enough understand such a reasoning on the part of Paul's Jewish-Christian opponents. For them καταλύω was a negative, sinful action. Building up again, then, is a retraction which manifests and confesses the wrong nature of the previous destruction.

Yet three reasons plead against this understanding. First, too much remains implicit, unsaid, in such a train of thought, more particularly the transition from "I show (now) that (then) I was a transgressor". Second, συνιστάνω does not elsewhere in Paul's letters have the nuance of "I recognize, I confess", although this verb occurs therein twelve more times. Third, one cannot see how the γάρ sentence of v. 19 explains and motivates v. 18 when this interpretation is accepted.

b) In view of the difficulties with this first proposal an alternative interpretation connected with law presents itself. If Paul builds up again what he has torn down, then, i.e., afterwards, by subsequent actions, he will prove himself a transgressor of that restored law. As arguments in favor of this proposal we mention: οἰκοδομῶ is the main verb of the protasis; it stands at the end; it corresponds in tense with συνιστάνω. The idea which is supposed to be present is very Pauline. In the same letter to the Galatians, in 3:10, Paul states that all who rely on the works of the law are under a curse because they do not keep all prescriptions of that law. In 3:19 Paul states that the law is added τῶν παραβάσεων χάριν till the offspring should come. If this verse is compared with 3:22 it appears that in Paul's view the law concretely functions as a factor which does not limit but increases sin. Moreover, an oppositional connection between "Christ, an agent of sin" (v. 17) and "Paul, future transgressor (of the law)" becomes evident.

Several factors, however, make us hesitate with regard to this second proposal as well. In the first proposal there could be no doubt about what Paul has transgressed: the law which contains the food prescriptions pointed to in v. 18a. In this second interpretation, however, the link between the object of transgressing in v. 18b and the ταῦτα ἃ κατέλυσα in v. 18a is not so clear since Paul is thinking in v. 18b of radical moral sin (cf. sinners and sin in vv. 15 and 17), not of breaking ceremonial prescriptions. Further, although theoretically speaking a future sense could be read into συνιστάνω, the reference to future transgressions is not so easy to accept in v. 18b. Moreover, it would have then the unusual sense "I will constitute myself". Finally, the logical connection between v. 18 and v. 19 is equally difficult.

c) To be sure, because of the Pauline use of παραβάτης and because of the specific content of v. 18a (restoration of law prescriptions) one expects after "transgressor" the objective genitive "law"; one tends spontaneously to supply its absence. Yet, immediately afterwards, v. 19a points to a new situation: Paul is dead to the law; and in v. 19b there is the ἵνα-clause which formulates the new command: a Christian must live for God. Does the transgression of v. 18b not precisely consist in the building up again of the law which would make obedience to that new command no longer possible? The transgressor does violence to the will of God as clearly revealed in Christ. In the second proposal above the restoration was not the transgression: the restoration would inevitably lead to transgression of the law. Here in our proposal it is the restoration itself which also transgresses the new command to live solely for God.

Yet one still hesitates and persists in asking whether it is not too far-fetched to look at "living to God" in v. 19a as a command that can be transgressed. Moreover, we have to admit, the content parallelism between vv. 18a and 21b as well as between vv. 18b and 21a is not perfect. On the other hand, three more remarks seem to corroborate the third interpretation. (1) Within this tentative interpretation the motivating sentence of v. 19 works nicely in a logical way. The underlying idea is that I am not permitted to re-establish the law because I died to it by becoming a Christian; I am not permitted to transgress the life-command that results from that death. (2) Just as the noun παραβάτης, the verb ἀθετέω is also a legal term. After this verb one expects as direct object a command, an agreement or a law. Just as in v. 18b the object in v. 21a is not the Torah; otherwise than in v. 18b, however, the object is mentioned: God's grace. (3) The idea of refusing and rejecting God's grace is present in other passages of Paul's letters as well. We may refer to the letter to the Galatians itself where Paul in 1:6 expresses his astonishment: "you are so quickly moving away from (μετατίθεσθε ἀπό) him who called you in the grace of God". In 5:4 he writes: "You are severed from (κατηργήθητε ἀπό) Christ, you who would be justified by the law, you have fallen away from grace (τῆς χάριτος ἐξεπέσατε)", and in 5:11 he states that the preaching of circumcision would mean that the stumbling block of the cross has been removed (κατήργηται). The most vigorous passage, however, is Rom 9:30–10:4 where Paul in 9:32 says about Israel that they have stumbled over (προσέκοψαν) the stumbling stone, in 10:2 that their zeal is not enlightened (οὐ κατ᾽ ἐπίγνωσιν), and in 10:3 that they were ignorant (ἀγνοοῦντες) of God's righteousness and did not submit (οὐχ ὑπετάγησαν) to it (see also 10:21: λαὸς ἀπειθοῦν καὶ ἀντιλέγων).

Of course, all these remarks do not directly prove that in Gal 2:18b Paul had in mind a transgressor of God's new initiative in Christ and the command it implies, but at least they indicate for Paul the possibility of that idea. If our own proposal possesses any value, as we think it does, then one will notice that there is a kind of identification between nullifying (v. 21a) and transgressing (v. 18b), in so far as one who nullifies God's grace by the same token transgresses the life command it contains. As a matter of fact, by the restoration of the law Paul would destroy God's grace and become ipso facto a transgressor of that new command to live for God. What further commends this third understanding of παραβάτης is the fact that in it vv. 18–21 form a small unit, framed by v. 18b and v. 21a, expressing the same idea: I am not going to be a transgressor, I am not going to nullify God's grace. In the final analysis Paul does not want to become a transgressor by nullifying the grace of God!

II. Argument

It would seem that the center of Paul's reasoning in the whole letter is given in 2:16: Nobody is justified by works of the law but through faith in Jesus Christ. Paul put forwards his basic conviction; he formulates the essence of what he believes: justification through faith. With this one argument he defends his apostolate and the concrete way he preached the gospel among the Gentiles. For Paul and for Peter, for Gentile and Jewish Christians alike, this faith is the same. In Paul's mind, 'justification by faith' applies to all Christians. This conviction of Paul, moreover, is his sole apology.

1. One Gospel

In the letter to the Galatians Paul's emphasis on the 'gospel of Christ' (see 1:6–10) is no doubt remarkable. True, Paul stresses the fact that this is precisely the gospel which he himself preached to the Galatians and which they received (see 1:8 and 9). But there is no alternative gospel (see 1:7), he argues. It is universal, the same for all Christians and meant for all humankind. This 'catholic' character is also evident from the fact that the gospel which was preached by Paul is not a human gospel; he received it not from any human being but through a revelation of Jesus Christ (cf. 1:11–12). Because of this sameness of the gospel, Paul can say in 2:14 that Peter and the others in refusing table fellowship with the Gentile Christians were not straightforward about the truth of the gospel. On referring to this universally valid gospel in 1:23 Paul uses the singular expression εὐαγγελίζομαι τὴν πίστιν.

2. Yet Two Different Gospels?

It cannot but strike the readers of Galatians that after 1:6–12, with its stress on the one gospel, Paul distinguishes in 2:7–10 between two gospels: τὸ εὐαγγέλιον τῆς περιτομῆς and τὸ εὐαγγέλιον τῆς ἀκροβυστίας (v. 7), equally between two 'apostolates' or missions (v. 8) and, implicitly, between two graces (v. 9). Can each of these gospels be characterized? As far as the text of Gal 1–2 goes, three factors which make Paul's own gospel different may be listed. (1) Paul does not require that Gentile Christians be circumcised (cf. 2:3–5: Titus as 'test-case'; see also, e.g., 5:2, 11 and 6:13). (2) Paul's Gentile Christians do not observe the Jewish food laws (cf. 2:11–14). (3) And Paul, in a more general way, does not "compel the Gentiles to live like Jews" (2:14). Obviously at least some works of the law can be neglected by the Gentile Christians, not only circumcision and food laws but, as 4:10–11 seems to say, also Jewish feastdays.

In 2:7–9 Paul apparently defends the good rights of both gospels. He himself "had been entrusted with the gospel to the uncircumcised, just as Peter had been entrusted with the gospel to the circumcised" (v. 7). The God who worked through Peter for the mission to the circumcised also worked through Paul for the Gentiles (cf. v. 8). The grace is given to Paul (just as it was given to others, we could add; cf. v. 9).

Yet, it would go too far, I think, if we infer from this evident parallelism that in Paul's mind God himself wants to seal or perpetuate the specific differences between the two gospels. In the reasoning of vv. 7–9 Paul defends his apostolate and his own way of acting, i.e., mainly the freedom of his Gentile Christians. What he says regarding Peter is but the point of departure for that focus. A specific 'gospel to the Jews' is as it were taken for granted or, better, for the time being conceded by Paul. Therefore, we must not assume that in Paul's conception God really sanctions the Jewish distinctive particularities.

3. Paul's Way of Reasoning

When Paul wrote his letter to the Galatians, the situation in Galatia was analogous to that of about six or seven years earlier. Paul could therefore refer to the Jerusalem council and use that past conflict to clarify the new difficulties. Yet three specific factors must be pointed out. (1) In Galatia also there are those who cause trouble; according to Paul they preach another, a different gospel; they block, he says, the gospel of Christ (cf. 1:6–9). Most probably they are Jewish Christians. Do they come from Jerusalem? How far do they rely on James (as those in 2:12 do)? This is not clear. (2) Further, Paul is full of anxiety because he fears that his Galatian Christians will be led astray. Throughout the whole letter he pleads and tries to convince them, to win them back. It can be presumed that the same danger and fear also existed in the earlier period. But this poignant character is very prominent in the letter. Moreover, Paul must defend himself. He stresses that he really is God's apostle and does not seek human favor. (3) In this letter Paul uses a rather strange, somewhat sarcastic vocabulary where he refers, now after six or seven years, to the Jerusalem authorities. In 2:2 he writes: οἱ δοκοῦντες, they who are of repute. In 2:6 he explains: οἱ δοκοῦντες εἶναί τι, they who were reputed to be something, and he adds: "what they were makes no difference to me; God shows no partiality". Further, in 2:9, he calls them οἱ δοκοῦντες στῦλοι εἶναι, they who were reputed to be pillars. The language is obviously not without a bitter tone.

Paul is deeply convinced that he preached the pure gospel of Christ to the Galatians (see 1:7). Judging from Gal 1:4 its kernel is 'redemption'. Jesus gave himself for our sins to deliver us from the present evil age. There is no alternative gospel. If other missionaries, even if an angel from heaven should bring a gospel contrary to that which Paul preached to the Galatians, let them be accursed.

With such a conviction how can Paul then in 2:7 distinguish between the gospel τῆς ἀκροβυστίας and that τῆς περιτομῆς? Paul certainly understands these expressions as pointing to the addressees: the gospel to the uncircumcised and that to the circumcised. Vv. 8 and 9 corroborate such an understanding: in v. 8 'the apostolate εἰς τὰ ἔθνη' corresponds to 'the apostolate τῆς περιτομῆς', and in v. 9 we encounter in parallel construction ἡμεῖς εἰς τὰ ἔθνη, αὐτοὶ δὲ εἰς τὴν περιτομήν. However, these gospels are not completely the same. The whole context teaches us that Jewish Christians still observe the law. As far as we can judge, their Jewish way of life (with circumcision, food laws and sabbath) is not experienced as contrary to their faith in Christ.

The surprising feature now appears to be that the different gospel put forward by both the troublemakers in Galatia and, years earlier, by the people from James in Antioch, and in 1:6–9 so vehemently rejected by Paul, is precisely that εὐαγγέλιον τῆς περιτομῆς which he accepts without any difficulty in 2:7–9. What is then wrong with it? At first one would like to state that the point of friction lies only in the fact that Jewish Christian missionaries compel Gentile Christians to live as Jews. Under no condition can Paul accept this interference. Paul's fight for freedom is thus certainly a fight for a 'Gentile' gospel which no longer contains those Jewish 'identity markers'.

But as we continue to read the letter we detect that that liberation is far from being just an external matter. Paul reflects on the implications; he reasons and tries to convince the others. In 2:14b–21 and elsewhere in Galatians (and in

Romans) he grounds his position. Nobody is justified by works of the law. Redemption occurred through Jesus crucified. The Spirit is given through faith in Christ. It would seem that Jewish Christians spontaneously still attach salvific effect to these 'identity markers'. Such an understanding of their εὐαγγέλιον τῆς περιτομῆς is intrinsically vitiated.

In Gal 4:3 Paul reminds his Galatian Christians in passing that by becoming believers they were liberated from slavery to the former pagan regulations (τὰ στοιχεῖα τοῦ κόσμου). Their freedom is thus twice negatively defined, namely vis-à-vis the Jewish particularities and vis-à-vis their own Gentile past. As far as Galatians is concerned no word is spoken of a new, 'Gentile' inculturation or contextualisation, more or less analogous to characteristics of the gospel τῆς περιτομῆς. On the contrary, Paul's whole attention is apparently focused on the essential content and the liberating effect of Christ's gospel.

III. Three Points of Discussion

In this third section explicit attention is given only to the second part of the pericope, Paul's address. Even within this address we must omit a discussion of v. 16 and vv. 19–20; moreover, within the actual treatment of the three points only certain aspects of their problems will be dealt with.

Before we begin our discussion a word may be said about our proposed threefold structure of 2:14b–21 (see p. 55). Michael Bachmann has devoted large sections of his monograph to the analysis of the structure of 2:15–21[5], while Andreas Wechsler appears more or less to adopt our proposal[6]. In his comment Wechsler even confirms this view on structure by pointing to the fact that both main sections of that address (vv. 15–17 and vv. 18–21, "zwei Gedankenlinien") end in a conditional period "dessen Apodosis eine unmögliche Aussage über Christus enthält"[7]. He adds: "Die beiden ARA-Sätze enthalten also jeweils eine Absurdität in sich [Christ agent of sin; Christ's death in vain] und treffen voll in die Galatische Krise, weil sie die gegenseitigen

---

[5] M. Bachmann, *Sünder oder Übertreter. Studien zur Argumentation in Gal 2,15ff.* (WUNT, 59), Tübingen, 1992, pp. 25–54: "Zu Struktur und Intention von 2,15–21"; and 55–83: "Architektonisches". Two remarks are in order: v. 14b is omitted in this analysis; v. 17 receives a special treatment in regard to its structural status: it stands "zwischen dem ersten ... und dem zweiten Teil" (p. 85). According to Bachmann Gal 2:15–21 is "eine wohlüberlegte Komposition" (ibid.). V. Jegher-Bucher, *Der Galaterbrief auf dem Hintergrund antiker Epistolographie und Rhetorik* (ATANT, 78), Zürich, 1991, proposes a division which separates 2:17–3:5 ('Transitio') from 1:13–2:16 ('Argumentationseinheit'); this proposal is unconvincing.

[6] A. Wechsler, *Geschichtsbild* (n. 3), pp. 394–395.

[7] Ibid., p. 395.

Vorwürfe markieren"[8]. Wechsler also mentions that the caesura at v. 18 is after all not so strange: "Der Bruch nach μὴ γένοιτο erklärt sich am besten aus der blasphemischen Ungeheuerlichkeit von V. 17b [Christ agent of sin], die freilich in dem nicht weniger herausfordernden ἄρα Χριστὸς δωρεὰν ἀπέθανεν gekonterd wird"[9].

1. Verse 14b

What does Peter's "living like a Gentile" mean? The position of Paul Böttger is extreme and hardly deserves much attention[10]. The fact that Peter separates himself from the Gentile Christians and takes up the Jewish way of life would paradoxically make him to a Gentile sinner: "Gerade der zum orthodoxen Judentum zurückkehren wollende Petrus hat dieses paradoxerweise völlig verfehlt und ist auf die Stufe des Heidentums zurückgesunken …"[11]. And again: "Indem Petrus ὑπὸ νόμον zurückgekehrt ist …, steht er im Bereich seiner in die Sünde führenden und deswegen von Gott trennenden und verurteilenden Macht"[12].

More interesting are the brief, perhaps somewhat forced remarks which Martin Karrer devotes to Gal 1–2 in his article "Petrus im paulinischen Gemeindekreis"[13]. From 1:18 and 2:1–10 one can deduce that for Paul Peter is the highly respected 'Zentralgestalt'[14]. The Antioch incident is the anti-climax to this. Peter stands condemned (by God) because he yields to human pressure. The passage "demonstriert die Richtigkeit der 1,10 vorangestellten These, daß Paulus sich durch Menschen nicht bestimmen lasse, am Unterschied zum großen Petrus. Paulus widersteht, Petrus aber erliegt"[15]. Yet, according to Karrer, Peter was certainly not a 'Judaizer'. The Antioch incident was an exception to his behavior. The present tense ζῆς in 2:14b (as well as Acts 10:1–11:18) shows his basic attitude. "Er paßt sich, obwohl jüdischer Herkunft und mit dem Apostolat unter den Beschnittenen beauftragt, grundsätzlich und in der Dauer seines Wirkens den Lebensgewohnheiten der 'Völker' an. Im Bruch der Tischgemeinschaft in Antiochien bricht er … seine eigene Regel"[16]

---

[8] Ibid. Yet Bachmann, *Sünder* (n. 5), p. 57, rightly warns us that there is no strict parallelism between v. 17ab (with its rhetorical question) and v. 21bc. As has already been mentioned in this paper, v. 18 corresponds with v. 21bc. See also pp. 73–74.

[9] *Geschichtsbild* (n. 3), p. 395.

[10] P.C. Böttger, *Paulus und Petrus in Antiochien. Zum Verständnis von Galater 2. 11–21*, in *NTS* 37 (1991) 77–100, esp. pp. 79–82.

[11] Ibid., p. 81.

[12] Ibid., pp. 81–82.

[13] M. Karrer, *Petrus im paulinischen Gemeindekreis*, in *ZNW* 80 (1989) 210–231, esp. pp. 213–221.

[14] Ibid., pp. 214–216.

[15] Ibid., p. 217.

[16] Ibid., p. 219. Cf., e.g., Stowasser, *Konflikte* (n. 3), p. 76.

The new proposal by James Dunn is put forward with great emphasis[17]. He first mentions the double problem: the present tense of the verb (ζῇς; is Peter still living like a Gentile when Paul speaks?) and the force of the expression itself ("does Paul imply that Peter had totally abandoned all characteristic and distinctive Jewish practices?"[18]). To maintain that Peter still continues to live like a Gentile in other matters than table fellowship is no good solution since the Jewish way of life is an indivisible whole. Equally, to maintain that the phrase "to live like a Gentile" can objectively be used for a minimum of Torah observance like that required by the apostolic Decree – Dunn here refers to his own earlier thesis – is also hardly acceptable[19]. Dunn now proposes as "the key to the most plausible solution" that Paul is "probably picking up the actual words used by the James group in their rebuke of Peter, 'How can you, Peter, a Jew, live like a Gentile?'"[20]. It is *not the language of objective description but … the language of inter-Jewish factional dispute*"[21]. Conservative Jews denounce every failure to conform to their positions as complete treason, as a following of the Gentile way of life.

Dunn's suggestion that we have here an "an echo of intra-Jewish polemic", however attractive, remains quite hypothetical. To be fair, in his study he discusses two more echoes in Gal 2:15–16 ("Jews by nature, not Gentile sinners" and "works of the law") and possible hints in 2:11–17 (furthermore also the calendar piety mentioned in 4:10 and Paul's accusation in 4:17). Yet, it appears to me that the number of so-called instances scarcely increases the probability of Dunn's thesis. Moreover, there is still his hardly provable thesis that table-fellowship at Antioch showed "respect for the principal Jewish scruples against, say, eating blood and pork"[22] (cf. the apostolic Decree of Acts 15) and, therefore, did not mean completely free association between Christian Jews and Gentiles[23].

---

[17] J.D.G. Dunn, *Echoes of Intra-Jewish Polemic in Paul's Letter to the Galatians*, in *JBL* 112 (1993) 459–477. On 2:14 see also idem, *The Epistle to the Galatians* (Black's N.T. Comm.), Peabody, MA, 1993, pp. 126–130.

[18] *Echoes* (n. 17), p. 468

[19] Cf. ibid.

[20] Ibid., p. 469. See also idem, *The Theology of Paul's letter to the Galatians* (New Testament Theology), p. 74: "In the eyes of the James' group Peter had been 'living like a Gentile and not as a Jew' (2.14); he had been behaving like 'Gentile sinners' (2.15)".

[21] *Echoes* (n. 17), p. 469.

[22] Ibid., p. 468.

[23] See J.D.G. Dunn, *The Incident at Antioch*, in *JSNT* 18 (1983), 3–57, e.g., p. 25 (republished in idem, *Jesus, Paul and the Law. Studies in Mark and Galatians*, London, 1990, pp. 129–174, and Additional Note on pp. 174–182). Cf. now the critical discussion by Wechsler, *Geschichtsbild* (n. 3), pp. 353–355. We may quote Verseput, *Gentile Mission* (n. 3), p. 532, n. 34: Dunn "may be correct in his historical assessment that the Gentiles [= Gentile Christians] in Antioch were already observing some of the basic food laws and that Peter's action served only to raise the ritual barriers surrounding table-fellowship. Paul, however, ignores

2. Verses 17–18

For Dunn 2:17a is seemingly an irrealis, a statement not accepted by Paul but brought forward by the people from James. "Evidently the James faction's insistence that the Gentile believers at Antioch were still to be categorized as 'sinners' drew the corollary, obvious to all the Jewish factions represented, that those Jews who consorted with such 'sinners' and thus conducted themselves in ways repugnant to Torah loyalists would find themselves regarded by the Jewish 'righteous' as equally 'sinners'"[24]. Moreover, it is Dunn's opinion that 'sinner' in v. 17a (and 17b) has the same meaning as that in v. 15 and is an echo of the language used by the group from James. Gentiles are sinners 'by nature' because they are outside the law. Table fellowship is one of the great sins. According to this interpretation, in v. 17 Paul particularly thinks of that type of sin after becoming a Christian[25].

For the refutation of this exegesis we not only can refer to the first part of this paper (pp. 56–58) and the studies on which it relies, but also to the two already mentioned recent monographs. Wechsler accepts our three main decisions regarding verse 17: (1) V. 17a is a realis (Paul agrees with its content); (2) in v. 17a 'sinners' refers to the pre-conversional situation of the Jewish Christians and possesses a more radical sense (cf., e.g., Rom 3:23) than Dunn seems to suppose; (3) v. 17b (Christ agent of sin) should be explained according to what Paul says in Rom 3:8; 6:1 and 15: a law-free gospel provokes libertinism[26]. Moreover, Wechsler also assumes that after v. 17, notwithstanding the γάρ in v. 18, there is a break in the line of argument. There is, as it were, a new start; Paul returns to the Antioch incident[27].

---

this fact in the present context and concentrates wholly on the reality that Gentiles were being denied such fellowship".

[24] *Echoes* (n. 17), p. 465; see also idem, *Galatians* (n. 17), p. 141 and *Theology* (n. 20), p. 75. Cf. in the same vein J.M.G. Barclay, *Obeying the Truth: A Study of Paul's Ethics in Galatians*, Edinburgh, 1988, pp. 77–80. Dunn's understanding can be compared with the somewhat differing position of R.N. Longenecker, *Galatians* (Word), Dallas, TX, 1990, pp. 88–90: "… in saying 'we are found to be sinners' Paul is responding to a charge of his opponents and granting the truth of their underlying observation: that Christians, though claiming a higher standard for living, yet sin" (p. 90). In v. 17a Paul would be pointing to the Galatians' libertinism.

[25] *Echoes* (n. 17), pp. 462–465. Cf. F.J Matera, *Galatians* (Sacra Pagina Series, 9), Collegeville, MN, 1992, p. 95: "Faith in Christ results in ethnic Jews living as Gentile sinners because they no longer practice legal works such as the dietary laws".

[26] Wechsler, *Geschichtsbild* (n. 3), pp. 380–383. Cf. Th. Söding, *Die Gegner des Apostels Paulus in Galatien. Beobachtungen zu ihrer Evangeliumsverkündigung und ihrem Konflikt mit Paulus*, in *MüTZ* 24 (1991) 305–321, esp. pp. 313–314; Verseput, *Gentile Mission* (n. 3), pp. 54–55 and n. 44.

[27] Wechsler, *Geschichtsbild* (n. 3), p. 386. Cf. Verseput, *Gentile Mission* (n. 3), p. 55 and n. 46 as well as n. 48 (in v. 18 there is no reference to the behavior of Peter).

Bachmann has not been able to use the work of Wechsler. He himself also considers v. 17a as a realis[28]. V. 17a 'repeats' what is said in vv. 15–16: all verses refer to "die Zeit des Gläubigwerdens"[29]. He very much and rightly underlines the fact that in v. 17 a shift occurs, "ein gewisser Bruch zwischen V. 17a und V. 17b"[30]: while in v. 17a the sinful condition at the time of the conversion is pointed to, in v. 17 (and the following verses) Christian life is envisaged[31]. For Bachmann too, sinner and sin in v. 17 has a radical sense, although in Paul's view not sin but the Christ-event is dominant[32]. The author, however, does not see a break between v. 17 and v. 18[33].

3. Verses 18 and 21

One of the most important results of Bachmann's monograph is, I think, the way he explains παραβάτης of v. 18b. There can be no doubt about the negative character of "the building up again" (not of "the tearing down") in the protasis of v. 18a[34]. From his thorough 'diachronic' analysis of παραβάτης, παραβαίνω and παράβασις Bachmann draws the conclusion that 'transgressing' is not always linked with the law but may in particular cases refer to a "grundsätzliche Verfehlung des Willens Gottes"[35]. In v. 18b we must understand it "als einen fundamentalen Verstoß gegen Gottes Heilswillen und -handeln"[36]. He detects a "ringkompositorische, chiastische, sachliche Korrespondenz" between the conditional periods of v. 18 and v. 21bc[37]. All this can be

---

[28] *Sünder* (n. 5), e.g., p. 40 and p. 56. His conclusion is made on the basis of a lengthy investigation of all μὴ γένοιτο passages in Paul (pp. 30–54).

[29] Ibid., p. 38.

[30] Ibid., p. 40.

[31] Ibid., pp. 37–40. His claim is that "die inhaltliche Verschiebung von V. 17a zu V. 17b bringe das christliche Leben ins Spiel, das dann jedenfalls in den nachfolgenden Versen im Zentrum steht" (p. 62).

[32] See, e.g., ibid., pp. 81–83, 88, 90 and 101–102. Regarding the function of Christ for Christian life, cf., e.g., p. 64 and p. 68.

[33] Ibid. pp. 53–54: "Die ... Protasis V. 18a ... [vermittelt] zwischen V. 17b und V. 18b" (53). Cf. also pp. 32–33.

[34] Ibid., p. 56.

[35] Ibid., pp. 73–77 (quoted phrase on p. 77). Compare Longenecker, *Galatians* (n. 24), p. 91, who maintains that the term παραβάτης means 'violator of the law', 'law-breaker': "It has to do with not just breaking a specific statute of the law but with setting aside the law's real intent ... So here in v 18 Paul insists that to revert to the Mosaic law as a Christian is what really constitutes breaking the law, for then the law's true intent is nullified".

[36] Bachmann, *Sünder* (n. 5), p. 56. Cf., e.g., pp. 53, 67, 69, 83, 85: "παραβάτης, freilich nicht 'Übertreter' (lediglich) einer Einzelvorschrift des Gesetzes, vielmehr des heilvollen Wollens und Handelns Gottes in Christus, des Christusgeschehens". Otherwise recently Verseput, *Gentile Mission* (n. 3), pp. 55–56: "... παραβάτης is most naturally understood in relationship to the idea of covenant Law or command, in this context to the 'unjustified' status of the Jew outside of Christ ... Any return to the Law-service meant confinement in the role of transgressor".

[37] Bachmann, *Sünder* (n. 5), pp. 62–70.

seen as a corroboration and further clarification of what I myself proposed, especially in my study of 1991 (cf. pp. 59–66 of this paper)[38].

The treatment we find in Wechsler is much more concise[39]. Yet he too sees the transgression concretized in ταῦτα πάλιν οἰκοδομῶ (v. 18a). The transgressor who builds up the law again does not transgress that law but is "einer, der dem Rechtfertigungsgeschehen in Christus zuwider handelt"[40]. Like Bachmann, Wechsler also sees a parallelism between v. 18 and v. 21, but he equally refers to v. 14a: "to be not straightforward about the truth of the gospel". V. 18 must therefore be interpreted in accordance with these two framing verses: 2:14 ("Verstoß gegen die Wahrheit des Evangeliums") and 2:21 ("Verstoß gegen die Gnade Gottes")[41].

In his monograph Wechsler[42] refers to an old contribution by Richard Lipsius[43] where the same interpretation of 'transgressor' is already put forward. By way of conclusion we may quote from the related passage of this 1861 article. Lipsius states that for Jewish Christians 'transgression' "ist die Übertretung ausdrücklicher Vorschriften des Mosaischen Gesetzes"[44]. This sense, however, is unacceptable for 2:18. Yet 'transgression' is also "die Übertretung einer feierlich anerkannten Lebensnorm überhaupt; auch innerhalb der Sphäre des christlichen Glaubensprincips gibt es eine παράβασις, und grade dieser hat sich Petrus schuldig gemacht"[45]. Wenn Peter builds up again the things which he tore down, "so handelt er nicht nur inconsequent, sondern gibt zugleich die neue christliche Lebensnorm wieder auf, und eben dies ist zunächst seine παράβασις"[46].

The readers of this paper may judge the degree to which recent publications demonstrate the soundness of our exposition of Gal 2:14b–21 with its numerous sensitive issues.

---

[38] See the reference in n. 2. Cf. the mention of that study by Bachmann, *Sünder* (n. 5), p. VII of the 'Vorwort'.

[39] *Geschichtsbild* (n. 3), pp. 390–393

[40] Ibid., p. 391. He continues: "Der kausale Anschluß von V. 19 wäre dann folgendermaßen zu paraphrasieren: 'Weil ich durch das Gesetz dem Gesetz gestorben bin, ist die Wiederaufrichtung des Gesetzes eine aktive Übertretung meines neuen christlichen Standorts'" Wechsler calls it also: a transgression of the "neuen Christus-Existenz" (ibid., p. 392).

[41] Ibid., p. 393.

[42] Ibid., p. 387, n. 501 and p. 390, n. 524.

[43] R.A. Lipsius, *Über Gal. 2,17 ff.*, in *Zeitschrift für wissenschaftliche Theologie* 4 (1861) 72–82.

[44] Ibid., p. 79.

[45] Ibid.

[46] Ibid., pp. 79–80.

Defining the Faithful Character
of the Covenant Community

Galatians 2.15–21 and Beyond

by

BRUCE W. LONGENECKER

I. Preliminary Considerations

It may be unwise to incorporate the controversial word 'covenant' in the title of this essay, and I am tempted to avoid it and replace it with a far less problematic term, such as 'Christian'. Its appearance in the title has, I hope, less to do with imprudence than with the impression that the word 'covenant' encapsulates the primary dynamics at work within Gal. 2.15–21, where Paul has much to say about the law. Knowing that use of the word 'covenant' is a controversial matter in relation to Paul, I offer a few introductory remarks and observations prior to examining the passage itself.

While it is not infrequent to find the word 'covenant' used in relation to Paul and his epistolary presentations, there seem to be at least two ways in which the notion of 'covenant' is sometimes thought to be an inadequate characterisation his thought: for some, it seems not to say enough, while for others it says too much. On the 'not to say enough' front, 'covenant' is seen to be ill-suited to express the richness and depth of Paul's theological worldview.[1] This impression might be heightened by the way in which many recent ('post-Sanders') studies have employed covenant terminology in Jewish and early Christian literature almost as a sociological notion, focusing on matters of social identity and differentiation in relation to membership within or without the community of God's people (language such as 'getting in', 'staying in' and 'being in' are common in this kind of work). While such an enterprise has its own kind of validity (and is an important component of this essay), it nonetheless has a tendency to minimise or avoid some deep resources of covenant theology. And in this way I would affirm that, if covenant theology is simply a

---

[1] E. Grässer finds 'daß Paulus von sich aus keine Veranlassung hat, das mit dem Christusereignis eröffnete Heil als Bundestheologie zu explizieren' (*Der Alte Bund im Neuen* [WUNT 35; Tübingen: Mohr [Siebeck], 1985) 56.

matter of defining the membership of God's people, then the adjective 'cov-enant' does not do justice to the depths of Paul's theological worldview.

It is arguable, however, that a social and communal dimension is not ex-haustive of covenant theology itself; when viewed simply as a way of speak-ing about group identity, the 'full-blooded' dynamics of covenant theology can be flattened out. In the literature of early Judaism, a consciousness of the covenant between God and Israel is frequently one aspect of a much broader cosmic situation in which the reputation of God as the righteous sovereign of the world is ultimately at stake. It is not hard to see how covenant theologians in Early Judaism often engage in matters of theodicy – the attempt to explain the existence of evil within God's cosmos, evil that all too often affects the life of the community of God's people. The very fact that some of the best expres-sions of covenant theology are evident within extant Jewish apocalyptic lit-erature (Daniel; 4 Ezra; 2 Baruch; all of which are attempts at theodicy), where God triumphantly strides into the sphere of human history to effect a cosmic revolution by his all-engulfing reign of justice, should warn against posing a sharp contrast between (so-called) 'apocalyptic' and covenant world-views, as if the latter were somehow theologically underdeveloped in relation to the former; for these Jewish apocalyptic writers, the covenant relationship was part and parcel of the way in which God was, in the final consummation of this age of history, to show himself as the sovereign world-ruler, over whom no competing power would prevail. This sovereign, powerful and righteous God was Israel's covenant God, whom they trusted and served in faithful obedience to the Torah, the cherished revelation of his will.

At its heart, in fact, covenant theology is first and foremost about divine presence – both in relation to Israel as God's people, and ultimately in relation to the world as God's creation. In this way, all the signs of God's covenant presence with his people (not least, the Jerusalem temple) were themselves constant reminders of the grand events to come when God's presence was ex-pected to fill the whole world in a dramatically new fashion.[2] Until then, the covenant presence of God with his people served as a miniature version of what lay in store on a cosmic level, a microcosm of God's design and sover-eignty. It is little wonder, then, that Zechariah could proclaim the prophetic message of Israel's covenant hope: 'The Lord will be king over the whole earth. On that day there will be one Lord, and his name the only name' (14.9).

In general terms, then, a sharp dichotomy between 'apocalyptic' and cov-enant categories of thought and expression would seem to be unhelpful and

---

[2] This, of course, is why the destruction of the temple of God's presence in 70 C.E. re-sulted in the crisis of confidence in God's sovereignty and justice in this world, the issue that pervades 4 Ezra. See, for instance, B.W. Longenecker, *2 Esdras* (Sheffield: Sheffield Aca-demic Press, 1995).

unproductive. (Perhaps confusion over the adjective 'apocalyptic' has helped to perpetuate this unhelpful distinction.) The writings of the first Christians may themselves be the best evidence against forcing apocalyptic and covenant modes of thought into two separate categories. But even if early Christians in general explored covenant theology in relation to its apocalyptic dimension (or conversely perhaps, apocalytic theology in relation to its covenantal dimension), the question remains: to what extent is this true of Paul, particularly in his letter to the Galatian Christians?

This introduces a related complication that might plague any attempt to apply the adjective 'covenant' in relation to Paul's presentation in Galatians: not that it fails to say enough (as above), but that it says too much in relation to the history of the people of Israel. Here we are reminded of the stimulating work of J. Louis Martyn, who has argued repeatedly that Paul's presentation in Galatians involves 'the end of *Heilsgeschichte*', that the gospel there has no 'linear *pre*-history', that there is nothing in Galatians to affirm 'a salvific linearity prior to the advent of Christ', and that there is in Galatians 'no indication of a covenant-created people of God during the time of the Law'.[3] Instead, Paul 'passes clean by both covenantal nomism and the history of Israel in order to speak of the eschatological purpose of God'.[4] According to Martyn:

Galatians shows us a Paul who does not accept 'covenant' as a term indicating a fundamental building block of this theology. However disappointing it may be to have to say so, this apostle is not a covenantal theologian and thus scarcely one for whom covenantal nomism – however construed – constitutes a frame of reference within which he can preach and re-preach the gospel. Neither does he present as his theology a form of *Heilsgeschichte* in which Christ is interpreted in line with Israel's history.[5]

Martyn is disparaging of the view held by some that Paul adopted the agitator's covenantal agenda in Galatians and sought to redefine things within that context, thinking instead that Paul took up a completely different agenda that, despite making contact with the interests of the agitators, transcended those interests altogether.[6] Martyn sets up these two views of Paul's debate technique almost as contrasting opponents (rather like 'apocalyptic antinomies'), but caution is advisable here, and making an either-or of these two views may

---

[3] J.L. Martyn, 'Events in Galatia: Modified Covenantal Nomism versus God's Invasion of the Cosmos in the Singular Gospel: A Response to J.D.G. Dunn and B.R. Gaventa', in *Pauline Theology Volume 1* (ed. J.M. Bassler; Minneapolis: Augsburg Fortress, 1991) 160–179, 174.

[4] 'Events in Galatia', 176. Cf. too his 'Apocalyptic Antinomies in Paul's Letter to the Galatians', *NTS* 31 (1985) 410–424.

[5] 'Events in Galatia', 179.

[6] 'Events in Galatia', 162; another option, much like the second above only without the qualifying clause, is mentioned but not given any credence by Martyn.

be unnecessary and unhelpful. There is, for instance, no *a priori* reason why another scenario is not just as possible: that Paul employed different strategies in relation to the agitator's views, sometimes working within the context of their interests, sometimes working within a different context of thought altogether.

My assignment for this symposium is not, however, to examine issues of this sort but to set out some thoughts on Paul's statements about the law in Gal. 2.15–21. In my view, however, this is an impossible task without making mention of covenant theology. This significant passage not only makes matters of the covenant unavoidable, but puts them firmly on the map. The argument of this essay is that Paul's argument in Gal. 2.15–21 is animated by a covenantal agenda and operates within the framework of covenant theology. The letter to the Galatians is, of course, made up of many parts, and the relationship between the whole and its parts is a complicated one. Accordingly, in making a case in relation to one particular passage within the whole, I am not pronouncing judgement on the letter in its entirety, nor is it claimed here that Paul's theological programme as a whole is the result of theological reflection on God's covenant dealings with his people in history, or that Paul is everywhere and in every way a covenant theologian. Nonetheless, it seems that Paul's presentation within this short and somewhat opaque passage is informed by and operates with a covenant agenda in view. Whether this was to Paul's own liking and preference or was imposed upon him by the context of the Galatian crisis is another matter. Moreover, it is not my intention to consider whether or not Paul introduced this agenda to the Galatians initially or whether it was introduced later by the Jewish agitators,[7] nor will I advocate that Paul maintained this covenant agenda consistently throughout the letter. Instead, focusing on Gal. 2.15–21 and signalling its relationship to a few further developments in the letter, I hope to show how Paul could and, on this occasion at least, did employ covenantal categories to his own theological advantage. While this might be suggestive, it is by no means conclusive of whether or not Paul is best described as a covenant theologian, whether specifically in Galatians or in general.

---

[7] An issue explored, for instance, by T.L. Donaldson, '"The Gospel That I Proclaim among the Gentiles" (Gal. 2.2): Universalistic or Israel-Centred?', in *Gospel in Paul: Studies on Corinthians, Galatians and Romans for Richard N. Longenecker* (JSNTS 108, ed. L.A. Jervis and P. Richardson; Sheffield: Sheffield Academic, 1994) 166–193. Donaldson finds an Israel-centred gospel at the earliest strata of Paul's teaching in Galatia. While Donaldson's conclusions on this matter are interesting, he may arrive at them more by wishful thinking than by conclusive evidence.

2. Galatians 2.15–21

Identifying Gal. 2.15–21 as the *propositio* of Galatians, H.D. Betz has demonstrated that Paul's *propositio* here shares the character and function of a *propositio* in accordance with the standards of ancient rhetoric. So, as ancient rhetoricians would expect, Paul's *propositio* (1) identifies points that all parties agree upon, (2) identifies points that all parties do not agree upon, and (3) is marked out by conciseness and brevity, in order to be unpacked in more detail later.[8] The third characteristic explains why Gal. 2.15–21 bears such a close relationship to other passages throughout Galatians; the second characteristic animates much of Gal. 2.17–20, while the first characteristic appears within Paul's comments in Gal. 2.16, where points held in common within the Galatian situation are cited.[9]

Unfortunately, it is precisely here, in Gal. 2.16, where points of considerable disagreement arise within scholarly circles, as is the case with Jan Lambrecht's essay for this symposium and my own. The primary point of departure between us involves the now-controversial little phrase that appears twice in this verse, πίστις ['Ιησοῦ] Χριστοῦ. It seems inadequate simply to state, as Lambrecht does, that πίστις 'Ιησοῦ Χριστοῦ must involve an objective genitive ('faith *in* Jesus Christ') since it falls next to πιστεύειν εἰς. A substantial and seemingly ever-growing number of scholars do not find this kind of argument convincing,[10] and think that the genitive is not an objective but a subjective genitive ('faith/faithfulness *of* Jesus Christ').

The strength of the subjective genitive reading is determined one way or another by a mixture of grammatical, stylistic and exegetical considerations, which cannot be rehearsed here. On the whole, I find the subjective genitive to have a stronger case than the objective genitive reading. We await a serious response to S.K. Williams' consideration of relevant syntactical matters, demonstrating the strength of subjective genitive reading.[11] Recently, D.B.

---

[8] H.D. Betz, *Galatians* (Hermeneia; Philadelphia: Fortress Press, 1979) 114. So too, R.N. Longenecker, *Galatians* (Word Biblical Commentary 41; Dallas: Word, 1990) 80–81. Whether or not a rhetorical or epistolary analysis of the structure of Galatians is warranted in general, Betz's view on the character of Gal. 2.15–21 would not seem unnecessarily controversial.

[9] Already, then, we should be cautious about thinking that Paul's case in this section marches to the beat of a drum different to that of the agitators, who pounded out a covenantal beat to which the Galatian Christians were expected to march.

[10] M.D. Hooker calls the kind of case put forward by Lambrecht 'strange logic' ('Πίστις Χριστοῦ', in her *From Adam to Christ: Essays on Paul* [Cambridge: Cambridge University Press, 1990] 165–186, 166; originally published in *NTS* 35 [1989] 665–674).

[11] 'Again *PISTIS CHRISTOU*', *CBQ* 49 [1987] 431–447, esp. 431–437. J.D.G. Dunn argues against a subjective genitive on the basis of grammatical considerations, which are then supported by his own reading of relevant passages ('Once More, ΠΙΣΤΙΣ ΧΡΙΣΤΟΥ', in *SBL 1991 Seminar Papers* [ed. E.H. Lovering, Jr.; Atlanta: Scholars Press, 1991] 730–

Wallace has considered the syntactical matter and found that the grammatical argument for the objective genitive 'has little to commend it', concluding that 'on balance grammatical considerations seem to be in favor of the subjective gen. view'.[12] If syntactical considerations favour the subjective genitive, these can be bolstered by contextual and exegetical arguments as well.[13] For my part, one neglected point clinches the matter in favour of the subjective genitive reading. In Rom. 3.25, Paul incorporates what is likely to be an established confession into his presentation. Within this confession, the phrase διὰ [τῆς] πίστεως is far more likely to be original to the confession than a Pauline insertion, and is most naturally understood to be an attribute of Jesus' life.[14] Here is an established confessional statement within earliest Christianity that speaks both of the righteousness of God, as Paul himself does in 3.21–2, and of the faithfulness of Christ.[15] This consideration provides a good control for understanding the πίστις Ἰησοῦ Χριστοῦ formulations in Rom. 3.22 and 3.26, both of which expect the subjective sense, as would all other occurrences of the phrase throughout the Pauline corpus.[16]

It seems justifiable to believe, then, that the notion of the πίστις of Jesus Christ is not a Pauline invention but is a central component of early Christian

---

744). His grammatical argument seems to rest primarily on the point that πίστις Χριστοῦ formulations are anarthrous (732–734), a point argued earlier by A.J. Hultgren ('The *Pistis Christou* Formulation in Paul', *NovT* 22 [1980] 248–263). But Dunn seems to have taken no account of William's compelling counter-arguments in response to Hultgren. D.B. Wallace finds Dunn's grammatical argument to contain some miscalculations (*Greek Grammar Beyond The Basics: Exegetical Syntax of the New Testament* [Grand Rapids: Zondervan, 1996] 124–126 in penultimate proofs). Moreover, Dunn seems to accept a subjective genitive reading of διὰ τῆς πίστεως αὐτοῦ in Eph. 3.12 ('ΠΙΣΤΙΣ ΧΡΙΣΤΟΥ', 733), a significant concession on his part!

[12] *Exegetical Syntax*, 125 and 126 in penultimate proofs.
[13] Most recently, see I.G. Wallis, *The Faith of Jesus Christ in Early Christian Traditions* (SNTSM 84; Cambridge: Cambridge University Press, 1995) 65–127.
[14] See B.W. Longenecker, 'ΠΙΣΤΙΣ in Romans 3.25: Neglected Evidence for the "Faithfulness of Christ"?', *NTS* 39 (1993) 478–480, part of a response in a Durham NT postgraduate seminar to Dunn's paper 'ΠΙΣΤΙΣ ΧΡΙΣΤΟΥ' which was later published in the SBL seminar papers. Dunn thinks that διὰ [τῆς] πίστεως in Rom. 3.25 might be a reference to God's faithfulness (742) rather than the believers faith.
[15] While recognising the inadequacy of translating πίστις by either 'faith' or 'faithfulness', I prefer the latter for two reasons. First, because it seems the broader of the two, in that it includes the other within its meaning, whereas the opposite is not immediately obvious; and second, because it seems to do better justice to the dynamics of Paul's case, as this essay seeks to show.
[16] I take almost all occurrences of πίστις which are not modified by a genitive in reference to Jesus (as in Gal. 2.16, 20; 3.22; Rom. 3.22, 26; Phil. 3.9; Eph. 3.12) to be references to the faith of the Christian, except for ἐπὶ τῇ πίστει in Phil. 3.9 which refers back to the just mentioned πίστις Χριστοῦ, and the πίστις of Rom. 3.25. Dunn rightly criticises Hays for finding Jesus' faithfulness lurking behind πίστις at a good number of unlikely places in Galatians ('ΠΙΣΤΙΣ ΧΡΙΣΤΟΥ', 735–736), as well as S. Stower's strained attempt to find it in Rom. 3.30–31 ('Ἐκ πίστεως and διὰ τῆς πίστεως in Romans 3.30', *JBL* 108 [1989] 665–674).

understanding about God's covenant righteousness processing triumphantly in eschatological splendour (ἐν τῷ νῦν καιρῷ). It is no wonder, then, that in Gal. 2.15–16 Paul writes as if all parties are in agreement (εἰδότες) over the fact that righteousness is through πίστις Ἰησοῦ Χριστοῦ, the 'faithfulness of Jesus Christ'. Part of Paul's purpose in citing the confessional formula of Rom. 3.25 was to assure the recipients of his Roman letter that, despite his controversial reputation, and although he had never met them face to face, he nonetheless affirmed, and had not strayed from, the Christian message as confessed by the corporate body of Christ. Something similar is happening in Gal. 2.15–16, where Paul goes back to the basics upon which all are agreed. These basics have to do first and foremost with πίστις (Ἰησοῦ) Χριστοῦ, which, as in Rom. 3.25, refers to the 'faithfulness of Jesus Christ'.

And just as is the case in Rom. 3.25, so too here in Gal. 2.15–16 and beyond, much of what is under discussion has to do with a theology of covenant relationship. This much is expected, at least, by Paul's tone in 2.15, where 'Jews by nature' and 'gentile sinners' function as stereotypical depictions of insiders and outsiders to the covenant – stereotypes common in much of Jewish literature of the time but soon to be disqualified by Paul. If the stereotypes are shown to be defective, however, the covenantal context is not. This is clear from the five occurrences of the δικαι- root in 2.15–21,[17] since 'righteousness' terminology is firmly rooted in the deep soils of Jewish covenant theology. The δικαι- root is flexible enough to connote various nuances, but all of them cohere within the broader context of the covenant relationship between the creator God and his elect people. To be marked out by righteousness, or to be justified, is primarily about having membership within the covenant people of the just and sovereign God whose righteousness will be established once and for all in the eschatological in-breaking of his reign.[18]

And it is this context of covenant theology that animates the common Christian belief that covenant relationship with God is operative not through one's own lifestyle of nomistic observance (ἔργα νόμου), but through the covenant faithfulness of Jesus Christ (πίστις Ἰησοῦ Χριστοῦ). This is why, as

---

[17] All five occurrences appear in strategic positions: points of agreement (2.16); points of disagreement (2.17); conclusion (2.21).

[18] See, for instance, K.L. Onesti and M.T. Brauch, 'Righteousness, Righteousness of God', in *Dictionary of Paul and His Letters* [ed. G.F. Hawthorne *et al.*; Downers Grove: InterVarsity, 1993] 827–837; S.K. Williams, 'The "Righteousness of God" in Romans', *JBL* 99 (1980) 241–90, 260–263; R.B. Hays, 'Justification', in the *Anchor Bible Dictionary*, vol. 3 (eds. D.N. Freedman *et al.*; New York: Doubleday, 1992 (1129–1133). Hays writes: 'righteousness should be interpreted primarily in terms of the covenant relationship to God and membership within the covenant community ... "Righteousness" refers to God's covenant-faithfulness which declares persons full participants in the community of God's people ... Paul's understanding of justification must be interpreted resolutely in terms of OT affirmations of God's faithfulness to the covenant, a faithfulness surprisingly but definitively confirmed through Christ's death and resurrection' (1131, 1133). While this helpful corrective

Paul says, εἰς Χριστὸν Ἰησοῦν ἐπιστεύσαμεν[19] in order that his covenant faithfulness might become effective for believers, just as in 3.22 Paul's dis-cussion of God's promise to Abraham to bless all the nations (3.15–22) is grounded in the assurance that this promise has been given τοῖς πιστεύουσιν through the faithfulness of Jesus Christ (ἐκ πίστεως Ἰησοῦ Χριστοῦ). By their faith, others enter into the sphere of covenant relationship centred in the faithfulness of Jesus. Paul's language of 'faith' in these verses is, then, funda-mentally a language of participation; whereas Paul can talk of being crucified with the crucified one, of dying with the one who died in order to live with the one who lives, and of Christian sonship arising out of participation in the sonship of Jesus, so he can talk of Christian participation in the πίστις of Jesus through their πίστις.

Martyn is one of the growing number of scholars for whom πίστις Χριστοῦ in Gal. 2.16 includes a subjective genitive, referring to the faith/faithfulness of Christ. Moreover, he criticises those who take it to include an objective genitive and who therefore contrast ἔργα νόμου and πίστις Χριστοῦ to be 'two human alternatives: should one observe the Law, or should one have faith in Christ?' According to Martyn, these two phrases are not about 'two alternative acts of human beings' but involve a contrast between, on the one hand, 'a deed of the human being' and, on the other hand, 'a deed of God'.[20] With this interpretation of πίστις Χριστοῦ, Martyn accentuates the 'apocalyp-tic' dimension of the divine invasion into the world in Christ. While I would agree with the general gist of Martyn's emphasis, I find him to have under-played the covenantal framework that surrounds πίστις Χριστοῦ in 2.16, a framework that should have further informed his talk of Jesus' 'faithful death'.[21] In some fashion, the apocalyptic in-breaking of God in Christ must, at least within the context in which Paul is working in Gal. 2.15–21, be under-stood as the eschatological inbreaking of true covenant faithfulness that elicits

---

earths 'righteousness' terminology in covenantal soils, the full-flowering of that terminol-ogy blossoms in images of the eschatological establishment of God's cosmic sovereignty and justice. In a sense, then, 'covenant theology' might be thought of as a sub-set within the context of a 'creation theology'.

[19] Williams argues for a strong participationistic sense of εἰς Χριστὸν Ἰησοῦν ἐπιστεύσαμεν, 'we believed *into* Christ', in parallel with εἰς Χριστὸν ἐβαπτίσθητε of Gal. 3.27 ('*Pistis Christou*', 442–443). Cf. too J.D.G. Dunn, *The Theology of Paul's Letter to the Galatians* (Cambridge: Cambridge University Press, 1993) 56; and somewhat differently D.J. Lull, 'Salvation History: Theology in 1 Thessalonians, Philemon, Philippians, and Galatians: A Response to N.T. Wright, R.B. Hays, and R. Scroggs', in *Pauline Theology, Volume I*, 247–265, 264 n. 52. R.B. Hays gives a different interpretation of the verbal clause in Gal. 2.16, translating it as 'we have placed our trust in Christ Jesus' ('ΠΙΣΤΙΣ and Pauline Christology', in *SBL 1991 Seminar Papers* [ed. E.H. Lovering, Jr.; Atlanta: Scholars Press, 1991] 714–729, 725).

[20] 'Events in Galatia', 168. Cf. Hooker, 'Πίστις Χριστοῦ', 180, 185.

[21] 'Events in Galatia', 169.

Christian faith as the sole means of participation and inclusion within that eschatological event.[22]

With this we can compare what Paul says in Phil. 3.9. Having listed the various reasons why he had grounds to boast in his Jewish identity and fervour for the law, Paul cites these to be for him now as 'loss' (ζημίαν) and 'excrement' (σκύβαλα) in order that he might be found in Christ (ἐν αὐτῷ). And so he states: μή ἔχων ἐμήν δικαιοσύνην τήν ἐκ νόμου ἀλλά τήν διά πίστεως Χριστοῦ – that is, 'a righteousness through the faithfulness of Christ', clarified further as τήν ἐκ θεοῦ δικαιοσύνην ἐπὶ τῇ πίστει, 'the righteousness of God that is based upon that faithfulness' (Christ's). This is a dramatic redefinition of covenant fidelity centred on the person of Christ and his faithfulness, in contrast to Paul's own nomistic observance. The most poignant note in this is the contrast between Paul's own 'blamelessness' with regard to righteousness 'in [the sphere of] law' (κατά δικαιοσύνην τήν ἐν νόμῳ γενόμενος ἄμεμπτος, 3.6) and the righteousness that comes through the faithfulness of Christ (τήν διά πίστεως Χριστοῦ, 3.9). Evidently there is a new order of 'power-existence' (3.10) operative through Christ that, when described in terms of covenant righteousness, can be spoken of as arising out of a faithfulness (Christ's own) that qualitatively surpasses all other expressions of covenant faithfulness. In fact, with Christ's faithfulness in view, Paul looks back with hindsight upon his own blamelessness in the law and sees it to be lacking, even as excrement.

Two things need to be recognised in relation to this contrast between Christ's covenant faithfulness and Paul's blamelessness 'in the law': (1) the context here is that of covenant theology, although (2) the traditional concepts and language of covenant theology are being stretched to breaking point in order to contain the contrast (that is, blamelessness in nomistic righteousness is discounted as dung). For our purposes, however, it is important to note simply Paul's contrast of, on the one hand, covenant righteousness through blameless nomistic faithfulness and, on the other hand, covenant righteousness through the faithfulness of Christ. To be in Christ is to have *his* (and only his) faithfulness as the mark of one's own covenant fidelity.[23]

The same notion is evident in Rom. 3.26. Having posited a contrast between covenantal fidelity in terms of 'works of law' (ἔργα νόμου, 3.20) and the 'faithfulness of Jesus Christ' (πίστις Ἰησοῦ Χριστοῦ, 3.22, 25), Paul claims in

---

[22] It is off-target to argue, as Dunn does, that πίστις Χριστοῦ cannot refer to the faithfulness of Christ without playing 'into the hands of his [Paul's] Jewish-Christian opponents' ('ΠΙΣΤΙΣ ΧΡΙΣΤΟΥ', 741).

[23] The participationistic note of ἐν αὐτῷ in 3.9 needs to be highlighted, lest an unnecessary criticism be thrown at the 'faithfulness of Christ' interpretation at this point in the manner of Dunn's charge: 'the vital means by which the righteousness actually comes to the individual is left unexplained' ('ΠΙΣΤΙΣ ΧΡΙΣΤΟΥ', 744).

3.26 that God 'justifies' (δικαιοῦν) the one who lives on the basis of the faithfulness of Jesus (τὸν ἐκ πίστεως Ἰησοῦ). This appears to mean that the faithfulness of Christ, through which God's eschatological righteousness has broken into this world (πεφανέρωται ... διὰ πίστεως Ἰησοῦ Χριστοῦ, 3.21–2; the eschatological note is reminiscent of ἀποκαλύπτεται in 1.17, and is restated again in 3.26; πρὸς τὴν ἔνδειξιν τῆς δικαιοσύνης αὐτου ἐν τῷ νῦν καιρῷ), is being replicated within the lives of those who believe, and only on that basis is a relationship of covenant righteousness established.[24] The one described there is one in whom the faithfulness of Christ is operating, as opposed to one whose identity is marked out by faithful nomistic observance.

Evidently, then, the logic of Paul's case in Gal. 2.15–16 is not idiosyncratic within the corpus of his extant writings. For him, but not always for others, to attach salvific significance to anything other than the covenant faithfulness of Christ is an affront to the covenant grace of God (2.21) and makes one a transgressor of the will of God (2.18).[25] If in this passage Paul's presentation is indebted to a theology of covenant relationship, it is a theology that has severed itself from the 'givens' of covenant theology typical of most forms of Early Judaism, where the will and grace of God are inseparable from νόμος. For Paul, living to God does not involve living in observance of the law but, instead, dying to law observance (2.19) since, as Paul maintains throughout 2.15–21, law observance has nothing to do with righteousness – that is, with living in covenant relationship to God.

Consequently, Paul redraws the boundaries of the covenant, resulting in a redefinition of the term 'sinners' in Gal. 2.17. Lambrecht's article for this symposium highlights two of the many interpretations of this verse: (1) that ἁμαρτωλοί describes the 'pre-conversion' recognition of Jewish Christians who, even prior to putting faith in Jesus, had recognised that they too were 'sinners' like the gentiles, and in need of redemption, and (2) that ἁμαρτωλοί refers to a 'post-conversion' recognition of Jewish Christians who could be called 'sinners' due to their eating with gentiles, a 'sin' against the law, although not actually a sin since the law is no longer in force.[26] The former interpretation, advocated by Lambrecht, views Paul's comment as being a *realis*

---

[24] Accordingly, Dunn's estimate is wrong on two accounts when he claims: 'To understand πίστις Χριστοῦ as referring to *Christ's* faithfulness would not only weaken the emphasis on human faith (like that of Abraham) but also confuse and even divert attention from the emphasis on *God's* faithfulness' ('ΠΙΣΤΙΣ ΧΡΙΣΤΟΥ', 742).

[25] Reading παραβάτης in the manner urged by Lambrecht, both in his essay for this symposium and in his 'Transgressor by Nullifying God's Grace: A Study of Galatians 2.18–21', *Biblica* 72 (1991) 217–236. Cf. G.S. Duncan, *The Epistle of Paul to the Galatians* (New York: Harper, 1934) 69. However, I find Lambrecht's term 'command' with reference to ἵνα θεῷ ζήσω (2.19) to be strained and unhelpful (above p. 65).

[26] Cf. Betz, *Galatians*, 120; F. Watson, *Paul, Judaism and the Gentiles* (SNTSMS 56; Cambridge: Cambridge University, 1986) 68.

that states an actual situation, while the latter views it as an *irrealis* that enter-tains a hypothetical situation on the basis of inadmissible factors (i.e. that the law defines the identity of the sinners and the righteous).

Perhaps neither alternative hits the mark squarely, Gal. 2.17 being animated by different dynamics than either interpretation allows. It might be better to understand Paul's meaning as following on naturally from the definition of covenant relationship given in 2.16. Much of the Jewish literature from Early Judaism demonstrates the way in which the definition of covenant member-ship could expand or contract according to the needs of self-definition within particular groups. Notions concerning who was to be numbered among the 'righteous' and who among the 'sinners' varied from group to group, context to context.[27] So, for instance, those Jews who appreciated a text like Pseudo-Philo (LAB) would have considered the covenant community to encompass most of the Jewish people, who were righteous, unlike the gentiles and a few Jews who were sinful outsiders to the covenant. Those within the Qumran community, however, drew the lines of covenant insider and outsider differ-ently, finding the covenant community to be restricted to the small number of those who were committed to the ways of the righteous sect, while all others, Jews and gentiles alike, fell within the category of sinners.

Paul's case in Gal. 2.16–17, I suggest, follows precisely the same simple rules of covenant definition, except that, for him, the embodiment of covenant faithfulness is not an ethic people, nor a sub-group within that people, but a single individual, Jesus Christ, whose covenant faithfulness alone is the catchment of covenant relationship with God, and the vehicle through which God's covenant righteousness is creating a new sphere of existence, a new order of life, a 'new creation'. For Paul, the obvious consequence is that the definition of 'sinners' needs to be adjusted accordingly.[28] The result of re-stricting the boundaries of covenant faithfulness to a single individual is that all others find themselves to be 'sinners', outsiders to the covenant. This has little to do with pre- or post-conversion sin, and more to do with the theologi-cal process of the marking out of covenantal boundaries.

If this is the case, then, εὑρέθημεν καὶ αὐτοὶ ἁμαρτωλοί is best seen (as Lambrecht agrees, although for different reasons) as a *realis* – a statement that Paul accepts to be a true: all people find themselves to be outsiders to the cov-enant, 'sinners' – a situation especially repugnant to Jews, the primary (but not exclusive) referent of αὐτοί (cf. 2.15). All this follows not from some 'pre-conversion' conviction nor from a 'post-conversion' situation, but from defin-ing the covenant boundaries as encircling solely the faithful Jesus Christ; the

---

[27] Cf. J.D.G. Dunn, 'Pharisees, Sinners and Jesus', in his *Jesus, Paul and the Law* (Lon-don: SPCK/Louisville: Westminster, 1990) 61–88.

[28] This can be recognised already in 2.15 where Paul gives his tongue-in-cheek reference to 'gentile sinners (ἁμαρτωλοί)' in opposition to 'Jews by nature'.

category applicable to all others is that of covenant outsider, 'sinner'. Some participants in the Galatian debate were uncomfortable with this label and sought to remove its disturbing effect through their nomistic observance. For Paul, however, 'sinner' remained the primary category of self-identity for πᾶσα σάρξ apart from Christ (2.16), a condition that does not find its remedy in ethnic identity (φύσις, 2.15) or nomistic practice (ἔργα νόμου, 2.16) – such things only build up that which has been torn down, thereby making one a transgressor of the will of God (2.18).[29] Paul's implication is clear: all those who would supplement the efficacy of the covenant faithfulness of Christ with their nomistic practice are themselves aiding the cause of sin rather than righteousness.

Here, Paul has turned the tables on those who belittle his understanding of the gospel, who find it to implicate Christ as a 'servant of sin' (2.17); in their view, by side-lining the law from the equation of covenantal definition, Paul has removed the guide for, and standard of, ethical living. For them, the faithfulness of Christ as the centre of covenant relationship has nothing to do with excluding the law from covenant relationship; such a move simply invites antinomian behaviour, making Christ in Paul's covenant definition little more than a puppet through which sin (or better, the power of Sin) promotes itself. Here we are witnessing the pulling apart of the common Christian theology of the covenant expressed in Gal. 2.16, as different parties understand that common core differently.

Rejecting this misconstrual of his gospel (μὴ γένοιτο), Paul places nomistic observance in opposition to the true will of God (2.18), and makes a rather enigmatic claim: ἐγὼ γὰρ διὰ νόμου νόμῳ ἀπέθανον (2.19). If various solutions have been proposed to explain what Paul meant by διὰ νόμου, another solution is proposed here that follows the lines of covenant definition. Within the scriptures and literature of the Jewish people, the law was understood to be a means to life for the covenant people, offering them the blessing of abundance (Deut. 28.1–14), 'prosperity and life' (Deut. 30.15). So in Pseudo-Philo, for example, God makes this pronouncement concerning the people of Israel: 'I gave them my Law and enlightened them in order that by doing these things they would live and have many years and not die' (23.10; cf. Ps. 1; Lev. 18.5; Pss. Sol. 14.2–3; 4 Ezra 7.127–31; 14.22, 29, 34). This function of the law with regard to covenant insiders contrasts sharply with the function of the law with regard to covenant outsiders, against whom it pronounced a curse (Deut. 28.15–68; 29.19–28) that resulted in 'death and destruction' (Deut. 30.15; cf. e.g. 4 Ezra 7.20–24, 46–48, 62–75; 9.32–37). A near-contemporary of Paul even talks of the Messiah destroying covenant outsiders 'by the law'

---

[29] Lambrecht's reading of γάρ as 'but' (above p. 58) may force 2.18 too far from the context of the issue in 2.17 (cf. his talk of 'a kind of break' after 2.17).

(Syr: *bnmwsh*, 4 Ezra 13.38; other versions are corrupt), by which the author probably means 'in accordance with the pronouncement of the law'.

When Paul speaks of having died *through* the law, perhaps his point is much the same: If the boundaries of the covenant have been drawn in such a way that πάσα σάρξ stands together outside the boundaries of the covenant, then the pronouncement of the law upon all is 'death',[30] a death that Paul says he has undergone already. Ironically, this death is νόμῳ – that is, death that severs all relationship with the law. The construction of 2.19a is important. The dative νόμῳ appears before the verb for the sake of emphasis, Paul's own clever spin in which he reworks the motif of the law's pronouncement of death to include the severing of the dead person's obligation to the law (cf. Paul's more elaborate statement of this in Rom. 7.1–5). In 2.19b Paul goes further into the unexpected by stating that this pronouncement of death actually results in life – that is, the life promised to those within the boundaries of the covenant, expanded in 2.19c to include those who, like Paul, have been crucified with Christ.

The whole of Gal. 2.19, then, might be paraphrased in this manner: 'For through the pronouncement of the law upon covenant outsiders, I died to the obligation to observe the law, in order that I might enjoy life within the covenant by being crucified with Christ'. This has the added advantage of not reading Gal. 2.19 in the light of Paul's train of thought in Gal. 3.10–13, as is generally done. The method of explaining an earlier verse by a later verse, while occasionally necessary, has an obvious weakness: such a method was not available to the original hearers of the letter. The general covenantal background suggested above provides a context out of which both Gal. 2.19 and 3.10–13 arise: the law curses those outside the boundaries of the covenant (3.10–13) and makes a pronouncement of death upon them (2.19). The agenda with which Paul is working still seems to be one rooted in covenant theology.

In Gal. 2.19c–21 Paul lays the basis for his rebuttal of the charge of antinomianism that seems to lie behind 2.17 (ἄρα Χριστὸς ἁμαρτίας διάκονος): Having been crucified with Christ, Paul claims that he no longer lives but that Christ now lives (continually) in him (ζῆ). This aspect of Paul's christology, 'Christ living in me', will later be developed to provide a full-blown rebuttal of the charge of antinomianism (Gal. 5.3–6.10).[31] But even here Paul lays the foundation for his refutation of that charge, expanding the

---

[30] In Romans 7, Paul elaborates upon the experience of 'the Jew' who is outside the boundaries of the covenant and for whom the law is *not* unto life; see B.W. Longenecker, *Eschatology and the Covenant: A Comparison of 4 Ezra and Romans 1–11* (JSNTS 57; Sheffield: Sheffield Academic Press, 1991) 225–245.

[31] On the paraenetical section of Galatians as following from the theological dispute concerning the law, see especially J. Barclay, *Obeying the Truth: A Study of Paul's Ethics in Galatians* (Edingburgh: T. & T. Clark, 1988).

'Christ living in me' motif by returning to the common core of Christian tradition and once again drawing upon the 'faithfulness of Christ' motif. Even in
the mortal body,[32] the believer is marked out by faithfulness to God precisely
because the life of the faithful Son of God is being lived out within the life of
the believer: 'I live (continually) by the faithfulness of the Son of God' (ἐν
πίστει ζῶ τῇ τοῦ υἱοῦ τοῦ θεοῦ).[33] In Paul's definition of the covenant, the
believer's life is marked out neither by nomistic observance nor by ethical
antinomianism, but by the faithfulness of the Son of God.[34]

This is expanded further in 2.20d,[35] where faithfulness in the life of Jesus is
defined concretely in terms of love and the giving of himself for the benefit of
others – a quality of Jesus' life highlighted right at the start of the letter: τοῦ
δόντος ἑαυτὸν (1.4). The point to note is that Paul has worked his theological
presentation so that a redefinition of covenant fidelity in terms of the faithfulness of Christ serves as the christological basis of his ethic, developed later
especially in Galatians 5–6, where again he has several things to say about the
law. The dispute in Galatia concerning the law was not simply about ethnic
identifying marks (e.g. circumcision), but about how life is to be regulated on
a daily basis. On that sorce, the agitators upheld the law as the means whereby
behaviour is governed and managed; without the law, Paul's gospel was seen
to promote antinomianism and libertinism. Accordingly, without his presentation in Galatians 5–6, Paul's explanation of the gospel within the Galatian crisis would have been incomplete; conversely, the ethical section of Galatians
5–6 is itself little more than an elaboration on the rudimentary ethic spelt out
in Gal. 2.20, where the Son of God, whose own faithfulness was expressed in
terms of love and the giving of himself, lives continuously in the very existence of Paul.[36] Thus, as a condensed version of the rudiments of Christian

---

[32] Paul speaks here of σάρξ, rather than σῶμα, perhaps, as Betz suggests, in order to
counter 'widespread enthusiastic notions, which may have already found a home in Christianity, according to which "divine life" and "flesh" are mutually exclusive' (*Galatians*, 125).

[33] Cf. R.B. Hays, *The Faith of Jesus Christ* (SBLDS 56; Chico, CA: Scholars Press,
1983) 167–169. Hays writes: 'If Paul intended to designate "the Son of God" as the object of
the verbal idea in the noun πίστει, he certainly chose a very odd way to do it' ('ΠΙΣΤΙΣ',
726).

[34] Precisely at this point the subjective genitive reading of πίστις ['Ιησοῦ] Χριστοῦ allows Paul's case a force that it does not otherwise have. If Paul is pressed to show how our
faith apart from 'works of law' does not deteriorate into antinomianism (an issue apparently
introduced in Gal. 2.17), the claim that 'I live by faith in the Son of God' would be simply a
feeble restatement of the problemmatic point, whereas 'I live by the faithfulness of the Son
of God' addresses the point directly.

[35] The three δέ connectives in 2.20 all serve to unpack the Χριστῷ συνεσταύρωμαι of
2.19c. Contrast Lambrecht's view that 'v. 20 opens with an opposing δέ' (above p. 59), followed by two more oppositional occurrences of δέ (above p. 61).

[36] R.B. Hays seems to hit the mark directly when he writes: 'Gal. 2.20–21, with its emphasis on union with Christ's grace-giving death, looks more and more like the hermeneutical centre of the letter' ('Crucified with Christ: A Synthesis of the Theology of 1 and 2

ethics in Galatians, Paul's use of the faithfulness of Christ motif in Gal. 2.20 opens the flood-gates to Paul's discussion of Christian ethics in Galatians 5–6, to which we briefly turn without abandoning the issue of 'Paul and the law'.

3. And Beyond

Paul's ethic in Galatians arises out of his understanding of the Spirit, identified as the Spirit of Christ (4.6). The activity of the Spirit brings to life characteristics within the believing community that resemble the character of Jesus' own life, being little more than dynamic extensions of the qualities he demonstrated. The christological model of faithfulness, manifest in love and self-giving (1.4; 2.20), becomes for Paul the paradigm of Christian character, so that social relationships between those who have been crucified with Christ are defined not by such things as circumcision or dietary regulations (and other 'works of law') but by 'faith working practically (ἐνεργουμένη) through love' (5.6). So in Paul's list of the fruit of the Spirit, love heads the list as the primary characteristic of Christian lifestyle (5.22–23).[37] This Christ-like character is to be formed in the midst of the corporate life of the believers (μορφωθῇ Χριστὸς ἐν ὑμῖν, 4.19), as its members are 'clothed with Christ' (Χριστὸν ἐνεδύσασθε, 3.27),[38] just as an actor clothes himself in another's character and so 'becomes' that person within a play.[39] In this way, Paul envisages the corporate life of the Christian community to be the social embodiment of the self-giving Christ. The faithfulness of Christ provides the context out of which arises the characteristics of the new-world order of Spirit-enabled love and self-giving.

Thessalonians, Philemon, Philippians, and Galatians', in *Pauline Theology, Volume I*, 227–246, 242). Cf. his 'Christology and Ethics in Galatians: The Law of Christ', *CBQ* 49 (1987) 268–290. In relation to this, the ἐν ἐμοί of Gal. 1.16 is in danger of being under-interpreted when translated 'to me'. The apocalyptic revelation mentioned there (ἀποκαλύψαι) did not result in an introduction of two persons and their first impressions of each other; the revelation is so comprehensive and all-encompassing that Paul himself became transformed in the process, so that the Son can be said to be revealed 'in me'. This is little different from Paul's words in 2.20, and in 4.19: μέχρι οὗ μορφωθῇ Χριστὸς ἐν ὑμῖν.

[37] Dunn: 'The understanding of the Spirit as the Spirit of Christ ... reflects a common perception within first-century Christianity that Christ (the character of Christ as remembered in the Jesus tradition and proclaimed in the gospel of the cross) provided a means of discerning and defining the Spirit' (*Theology*, 62 n. 55); cf. his *Jesus and the Spirit* (London: SCM Press, 1975) 324–326.

[38] ἐνδύειν involves 'the taking of characteristics, virtues, intentions' of another person, according to W.F. Arndt and F.W. Gingrich, (*A Greek-English Lexicon of the New Testament* [Chicago: University of Chicago, 1957] 263).

[39] So, Dunn, *Theology*, 119 n. 32; cf. his *The Epistle to the Galatians* (London: A. & C. Black, 1993) 204–205.

Paul's depiction of Christ-like character contrasts sharply with his depiction of the character of life fostered within those who observe the law; their
lives are characterised throughout Galatians in terms of zealous manipulation
of others (1.13–14; 2.4), self-interestedness and promotion (4.17; 6.13), and
fierce competitiveness and judgementalism (5.15, 26). It is little wonder, then,
that Paul can link the destructive inner motivations of the 'flesh' that oppose
the Spirit with the concern for social 'fleshly' things such as circumcision and
dietary regulations. In 3.3, to consider 'works of law' as necessary for covenant membership is to be 'in the flesh' (σαρκί) rather than 'in the Spirit'
(πνεύματι); in 4.29, to define Abrahamic heritage in terms of ethnic lineage is
to inherit fleshly rather than spiritual identity.[40] So too, those who are lead by
the Spirit are not ὑπὸ νόμον (5.18), just a those who have been crucified with
Christ have crucified τὴν σάρκα (5.24; cf. 2.19). The character induced by the
flesh is graphically portrayed in 5.19–21, where Paul's list of τὰ ἔργα τῆς
σαρκός calls to mind qualities such as those which, to many a Jewish mind,
mark out the decadence of the pagan world. In all this, Paul unmasks the
value-system of those who would observe the law and shows it to be nothing
but a web of corruption and perversity, in contrast to the work of God in Christ
ὅπως ἐξέληται ἡμᾶς ἐκ τοῦ αἰῶνος τοῦ ἐνεστῶτος πονηροῦ (1.4).

Moreover, this catalogue of τὰ ἔργα τῆς σαρκός provides no hope for the
health and longevity of a 'fleshly' community, but ensures its destruction
through the tearing apart of its fabric by chaotic internal forces (cf. 5.15, 26,
as well as Paul's attempts to destroy the community from outside its boundaries, described in 1.13–14). This has nothing to do with the cosmic power of
God to bring all things alive in a new creation. This fleshly kind of existence
runs directly counter to Paul's view of the character of the community of
God's people in Christ (e.g. 6.10), which knows and is known by God (4.9),
and which even in its diversity is to be marked out by unity and solidarity
(πάντες γὰρ ὑμεῖς εἷς ἐστε ἐν Χριστῷ Ἰησοῦ, 3.28), as both a demonstration
and a microcosm of God's eschatological power and in-breaking sovereignty.[41]

Paul's connection between fleshly attitudes and fleshly concerns for
nomistic observance demonstrates, then, that in Galatians the issue about law
observance involves more than simply a dispute over social boundary markers

---

[40] Compare too the relationship between circumcision and flesh in 6.12–13, as well as
the suggestive way that Paul includes σάρξ in his reading of Ps. 143.2 [142.2 LXX] to bol-
ster his rejection of ἔργα νόμου in 2.16.

[41] Gal. 6.1–10 seems primarily to be a generalised example of what a community looks
like when the Spirit of God is at work within its members. It involves neither the abandonment of ethical living nor the kind of watch-dog morality that marked out the agitators, but
the considered enactment of mutual responsibility in personal and social matters under the
auspices of God.

and group membership, although it certainly includes that dimension. For Paul, an ethnic definition of covenant is a full-blown case study of something far more fundamental within the human condition: the tendency towards ego-centrism and self-interestedness, a tendency that results in behaviour befitting only wild animals who bite and devour each other (5.15), and who provoke one another through envy (5.26). The chaos that results from such a condition fails to testify to the overthrow of the forces of evil in this present age. To understand the gospel in terms of 'works of law' is to incorporate matters of flesh into the gospel, thereby denuding the gospel of its testimony to the power of the sovereign God in bringing into existence a united believing community transformed into the image of Christ (e.g. 3.26–28; 4.19); instead, the gospel becomes a tool testifying to the power of those who would perpetuate their own self-interests by transforming others into their own image (e.g. 4.17; 6.13). At its heart, then, the issue in Galatia concerns the character, ethos and (in a word) 'spirituality' of the communal life of those in Christ who have been rescued from the present age of evil and are members of the new creation that God has inaugurated.

If the character of Christ-like service and love serves as the embodied manifestation and advertisement of God's eschatological in-breaking and the creating of a new sphere of existence, Paul strikes an unexpected note in 5.13–14 where this same eschatological character is also said to be the fulfilment of the law (5.13–14). It seems likely that the conceptual difference between 'doing the law' in 5.3 and 'fulfilling the law' in 5.14 lies primarily in the verb: Those who understand covenant relationship to involve 'circumcision' and other ἔργα νόμου must recognise that adherence to the law demands 'doing' (ποιεῖν) all the prescriptions of the law (5.3),[42] whereas those who walk by the Spirit in love and service to others 'fulfil' (πληροῦν) or 'meet the standard of' the Mosaic law by that love, even without doing its prescriptions (5.14; cf.

---

[42] Paul seems on occasion to portray Jewish nomistic observance as involving 'perfectionism' (which seems the best understanding of Gal. 3.10 and 5.3; cf. 6.13) and 'legalism' (cf. Rom. 4.4–5). If this does not do justice to the covenantal motivation of most/many practising Jews, it follows naturally from Paul's definition of the covenant. Since God's saving grace is restricted to the boundaries of the Christian community, non-Christian Jews have no recourse to the covenant grace of God (a view modified in Romans 11); accordingly, notions of repentance and atonement, which presuppose the grace of God, are excluded from typical definitions of 'doing of the law' and, as a consequence, Jewish observance of the law is no longer a response to God's saving grace (covenantalism) but an attempt to earn it (legalism) – an attempt which thereby demands perfect fulfilment of every legal prescription (perfectionism), an impossible task. See further, Longenecker, *Eschatology*, 211–14, 270. Cf. C.K. Barrett: 'No doubt – we are grateful to E.P. Sanders for emphasizing it – the gracious God was there in Judaism; but that is not where Paul found him' ('Paul and the Introspective Conscience', in *The Bible, The Reformation and the Church* [JSNTS 105, ed. W.P. Stephens; Sheffield: Sheffield Academic Press, 1995] 36–48, 47 n. 33).

Rom. 13.8–10; 8.4).[43] In this way, whereas 'law' and Christ seem to have been
at odds with each other throughout the letter thus far, in 5.14 Paul brings them
together in terms of a Christ-like attitude of service and love within the life of
the Christian community.

A similar phenomenon is evident in Gal. 6.2, where fulfilment of the law
(πληροῦν again) is seen in the relationship of those who live by the Spirit as
they bear each other's burdens. Says Paul, this fulfils ὁ νόμος τοῦ Χριστοῦ. It
is often claimed that ὁ νόμος τοῦ Χριστοῦ in this verse is not a reference to
the Mosaic law;[44] instead, it must refer to the social teaching of Jesus as a
form of Christian halakah,[45] or in a more general way to a 'norm' or 'principle'
of Christian living patterned on Christ's own model.[46] There is some cause to
think that Paul is significantly redefining things here, but it seems unwise to
evaporate all reference to the Mosaic law in this phrase; the links between
5.13–14 (where νόμος clearly refers to the Mosaic law) and 6.2 are too strong
to suggest otherwise, since both passages speak of relationships of Christian
mutuality and service in connection with πληροῦν and νόμος. So, as in 5.14,
in 6.2 Christian relationships of mutual self-giving and loving service are
themselves shown to be the fulfilment of Mosaic law. The concept of law has
undergone such a drastic redefinition with reference to the Spirit of Christ and
the community of Christ that Paul can go so far as to identify it as the 'law of
Christ' – that is, the Mosaic law that comes to its fullest and proper expression

---

[43] See especially, S. Westerholm, *Israel's Law and the Church's Faith* (Grand Rapids:
Eerdmans, 1988) 201–205; Barclay, *Obeying the Truth*, 135–141. H. Hübner locates the difference between 5.3. and 5.14 in the construction of the phrases ὅλος ὁ νόμος (5.3) and ὁ
πᾶς νόμος (5.14); the substantival construction of the former allows for a reference to the
Mosaic law, while the attributive construction of the latter demonstrates that something else
is in view, an ironic reference to a generalised sense of law that applies to the Christian
('Das ganze und das eine Gesetz: Zum Problemkreis Paulus und die Stoa', *KuD* 21 [1975]
239–256). The criticisms of this view are compelling; see, for instance, Barclay, *Obeying
the Truth*, 136–137. As A. van Dülmen writes, Paul 'spricht … hier dem Gesetz des Alten
Bundes volle Autorität und Gültigkeit zu' (*Die Theologie des Gesetzes bei Paulus* [Stuttgart:
Katholisches Bibelwerk, 1968] 60). In Rom 2.14, Paul speaks of non-Christian gentiles 'doing' (ποιεῖν) the law; there, however the context of Paul's case is quite different, his intent is
enormously polemical, and his train of thought itself is problematic (see Longenecker, *Eschatology*, 186–189, 194–195), to the extent that the occurrence of ποιεῖν there should not
be used to interpret its meaning in Gal. 5.3. Cf. Westerholm, *Law*, 203 n. 18.
[44] So D. Lührmann: 'Für Paulus … kann es [ὁ νόμος τοῦ Χριστοῦ] nur der Gegensatz
zum Gesetz vom Sinai (vgl. 3,19) sein' (*Der Brief an die Galater* [Zürich: Theologischer
Verlag, 1978] 97). So too van Dülmen, *Gesetzes bei Paulus*, 66–68.
[45] C.H. Dodd, ''Εννομος Χριστοῦ' in his *More New Testament Studies* (Manchester:
Manchester University, 1968) 134–148; W.D. Davies, *Paul and Rabbinic Judaism* (4th ed.;
Philadelphia: Fortress Press, 1980) 142–145.
[46] H. Räisänen, *Paul and the Law* (Philadelphia: Fortress Press, 1983) 79–80; Hays,
'Christology', 276. Räisänen finds similar meaning in the references to νόμος in Rom 3.27
and 8.2, two passages that I find to have the Mosaic law in view (*Eschatology*, 207–210,
241–45).

in the relationships of mutual service within the community of those whose lives are being transformed by the Spirit of Christ in conformity to the character of the faithful life of Christ.[47]

Accordingly, Paul's comments in 5.14 and 6.2 depict a dramatic shift in his tone about, and characterisation of, the law. In the earlier chapters of Galatians, observing the law in the eschatological era is shown to be a heinous error, since the function of the law has nothing to do with 'making alive' (3.15–25); instead, observance of the law involves enslavement to τὰ στοιχεῖα τοῦ κοσμοῦ (4.1–11), Mount Sinai being associated with children of slavery rather than children of promise in the allegory of 4.21–31. In these contexts where observance of the law is in view, Paul attacks nomistic performance as a threat to the singularity of the gospel. In Gal. 5.14 and 6.2, however, the context has shifted, allowing Paul to claim that the singular gospel embodies, in an indirect fashion, the fulfilment of the law. Although the period of law observance has come to an end with the eschatological arrival of Christ, Christian existence nonetheless fulfils the law.[48] In a sense, Paul has snuck the law in through the back door, the different context of Galatians 5–6 allowing him to make that manoeuvre.[49] Despite the eschatological novelty of God's self-revelation in Christ, that relevation incorporates within itself his previous revelation, even if it goes beyond it. If Paul's rhetoric and argument has shifted, the constant throughout it all is the singularity of the gospel, whereby observance of the law is excluded and whereby the law is indirectly fulfiled by means of Christian character.

Despite all that Paul has said against living in accordance with the prescription of the law, in the end he seems to want to demonstrate that his gospel not only excludes the charge of antinomianism but also provides the only possible avenue for 'fulfilling' the Mosaic law (as distinct from 'doing' it) within the community of those in Christ. This aspect of Paul's presentation compares well to that of Jewish covenantal theologians of Early Judaism, for whom definitions of 'law' and 'covenant people' were to cohere, dovetailing in relation

---

[47] For similar views, see Barclay, *Obeying the Truth*, 125–135; Dunn, *Galatians*, 322–324.

[48] Lull: 'The law finds its fulfilment in the fulfilment of the Abrahamic covenant' ('Salvation History', 261 n. 42).

[49] One interpretative option that has not been pursued is that Paul, having vented most of his exasperation with the agigators and their false gospel, relaxes some of his rhetoric late in the letter, so that 'law' and 'Israel' are allowed to make an appearance (redefined, in 5.14, 6.2 and 6.16), due to a waning of his level of irritation. If such an unlikely scenario could ever be demonstrated, it would provide a case study in S.J. Kraftchick's suggestion that on occasion Paul's presentation might undergo modification even within, and due to, the process of composition itself ('Seeking a More Fluid Model: A Response to Jouette M. Bassler', in *Pauline Theology, Volume II* [ed. D.M. Hay; Minneapolis: Augsburg Fortress, 1993] 18–34, 24).

to each other so that the two 'constitute a blended entity'.[50] If the indirect fulfilment of the law is an aspect of Paul's case that has surprised some interpreters, it is wholly expected within the grammar of covenantal self-definition,
despite all that Paul has said about the law earlier. It is perhaps here in Gal.
5.14 and 6.2, more than anywhere in the Pauline corpus, that we recognise
Paul's deeply-ingrained impulse to maintain a place for the law within his understanding of the gospel; in a letter where such a concern is least likely to
appear, even there Paul finds a way to situate the law within the context of the
gospel in a fashion (albeit highly polemical) that is not antagonistic to the gospel.

4. Concluding Observations

It may be no exaggeration to claim that Paul's christology, pneumatology, and
ecclesiology (if such terms are appropriate) throughout Galatians are animated by an understanding of the character of the life of Christ, in contrast to
the character of the life of nomistic observance. Whereas the scriptures record
the story of the life of ethnic Israel which had proven itself to be persistently
unfaithful to God, Paul recalls the story of the life of Jesus who had shown
himself to be *faithful* to God. By tapping into this traditional Christian story
and unpacking it with reference to those 'in Christ', Paul hopes to establish
the character of Jesus' faithful life as the identifying mark of all those who,
despite their various ethnic origins and identities, make up what he dares to
call, ὁ Ἰσραὴλ τοῦ θεοῦ (6.16)[51] – those whose lives of Christ-like service
fulfil the intentions of the law (5.13–14; 6.2), even if they do not observe the
prescriptions of the law.

Discussions of the issue of 'Paul and the law' occasionally give the impression that the issue primarily concerns matters of (so-called) 'doctrine'. But
this view of the matter is dangerously reductionistic, for Paul sees the issue to
be not so much one concerning doctrine and right thinking *per se*; behind his
presentation lies a more fundamental concern to nurture right behaviour and
attitudes within the Christian community of faith. For him, the issue is primarily about the character and ethos of the eschatological community of the sov-

---

[50] S. Sandmel, *Judaism and Christian Beginnings* (Oxford: Oxford University, 1978)
182. Compare E.P. Sanders' observation of the 'two pillars to all forms of Judaism: the election of Israel and faithfulness to the Mosaic law' (*Paul, The Law and the Jewish People*
[Philadelphia: Fortress Press, 1983] 208). Paul's presentation, even in Galatians, seem to
involve the redefinition of these two pillars in the light of his christology and pneumatology,
but not the abandonment of them.

[51] For a defence of this reading of τὸν Ἰσραὴλ του θεοῦ, see especially J. Becker,
Paulus: Der Apostel der Völker (Tübingen: Mohr [Siebeck], 1989) 492–94. An opposing
view is defended by Dunn, *Galatians*, 345–346.

ereign God, about the 'spirituality' of that community as it expresses itself within social relationships of mutual love and care, relationships that speak of the transforming power of the sovereign God. As such, this concern encompasses both the personal and the communal, both the individual and the social, and runs like a thread throughout the whole of the Pauline corpus. Paul perceived social character to be demonstrative of a fundamental spiritual condition of a community's constituency, as the re-formation of an inner condition results in a re-formed community. His case throughout Galatians is, then, primarily a charter and blueprint for social relationships within the eschatological community in which the sovereign creator is transforming his people in conformity with the character of his Son.

This is where Paul's critique of the law finally becomes earthed – in the establishment of a united community of transformed people whose relationships are marked out not by the kind of character that results from observing the law or any other pattern of life (all of which are enslaved to τὰ στοιχεῖα τοῦ κόσμου that oppose God's sovereign reign; 4.3, 9), but by the kind of love and self-giving that marked out the faithful life of Jesus Christ. The formation of Christ's own faithful character within the life of the Christian community is itself the social advertisement of the fact that the creator God has acted powerfully to establish his sovereign reign 'in Christ'; character of any other sort advertises the influence of forces at work (e.g. σάρξ, στοιχεῖα) other than the power of the Spirit of the Son sent by God 'when the time had fully come'.

And so, we return to the matter with which this essay began: the appropriateness of the term 'covenant' as applied to Paul's perception of what God has done in Christ. So far, we have seen nothing to suggest that a covenant agenda says too little by way of God's eschatological action to establish a new creation; to affirm that covenant theology is evident in Gal. 2.15–21 is not, then, to deny that '*Paulus war ... Apokalyptiker*! ... seine Theologie ist maßgeblich von der Apokalyptik geprägt',[52] just as the apocalyptic dimension of Paul's presentation does not deny its covenantal dimension.[53]

Nor is it evident that the covenant agenda says too much in terms of the history of the people of Israel, although this needs careful nuancing. Paul's handling of the traditional 'faithfulness of Christ' motif includes an inherent contrast with the people of Israel; Paul seems to envisage Jesus entering into Israel's own history, albeit in a distinctive fashion, so that his distinctive faith-

---

[52] L. Goppelt, *Christologie und Ethik: Aufsätze zum Neuen Testament* (Göttingen: Vandenhoeck & Ruprecht, 1968) 237, emphasis his.

[53] Cf. N.T. Wright: 'I believe in the essentially apocalyptic nature of Paul's covenant theology, and vice versa ... What has been left behind in the relation of the new world through the gospel is not covenant theology itself, but the restriction of covenant membership to "those of the Torah" ('Gospel and Theology in Galatians', in *Gospel in Paul*, 222–239, 237–238).

fulness within that history becomes the sphere of covenant fidelity in which the eschatological creation has come into existence. Such seems to be the case also in Gal. 4.4–5, where God's eschatological activity is manifest in Christ who γενόμενον ὑπὸ νόμον, ἵνα τοὺς ὑπὸ νόμον ἐξαγοράσῃ, with the ensuing effect of his sonship extending to all believers.[54] The same line of thought is likely in Gal. 3.13–14, where Christ enters into the Jewish condition of being under the law's curse and redeems that condition (taking ὑπὲρ ἡμῶν in 3.13 as a reference to Jewish Christians),[55] thereby precipitating the inauguration of a new age of salvation for all.[56]

These passages are suggestive of a view in which the situation of Israel is the historical context that requires redemption in order for a new eschatological context to emerge from it; the former is the prerequisite for the latter.[57] Therein lies the basis of, and rationale for, Paul's application of the title ὁ Ἰσραὴλ τοῦ θεοῦ to the believing community; the title evokes remembrance of God's dealings with a people into whose situation Christ came and out of which a new creation has emerged, while at the same time being redefined to match the constituency and identity of God's eschatological people. While there is little in Galatians that might suggest a developmental and evolutionary unfolding of salvation history progressively leading up to an eschatological climax in Christ, there is a sense in which Israel's history has been, and needed to be, dealt with rather than avoided, averted, neglected, trivialised or rendered irrelevant. For Paul, in ways reminiscent of Jewish apocalyptic theologians of his day, the redemption of Israel's predicament, not its abandonment, is the necessary pre-condition for the establishment of the new creation, lest God's reputation as the cosmic sovereign be in jeopardy. That redemption is earthed in, and issues from, an historical context in which God

---

[54] Martyn makes the following claim: 'Christ's being born "under the law" refers to his real entry into the human state of enslavement, not to his coming into the history of Israel … The resulting picture is, I think, apocalyptic' ('Events in Galatia', 178, note 41). Without denying that Paul viewed the human condition as conditioned by enslavement, Martyn's rejection of *Heilsgeschichte* in relation to Israel seems particularly strained at this point; the point for Paul is that the form of enslavement that Christ took was precisely that of Israel, 'under the law'.

[55] See especially, T.L. Donaldson, 'The "Curse of the Law" and the Inclusion of the Gentiles: Galatians 3.13–14', *NTS* 32 (1986) 94–112; N.T. Wright, *The Climax of the Covenant* (Edingburgh: T. & T. Clark, 1991) 143–144.

[56] To say that Paul's claim in Gal. 3.13 ('Christ … became a curse for us') 'is not directly relevant to our theme' of Paul and the law, as G.N. Stanton does in his essay for this symposium ('Paul and the Law: Galatians 3 and 4', [below p. 110 n. 29], seems ill-considered.

[57] So Donaldson writes: 'the redemptive road passes through the territory of the law (and its people) … it was not possible to make an end run around the law and those in its domain. Rather, the way forward for both Jew and Gentile required the redemption of Israel from its plight … For Paul the law was not a dead end side trail but rather something lying squarely on the path of redemptive history' ('Curse of the Law', 102–103; cf. 106).

had already been at work,[58] although that context has itself been magnificently transformed in the establishment of an eschatological sphere of existence. Deliverance ἐκ τοῦ αἰῶνος τοῦ ἐνεστῶτος πονηροῦ certainly involves transfer from one realm into another, but a transfer not in terms of substitution and displacement but in terms of metamorphosis and transfiguration; the end result is the same (there's no going back!), but the mechanism is altogether different.

In the end of the day, however, it may be that Paul is, in fact, not so much a covenant theologian as one who occasionally (whether by his own chosing or otherwise) employs covenantal patterns of thought as a kind of metaphorical context in which to speak about what God has done in Christ.[59] 'Covenant' may not describe Paul's 'theology' as much as it describes one means whereby his conviction of divine presence 'in Christ' finds theological articulation. W.S. Campbell's reflections on Paul as a theologian are worth calling to mind in this regard:

> Those scholars who have insisted that Paul is no systematic theologian are perfectly correct … It is … probably wrong to look for any one key or central element to elucidate Paul's theology. It is a body of tradition rather than a system of theology with which Paul interacts. But if the creative reformulating and transforming of inherited images and metaphors are what constitutes doing theology, then Paul is certainly a theologian par excellence.[60]

In the final analysis, we should not be surprised, nor can we help but be impressed, by crucial passages, such as Gal. 2.15–21 and beyond, in which Paul demonstrates his theological profundity by exploring and exploiting the rich resources of the covenant theology of his Jewish heritage in relation to what God has done in Christ.

---

[58] So, for instance, the law had been given by God through angels to be Israel's pedagogue. All this needs more defence and nuancing than can be offered here.

[59] Most people are proficient in their use of language, despite rarely identifying explicitly the grammatical structures on which that language is based. So too, identifying covenantal patterns of thought in Paul is not simply a matter of counting the frequently of the term 'covenant' (indeed a rare term in Paul) and its associates.

[60] W.S. Campbell, 'The Contribution of Traditions to Paul's Theology: A Response to C.J. Roetzel', in *Pauline Theology, Volume II*, 234–54, 254.

The Law of Moses and the Law of Christ

Galatians 3:1–6:2

by

GRAHAM STANTON

My brief for this Symposium is surely the most difficult of all. There are several reasons why this is so. Galatians 3 to 6 are related even more intimately than Paul's other discussions concerning the law to a quite specific historical, social, and theological context. Although most scholars agree that this context can be reconstructed in general terms, exegesis of these chapters often totters precariously on shaky reconstructions of particular details of that context. Paul's terse comments on the law continue to puzzle and confuse his readers.[1] Reconstruction of the premises on which Paul grounds some of his statements is at least as difficult as reconstruction of the views of his opponents.

Gal 3 and 4 contain a number of passages which have always been central in discussions of Paul and the law. I shall insist that consideration of them must start at Gal 2:15, if not even earlier in the letter. And in order to appreciate fully the vigour and subtlety of Paul's teaching on the law in Galatians, one must not overlook the surprising twist introduced in Gal 4:21b, 5:14 and 6:2. Since it is all but impossible to excise Paul's comments on the law from his sustained argument in Galatians, our agenda turns out to be the whole letter.

And to complicate matters further, we have Romans! To what extent should Romans be used as a commentary on Galatians? Where terse or enigmatic statements in Galatians seem to be expressed more fully or more clearly in Romans, is it always illegitimate to refrain from referring to Romans? Some would urge us not to do so on the grounds that Paul's views changed considerably between the writing of Galatians and Romans.[2] I shall not join that debate. As far as possible I shall try to interpret Galatians by Galatians, even

---

[1] Richard B. Hays describes the central 'theological' section of Galatians as 'a vexing exegetical puzzle': *The Faith of Jesus Christ: An Investigation of the Narrative Substructure of Galatians 3:1–4:11*, (Chico, Calif.,: Scholars, 1983) 193. His own discussion is a major contribution to many of the puzzles of Galatians.

[2] See especially Hans Hübner, *Law in Paul's Thought* (Edinburgh: T&T Clark, E.tr. 1984). On p. 36 he rightly notes that familiarity with Romans often leads us to read Galatians in the light of Romans – with harmonising presuppositions.

though recent writers on Galatians have frequently used passages from Romans to clinch exegetical points they wish to make.

I do not propose to summarise and assess critically recent discussion of Galatians 3 to 6.[3] I shall focus on some of Paul's key points concerning the law in these chapters. An adequate discussion of Paul's thirty two references to the law in Galatians would involve detailed exegesis of the whole letter, a task which cannot be attempted here.

Before I set out my observations on the passages in these chapters which relate most directly to the theme of this symposium, I would like to make a preliminary point which has not been prominent in the plethora of recent writing on these chapters, a point which needs to be worked out much more fully in due course.

Galatians is an oral text. Paul dictated most of this letter to a secretary (6:11). It was written to a cluster of ἐκκλησίαι in Galatia (1:2): presumably a messenger took the written text from community to community, as was the case with I Peter. Some of the initial recipients of Galatians may have *studied* the written text closely; when they did so, they would almost certainly have read it aloud themselves, for silent reading was rare in antiquity.[4] However most of the recipients are likely to have *heard* Galatians read aloud, presumably in the context of worship – and perhaps on several occasions. On hearing the text, they would have learned it by heart much more readily than we do today.

Since Galatians was composed and received initially as an oral text, we need to attend to the 'sound map' of this letter.[5] We need to listen attentively to the stylistic devices used in antiquity in oral texts: to the repetition and parallelism of key words and phrases, to the use of alliteration, to the repeated use of rhetorical questions, to sentences which round off sections of the argument pithily, to the ways in which key points are set out forcefully and then explained and developed later. In short, rhetorical analysis of Galatians should not be confined (as in much recent discussion) to examination of the literary genre of this letter; the rhetorical techniques used in oral persuasion within short sections and even within individual sentences also need to be considered.[6]

---

[3] See especially Douglas Moo, 'Paul and the Law in the Last Ten Years', *SJT* 49 (1987) 287–307, and Stephen Westerholm, *Israel's Law and the Church's Faith* (Grand Rapids: Eerdmans, 1988).

[4] See G.N. Stanton, *A Gospel for a New People: Studies in Matthew*, Edinburgh: T&T Clark, 1992, 73–6.

[5] I owe this term to a stimulating paper by Brendan B. Scott and Margaret Dean, 'A Sound Map of the Sermon on the Mount', in ed. E.H. Lovering, *SBL Seminar Papers 1993* (Atlanta, Scholars Press, 1993).

[6] In his fine commentary (26–8) H.D. Betz touches on but does not develop this point. Betz seems to envisage that Paul uses key phrases from his own initial oral preaching. Betz draws attention to Paul's use of numerous 'theological abbreviations' – '... brief expressions, most of them prepositional phrases. All of them are abbreviations of theological doc-

Let me develop this point briefly. On listening again and again to the text of Galatians, I have been struck, as have many other exegetes, by the way 2:16 functions as a 'text' which is then expounded at length from many angles throughout the rest of the letter. The strong antithesis between those who are ἐξ ἔργων νόμου and those who are ἐκ πίστεως is sustained right through chapters 3 and 4, with later echoes. νόμος and πίστις function like key musical notes in contrasting thematic phrases which are developed with subtle variations in a movement in a symphony. In chapter 3 the πίστις word group is used sixteen times; νόμος is used fifteen times.

Alongside both πίστις and νόμος are set 'satellite' words and phrases which are repeated and expounded. On the πίστις side are ranged the διχ- word group, υἱοί and τέκνα (of Abraham, of God), ἡ ἐπαγγελία, ἡ κληρονομία, and, finally, the ἐλευθερία word group. On the νόμος side, ἡ κατάρα and, more and more strongly in ch. 4, the δοῦλος word group. At the climax of the argument in 4:31 and 5:1 we have a sharp antithesis between freedom and slavery, an antithesis which I take to be synonymous with the antithesis first set out in 2:16 between those who are ἐξ ἔργων νόμου and those who are ἐκ πίστεως.

In view of the repetition of these key words and phrases, and their 'satellites', I do not think that the initial listeners could possibly have missed the main point Paul was making. Modern exegetes ponder (quite rightly) the precise nuance of every word and phrase, and the precise line of Paul's argument. They then use words like 'difficult', 'terse', 'enigmatic', 'contorted' to describe this letter. But there is a real risk that we shall miss the wood for the trees. If we attend to the 'sound map' of these chapters, Paul's main point is crystal clear: πίστις and νόμος are at odds with one another.[7]

. There is an important corollary. Paul's comments on the law in Gal 3 to 6 are all set within this sharply antithetical line of argument which I have sketched. In this rhetorical context it is not surprising that Paul refers repeatedly to the law in such negative ways. As we shall see, what is surprising is the way Paul changes direction radically in 4:21b, 5:14 and 6:2.

---

trines. Their origin is unknown, but they can be most likely explained as coming from the oral transmission of Paul's theology.'

See esp. P. Achtemeier, '*Omne verbum sonat*: The New Testament and the Oral Environment in Late Antiquity', *JBL* 109 (1990) 3–27. G. Walter Hansen, *Abraham in Galatians: Epistolary and Rhetorical Contexts* (Sheffield: Sheffield Academic Press, 1989, 55) notes that Galatians is 'similar in many ways to oral speech', but largely confines himself to questions of genre and structure.

[7] My colleague Dr Francis Watson helpfully notes that the general point I have been making in the preceding paragraphs would also apply if the text were read rather than heard. I take this point, but I think that many of the 'patterns of persuasion' used in Galatians are particularly appropriate when the text is read aloud and heard. Further consideration needs to be given to the difference between reading and studying a text, and reading it aloud and hearing it.

There is one further point to be mentioned at the outset. From time to time I shall refer to Justin's *Dialogue with Trypho*. The differences between Galatians and the *Dialogue* go far beyond different literary genres and a chronological gap of just over one hundred years. Whereas Paul is terse, Justin rambles. Whereas Paul quotes explicitly only a handful of brief passages of Scripture, Justin quotes numerous enormous chunks of text. Whereas Paul is countering the influence of Jewish Christian agitators, Justin is primarily concerned with objections raised by his Jewish opponent, Trypho. Whereas Paul alludes to, but does not spell out the arguments of his opponents, Justin allows Trypho to state his case.[8] Whereas Paul only hints at the existence of more radical Christians who stressed the 'newness' of Christianity even more strongly than he himself did, Justin is regularly looking over his shoulder at gnostics and Marcionites.

None the less there are sufficient similarities in both social context and theological argument to make comparison fruitful. Paul and Justin are both struggling to hold together the continuity and the discontinuity of the church with Israel and her Scriptures. Neither Paul nor Justin will tolerate Jewish Christians who stress continuity and who are not in full fellowship with Gentile Christians, nor will either tolerate Jewish Christians who persuade Gentile Christians to keep the law. In the latter case Justin suspects that under their influence some Gentile Christians may move over completely to the Jewish polity. Similar fears may well have been in Paul's mind, even though they are not expressed explicitly in Galatians.[9]

There is now broad scholarly agreement concerning Paul's purposes, and at the moment I see no reason to challenge the consensus. Justin's purposes in writing the *Dialogue* are less clear. I do not think that his *main* aim was to 'win over' Jews such as as Trypho, or Gentiles already as closely attached to Judaism as Trypho's companions. If that had been his expectation or hope, he would not have allowed Trypho and his Gentile companions to go their own way untroubled and unmoved by Justin's proclamation and apologetic. I think that Justin wrote with more than half an eye on Gentiles broadly sympathetic to both Judaism and Christianity – Gentiles who did not appreciate the differences. Although Paul's immediate aim in writing Galatians was very different, is it not possible that in some of the Galatian churches his letter *functioned* similarly?

---

[8] In places Trypho is no more than a 'straw man', but in many passages Trypho expresses widely held Jewish convictions and well-known Jewish objections to Christian claims.

[9] In a forthcoming paper, 'Justin Martyr's *Dialogue with Trypho*; Group Boundaries, "Proselytes", and "God-Fearers" ' I have argued that in Justin's day there were different levels of attachment to both Jewish and Christian communities, as well as keen 'on the ground' rivalry. I strongly suspect that in the Galatian churches in Paul's day there were more strands of opinion and levels of commitment than the text of Galatians would lead us to suppose.

Justin did not know Galatians, and used Romans only to a very limited extent.[10] And yet (as I hope to show below) there are several similarities in the lines of argument developed by Paul and Justin. Of course we cannot solve the exegetical problems of Galatians by appealing to Justin's *Dialogue*, but Justin does help us to approach Galatians with some fresh questions in mind.

I. Galatians 3:1–5: By works of the law or by believing?

These verses are notable for the striking emotive language Paul uses to counter the success of the agitators in the Galatian communities. They are also notable for the fact that Paul's argument is not grounded on Scripture, as it is at nearly all the key points in chapter 3. Instead Paul appeals to the Galatians' initial reception and continuing experience of the Spirit. And most important of all for my present purposes, Paul sets out a sharp antithesis between ἐκ ἔργων νόμου and ἐξ ἀκοῆς πίστεως as the ground of the Galatians' Christian experience. This contrast is first developed in the initial statement of his central conviction in 3:2b; it is then repeated in 3:5 which rounds off the argument of this short section.

The phrase, 'the works of the law', is used five times within eleven verses (2:16 three times; 3:2, 5). The repetition of this phrase as part of a sharp antithesis was intended to make a strong impact on the initial hearers: the initial recipients could hardly have missed the contrast Paul was drawing between two different ways of establishing one's standing before God. We are clearly touching the nerve centre of Galatians.

It is generally agreed that 2:15–16 is a programmatic statement which is expounded and underlined in the sections of Galatians which follow.[11] To what does the phrase 'works of the law' refer in 2:16, and then in the partial development of this verse in 3:1–6? I am convinced that Paul is refuting the agitators' claim that one's standing before God was dependent on carrying out the requirements of the Mosaic law.

I am well aware that my previous sentence is controversial. I concede that Paul's first use of the phrase 'works of the law' in 2:16a is triggered by the issues which dominate the preceding discussion in Gal 2, circumcision and food laws. But as the initial listeners heard the argument of the following verses unfold, they were left in no doubt that Paul was concerned about far

---

[10] See further below. It is difficult to account for Justin's failure to mention Paul, and his minimal use of Paul's writings. However, I hope to show that this is not to be attributed to dislike or suspicion of Paul.

[11] James Dunn, *Galatians* (London: SPCK, 1993) aptly refers to G.S. Duncan's comment: "This is the text on which all that follows in the Epistle is commentary."

more than these 'test cases of Jewish distinctiveness over against Gentiles'[12]: Paul rejects the agitators' claim that one's standing before God (past, present, and future) is determined by carrying out the requirements of the law.

In later sections of this paper I hope to offer some support for this view. For the time being I want to draw attention to two points. (i) The future passive tense in 2:16d, δικαιωθήσεται, should not be swept aside as a mere fossil which has survived as a result of Paul's quotation of the LXX of Psalm 143:2. In fact Paul does not give his listeners any explicit indication that a citation is being offered:[13] he could have altered the tense of the verb, but chose not to do so. Hence 2:16d offers a broad hint that (*pace* E.P. Sanders) it is not just *maintenance* of one's standing before God which is at stake, but one's ultimate status.

(ii) 3:5 also calls in question the distinction which has become familiar in recent discussion between 'getting in' ἐξ ἀκοῆς πίστεως and 'staying in' ἐξ ἔργων νόμου. Once again Paul's choice of tense is important: in this verse both participles are in the present tense. Paul uses a rhetorical question in order to elicit the close attention of his listeners: he hopes they will agree that God *continually* gives his Spirit and works miracles among the Galatians ἐξ ἀκοῆς πίστεως and not ἐξ ἔργων νόμου.[14] 'Faith' is not to be confined to 'getting in': it is a continuous process – it is as necessary for 'staying in' as it is for 'getting in'.[15]

The question which Paul presses in 3:2b is instructive. Since reception of the Spirit cannot be distinguished from 'getting in', it seems likely that the agitators claimed that 'getting in' as well as 'staying in' was on the basis of carrying out the requirements of the law. Does Paul's question in this verse imply that his opponents taught that salvation, 'getting in', was on the basis of keeping the law? This 'traditional' line of interpretation runs against the grain of much recent writing: ever since the publication of E.P. Sanders's *Paul and Palestinian Judaism* in 1977, it has found few supporters. I am convinced that Sanders (and others) have shown that in the past too many Christian scholars have accepted uncritically that all strands of early Judaism were legalistic.

---

[12] The quotation is from James Dunn's commentary, 136. In a lengthy discussion of 2:16 in his commentary, and also in 'Yet Once More – "The Works of the Law": a Response', *JSNT* 46, 1992, 99–117, and in *The Theology of Galatians* (Cambridge: CUP, 1993) he clarifies and modifies some of his earlier comments on 'works of the law'. Note, for example, 'Yet Once More', 100: '... 'works of the law' characterize ... the conviction that status within the covenant (= righteousness) is maintained by doing what the law requires (works of the law').'

[13] So too Christopher D. Stanley, *Paul and the Language of Scripture*, (Cambridge: CUP, 1992) 234 n. 179.

[14] For a fuller discussion, see especially Heikki Räisänen, *Paul and the Law* (Tübingen: Mohr, 1983) 189.

[15] Similarly John Barclay, *Obeying the Truth* (Edinburgh: T&T Clark, 1992) 237: 'If Paul requires 'faith in Christ', this is not just as an 'entry requirement', but it is the fundamental determinant of all Christian behaviour.' See also R.H. Gundry, 'Grace, Works, and Staying Saved in Paul', *Biblica* 66 (1985) 1–38; here, 8–12.

However I am not yet convinced that early Judaism was univocal on this point. At least some of the evidence discussed by Sanders is not clear-cut. And in spite of its polemical thrust, surely some of the evidence of the gospels and of Paul's epistles points in another direction, and is relevant in a reconstruction of the 'pattern of religion' of early Judaism.[16]

As far as I am aware, important evidence in Justin's *Dialogue* has been overlooked in the recent vigorous discussions of this point.[17] Following Justin's autobiographical sketch which is designed to legitimate his Christian claims (cf. Galatians!), Justin and Trypho both state their central convictions vigorously in chapter 8, a passage which sets the agenda for the discussions which follow (cf. Gal 2:15–16!). In a quite un-Pauline way Justin urges Trypho to follow his example and pay attention to the words of Christ: 'rest most delightful comes to those who carry them out in practice.' If Trypho is sincere in his quest for salvation, he should 'trust in God', 'know the Christ of God and become an initiate' (τελείῳ γενομένῳ).[18]

In response, Trypho pleads with Justin: 'first be circumcised, then keep (as the law commands) the sabbath, and the feasts and God's new moons, and, in a word, do all the things that are written in the law (τὰ ἐν τῷ νόμῳ γεγραμμένα πάντα ποίει), and then you will indeed find mercy from God (ἴσως ἔλεος ἔσται).[19] In this passage a learned Jew expresses the view that one's standing with God is dependent on carrying out the whole law. No doubt some will recall the evidence set out by E.P. Sanders and others which confirms that for early Judaism, 'getting in' was by grace, and not, as Christians have so often believed, by 'works of the law'. They may then conclude that Trypho is here simply a mouthpiece for Justin's mistaken Christian perception of Judaism.

However before we rush to this conclusion, two points need to be borne in mind. Is it likely that two Christian thinkers who both wrestled with the question of the law should have operated independently with a mistaken view of Jewish opinion on such a crucial point? Although Trypho is sometimes no

---

[16] Similarly, D. Moo (1987) 292. In a written comment on an earlier draft of this chapter, my colleague Dr Francis Watson makes the following interesting observation: 'How can a requirement be unnecessary for getting in but necessary for staying in? If, as I consider getting in, I learn that I must keep the law in order to stay in, then a willingness to keep the law is integral to getting in'.

[17] Heikki Räisänen (1983) does discuss helpfully and at some length Justin's disputes with Trypho concerning the law, but not the passage to which I am drawing attention. E.P. Sanders does not discuss this passage in his *Paul and Palestinian Judaism*.(London: SCM, 1977).

[18] This is probably a reference to baptism.

[19] In the most widely used English translation of the *Dialogue* A.L. Williams (London: SPCK, 1930) translates ἴσως conventionally as 'perchance'. However this hardly makes sense in the context. T. Stylianopoulos, *Justin Martyr and the Mosaic Law* (Missoula: Scholars, 1976) 8 n. 4 (following J.K.T. von Otto, 1876–81) shows that ἴσως was sometimes used with the meaning 'indeed'.

more than a puppet who feeds Justin lines which can then be readily refuted, in numerous passages it can be shown that Trypho does indeed set out Jewish views which are well-attested elsewhere. So why should we not at least consider this possibility in *Dialogue* 8:4?

In short, I am inclined to think that Galatians and the *Dialogue* suggest that for at least some strands of Jewish opinion, 'getting in' was on the basis of keeping the law of Moses. I do not think it at all unlikely that many Jews in the first and second centuries would have accepted that entry into the people of God was on the basis of acceptance of God's gracious covenant with his people *and at the same time* have maintained that carrying out the law was a *sine qua non* for past, present and future acceptance by God.

II. Abraham: Galatians 3:6–9 and 15–18 and 4:21–5.1

In 3:6 Abraham is introduced for the first time; he remains on stage until 5:1, though at times he lurks in the background. Given the prominence of Abraham in numerous early Jewish writings, it is not surprising that Paul should also appeal to parts of the Abraham story.[20] Paul's main aim is to use the story of Abraham to support his own argument. Is he also refuting the agitators' version of Abraham traditions? I think that this is likely, though the dangers of 'mirror-reading' must be kept in mind.[21] Paul and the agitators were both giving priority to different parts of the Abraham traditions; they were probably appealing to some of the same traditions, but interpreting them very differently. I shall comment briefly on the parts of the 'Abraham' passages in Gal 3 and 4 which are most closely related to the theme of this symposium.

Paul takes his listeners immediately to Gen 15:6 and then to his adapted version of Gen 12:3 in order to argue that οἱ ἐκ πίστεως (including Gentiles) are sons of Abraham. Longenecker notes that 'Paul cites Gen 15:6 without any reference to Abraham's meritorious deeds of Gen 14 as a basis for his reception by God or to Abraham's acceptance of circumcision in Gen 17 as a condition.' He suggests (as have other exegetes) that in Gal 3:6ff. Paul is refuting the Judaizers' use of these passages.

There is plenty of evidence which suggests that in his interpretation of Gen 15:6 Paul is at odds with the way this passage was understood by many Jews

---

[20] See the helpful Appendix, 'Abraham in Jewish literature' in G. Walter Hansen, *Abraham in Galatians* (Sheffield: Sheffield Academic Press, 1989). Hansen shows that the story of Abraham was used in different ways by different writers. See also the excursus, 'Abraham's Faith and Faithfulness in Jewish Writings and in Paul' in Richard Longenecker's fine commentary, 110–2.

[21] On the dangers of 'mirror-reading', see John Barclay, 'Mirror-Reading a Polemical Letter: Galatians as a Test Case', *JSNT* 31 (1987) 73–93.

at the time, and probably also by the agitators in Galatia. References to the circumcision of Abraham (Gen 17:4–14) are less common.[22] None the less I think it is likely that the agitators did refer to this passage. Since we can be certain that the agitators were promoting circumcision (6:12), and since circumcision and the covenant with Abraham are linked in a number of early Jewish traditions, we may be confident that the agitators referred to Abraham's circumcision.[23] This is made a little more likely by the evidence of Justin's *Dialogue*, evidence which seems to have been overlooked in recent discussion of Galatians.

The very first passage of Scripture which Trypho throws at Justin is Gen 17:14: 'That person who is not circumcized on the eighth day will be cut off from his people.' Trypho goes on to remind Justin that this command refers alike to 'strangers (ἀλλογενῶν) and to purchased slaves'. Those who despise this covenant (with Abraham, with circumcision as its sign) necessarily neglect all the other commandments of the law. Trypho completes his initial challenge to Justin by urging him to show him how Christians can have any hope at all, if they do not keep the law (*Dialogue* 10:3–4). Justin knows just how strong this opening gambit is, so he replies (not very convincingly) at length. Even if Justin has placed this reference to Gen 17:14 into the mouth of Trypho, its importance for the rhetoric of the whole *Dialogue* can hardly be over-estimated. Justin knows that the issue at the top of the agenda in any discussion with Jewish opponents (and with Jewish Christians, cf. *Dialogue* 46 and 47) is circumcision and the law, and he knows he must support his case with Scriptural argument.

I am not claiming that a line can be traced back from Justin to Paul. But the *Dialogue* does suggest that the relationship between Gen 15:6 and Gen 17:14 is likely to have been prominent in the disputes in Galatia. So why does Paul not discuss Gen 17? Perhaps his failure to do so was deliberate: his silence may have been a shock tactic, designed to set the Galatians thinking. Perhaps Paul was saying in effect: Gen 15:6 is the key passage, not Gen 17:14; I know what the agitators have been saying about this verse, but here is its true meaning.[24]

Paul clinches his argument forcefully in 3:9: 'Those who have faith are blessed with Abraham who believed.' He repeats it and develops it further at 3:14, the climax of the next step in his argument: Christ redeemed us from the curse of the law that the blessing given to Abraham might come to the Gentiles through Christ Jesus, so that by faith we might receive the promise of the Spirit.

---

[22] See the evidence gathered by Hansen and Longenecker, as in n. 20.

[23] So also G. Walter Hansen, *Galatians* (Downers Grove, Ill.: IVP, 1994).

[24] Similarly, C.K. Barrett, 'The Allegory of Abraham, Sarah, and Hagar in the Argument of Galatians', in his *Essays on Paul* (London: SPCK, 1982) 159.

Abraham continues to be prominent in the verses which follow. In 3:16 Paul cleverly accepts the slogan repeated ceaselessly by the agitators: 'The promises were spoken to Abraham and his seed.' Paul even agrees that the phrase in the singular, 'and to your seed' is crucial, but he claims that it refers to a single person, Christ. For our present purposes, the next verse, which concludes the argument of this section, is even more important.

The agitators were insisting that God's covenant with Abraham was based on his good works (cf. 3:6) and probably that Abraham's circumcision was the sign of the covenant (Gen 17:10–14). They may well have echoed several strands of Jewish opinion which claimed that Abraham's circumcision confirmed that he kept the whole Mosaic law. As C.K. Barrett notes, 'They probably took the view that the Abrahamic covenant had been redefined by the Sinaitic.'[25] Paul will have none of this. God's covenant with Abraham was based on faith; it was not set aside, supplemented, or reinterpreted by the law, given 430 years later.

Like most Jewish teachers, Paul appealed to the Scriptural traditions about Abraham. But his priorities were often different, and when he did turn to the same passages as the agitators, he interpreted their favourite verses along radically new lines. In the Abraham passages I have considered briefly so far, there is a consistent pattern: Paul rejects firmly any suggestion that God's covenant with Abraham was based circumcision rather than faith, or that it was modified in any way by the Mosaic law introduced 430 years later. In short, Paul removes circumcision and the law from the pedestal on which they had been placed.

Is the final reference to Abraham in Galatians, the allegory in 4:21–5:1 concerning Abraham's two sons, consistent with the earlier Abraham traditions as far as the law is concerned? There are two main reasons which confirm that this is the case.

(i) Once again Paul is refuting the agitators' reading of some of the Abraham traditions. Along with a number of recent writers, I find Barrett's 1976 article compelling. He begins by noting that the Hagar-Sarah allegory has often been neglected or treated as a mere appendix to Gal 3 and 4. The same tendency can be observed in more recent exegesis. R. Longenecker and G. Walter Hansen both pay careful attention to the Abraham traditions in Galatians, but they downplay the lines of continuity in Paul's references to Abraham by assigning Paul's two main uses of the Abraham story to different sections of the letter: 3:6–29 is said to substantiate Paul's *rebuke* to his Galatian converts for their desertion from the gospel, while the Hagar-Sarah allegory belongs to the *request* section of the letter and serves as scriptural

---

[25] 'The Allegory', 167.

support for his ethical imperatives. I am not yet persuaded by their claim that Galatians is an example of a rebuke-request letter.[26]

Barrett notes that Paul is unlikely to have introduced the Hagar-Sarah allegory of his own accord, for its value from his point of view is anything but obvious, and the method of interpretation is unusual with him. In fact, 'its plain, surface meaning supports the Judaizers, not Paul'. Hence it stands in Galatians 'because Paul's opponents had used it and he could not escape it.'[27]

The agitators seem to have claimed that they were the sons of Isaac, the legitimate children of Abraham; that belonging to the people of God must involve circumcision and keeping the law; that the church in Jerusalem supported their views; that Paul and and those who accepted his views were like the Ishmaelites, illegitimate children.

Paul subverts their claims by insisting that those freed by Christ (both Jews and Gentiles) belong to the Sarah-Isaac line as children of promise; those under the law belong to the line of the slave woman Hagar and her son Ishmael. For our present purposes v. 25 is important: here by means of the theme of 'slavery', Paul links Hagar, Mount Sinai in Arabia (= the law) and the present city of Jerusalem. Heikki Räisänen's conclusion cannot be avoided: 'It is the law itself that enslaves those under it'.[28]

In Paul's re-interpretation of the traditions concerning Abraham's two sons, those who belong to Christ trace their line of descent directly back to Abraham, by-passing completely Mount Sinai and the law.

(ii) The original listeners in the Galatian churches may have had as many difficulties with this passage as many modern commentators. But the introduction, the conclusion, and the sustained antithetical contrast are crystal clear. Paul addresses 'those who want to be under the law' and contrasts their slavery with the freedom Christ has brought (4:21, 31 and 5:1). In view of the sustained contrast which begins at 2:15 between those whose standing before God is based ἐξ ἔργων νόμου and those whose standing is ἐκ πίστεως, the original listeners would have grasped readily that 'faith' and 'freedom' on the one hand, and 'law' and 'slavery' on the other were diametrically opposed to one another. The link between the law and slavery had already been established in 3:22–4 and 4:1–10; the contrast between circumcision – law – slavery, and freedom in Christ Jesus had already been drawn in 2:3–4. The Hagar-Sarah allegory is no mere awkward appendix; it recalls one of the passages in the narrative section of Galatians, and brings to a climax the argument Paul has been developing since 2:15–16.

---

[26] See my review of Hansen, *Abraham in Galatians* (1989) in *JTS* 43 (1992) 614–5.

[27] 'The Allegory', 163. So too John Barclay, *Obeying the Truth*, 91, in spite of his hesitations over mirror-reading.

[28] *Paul and the Law*, 44.

III. The Curse of the Law: Galatians 3:10–12

Although it is difficult to establish the precise meaning of these verses and to be certain of their relationship to one another, Paul's basic point is clear: those who rely on carrying out the requirements of the law are under the curse of the law. But why does the law bring a curse, rather than a blessing? What is wrong with the law? There are three major *cruces*. What does 3:10 mean? What do 3:11 and 12 mean and how are they related to 3:10? And what is the relationship of the three citations of Scripture in these verses to one another?[29]

In the preceding verses, 3:6–9, Paul has been insisting that οἱ ἐκ πίστεως are sons of Abraham and blessed with Abraham who believed. In verse 10 Paul turns to οἱ ἐξ ἔργων νόμου. Once again Paul draws a strong contrast between those who are ἐξ ἔργων νόμου and those who are ἐκ πίστεως, a contrast which is first worked out in 2:16, and which must have sounded to the first listeners like a refrain by now.[30]

Why does the law bring a curse? Paul answers the question by quoting Deut 27:26, but his answer has been understood in two very different ways in modern discussion.[31] Some (the majority, according to Räisänen)[32] assume that Paul is implying that it is impossible to carry out the requirements of the law: since those who try to carry out the requirements of the law fail to keep the law completely, they are accursed. On this view there is a solemn warning to the Galatians: beware of the law's siren voice, for it brings a curse, not a blessing.

Räisänen defends this view strongly by appealing to Gal 5:3 and Romans 1:18–3:20. He accepts Hübner's view that taken together, Gal 3:10 and 5:3 seem to reveal 'an enormously rigorous attitude.' The corollary of this line of interpretation is that 3:11 and 12 make a rather different point. Although 3:11

---

[29] 3:13, 'Christ … became a curse for us …' will not be discussed since it is not directly relevant to our theme.

[30] Although 3.10 is related to 3.9 by a simple γάρ, the antithesis is so stark that the REB translation of the opening of 3.10, 'on the other hand', is not out of order.

[31] See the references to the supporters of the two views in Räisänen, *Paul and the Law*, 94, notes 2 and 4.

Justin also cites Deut 27.26, at *Dial* 95. 1ff. Since the wording of his quotation is very similar to Paul's, and since both seem to agree against the LXX, several scholars have concluded (largely on the basis of this passage) that Justin knew Galatians. For example, O. Skarsaune, *The Proof from Prophecy* (Leiden: Brill, 1987) writes, 'No doubt Justin had Gal 3 before his eyes when writing *Dial* 95f.' However Skarsaune and T. Sylianopoulos (n. 19) fail to note that Paul's citation of Deut 27:26 includes phrases from Deut 28:58 and 30:10. The key phrase τοῖς γεγραμμένοις ἐν τῷ βιβλίῳ τοῦ νόμου recurs as a formula throughout Deut 28–30; this 'makes it hazardous to rule out the possibility that the words might have crept into Paul's *Vorlage* as a result of scribal harmonization, despite the lack of manuscript support for such a reading.' C.S. Stanley, *Paul and the Language of Scripture* (Cambridge: CUP, 1992) 240.

[32] H. Räisänen, *Paul and the Law*, 94.

is introduced as if it were a proof for v. 10, 'from the point of view of its content it looks more like a new argument.'[33]

Other exegetes have interpreted 3:10 rather differently and more closely in line with the view of the law which seems to underlie 3:11 and 12.[34] The fault with the law is not that it cannot be carried out completely, but 'rather that it drives man to *do* things'; v. 10 shows that 'what is important in the sphere of the law is doing.'[35]

The citation of Lev 18. 5 in 3. 12 has baffled some exegetes. How is this citation related to the quotation of Hab 2. 4 in 3. 11? The former seems to have been ruled out of court by the latter: living by faith leaves no room for living by the requirements of the law.[36] Christopher Stanley has recently shown that by dropping ἄνθρωπος from the LXX of Lev 18. 5 Paul has brought the two quotations into near-perfect parallelism, 'thus throwing into sharp relief the inherent contradiction (in Paul's way of thinking) between their respective contents.' Stanley goes on to draw attention to the importance of verbal cues to meaning in antiquity, a point I have emphasised above.[37]

Surely the two citations are intended to form yet another strong contrast. In v. 11 Hab 2. 4 underpins Paul's argument concerning faith; in 3. 12 Lev 18. 5 confirms that the law has to do with carrying out the requirements of the law and living by them. J.L. Martyn has recently noted that in 3:11–12 Paul uses the rhetorical form of contradiction in order to distinguish the *true* promise of Hab 2:4 from the *false* one of Lev 18:5.[38]

In Gal 3:10–12 we are looking at only one side of the coin: Paul's comments on the law are pointed and harsh. But the other side of the coin, the verses which follow immediately in 3:13–14, is much more attractive. These verses form the climax of Paul's argument: Christ redeemed us from the curse of the law ... so that we might receive the promise of the Spirit through faith. In focussing on Paul's attitude to the law we do not do justice to the richness of the apostle's thought.

[33] H. Räisänen, *Paul and the Law*, 95.

[34] For a recent defence of this view, see James Dunn's commentary. He does not refer to Gal 5:3, the verse which is a pillar in Räisänen's case.

[35] This is Räisänen's summary (94) of Chr. Maurer's view (1941). In the version of this chapter prepared for the Symposium in Durham, I noted that since proponents of both views would be sitting around the same table, they could well debate the exegesis of 3: 1–12. No doubt mainly because of the complexity of the exegetical issues, they failed to take up my challenge.

[36] See John Barclay, *Obeying the Truth*, 67.

[37] C.D. Stanley, *Paul and the Language of Scripture*, 244–5.

[38] J.L. Martyn, 'Christ, the Elements of the Cosmos, and the Law in Galatians', in ed. M. White and L. Yarbrough, *The Social World of the First Christians*, Essays in Honor of Wayne A. Meeks (Minneapolis: Fortress, 1995) 16–39, here 36 n. 53. For a rather different line of exegesis, see J. Lambrecht, 'Curse and Blessing: a Study of Galatians 3, 10–14' *Collationes* 21 (1991) 133–157, now included his *Pauline Studies* (Leuven: University Press, 1994) here 284–5.

IV. The origin and purpose of the law: Galatians 3:19–25 and 4:1–10

The general pattern of 3:10–14 is repeated in 3:19–29. Negative comments on the origin and purpose of the law in 19–25 are a step towards the positive finale of 3:26–9, verses which are as theologically powerful and positive as any other passage in Paul's writings. There can be no doubt that in 3:19–25 Paul comments negatively on the origin and role of the law. It is by no means easy to determine just how negative his statements are. Once again we need to bear in mind the overall impact this set of comments on the law would have had on the first listeners. Although it is possible to interpret one or two of Paul's comments, taken in isolation, in a 'neutral' or possibly even in a positive sense, the thrust of the whole argument is inexorable: Paul is even more antagonistic to the law in this passage than elsewhere in Galatians. The main points will be considered briefly in the order in which they occur.

(i) Gal 3:19a and b: The law was added (to the promises) because of transgressions, until the Seed ... had come.

There can be little doubt about the force of προσετέθη: it 'marks the law as supplementary, and hence subordinate to the covenant.'[39] χάριν is not so straightforward. Here there are two main possibilities.[40] Was the law given 'to bring about a knowledge of transgressions',[41] or was it given 'to cause or increase transgressions'? On the former view, the law has a positive role: it enables us to recognise sin for what it is. Since this positive note is out of character with the comments which follow immediately, and with the general tenor of Galatians as a whole, the latter sense is preferable. However, unless passages in Romans are allowed to settle the matter, a confident decision is not possible.

The verb προσετέθη had already hinted at the temporary nature of the law. ἄχρις οὗ is explicit: the law's role is limited to the period between Moses and Christ. In nearly all strands of Jewish thought, and presumably in the view of the agitators, the law had been given by God permanently. Paul strikes a very different note. The temporary character of the law which is stated so unequivocally here prepares the way for the παιδαγωγός metaphor which follows in 3:24.

(ii) 3:19c and 20: The law was ordained through angels by a mediator. Now a mediator involves more than one party; but God is one. (NRSV)[42]

---

[39] E.D. Burton, *Galatians*, ICC, (Edinburgh: T&T Clark, 1921) ad loc.

[40] H. Räisänen, *Paul and the Law*, 141, lists the most influential supporters of these two views and notes a third: the intervention of the law makes sin a conscious and wilful activity; it makes man guilty.

[41] James Dunn takes an even more positive line here: '(the law was added) in order to provide some sort of remedy for transgressions.'

[42] διαταγείς is translated as follows: REB: 'promulgated through angels'; NIV 'put into effect through angels'; GNB: 'handed down by angels, with a man acting as a go-between' (!).

The precise sense is much disputed. There are plenty of traditions which associate angels with the giving of the law, starting with Deut 33:2 (LXX); the involvement of angels is usually set either in a neutral or a positive light. But what is their role here? Is Paul simply saying that God allowed angels to pass on his laws to Moses? Or is he hinting that the angels were the *source* of the law, perhaps even as demonic beings? Or is there a *via media*: not an outright denial of the role of God, but a subtle distancing of God from the giving of the law? Supporters of the first view take διαταγείς as a 'divine passive'. Although this interpretation is just possible, it is by no means necessary; the context and (as we shall see in a moment) 3:20 rules it out. Since weighty objections have been made to the second view,[43] I think the latter view is the most likely.

The immediate context confirms that the first listeners were bound to notice the absence of explicit reference to the involvement of God in the giving of the law. I have drawn attention repeatedly to the antithetical words and phrases which are found almost right through Gal 3 and 4. In this case 'promise' and 'law' are set opposite one another. Gal 3:18 refers to God's gracious gift to Abraham through a promise; God's role is emphasised by the placement of ὁ θεός at the end of the sentence. In the very next verse the giving of the law is referred to, but 'God' is not mentioned explicitly; the silence is telling.

The most natural interpretation of 3:20 supports this conclusion. Räisänen (1986) p. 130, notes that 3. 20 is a famous *crux*, 'but mainly because interpreters are not willing to swallow Paul's message ... God, being One, needs no mediator between himself and mankind. A mediator was needed, therefore God was not involved. A mediator was necessary, because both parties involved consisted of many persons; unlike God, neither party was 'one'.' Of course the idea is strange, as Räisänen concedes, but the gist of it is clear.

(iii) Gal 3:24–5: The law was our παιδαγωγός. Paul's striking metaphor has been understood in various ways. In recent years an enormous amount of material has been gathered concerning the role of the παιδαγωγός in antiquity.[44] But this huge Pile of references has only muddied the water: the role of the παιδαγωγός was thought of in very different ways in different circles, many of which can be applied plausibly to the law. Which one did Paul have in mind? Is the law, like the παιδαγωγός, seen primarily in an educative role, a disciplinary role, or in a temporary restrictive role?

Paul's metaphor could have been understood by the listeners in many different ways. In this respect it is not unlike Matthew's use of the metaphor of

---

[43] Räisänen rejects Hübner's claim (which is similar to Albert Schweitzer's) that the angels were 'demonic beings', with evil intentions.

[44] See especially D.J. Lull, 'The Law was our Pedagogue' *JBL* 105 (1986) 481–98; N.H. Young, "Paidagogos: The Social Setting of a Pauline Metaphor', *NovT* 29 (1987) 150–76; R.N. Longenecker, *Galatians* (1990).

'salt' for disciples in 5:13. Metaphors are often 'open' comparisons which need a context in order to allow their precise sense to become clear. Paul has already given his listeners clear guidance in 3:23 concerning the sense of παιδαγωγός: before faith came, we were 'kept in custody', 'confined' until faith should be revealed. The law, like the παιδαγωγός, provided unpleasant restraint for a limited period.[45]

(iv) Gal 4:1–10: The law and τὰ στοιχεῖα. In these verses Paul draws a comparison between the Galatians' present plight as they hanker after the law, and their plight before they became Christians. Formerly they were enslaved to the στοιχεῖα; now they want to be enslaved all over again. But does Paul go further than this and, as some have suggested, include the law among the enslaving στοιχεῖα?

What are the στοιχεῖα? Two suggestions have been prominent in discussion. If the στοιχεῖα are understood as 'demonic powers', then this would not square with even the most negative points Paul has made about the law in the preceding verses. But in fact a link between στοιχεῖα and the demonic is hard to establish until much later than Paul's day.[46]

If, however, στοιχεῖα means 'the basic elements from which everything in the natural world is made and of which it is composed', then a direct link with the law is probable. J.L. Martyn has recently argued persuasively that the Galatians are almost certain to have taken the expression 'the elements of the cosmos' long before they laid eyes on either Paul or 'the Teachers' to refer to the earth, air, fire, water, with the possible addition of the stars. When Paul speaks in 4:3–5 of liberation from the enslaving elements of the cosmos, he has in mind 'not earth, air, fire, and water, but rather the elemental pairs of opposites listed in 3:28, and emphatically the first pair, Jew and Gentile, and thus the Law and the not-Law.'[47] On this view once again Paul speaks negatively about the law, though his primary concern is to remind the Galatians of their liberation from the στοιχεῖα, and so to encourage them to turn aside from further enslavement.

V. The Law of Christ:4:21b, 5:14, and 6:2.

Right up until 4:21b Paul speaks negatively about the law, and in every case he has the law of Moses in mind. It is no exaggeration to claim that from 2:16

---

[45] Similarly, S.Westerholm, *Israel's Law and the Church's Faith*, 1988) 196. Longenecker puts the cart before the horse when he interprets 3:23 in the light of his conclusions about the role of the παιδαγωγός.

[46] See especially R.N. Longenecker, *Galatians*, 165; J.L. Martyn (n. 37) 19.

[47] J.L. Martyn (n.37) 31.

to 4:21a, Paul's portrait of the law is 'consistently malignant'.[48] ὁ νόμος, ἐξ ἔργων νόμου, ἐκ νόμου, ἐν νόμῳ and ὑπὸ νόμον have been pounding relentlessly in the Galatians' ears since 2:16. However in 4:21b, 5:14 and 6:2 Paul's tone changes dramatically: νόμος is clearly used in a positive sense.

In the first clause of 4:21 Paul speaks with heavy irony: 'Tell me now, you that are so anxious to be under law.'[49] Here ὑπὸ νόμον is used in what has become a familiar way to Paul's hearers. But in 4:21b Paul urges his hearers to listen to what the law really says: the law suddenly and unexpectedly does have positive things to say. Paul does not speak about a different law in 4:21b, or a principle: as in all the earlier uses of νόμος in Galatians, it is the law of Moses which is referred to. J.L. Martyn paraphrases Paul's point: 'Do you really hear what the law says when it bears its evangelistic witness?'[50]

Paul had partially prepared his readers for this important positive role for the law of Moses in 3:8. There ἡ γραφή, foreseeing that God would justify the Gentiles through faith, had declared the gospel to Abraham beforehand. In 4:21b it is not ἡ γραφή but ὁ νόμος, heard aright, which bears witness to the gospel in the allegory of Hagar and Sarah which follows.

In the light of this understanding of 4:21b, 5:14, with its reference to fulfilling the law in loving one's neighbour, is not 'the most unexpected development of Paul's thought in this letter.'[51] There is an important distinction between 5:3, 'keeping the entire law', and 5:14, 'fulfilling the whole law': it is not the difference between ὅλος ὁ νόμος and ὁ πᾶς νόμος, or the difference between the law of Moses and some other 'law',[52] but the difference between the verbs. In 5:14 πληροῦν is used, a verb not used with νόμος in the LXX or in Greek Jewish literature.[53] Barclay notes that in 5:14 Paul uses the verb 'to describe the total realization of God's will in line with the eschatological fulness of time in the coming of Christ.'[54]

As many exegetes have observed, 6:2, with its reference to the law of Christ and its use of ἀναπληροῦν, is closely related to 5:14. Although 'Christ' and 'law' have regularly stood in stark contrast earlier the letter, in 6:2 they are

---

[48] J.L. Martyn (n.37) 36.

[49] In his commentary at this point James Dunn refers appropriately to Paul's bantering tone.

[50] J.L. Martyn (n. 37) 37. H.D. Betz's comment is similar: '... to understand Torah is to understand its allegorical meaning.'

[51] Graham Shaw, *The Cost of Authority* (London: SCM, 1983) 50. I owe this reference to John Barclay, *Obeying the Truth*, 126.

[52] H. Hübner's denial that Paul is referring to the law of Moses is dubbed 'ingenious' by John Barclay, but rejected. See Barclay's discussion, with further references to the secondary literature on this point, *Obeying the Truth*, 137.

[53] See J. Barclay, *Obeying the Truth*, 138.

[54] *Obeying the Truth*, 140. Barclay also suggests that Paul chose this vocabulary partly because of its *ambiguity*! To say that 'the whole law is fulfilled in one command' leaves unclear the status of the rest of the commandments.

brought together in a striking and memorable phrase. Since 'fulfilling the law' in 5:14 refers to the law of Moses, the use of the similar verb in 6:2 strongly suggests that 'law' here also refers to the law of Moses – as 'redefined through Christ', as 'redefined and fulfilled by Christ in love' (John Barclay), or, 'as it has fallen into the hands of Christ' (J.L. Martyn).[55]

4:21b, 5:14, and 6:2 stand in counterpoise to Paul's other references to the law of Moses in Galatians. These verses confirm that in spite of the numerous negative comments on the law elsewhere in this letter, Paul did not repudiate the law of Moses. We might reasonably wish that he had explained a little more fully what he meant by 'the law of Christ'. Paul does so in Romans (albeit only indirectly), but that is another story.

---

[55] J. Barclay, *Obeying the Truth*, 134 and 141; J.L. Martyn (n. 37) 39 n. 60. Similarly (with further references to the secondary literature), James Dunn: 'it means 'that law (Torah) as interpreted by the love command in the light of the Jesus-tradition and the Christ-event.'

Letter and Spirit in 2 Corinthians 3*

by

KARL KERTELGE

Introduction: The Question

The antithesis of γράμμα and πνεῦμα, used by Paul in 2 Cor. 3:6, and also in Rom. 2:27-29 and 7:6, poses a basic theological question in Pauline thinking, as it does for all Christian theology subsequent to Paul. Among the fathers Augustine discusses the issue in *De Spiritu et Littera*. For Luther and the Reformation churches the antithesis was a central aspect in the doctrine of justification; it depicted the issue more comprehensively than did law and gospel. The fundamental theological question causes division in Pauline exegesis right up to our own time. The exegetical essay of O. Hofius upon this theme deals with 2 Corinthians 3 under the heading of law and gospel according to 2 Corinthians 3.[1] It does this even though neither νόμος nor εὐαγγέλιον occurs in the text. εὐαγγέλιον does, of course, introduce what follows in 4:3f., indicating the pregnant theme. The point of 2 Corinthians 3 is to demonstrate the Spirit in the ministry of the new covenant. Paul provides this demonstration by profiling the antithesis of letter and spirit in 3:6. Naturally the reality of the Mosaic law

---

* The first version of this paper was given at a meeting of Protestant and Roman Catholic theologians on March 21-24, 1994, at Friedewald. It was then slightly revised for the Durham symposium on Paul and the Law on September, 19-23, 1994, then revised again for publication.

1. In *Paulusstudien* (WUNT 51), Tübingen, 1989, 75-120. The divisive significance of 2 Cor. 3:6 relative to the Pauline doctrine of justification is also brought out by E. Käsemann, *Paulinische Perspektiven,* Tübingen, 1969, 237-285 ("Geist und Buchstabe"), where it serves as an expository criterion for the whole chapter. Cf., too, E. Grässer, "Paulus, der Apostle des Neuen Bundes (2 Cor. 2:14f.)" in L. de Lorenzi (ed.), *Paolo Ministro del Nuovo Testamento* (SMBen, BE 9), Rome 1987, 7-43, which states on p. 33: "The letter kills, but the Spirit gives life! this brief classical summation of Paul's theology of justification to my mind removes every doubt."

plays an important part in the context of the antithesis. We must not overlook this fact. The word γράμμα points to an important aspect of the Pauline doctrine of the law.

In our own day the antithesis has aroused attention in another respect, namely, as a hermeneutical direction for the exposition of scripture that commends the spiritual sense of the biblical texts in opposition to an analysis and interpretation that deals critically with the letter or attempts historical reconstruction.[2] This enduring desire, rekindled again today, now seeks a theological interpretation that will transcend historical-critical exegesis. But it should not lead us to treat the original meaning of the Pauline antithesis as though it were dealing only with the hermeneutical question, or to see here only a polemical opposition between historical criticism and theological and spiritual disclosure.

We shall not ignore the views presented, but our primary task here will be to expound the antithesis in the context of 2 Corinthians 3. The antithesis of letter and spirit in v. 6 is closely linked to Paul's description of himself as a minister of the new covenant. The antithesis obviously offers us a leading definition of the new covenant, and it does so by discussing in vv. 7-18 the relationship between the new covenant and the old. We must pay particular attention to this fact.

I. 2 Corinthians 3:6 As a Pointer to Paul's Themes

I.1. Verse 6 in Context

The third chapter forms an integral part of the discussion running from 2 Cor. 2:14 to 7:4. According to the hypothesis of G. Bornkamm,[3] this is a separate

---

2. For a brief survey of the reception and impact of the antithesis and of its hermeneutical significance cf. J. Kremer in his informative article, " 'Denn der Buchstabe tötet, der Geist macht lebendig.' Methodologische und hermeneutische Erwägungen zu 2 Kor. 3:6b," J. Zmijewski and E. Nellessen (eds.), *Begegnung mit dem Wort,* Festschrift H. Zimmermann (BBB 53), Bonn 1980, 236-39. Cf. also J. Eckert, "Die geistliche Schriftauslegung des Apostels Paulus nach 2 Kor. 3:4-18," *Dynamik im Wort,* Festschrift on the occasion of the 50th anniversary of the *Kath. Bibelwerks,* Stuttgart 1983, 247f, which states that although we must not oppose a literal interpretation and plead for an allegorical (as Origen did when he claimed that the antithesis establishes a right to understand the OT allegorically), yet we still have to note that the use of this pair shows that for Paul a purely literal interpretation was inadequate.

3. G. Bornkamm, *Die Vorgeschichte des sogenannten Zweiten Korintherbriefes,* SHAW.PH, Heidelberg 1961.

letter not attached to the whole epistle and commonly defined as an apology for the apostolic office. Paul, in v. 6, describes the leading theme as his divine empowering as a minister of the new covenant. He thus differentiates himself from rivals who operate in the church that he founded, and who have a different understanding of the apostolate. His argument is a theological one based on his view of the apostolic ministry that is pledged to the gospel that he proclaims. He qualifies this ministry of the gospel by using the catchword "new covenant" and giving it the distinctive definition of a covenant, not of the letter, but of the Spirit. The way was prepared for a closer definition of this antithesis. We find this in the preceding context of 3:1-3.

In these verses the apostle's position is plain. As new apostles might penetrate into the community, the Corinthian Christians will offer the valid proof that ought always to be expected of an apostle. These are the marks of an apostle (12:12) that show him to be a bearer of the Spirit. In 3:3 Paul speaks more soberly of letters of commendation by which a community in which an itinerant apostle has worked can commend him to other churches. The validity of Paul's own apostleship is at stake. As Paul sees it, looking at the outward marks of possession of the Spirit is wholly inappropriate. Only at a distance and relatively can he refer to his possible ecstasies (cf. 12:1: "revelations"). As the first to preach the gospel to them he was their "father" (1 Cor. 4:15).[4] A subsequent attack upon his authority thus seems to be absurd. The church itself, which is so closely related to the apostle, provides the validity that is in question. This relationship is grounded in the working of "the Spirit of the living God" (3:3), and the church ought to know that it has its basis in the *pneuma*.

In v. 3, therefore, we find the word *pneuma* that is so important throughout the section. According to vv. 1-3 we can say that the congregation of believers has the Spirit of God as its basis. Paul is not operating with the Spirit in terms of charismatic distribution to individuals but rather with the Spirit who imparts himself to the community through the preaching of the gospel. The Spirit is the Spirit of the living God, God's life-giving power. Already, then, Paul announces the theme of v. 6. He does so by using two corresponding pairs of concepts, thus giving antithetical force to what he says: "Not with ink but with the Spirit of the living God," and: "Not on tablets of stone but on tablets of human hearts." The further development of the main statement in v. 3 helps to motivate

---

4. "More than just a metaphor," H. Merklein, *Der erste Brief an die Korinther. Kap. 1–4* (ÖTK 7,1), Gütersloh 1992, 325.

the outworking of the theme in v. 6. The OT is the background. Exodus 31:18 refers to the tablets of Moses and Ezek 11:19 and 36:26 speak of the gift of hearts of flesh that will replace hearts of stone. The themes come together in v. 3. The connecting point is the "letter from Christ" that is the result of Paul's (apostolic) ministry. Paul does not later abandon the theme of himself and the church. At least we should not overlook the fact that in the ensuing verse what is stressed is that the apostolic office has its basis in God himself, or, more precisely, in the working of the Spirit of God.

The theocentric dimension of vv. 4-6 is obvious. The confidence (πεποίθησιν) of the preaching ministry is to be found in God. We can thus read in v. 12 that the apostle speaks with great openness (παρρησία). The motif of freedom then occurs in v. 17. We might also think of 4:2. Here Paul refers to his self-commendation before every human conscience and before God, namely, that he can openly proclaim the truth of the gospel. His immediacy to God through Christ is his divine qualification. By this qualification he is a minister of the new covenant. The more precise antithesis of the letter and the Spirit gives full weight to Paul's assertion that he is a minister of the new covenant. His ministry comes from God and is defined by the Spirit. Spiritual phenomena do not charismatically express this definition. At least, they do not do so primarily. It finds expression in the proclamation of the gospel that lays bare the truth of God. Paul gives voice to this apostolic self-understanding when in vv. 7-11 he strengthens what he says about the ministry of the new covenant by very favorably comparing it with the ministry of the old covenant. Then in vv. 12-18 he states, not unpolemically, the goal of a Spirit-filled ministry of the new covenant, which far surpasses that of the ministry of the old covenant, for it takes away the veil which covers the old covenant, and points Israel to the Kyrios.

2. The Thesis of 3:6 As a Profile of the Theme of the Apology

After 3:1-3, and even 2:14, Paul has to defend polemically the validity of what he is doing. He does not defend himself but offers the commendation of his understanding of what the ministry of an apostle involves. In v. 5 he shows that his equipment for the office came directly from God. He thus claims a different norm of judgment from that of his opponents. He had already stated this norm in 1 Cor. 2:14 when he had reconsidered what it means to speak words of wisdom, claiming that one must be fully gifted with the Spirit for the proclamation and the proper understanding of the gospel: "A natural person (ψυχικὸς ἄνθρωπος) does not understand the things that come from the Spirit; they are foolishness to him, and he cannot understand them, because they are spiritually (πνευματικῶς) discerned. The spiritual person (πνευματικός) judges all things but is not judged by anyone."

Spiritual things are to be judged spiritually. Paul bases himself on the "Spirit of the living God" who is at work in his gospel (2 Cor. 3:3). His ministry is defined by this Spirit. This leads on to the core statement that God has empowered him for this ministry (v. 6). When his ministry is thus qualified, it can then be expounded by the sharp antithesis of γράμμα and πνεῦμα. The gnomic saying that concludes the sentence: "For the letter kills, but the Spirit gives life," gives an edge to the contrast. This statement, and the whole of v. 6, prepares the ground for the development of the motif of the chapter.

The term "minister of the new covenant" calls for exposition, as does also the use of the antithesis of letter and Spirit in this context.

a. Minister of the New Covenant. The catchwords διάκονος and διακονία occur frequently in the wider context of the apology. In 6:3., looking back on what he had said before about this ministry, Paul says: "We put no stumbling blocks in anyone's path lest our ministry be discredited. Instead, we commend ourselves in every respect as servants of God, through great endurance in troubles, hardships, distresses. . . ." There then follows the list that continues up to v. 10 and that gives the apostle true validity if convincing criteria are to be sought. In this connection διακονία and διάκονος are used to define the apostolic office. This had been the case in 1 Cor. 3:5, in which Apollos and Paul were "διάκονοι through whom you came to believe as the Lord had given them." In 2 Cor. 11:13-15 Paul uses the term polemically when speaking of false apostles, deceitful workmen, camouflaging themselves as apostles of Christ, yet still claiming to be "servants of Christ" (v. 23). Yet Paul is far more so. Servant of Christ in the sense of a designation of office was obviously in use before Paul and along with him. The question is raised by 3:6, however, whether "servant of the new covenant" was a creation of Paul's or whether it was already used by his adversaries, so that the antithesis at the end of the verse makes a decisive distinction.[5]

---

5. Cf. J. Murphy-O'Connor, "A Ministry Beyond the Letter (2 Cor. 3:1-6)," *Paolo-Ministro del Nuovo Testamento,* L. de Lorenzi (ed.), who says on p. 117: "The intruders claimed to be ministers of the New Covenant, and the Apostle had to distance himself from them . . . by distinguishing between 'letter-ministers' and 'spirit-ministers' of the New Covenant." Yet, it here remains to be seen whether Paul's use of the term was primarily positive. The volume cited above offers important con-

We must also put the question regarding the use of the term καινὴ διαθήκη. How did Paul come to use this specific description of this ministry, and what does it mean in this context?

We find the term καινὴ διαθήκη, as we all know, in the tradition concerning the Last Supper according to 1 Cor. 11:25: "This cup is the new covenant in my blood." We find the same saying in Luke 22:20. In the eucharist the primitive Christian community celebrates the new covenant that had been instituted by the blood of Jesus. The reference is to the saying in Jer. 31:31-34 and also to the blood rite at the institution of the covenant in Exod. 24:8. According to E. Kutsch[6] and O. Hofius[7] the new covenant is a new dispensation unmistakably containing a basic order resting on a revelation of the divine will which establishes fellowship.[8] Newly qualified eschatologically, it is thus a new and eschatologically final way of salvation. That Paul in this sense can call himself a servant of the new *diatheke,* presupposes at least a positive recognition of the primitive Christian use of *diatheke* which derives from its self-understanding according to a valid but distinctive view of the people of God. Paul's understanding, then, is not itself distinctive, but his use of the antithetical addition is.

b. The Antithesis of γράμμα and πνεῦμα   The new covenant of which Paul is a servant is a covenant of the Spirit, not of the letter.[9] He obviously has his opponents in view. In v. 7 he accuses them of being servants of the letter. He himself had claimed in v. 3 that he had been active for the Corinthian church as a minister of "the Spirit of the living God." His adversaries, whose practice of sending letters of recommendation he is rejecting, are on the opposite side denoted by tablets of stone. The ministry of the letter plainly has to do with the Mosaic law represented by the stony tablets of the decalogue. But can we identify the ministry of the letter, set in antithesis to that of the Spirit, simply with the law of Moses? Not completely so, but only in one respect, namely, that we find the law in the form of γράμμα. This is the situational aspect of the antithesis. We should not overlook it, even though we have to maintain that it does basically touch also on the authority and theological dignity of the Mosaic law.

---

tributions to the exposition of 2:14 to 4:6 (M. Carrez, A. Vanhoye, M. E. Thrall, H.-J. Klauck). These essays have bearings on our own theme.

6. THAT I, 339-52.

7. Op. cit., 75f.

8. C. Wolff, *Der zweite Korintherbrief,* ThHK 8, Berlin 1989, 61.

9. Wolff, loc. cit., notes that it is a common misunderstanding to think that the contrast is between the external and the internal, between the wording and the deeper meaning.

This becomes apparent when we think of the gnomic character of the final sentence of the antithesis: "The letter kills, but the Spirit gives life" (3:6). Death and life are the contrasting results of the law on the one side and the gospel on the other according to Paul's doctrine of justification. We see this in the brief formula of Rom. 8:2: "The law of the Spirit of life in Christ Jesus has freed us from the law of sin and death."[10] This recognition, defined by faith in Christ, forms the background of 2 Cor. 3:6. Seen in relation to Paul's argument in chapter 3, it tells us that Paul's apostolic ministry has a basically different quality from that of his opponents, just as the gospel that he serves is so very different from theirs, for Paul's gospel is an effective means to free us from sin and death, which the law had no power to do (Rom. 8:3). The theology of 2 Cor. 3:6 has less to do with soteriology, however, and more to do with the apostolate. Nevertheless, the power of the Spirit that frees us from sin and death is the content of the gospel. This is indicated by the use of πνεῦμα and the explanation of πνεῦμα as a life-giving Spirit. In 2 Cor. 5:14-21 we will be told that the ministry of the apostle will also mediate salvation. It is a ministry of reconciliation based on the sacrificial death of Jesus Christ, effected by God, and entrusted to the apostle.[11]

As regards 3:6 the antithesis of πνεῦμα and γράμμα does, of course, merit special attention. According to v. 7 it points us to two ministries, that of death embodied in letters of stone, and that of the Spirit, which Paul claims for himself as an apostle. γράμμα denotes the death-dealing reality of the Mosaic law when viewed only in an exclusive sense.[12] γράμμα denotes the "writtenness" of the law. It leads the reader or hearer of the law into a restrictive and fatal fixation upon it, for they do not see that salvation comes through the Spirit, not the letter. Fixation on the Mosaic law prevents the further step toward the life-giving Pneuma. The law and the gospel, from the standpoint of fixation on the gramma, are radically different. Fixation on the gramma leads us to focus upon our own possibilities of observing the law. With this blocking fixation the law,

---

10. Cf. U. Wilckens, *Der Brief an die Römer,* Vol. 2, EKK VI,2, Zurich 1980, 123, who sees that for Paul a change in the law itself took place with our common condemnation and exaltation in Christ.

11. Cf. J. Schröter, *Der versöhnte Versöhner. Paulus als Mittler im Heilsvorgang zwischen Gott und Gemeinde nach 2 Kor. 2:14–7:4,* TANZ 10, Tübingen and Basel 1993.

12. Cf. E. Kamlah, "Buchstabe und Geist. Die Bedeutung dieser Antithese für die atl. Exegese des Apostels Paulus," EvTh 14, 1954, 277: "Indicates only the negative side of the νόμος"; also U. Luz, *Das Geschichtsverständnis des Paulus,* BEvTh 49 Munich 1968, 124: "*Gramma* stands for law only in a specific operation, in a specific regard, and in a specific usage or misusage."

which according to Rom. 7:14, is πνευματικός (ἐγὼ δὲ σάρκινός εἰμι, πεπραμένος ὑπὸ τὴν ἁμαρτίαν) cannot achieve its divinely appointed end. Salvation history, therefore, calls for a new institution, the καινὴ διαθήκη, in which the power of God is present that can overcome the incapacity of the old gramma-law. Paul does not concentrate upon the blocking anti-force of the gramma but on the gospel which proclaims the new covenant, in which the superior power of the Pneuma is displayed.

The antithesis of γράμμα and πνεῦμα in 3:6 thus sets forth the specific eschatological character of the new covenant of which Paul is a minister. While the stress is plainly upon the πνεῦμα as the eschatological power of God to give life, we must not overlook the fact that the contrast with γπάμμα was occasioned by a specific challenge. Paul uses γπάμμα to denote the giving and displaying of letters of recommendation, and the demonstrating of apostolic possession of the spirit, that are contrary to the true nature of "the Spirit of the living God." These are the expression of an order which has been outdated by the operation of the Spirit of God in the gospel. He goes on to prove this by a comparison of the two ministries based on the texts of the OT.

2. 2 Corinthians 3:7-18 as an Exegetical Development of the Saying in 3:6

Verses 7 and 8 show the connection between this section and the themes of v. 6. Yet surveys make it plain that vv. 7-18 are relatively independent over against the subject of apostolic self-commendation in vv. 1-6.[13] On the basis of Exod. 34:29-35 the figure of Moses is introduced as a representative of the ministry of death and judgment, not of the Spirit and righteousness. The reference to Moses persists through v. 18, though in vv. 14f. the Bible of the old covenant that he represents replaces him. Verses 7-11 bear a stronger reference to the theme of ministry in v. 6. In vv. 12-18 Paul's exposition deals more fundamentally with the concept of the παλαιὰ διαθήκη, though the contrasting pair of old covenant and new covenant (v. 6) still finds a place. We should pay particular attention to the expansion of the theme of the old covenant in vv. 12-18.

---

13. H. Windisch, *Der zweite Korintherbrief* (MeyerK 6), Göttingen 1924 (reprinted 1970) calls it a literary insertion, a Christian midrash on Exod. 34:29-35 demonstrating the surpassing glory of the new covenant as compared with the old.

2.1. The Twofold Ministry in Verses 7-11

The theme of this passage is denoted by the catchword, διακονία, which occurs four times in an antithetical arrangement. We have two parallel columns under this heading, the ministry of death (v. 7) and the condemnation (v. 9) on the one side, that of life (v. 8) and righteousness (v. 9) on the other. The two are held together by the motif of δόξα, which applies, though in different ways, to both ministries. Verse 7 makes it quite obvious that this motif is taken from Exod. 34:29-35, which refers to the glory on the face of Moses when he came down form Sinai. The theme of δόξα occurs throughout our present section,[14] even in the more generalized verses 10 and 11, in which it is a reality of the covenant that both ministries represent. δόξα, then, is assigned to both ministries as covenant realities, but in such a way that the incomparable (v. 10) reality of the new covenant far surpasses that of the old,[15] just as the Pneuma (v. 6) infinitely excels the gramma.

While stressing this superiority, Paul wants to do justice to Exodus 34. He, therefore, accords a certain glory to Moses. But his way of viewing the two sides gives rise to not a little tension. A continuity of glory is maintained as Paul looks at both the old covenant and the new, but his interpretation, especially in v. 10, makes a definite point of the truly incomparable reality of the eschatological new thing.[16] Against the relative δόξα of the old covenant Paul stresses the discontinuity between the old that has perished (in Christ).

The practical epitome of this presentation is the orientation of Christians to what is lasting (v. 11). This is how the Corinthians ought to see their situation. The adversaries of Paul are chained to what is perishing. the reality of the new covenant underlined by Paul offers a firm basis for the apostolic office adopted by him.

---

14. δόξα occurs eight times in 3:7-11, and δόξαζειν twice in 3:10, and the motif persists in 3:18 (twice) and ch. 4 (4 times).

15. For a basic discussion of the superiority or super-abundance of glory in the new covenant cf. M. Theobald, *Die uberströmende Gnade. Studien zu einem paulinischen Motivfeld* (FzB 22), Würzburg 1982, 167-239.

16. Cf. the consistent interpretation of the flow of the text in E. Grässer, op. cit., 16: "The radical antithesis of the ministries (of death and life) in vv. 7-11 negates the comparison of the doxa of the old covenant with that of the new (v. 10)." But M. Theobald, op. cit., 182 rightly observes that the constant motif stated in v. 11 is that of surpassing, so that though there is antithesis in relation to doxa, Paul steers clear of dualism. Paul allows glory to the ministry of Moses even though this usage is improper when no comparison is made with the normative glory of the new covenant.

2.2. *The Opening Up of the Old Covenant in Verses 12-18*

In v. 12 Paul uses the first person plural in relation to the theme of v. 6. In both context and content this saying must be compared with v. 7. Confidence and hope characterize the apostle no matter what questions his opponents raise. The word "hope" points back to what he had been saying in vv. 7-11, in which he showed what was the basis of his own *Christian* hope. But v. 12 also opens up a new aspect of the theme, that of openness (παρρησία). This is a feature of his proclamation, which, according to v. 13, distinguishes him from Moses, who had to use (Exod. 34:33) a cover (Luther) or a veil to hide his face. The subject here is the openness or freedom (v. 17) which marks the preaching of the gospel in contrast to the concealment of the Mosaic order. This motif of concealment plays a role in the verses that follow until we reach the unveiled face of all be- lievers in v. 18.

From Exodus 34 in the Old Testament we note that Paul shifts the emphasis in relation to this veil. The veil did not denote the limited ability of the people to see and to receive.[17] What it concealed was the fading away of the temporary glory of Moses. The Sinai Torah is thus presented in a bad light. Old Testament scholars, who want us to recollect the positive significance of Exodus 34, have a complaint to bring, at this point.

H.-J. Klauck,[18] too, accuses Paul of newly interpreting the veil over the face of Moses. The Old Testament, he says, never speaks about the fading away of this glory. That is Paul's own exegetical conclusion, which we can understand only as a pious strategic deception. Klauck has a different translation for v. 13: "In order that the Israelites should not see the end (or goal?) of the fading away." His explanation is that what the Israelites did not perceive was the fact that the radiance of Moses was prefiguring the glory of Christ in his fulfillment of the first covenant. The failure to see was part of the divine plan of salvation. The hiding of the transitory nature of Moses was beneficial for Israel.[19]

This is indicated by the motif of obduracy in v. 14a. Verse 14 explains that the veil is present when the Israelites read the παλαιὰ διαθήκη. This concealed reading, however, will be opened up in Christ (v. 14c). We have to ask, how- ever, whether Paul really does interpret the radiance of Moses as a prefiguring

---

17. Cf. F. L. Hossfeld exegeting Exodus 34 in 2 Cor. 3:7-18 in the ecumenical meeting of March 21-24, 1994.

18. H.-J. Klauck, *2 Korintherbrief* (NEB 8), Würzburg 1986, 39f.

19. C. Wolff, op. cit., 72.

of the glory of Christ in his fulfillment of the first covenant (Klauck). If that is true, we must relativize the contrast of γράμμα and πνεῦμα along the lines of a model of continuity. The παλαιὰ διαθήκη then becomes the "first covenant." But in v. 14 Paul speaks of the "old covenant," contrasting it with the "new." It is the covenant written on tablets of stone at Sinai.[20] This sense finds confirmation of v, 15, which equates the reading of the old covenant with the reading of Moses. Paul has in view both reading and understanding relative to the synagogue. The typology of the stone tablets in verses 3 and 7 is equated with the present reading practices of the synagogue. This gives a new application to the typology, that of correctly understanding the Mosaic law. The Mosaic law needs to be "opened up,"[21] and this will take place only "in Christ."

Students are usually inclined to view this passage as one that handles the theme of a Christian interpretation of the OT. In my opinion the hermeneutical subject arises only in v. 14c ("done away only in Christ") and v. 16, which raises the problem of Israel. The conclusion of this verse opens the door to freedom. We should not overlook the fact that Christian freedom is the dominant theme in the matter under discussion in vv. 12-18.

Verse 16 refers to a liberated turning to the Kyrios. Plainly recollected here is the meeting between Moses and Yahweh (LXX κύριος) in the tent of revelation according to Exod. 34:34. Yet Paul does not speak of Moses; on the basis of v. 13f, he speaks of all Israel. He presupposes a christological identity of the Kyrios, and thus he hints, at least in v. 16, that Israel will be converted to Christ.

This exposition is confirmed by v. 17. The Kyrios is the Pneuma. On the basis of v. 16 we would expect Paul to say that the Kyrios is Christ. The saying is anticipated, however, by the use of Kyrios in v. 16. Thus in v. 17 all the emphasis falls on the equation of the Kyrios with the πνεῦμα of v. 6. The Kyrios may be found in the working of the Spirit through the gospel.[22] We then find the result in v. 17: "Where the Spirit of the Kyrios is, there is freedom." The working of the Spirit through the gospel confers this freedom as Paul proclaims his apostolic message πολλῇ παρρησίᾳ (v. 12).

---

20. The term παλαιὰ διαθήκη occurs for the first time in the Christian tradition, and only here in the NT. It does not mean the OT in common Christian usage, but its use prepares the way for that identification (C. Wolff, op. cit., 73). Cf. E. Kutsch, art. "Bund," TRE 7, 397-410, which says on p. 408, with 2 Cor. 3:14 in view, that this term does not denote the whole of the OT but the law of Moses or the Pentateuch (cf. 1 Cor. 9:9).

21. E. Hübner, Art. "γράμμα," EWNT I, 622-624 remarks with reference to 3:3 that the law according to v. 12 has to be written on tablets that are human hearts.

22. Cf. E. Schweizer, TDNT VI, 419: "πνεῦμα is defined as the mode of existence of the κύριος."

Verse 18 conclusively strengthens the theme of freedom by referring to "all of us" who with unveiled faces reflect the glory of the Kyrios, that is, by the mediation which comes through the gospel of which the apostle is a minister. We are to take the transformation into his image quite literally. The logos proclaimed by the apostolic ministry is that into which believers are to be transformed. This will prove itself effective in their living the life of faith.

Like the preceding section (vv. 7-11), the passage in vv. 12-18 is oriented to motifs from Exod. 34:29ff. The subject is freedom as a mark of the new covenant which in Christ opens up the old covenant that once was read under a veil. Paul's assessment is based on his ministry, which is defined by the working of the Spirit.

3. Conclusions

1. We cannot simply understand the antithesis of letter and spirit in 3:6 in terms of two opposing and exclusive orders of salvation. Instead, they point to the life-giving power of the Spirit at work in the gospel, which overcomes the death-dealing power of the law. The demonstration of the Spirit in the gospel erases the death-dealing power of the law, but not the (Mosaic) law as such. This law finds its new expression as the "law of Christ" (Gal. 6:2) which is binding on Christians.

2. The catchword παλαιὰ διαθήκη in 3:14 forms a challenge for theological thinking as this tries to find a biblical theology that will embrace both testaments. We must consider this challenge from various angles.

3. The term is first used here by Paul as, in antithesis to the καινὴ διαθήκη of v. 6, he seeks to express the obstructive character of the Mosaic law that hampers the knowledge of faith. yet in this context a hope accompanies the term "old covenant," namely, the hope that the veil that lies over the law as a book that is just read will be done away in Christ. In a way that differs from the motif of γράμμα in v. 6, there is held out here the possibility of turning to the Lord. This interpretation checks the conclusion that Paul can view the "old covenant" as one that has been eliminated and nullified.[23] The transitory nature of the glory of the Mosaic cove-

---

23. Wolff, op. cit., 73. Similarly Hofius, op. cit., 81, who says that the new διαθήκη has dissolved and replaced that of Sinai. Cf. Bultmann, *Der zweite Brief an die Korinther* (ed. E. Dinkler, KEK), Göttingen 1976, 89, who says, relative to 3:14, that the subject of καταργεῖται has to be the παλαιὰ διαθήκη (or its δόξα). This is not destroyed but covered and hidden. Cf. 90, which states that the παλαιὰ διαθήκη comes only as the διαθήκη of death and κατάκρισις and thus as the καταργούμενον. Paul does

nant is revealed in Christ (Wolff), but so, too, is the glory itself as an anticipatory reflection of the abiding glory of the new covenant.

4. In 3:14 παλαιὰ διαθήκη does not denote the whole of the Christian OT, though it is well on the way to doing so. The question thus arises: What is its authority for Paul and what is its application as γραφή?

We must insist that the OT is γραφή (not γράμμα) and that it gives instruction to Christians (1 Cor. 10:11). Christians are in the end-time. An end-time perspective permeates all of scripture according to Paul. Instruction is given as we perceive the prefigurative character of biblical events viewed both positively and negatively, as promise, admonition, and warning. In particular Paul points us to the nature of the OT as promise. The promises that God gave to our forebears have now been fulfilled in Christ, and more than fulfilled according to the eschatological outlook of the understanding of salvation in the primitive Christian community.

5. The OT is the Word of God insofar as the tradition it embodies is brought into the sphere of the working of the Spirit that takes concrete form in the ecclesia of God. It therefore helps to articulate the message of the gospel as an abiding expression of this work of the Spirit, thus opening it up to the understanding of believers.

6. If we are concerned about a relevant Christian view of scripture, the antithesis of gramma and pneuma in 3:6 will always tells us what hermeneutical indications to look for if we are not to read the OT, which was the presupposition of primitive Christianity and the NT, simply according to our own historical and religious assumptions, but to read it from a NT point of view, that is, with a theological perspective that corresponds to the fact that the OT tradition is the Word of God.

---

not say that it is a book of revelation containing prophecies of Christ and therefore of his δόξα, when rightly understood. Nor is it his point that the law is a παιδαγωγὸς εἰς Χριστόν (Gal. 3:24) and that it therefore has a significant role in salvation history. His argument here is that it leads only to death, and that Christ is its τέλος (Rom. 10:4). Bultmann thus opposes the view of Barth in his *Evangelium und Gesetz* (ThEx 32,1935) 18. Here, on the basis of 3:15, Barth argues that while we do not acknowledge that the law proclaims our justification by God, we do see that it bears witness to the grace of God (13), so that it is a necessary form of the gospel whose content is grace (11). In Bultmann's opinion, this is the very opposite of what Paul is stating. For a rebuttal of Bultmann cf. P. von der Osten-Sacken, "Geist und Buchstabe. Vom Glanz des Mose und des Paulus," EvTh 41 (1981), 230-235, who, concerned about a fresh approach to scripture in debate with Paul (230), says about 3:13f. that even if we translate τέλος as end, the meaning is that Moses hid his face so that the children of Israel would not see the end of his *doxa,* not that the end had already come. Paul himself is aware of the continued existence of Moses in the form of the Torah (231).

Since the two testaments are united (in tension) to form holy scripture, the question of their theological unity inevitably arises. This unity is present in the witness that is given to the God who has revealed himself in the history of his people. In both testaments the unity of the Word of revelation may be seen in the converging form of the promise to God's people and of its eschatological fulfillment manifested in Jesus Christ, or, in other words, in the law of God that the Spirit has written on human hearts.

The Law in Romans 2

by

N.T. Wright

Introduction

Romans 2 is the joker in the pack. Standard treatments of Paul and the Law have often failed to give it the prominence that one might expect it to have, judging by its position within his most-discussed letter. But generations of eager exegetes, anxious to get to the juicy discussions that surround 3.19–20, 3.21–31, and so on, have hurried by Romans 2, much as tourists on their way to Edinburgh hurry through Northern England, unaware of its treasures.

There are at least two reasons for this, which are worth considering as we set the scene for a brief discussion and some proposals.

The first reason for the neglect of Romans 2 has to do with a powerful consensus about the flow of the argument in Romans, or at least Romans 1–8, as a whole. One commentary after another has set out the scheme, according to which these chapters deal with human sin (1–3), the divine remedy in Christ, and justification by faith (3–4), and, one way or another, the new life the Christian enjoys (5–8). The epistle thus far, in other words, is imagined to follow and expound some sort of *ordo salutis*. Within this, Romans 2 has no business to be speaking either of how one is justified or of the results of justification. It is part of a section (1.18–3.20) about which there has been an unusually strong consensus: the passage is supposed to say, neither more or less, that all human beings are sinful. The various twists and turns in the actual of ch. 2 must somehow fit in to this scheme. Part of the reason why there has been such a strong consensus is, of course, because it has a strong grain of truth in it. But I shall suggest that at certain points it needs quite severe modification. 'Big-picture' exegesis that loses sight of the details in always in danger.

The second reason for the neglect of Romans 2 is that, even where the consensus has been challenged, the challenge has not so far penetrated as far as a fresh contextual exegesis of this chapter. Notoriously, Sanders in *Paul, the Law and the Jewish People* declared that the passage was not a legitimate part of Paul's argument; it was an old synagogue sermon, with minimal Christian updating. I suspect that Sanders here said out loud what a lot of exegetes have thought privately, but it still comes as something of a shock to be told that the second chapter in a major theological letter must be put in brackets. My hunch is that Sanders' reforms in Pauline studies have not yet, in fact, gone far enough; that, when they are taken further, there will be more room for a chastened Protestant exegesis than is currently imagined, either by Sanders or his Lutheran objectors; and that Romans 2, for so long the Achilles heel of schemes on Paul and the Law, may make a vital contribution to some eventual solutions, both to the theological questions which surround all of Paul's writings and, of course, to the exegesis of Romans itself.

There are three particular issues which must concern us in this paper, corresponding to the three paragraphs in the chapter in which Paul speaks of the law. I propose to take them in reverse order, for the very good methodological reason that one should start from the clearer parts and build towards the less clear. The first question has to do with the meaning, and especially the referent, of 2.25–9, and of the role of the law within this dense little passage. The second concerns the nature of the critique launched in 2.17–24; what is Paul saying about 'the Jew', and how does the law fit into this critique? The third question, in my view the hardest, concerns 2.12–16, and divides into two sub-questions: first, what is the role of the law in the justification spoken of in 2.12–13? and second, who are these Gentiles in 2.14–15 who 'do the things of the law', and in what sense are they 'a law to themselves', with the law 'written on their hearts'? (There is a fourth question, but it does not so directly connect with the question of the law: who is being addressed in 2.1–16?)

These questions are no more new than they are easy. I have spent years, on and off, reading and writing about them.[1] In what follows, I shall try not to repeat what I have said elsewhere, though some overlap will be inevitable. Further, at the risk of failing to address some turns and twists in the discussion, I shall not attempt to enter into debate with colleagues who have written, often at great length, about this chapter. I have learnt a great deal from commentaries and monographs, but there is no room to cite and engage with them here.

1. Beginning at the End: 2.25–9

One of the peculiarities of Romans is the number of times when it is by no means clear, to contemporary readers, who Paul is talking about at given points in the letter. This problem is, of course, notorious in Romans 7. But it is, I think, no less acute in the end of Romans 2. In both cases the passage has to do

---

[1] For a recent treatment of Romans as a whole, cf. N.T. Wright, 'Romans and the Theology of Paul', in E.H. Lovering (ed.), SBL 1992 Seminar Papers, 184–214. Atlanta: Scholars Press. For more general reflections on Pauline theology, esp. the law, cf. N.T. Wright, *The Climax of the Covenant: Christ and the Law in Pauline Theology*. Edinburgh and Minneapolis: T & T Clark and Fortress Press.

with the law; and indeed it may be because of our theological confusions about the law that we find it hard to identify the people referred to, who stand in each passage in a particular relation to the law. If, in this case, we can discover who is being spoken of, we ought to arrive at some quite clear conclusions about the law. The two questions are not separable.

The passage sets up a running contrast between two categories of people. The first should not be in doubt: it consists of Jews who do not keep the law.

If you transgress the law, your circumcision becomes uncircumcision ... (2.25) ... they will condemn you, the one who through letter and circumcision transgress the law ... (2.27)
... the [Jew] in manifest visibility is not the Jew; [circumcision] in manifest visibility and in the flesh is not circumcision ... (2.28)

The singular ('the Jew') is a rhetorical device, through which Paul addresses all Jews to whom this applies, presumably including his own pre-conversion self. And the offence with which he charges 'the Jew' is, in this passage, clearly not 'boasting' in the law, or the attempt to keep the law and so earn status, or 'righteousness', or indeed anything else, through the law. The offence with which he charges 'the Jew' is *breaking* the law. This, of course, must ultimately be set within the wider context of Pauline passages in which the charge is amplified – indeed, not least alongside 2.17–24, on which see below – but at least in this passage the matter is clear. As in 7.7–25 (despite some continuing opinion to the contrary), the problem with 'the Jew' is that this person is a παραβάτης νόμου.

This understanding of the reason for the condemnation of 'the Jew' is exegetically confirmed by, and may indeed have been the logical reason for, Paul's statements about the person with whom 'the Jew' is contrasted:

If then the uncircumcision keeps [φυλάσσῃ] the commmandments of the law, will not his uncircumcision be reckoned as circumcision? And the uncircumcision by nature [ἐκ φύσεως] which fulfills [τελοῦσα] the law will condemn you ... (2.26f.)
But the [Jew] who is in secret is the Jew, and [circumcision] is circumcision of the heart, in the spirit not in the letter; the praise of this one is not from humans but from god. (2.29)

Clearly in 2.26f. the person – again the singular is obviously to be read as collective – is a Gentile. (In 2.29 Paul has widened the category, and his 'real Jew' could of course be Jewish or Gentile; but the purpose of 2.28f. is to assert the larger point, which entails the statement in 2.26f.; hence the γάρ in 2.28.) The question is: is he (it is pointless to say 'or she', since the question concerns circumcision) a Christian, or not? Upon this will hinge what precisely is meant by 'keeping the commmandments of the law', and by 'fulfilling the law'.

The reading suggested by the old consensus about Romans 1–3 is that this person is a non-Christian. Since these chapters describe humankind under the grip of sin, why would Paul suddenly throw in a description of a Christian? Clearly, on this view, all that he indicates is that, *if* such people as law-fulfilling Gentiles were to be found, they would condemn law-breaking Jews. But the only point of the argument, on this theory, is to assure the Jews that they are indeed condemned, not to assert that such people as law-fulfilling Gentiles exist; so there is no need to hypothesize them to make sense of what he says. Alternatively, Paul may be thought here to envisage momentarily that there might after all be some Gentiles who by the light of nature (i.e. without Christian faith) do in some sense 'keep the law', but that then he reverts to his normal bleak view of humankind and declares everyone condemned anyhow in 3.9–20. The class of law-keeping Gentiles is a possible one, but, according to this view, it turns out in fact to have no members.

One of the comparatively few points agreed on by those two great modern commentators on Romans, Charles Cranfield and Ernst Käsemann, is that this line of thought is wrong. Paul here speaks of Christian Gentiles. In fact, I think this is the easiest point to prove of all the contentious things I wish to argue about Romans 2, and this is why I have started with this paragraph. Out of the numerous arguments that have run back and forth, I select the following as particularly important.

1. The language of 2.29 is closely reminiscent of three other passages in which Paul is clearly talking about Christians:

a. Romans 7.6: νυνὶ δὲ κατηργήθημεν ἀπὸ τοῦ νόμου ἀποθανόντες ἐν ᾧ κατειχόμεθα, ὥστε δουλεύειν ἡμᾶς ἐν καινότητι πνεύματος καὶ οὐ παλαιότητι γράμματος. The spirit/letter contrast belongs closely, in Paul's mind, with the contrast between the life in Christ on the one hand and the life in the flesh, and/or the life in Judaism, on the other. The context is somewhat different, not least because in Romans 7 Paul speaks of those who are 'freed from the law'; this was unnecessary for Gentiles, since they had never been 'under the law' in the first place. The idea of fulfilling the law, likewise, is not present in 7.6, though it is, arguably, in 8.4–9 and elsewhere (see below). But the critical thing is the letter/spirit contrast. Unless Paul is using his own terminology extremely loosely (which cannot be ruled out from the start, of course, but the methodological assumption must be that he means more or less the same thing by the same words within the same letter), 7.6 should be enough to indicate that the Gentile in 2.29 is a Christian.

b. 2 Corinthians 3.6: ὃς καὶ ἱκάνωσεν ἡμᾶς διακόνους καινῆς διαθήκης, οὐ γράμματος ἀλλὰ πνεύματος. τὸ γὰρ γράμμα ἀποκτέννει, τὸ δὲ πνεῦμα ζωοποιεῖ. Within the context of the whole passage,[2], there can be no doubt of Paul's intention. The letter/spirit contrast is directly linked to the contrast be-

---

[2] On which see Wright 1991, ch. 9.

tween the ministry of Moses and of the Jewish law on the one hand and the gospel ministry of Paul on the other.

c. Philippians 3.3: ἡμεῖς γὰρ ἡ περιτομή, οἱ πνεύματι θεοῦ [v.1. θεῷ] λατρεύοντες ... καὶ οὐκ ἐν σάρκι πεποιθότες ... Circumcision; spirit; not trusting in the flesh: we are observing a cluster of terms which clearly belong closely with one another in Paul's mind. Here, as before, Paul contrasts Christians, himself and his Gentile converts included, with his own former self, in 'the flesh', as an unconverted Jew. We may note that, as in Romans 2.29, he does not say 'true' circumcision, though this is the implication. Grammatically, of course, ἡ περιτομή is the subject of the first clause, and ἡμεῖς the complement: 'Circumcision – that's us!'.

These parallels (to which we might add that between Rom. 8.3f. and 2.26) are quite sufficient in themselves, I believe, to compel the conclusion that the Gentiles in question in Romans 2.25–9 are Christians, to whom Paul is ascribing what is essentially *covenant* language (explicit in the 2 Corinthians text, strongly implicit in the others). But there are other arguments to back this up.

2. This language and concepts Paul uses in 2.25–9 evoke biblical and extra-biblical Jewish texts in which the explicit subject is the renewal of the covenant. Thus:

I will take you from the nations, and gather you from all the countries, and bring you into your own land. I will sprinkle clean water upon you, and you shall be clean from all your uncleannesses, and from all your idols I will cleanse you. A new heart I will give you, and a new spirit I will put within you; and I will remove from your body the heart of stone and give you a heart of flesh. I will put my spirit within you, and make you follow my statutes and be careful to observe my ordinances. Then you shall live in the land that I gave to your ancestors; and you shall be my people, and I will be your God. (Ezekiel 36.24–8; cp. 11.19f.[3])

Ezekiel, of course, envisages these people coming 'from the nations' as Jews, returning from exile. Paul may perhaps have taken this in an extended sense, seeing Gentiles themselves as the ones coming 'from the nations', who are, in the process, cleansed from their idolatry. But, whether that echo should be heard or not, there should be no doubt that this passage is in mind; not least because, the verse before our present section (2.24), Paul refers to the passage immediately preceding, namely Ezekiel 36.20, 'the name of God is blasphemed among the Gentiles because of you'.[4] The rest of the themes fall into place, despite the superfical mismatch between the 'heart of flesh' in Ezekiel and Paul's rejection of 'the flesh'. The new heart, the new spirit, the following of

---

[3] Other refs., and discussion, in N.T. Wright, *The New Testament and the People of God*. Volume I of *Christians Origins and the Questions of God*. London and Minneapolis: SPCK and Fortress Press 1992, p. 301 (and the whole chapter).

[4] Paul's exact words quote Isa. 52.5, but the context is so similar that the allusion to the Ezek. passage is perfectly natural as well.

the statutes and ordinances (nb. 36.27: καὶ ποιήσω ἵνα ἐν τοῖς δικαιώμασίν μου πορεύησθε καὶ τὰ κρίματά μου φυλάξησθε καὶ ποιήσητε; Paul is not quoting this directly in 2.26, but it is difficult to doubt the deliberate allusion) – all these add to the impression that Paul is describing *the 'returned exiles', the people of the new covenant*. This is not a hypothetical category, soon to be proved empty. It is alive and well. It consists, not least, of Gentile Christians.

3. Third, a small point, sometimes overlooked. In 2.26 Paul speaks of uncircumcision being 'reckoned' as circumcision. The other passages where Paul uses this language are of course those dealing with justification, e.g. 4.3ff. The language denotes a change of status; the passive indicates, presumably, divine action. It is of course possible that Paul has used this language to describe two quite different transactions, but it is simpler to see them both as part of the same event. The people here described are those whom God also declares to be 'righteous'.

4. The fourth argument undermines the assumption upon which the 'non-Christian' reading was based, namely that throughout this passage Paul's sole concern is to declare that all are sinners. That, of course, is one major point he is indeed making; but it is not the only one. I think it is increasingly recognised within the discipline of Pauline studies that Paul is quite capable of interjecting into a letter hints of things yet to come, suggestions of themes to be developed later on. An excellent example is to hand in the next chapter, where in vv. 1–9 Paul anticipates, so briefly as to be decidedly cryptic, a good deal of the argument of ch. 9. It is quite wrong to suppose that Paul's specific *argument* follows the line of the *theological* scheme which we may or may not be able to reconstruct from his letters. Like a symphonic composer, he is well able to state part of a theme a good way in advance of its full introduction. This, I suggest, is what has happened here.

I conclude therefore that in 2.25–9 Paul is principally describing the contrast between the Jew who breaks the law and the Gentile Christian who apparently 'keeps' or 'fulfills' the law. Such a person has somehow been inluded in the 'new covenant' category, designated simply as 'Jew' and 'circumcision'. We, to make this point clear, might explicate these words with the adjective 'true', while recognising that Paul, with more consequent polemic, simply transfers the titles themselves. This category ('Jew'/'circumcision') is of course, for Paul, made up of both Jews and Gentiles who are in Christ, indwelt by the Spirit. But the point of the critical turn in the argument, 2.25–7, is that there now exists a highly paradoxical category of persons: Gentiles who, despite remaining uncircumcised, seem to have (to put it in general terms for the moment) a highly positive relation to the Jewish law. It is this puzzle that must now occupy us for a few minutes, as we home in on the theme of 'Paul and the law' in this passage.

We have already seen that the problem faced by the Jew in this passage is not the wrong use of the law, not the attempt to keep it and thereby to earn a status before God, but simply the breaking of the law. What can Paul mean by the 'keeping' of the statutes of the law (2.26) and the 'fulfilling' of the law (2.27)?

He clearly cannot mean that these Gentiles have now become law-observant Jews. Not only is that the position against which the whole of Galatians launches its fierce polemic. Not only is the argument of Romans, from its very different point of view, hostile to such an idea. It is clear from the context of this very passage that they cannot be observant Jews, since *ex hypothesi* they are not circumcised. As in the notorious 1 Corinthians 7.19, Paul is expressing a sharp paradox, and must have known it. It would be quite wrong to press this passage for a full exposition of how he conceived, and indeed justified, such an oxymoron as an 'uncircumcised law-keeper'. But the allusion to Ezekiel 36, and hints throughout the rest of Romans, may give us a suggestion as to how his mind worked on this issue, which remains near the heart of the question of Paul's view of the law. To see this clearly we must take a step back from the argument for a moment.

Is has been argued, by Sanders and Räisänen in particular, that Paul's mind moved 'from solution to plight' instead of vice versa. According to them, the old view of Paul starting with a problem and receiving the answer on the road to Damascus will not hold water. Rather, Paul's new experience caused him to lash out with what looks like a reasoned 'critique', but which in fact is a series of scattered and inconsistent remarks, charging the Jews with anything that comes to hand. I regard this as very misleading, as I have argued elsewhere. But I do think that something somewhat analogous may have happened when it came to what Paul said about the way in which Christians, including Gentile Christians, 'keep' or 'fulfill' the law.

Several times Paul says, more or less, that Christians do keep the law. The most obvious passage is Romans 13.8 (not to mention 1 Cor. 7.19, already referred to). But we should note, as in fact more important, three other passages.

First, there is Romans 8.4–9, in which it is the mind of the flesh that 'does not and cannot submit to God's law'. The clear implication is that the mind of the Spirit can and does.

Second, there is Romans 10.4–11. Without providing a fuller exegesis than is here possible, we may suggest that Paul is using Deuteronomy 30, another 'new covenant' passage, as his basis for saying that when someone believes the Christian gospel, that person is thereby 'keeping the law', whether or not they have heard it, and despite the fact than in several points such as circumcision they are not doing what the law apparently required.

Third, there is the equally vexed νόμος πίστεως in Romans 3.27. This is of course likewise controversial, but I am increasingly persuaded that the best course is to treat νόμος as referring to the Jewish law throughout, and to see this passage as another hint of what is to come. Putting 2.26–9, 3.27, 8.4–9 and 10.4–11 in a sequence, I believe we have something of a crescendo of passages in which Paul says, sometimes very cryptically (whatever we do with 3.27, it will never cease to be cryptic!) and sometimes with more elaboration, that Christians do in fact fulfill the law, even though, if they are Gentiles, they have not done what to a Jew was one of its most basic commands. What did he mean by this? Why did he say it?

I think he said it because he knew it *a priori*. This is the point where he is making an assertion, reaching out into unknown (because not previously charted) realms of new theological possibilities. He knows (a) that those who are members of the new covenant fulfill the law; Ezekiel said so, backed up by Jeremiah 31 and Deuteronomy 30. He also knows (b) that the new covenant now has bona-fide members who have not been, and do not need to be, circumcised; that is the whole argument of Galatians, and the evidence is that these people have the Spirit and believe in the gospel. Therefore, without needing either to have a previously existing Jewish category of 'keeping the law' in some attenuated or limited sense to draw upon, or to have worked out the implications of what he is saying in more than rudimentary detail, he is able to assert as a matter of theological logic (compare λογισθήσεται in 2.26) that (c) uncircumcised Gentile Christians do in fact 'keep the statutes of the law', as Ezekiel said. The prophecies of covenant renewal and blessing upon the Gentiles have come true. The beneficiaries *must be* 'fulfilling the law' by their very existence. The question of an ethical 'fulfilment' such as that of 13.8 (corresponding very broadly to Luther's *tertius usus legis*) is not yet in view. The fulfilment of which Paul speaks is, I think, first and foremost a matter of status.

It is also involved, and indeed stressed by repetition, in this passage because Paul is using this theological deduction as a polemic tool. Does 'the Jew' break the law? Very well, he shall be constrasted with the Gentile Christian, who 'keeps the law'. This contrast, again, comes straight out of Ezekiel 36 and similar passages. There, the Jews in exile, guilty of idolatry and of all manner of evil through which God's name is dishonoured, are contrasted with the exiles who will return, with whom God will re-establish his covenant. My suggestion is that Paul has not worked out in detail, and I think in fact nowhere works out in great detail, exactly what this 'keeping the law' involves. Like 'circumcision', which becomes for him a polemical title, snatched from the physically circumcised, for Christians whether circumcised or not (Phil. 3.3), he refers to Christians as 'lawkeepers', not because they have observed every one of the Torah's commandments but because, as he says in 8.3, that which the law intended but could not do has been brought to fulfilment in them. This will only appear illogical to those who have not grasped the covenantal context and dimensions of Paul's thought.

I am proposing, therefore, that in 2.25–29 (1) we should understand Paul's critique of the Jews in terms of their lawbreaking; (2) we should see the Gentiles in question as Gentile Christians; (3) we should hear the overtones of the whole passage in tune with Ezekiel 36 and similar passages; and that (4) the 'keeping of the law' which Paul ascribes to these Gentile Christians should be seen as a new sort of theological category, derived from the 'new covenant' theme, ranged polemically against the failed Jewish 'lawkeeping', but yet to be worked out fully. It is a matter, not of achievement, nor yet of ethics, but of status.

2. Boasting in the Torah: 2.17–24

Is not the first of these conclusions at once undermined by the immediately preceding paragraph? μὴ γένοιτο. As we work backwards into the centre of the chapter, Paul seems to be charging the Jews not, or not primarily, with breaking the law, but with boasting in the law. Is this not the legalism, the 'nomism', with which we are familiar from so much exegesis, not least within the Protestant tradition?[5] Does it not mean that the charge of breaking the law is therefore misplaced?

No; or not exactly. I have argued in various places that Paul's basic critique of Israel was double-edged. As we have seen, and indeed as 2.17–24 bears ample witness, he accuses his fellow Jews of breaking the law (2.21–3, with several examples). But the wider category, within which this lawbreaking is to be seen, is what I have termed 'National Righteousness'. This is not the attempt to use the law as a ladder of good works up which to climb to a moral self-righteousness. It is the attempt to use the law as the covenant badge which would keep membership within that covenant limited to Jews and Jews only. It is this, I believe, which drives Paul's argument in this controversial little passage.

Verses 17–20 set out the Jewish claim – which, we may suppose, Paul would have known quite well, having made it on his own behalf somewhat stridently in the past. But this claim would be quite misunderstood if we were to imagine that it referred to the *individual* Jew, boasting in his (or, less likely, her) moral achievements. Indeed, Paul will argue that the lack of moral achievement vitiates the boast (2.23). The boast, rather, here and elsewhere, consists in the belief that ethnic Israel is inalienably the people of the one true god, and that her possession of the law, quite irrespective of her keeping of it, demonstrates this fact. Paul's list of the Jewish status-markers and privileges in 17–20 reads

---

[5] Lest I seem dismissive of the Protestant tradition, let me add that, as an Anglican, it is one I too claim to share. Equally, Anglicans, like first-century Jews, encourage at least in theory the principle of critique from within. We are, or aspire to be, *ecclesia catholica semper reformanda*.

as though it were an allusion, say, to the implicit boast made throughout the Wisdom of Solomon or Ben-Sira: that Wisdom/Torah has been given to Israel, setting her for all time in a superior position to the Gentiles round about her.

The start of the paragraph (εἰ δὲ σὺ Ἰουδαῖος ἐπονομάζῃ) makes a κύκλος with 2.29, and this, as well as reinforcing the conclusion reached in the previous section, suggests that 2.17–24 is intended as one half of a fuller statment of which 2.25–29 is the second half. Instead of the Jews being the teachers of the Gentiles, Gentiles (i.e. Gentile Christians) will be judges of the Jews! This again points us to the correct way of reading the passage. *Paul's charge against his fellow-Jews is not that they are all immoral, nor yet that they are all self-righteous legalists, but that they seek to claim for themselves the status of being the true, final people of God, while they are in fact still in exile.*

The quotation from Isaiah 52.5, with its overtones of Ezekiel 36.20, highlights the theme, which I am convinced is crucial, of Israel's exile. Contrary to popular assumption, most Jews of the second-temple period did not believe the exile was really over. I and others have argued this point at some length in various places, based on such passages as Nehemiah 9.36f., Ezra 9.8–9, CD 1.3–11, Tobit 14.5–7, Baruch 3.6–8, and 2 Maccabees 1.27–9.[6] Since that argument has not, apparently, been properly understood, it may be worth indicating its main line once more.

The Jews had, of course, returned to the land of Israel after the exile. But nowhere in all second-temple Jewish literature do we have the slightest suggestion that the great promises and prophecies of Isaiah, Jeremiah, Ezekiel and the rest – including those of Deuteronomy 30, which were important for Paul – had been fulfilled. Israel had not been restored to her proper position; she was not ruler in her own land; the Temple was not properly rebuilt; YHWH had not returned to dwell in the midst of his people; justice and peace were not yet established in Israel, let alone in the rest of the world. The 'post-exilic' prophets such as Haggai, Zechariah and Malachi indicate pretty forcibly that things are still in poor shape; Israel is not yet all she should be, and a further great act of YHWH will be necessary. Qumran proves the point exactly: the self-understanding evident in (e.g.) CD is precisely that of people who see themselves as *the advance guard of the real return from exile*, which means that everybody else is still in exile, and that they are the first, secret 'returnees', who will be vindicated as such when YHWH finally acts.

Few will doubt, in fact, that the great majority of Jews in Jesus' day were looking for a major action of their god within history to liberate his people. Even those who want to minimize this have to allow for a huge groundswell of this belief bursting out in the mid-60s of the first century. The point here is

---

[6] Cf. Wright 1992, 269ff., with refs., esp. to Knibb, Scott and Steck; and several works by Dr Paul Garnet of Concordia University, Montreal. The whole theme cries out for further serious attention.

that, in thinking about and longing for this event, they did not merely draw upon patterns and types, such as the Exodus, culled at random, allegorically or typologically, from a past conceived as a scattered bunch of unconnected events. Rather, they saw themselves *in sequence with*, and continuing, Israel's whole past story, waiting for that story to reach its promised goal. They were not living in an ahistorical mode, in which the only question of weight were timeless salvation or ethics, with such issues being 'illustrated' by ideas taken in a fairly random fashion from her distant past. Rather, they read that past not least as a story; as a story which was continuing, and in which they themselves were characters; as a story with an ending, which can variously be characterized as 'return from exile'; 'return of YHWH to Zion'; 'salvation'; 'forgiveness of sins'; 'new covenant'; 'new exodus'; and perhaps even, for some at least, 'new creation' and 'resurrection'. And one of the greatest concentrations of all these themes in biblical literature is of course Isaiah 40–55, from which Paul quotes in Romans 2.24. Anyone who supposes that first-century Jews thought that any or all of those great events had already taken place has simply not, I think, understood the texts (with, again, Qumran being the exception that proves the rule). Anyone who supposes that 'return from exile' is thus, so to speak, one metaphor among many others for an essentially ahistorical 'salvation' has not, I think, grasped the whole worldview which Saul of Tarsus shared, and which his letters still reflect.

To suggest, therefore, as some have done quite stridently, that Saul of Tarsus did not have a 'problem', which needed a 'solution' is to abandon history and engage in fantasy. To suggest, however, that this 'problem' had to do only, or chiefly, with the state of his soul, the question of salvation after death, or the attempt to gain justification in an individual or private sense, is again strictly non-historical. The problem, rather, faced by every serious Jew of Paul's day, and not least by those who, as he seems to have been, were on the more extreme wing of the Pharisaic party,[7] was the tension between the glorious future promised by YHWH to Israel and the gloomy fate she currently experienced. Israel needed a Messiah; Israel needed redemption; Israel needed the forgiveness of sins – not simply as a nation composed of sinful individuals, but because 'forgiveness of sins' was a shorthand for 'return from exile'. Paul did not need to reason backwards, after the Damascus Road experience, that there must have been a problem somewhere within Judaism, if only he could work out what it was. Of course there was a problem. The only Jews who blinded themselves to it were the Chief Priests, and perhaps the Herodians.

Part of this problem, as all the biblical prophets and most of the surviving postexilic literature perceived, was the further tension between the vocation of

---

[7] On the Pharisees in this period, particularly their 'zeal', cf. Wright 1992, 189–95, with refs. I incline strongly to the view that the pre-conversion Paul was a Shammaite, despite his Hillelite teacher Gamaliel.

Israel to be the true people of the creator god and the actual condition of Israel as a people deeply compromised with lawbreaking. One of the great looked-for blessings of the end of exile was that Israel would no longer be a sinful nation. Ezekiel promised the moral renewal of the nation; so, in various ways, did Isaiah and Jeremiah. It had not yet happened, as Ezra and Nehemiah had complained. Or rather, from Paul's point of view, it had not yet happened *to ethnic Israel*. Paul's claim, advanced briefly in 2.25–9 and developed more fully elsewhere (not least in Romans 6–8) was that it had indeed happened – in Jesus Christ, and through his Spirit. But where did that leave ethnic Israel?

According to Romans 2.17–24, it left ethnic Israel making an *ethnic* boast, and using the Torah to support that boast, while the Torah itself in fact rendered that boast null and void. The charge against Israel in this passage is not that all Jews steal, commit adultery, and rob temples. That absurd suggestion, and its equally absurd triumphant refutation by some scholars, are quite beside the point. The point is that if Israel was truly redeemed, *none of these things would be happening at all*. The charges of 2.22f. are not individualistic, because the passage is not simply about the sinfulness of every human being. It is about the impossibility, granted universal sinfulness in the Gentile world at least, of Israel's claiming a 'favoured nation clause' on the grounds of the Torah-based covenant. The claim is impossible for this reason: that the existence within Israel of *any* thieves, adulterers or temple-robbers shows that Israel cannot be affirmed as she stands. The exile has not ended, at least not in the way that had been expected. Israel as an ethnic nation has not been redeemed.

The quotation from Isaiah 52.5 in Romans 2.24 sums this up. The chapter as a whole is precisely about exile: Israel has been exiled for her sins, as a result of which the Gentiles have had cause to blaspheme YHWH. Now, however, YHWH is doing a new thing; his kingdom is being announced; the people are to be redeemed. Paul believes, clearly, that all this has come true in Jesus Christ; but the significance of this is not always fully grasped. For Paul, *in Jesus Christ the exile has come to an end*. That is for him, perhaps, the primary significance of the resurrection. But if this is so, it means that the problem of which Paul was already aware – the continuing exile of Israel – is not avoided by intensifying Torah-observance, or by acting with 'zeal' to bring in YHWH's kingdom. All such efforts fail to take account of the fact that ethnic Israel cannot be affirmed as she stands. The only way forward is in the spirit, not the letter; in the secret of the heart, not in the badge of circumcision; in the praise of the true god, not the praise of humans. Nor is this (as has recently been argued) to shift away from history into Platonism, to move simply from the material to the 'spiritual'.[8]

---

[8] Cf. D. Boyarin, *A Radical Jew: Paul and the Politics of Identity* (University of California Press, 1994), with my review article (in *Reviews in Religion and Theology* 1995/3 [August], 15–23).

What role, then, does the Torah play within the sequence of thought of 2.17–24? First, it is the apparently secure base upon which Israel builds her 'boast in god', that is, the boast that the creator god is the god of Israel. This Torah-base, upon which she 'rests' (ἐπαναπαύῃ, v. 17), is not the legalist's ladder of merit. It is Israel's national charter. Second, it is the repository of wisdom, possession of which means that Israel, through it, possesses 'the form of knowledge and truth' (v. 20). There is no need to suppose that Paul was insincere or sarcastic in making this comment. The law is, after all, 'holy, just and good' (7.12). Thirdly, the 'boast in god' of 2.17 becomes the 'boast in the law' of 2.23. We might illustrate this from (e.g.) Ben-Sira 24: Wisdom, identified as Torah, looks for somewhere to live among human beings, and chooses Israel. But, fourthly, the law cannot effect among Israel the wisdom, the holiness, the utterly human life, which it holds out. The problem of Israel, in Paul in general and Romans in particular, is not that there is, as is sometimes said, a 'hidden Jew in all of us'. Rather, it is the hidden Adam in the Jew. The Jew, called to be the people of the true god, dishonours her god by breaking his holy law. Israel is the people of the Messiah, but only 'according to the flesh' (9.5).

I suggest, therefore, a reasonably radical re-reading of 2.17–24. The passage has to do with the nation as a whole, not with a collection, even a complete collection, of individuals. Paul does not want to unsay any of the fine words in 2.17–20. Indeed, he reaffirms them in 3.1f. The problem is that they do not accurately describe the still-exiled nation. They describe only the one who will be faithful to the nation's vocation, the one through whom YHWH will do what the law could not.

3. Written on the Heart: 2.12–16

It goes against the grain to cut off a Pauline sentence beginning with γάρ from that which precedes it, but for the sake of brevity and clarity we may turn now to the paragraph which precedes 2.17 in the Nestle-Aland text, i.e. 2.12–16. This is, as far as I am concerned, the hardest part of the chapter, and the place where most uncertainty may still lurk about the place and meaning of the Torah in Paul's argument.

It is the addition of the law to the argument already in progress, in fact, which marks out these verses from 2.1–11. Up until now, the chapter has set up a picture of general judgment, in which some will be justified and others condemned. At this point Paul introduces the law into the picture. Some have the law, others do not: all will be judged, but only according to where they have been on this scale.

It is vital to note, first, that the justification and the judgment spoken of in this paragraph are inalienably *future*. This is not *present* justification; Paul will come to that in chapter 3. Nor can the two be played off against one another. They belong together: present justification, as Romans makes clear, is the true anticipation of future justification. And in Romans, as elsewhere in Paul, it is present justification, not future, that is closely correlated with faith. Future justification, acquittal at the last great Assize, always takes place on the basis of the totality of the life lived (e.g. Romans 14.11f.; 2 Corinthians 5.10). It is because the relation between the two has by no means always been understood (that is not the only thing that is not understood about Paul's doctrine of justification, but that is the subject of another paper) that exegetes have glossed uneasily over this passage, and have flattened it out into a general treatment of the sinfulness of all human beings.

Verse 12 provides a typically Pauline general statement, in two parts. Sinning without the law means destruction without the law; sinning under the law means judgment by the law. Verse 13, to explain this, offers a more specific assertion: it is not the hearers, but the doers, of the law who will be justified (at the future great judgment; i.e. the future tense is temporal, not merely logical). But who are these 'doers of the law'? Verse 13 is at once further explained (γὰρ) by verse 14: 'when Gentiles, who do not possess the law, do the things of the law, they are a law to themselves, even though they do not possess the law.' I have deliberately omitted to translate the word φύσει, which occurs in the middle of the verse, since it is precisely the point at issue, the little rudder around which the whole ship of Paul's argument here will turn. Who, we repeat, are these Gentiles who 'do the law'?

The reader may guess that I would prefer to give the same answer as I gave to the similar question in 2.25–9, and this guess would be correct. But it is important, before we reach the conclusion of the argument, to examine the more usual answer. Most exegetes still support some form of the following conclusion: that Paul here hypothesizes an imaginary category (Gentiles who, in their pagan state, somehow 'do the law by nature'), which he will later show to be void. Alternatively, some have suggested that Paul here allows the mask of severity to slip for a minute from his exposition of universal human sinfulness, revealing a more liberal approach in which, despite the conclusion of 3.19f., some Gentiles are recognised as being quite reasonable people, living up to their consciences and being, in the best sense (rather than in the bad sense in which the phrase is now regularly used) 'a law to themselves'.

These two alternatives both belong with the usual belief that chapters 1–3 are simply designed to demonstrate the universality of sin. Either Paul is saying 'supposing there were Gentiles who did what was right; they would be judged favourably; but of course there aren't any'. Or he is saying 'despite what I said above, and what I shall say below, I know perfectly well that some of my pagan neighbours live perfectly decent moral lives, and that God is quite pleased with them'. Both of these readings are inadequate. The critical word, again, is φύσει.

The majority of exegetes have taken φύσει with what follows, τὰ τοῦ νόμου ποιῶσιν. These Gentiles 'do by nature the things of the law'. But the next use of the word in the letter, a mere thirteen verses later, suggests strongly that this is the wrong way to take it. In 2.27 the Gentiles are described as ἡ ἐκ φύσεως ἀκροβυστία, 'that which is by nature uncircumcision'. Here 'nature' refers clearly to that which the Gentiles are/have, as we say, 'by birth'. Their φύσις, their 'natural state', is that they are uncircumcised.[9] I suggest that this strongly supports taking φύσει with what precedes, τὰ μὴ νόμον ἔχοντα, 'who do not have the law'. The point about the Gentiles is that they are 'lesser breeds outside the law'. The are, in that strict technical sense, 'sinners', ἁμαρτωλοί (cf. Gal. 2.15). By 'nature', that is, by birth, they are outside the covenant, not within Torah. And yet they 'do the things of Torah' (v. 14).

The most forceful objection to this way of reading the verse has to do with word-order. If Paul had meant 'Gentiles who do not by nature have the law', why did he put φύσει after τὰ μὴ νόμον ἔχοντα, instead of writing τὰ φύσει μὴ νόμον ἔχοντα? We may grant that the latter feels more natural. But Paul is quite capable of using a substantive participle followed, rather than preceded, by its modifying dative, as in Romans 14.1: τὸν δὲ ἀσθενοῦντα τῇ πίστει προσλαμβάνεσθε, where τῇ πίστει is naturally taken with τὸν δὲ ἀσθενοῦντα, not with προσλαμβάνεσθε.[10]

If this argument is still resisted, the main alternative is that now articulated in Fitzmyer's commentary:[11] 'Following the guidance of *physis* [in the sense of 'the regular, natural order of things'], Gentiles frame rules of conduct for themselves and know at least some of the prescriptions of the Mosaic Torah." This is, of course, possible, but seems to me far weaker as a contribution to the argument of 2.12–16, and of the chapter as a whole, forming more of an aside than an integrated stage in the discussion. Paul is, of course, capable of asides, but if in doubt we are, I suggest, justified in going for the meaning which ties the argument more tightly together.

---

[9] We may compare the other uses of the word in Paul: 1.26; 11.21; 11.24 (three times); 1 Cor. 11.14; Gal. 2.15; 4.8; Eph. 2.3. Of these, only 1 Cor. 11.14 (cited by e.g. J.A. Fitzmyer, *Romans* [New York: Doubleday 1993], 310 in favour of 'do by nature') points in the direction of an abstract 'nature'; in all the others, it refers to the status people have by birth or race. In addition, every time Paul uses φύσει, it is adjectival rather than adverbial (so P. Achtemeier, *Romans* [Atlanta: John Knox, 1985, 45). On the whole question see C.E.B. Cranfield, *A Critical and Exegetical Commentary on the Epistle to the Romans*, T & T Clark, Edinburgh, vol. 1 (1975), 156 n. 7.

[10] Cranfield *op. cit.*, 1.157 n. 2 lists several occurrences of substantival participals with dependent words following, but in most of them the dependent word is the direct object of the participle, which is hardly a direct parallel to 2.14.

[11] *op. cit.*, 309–11, here at 309.

I suggest, therefore, that 2.13–14 should be taken quite closely with 2.25–29, as described above. There are, however, two further points on the passage which need to be added.

First, we may consider the peculiar situation of those described here. 2.13 and 2.14, taken together, indicate quite clearly that those described in the latter as 'doing the law' will, according to the former, be justified (remembering, again, that we are here dealing with *future*, not present, justification). This is clear from putting together 2.13: οἱ ποιηταὶ νόμου δικαιωθήσονται with 2.14: ἔθνη ... τὰ τοῦ νόμου ποιῶσιν. The 'doing of the law' spoken of here and in 2.26f., then, has to do with nothing less than justification, albeit in the future. But why then will there be uncertainty, as suggested in the very strange passage in v. 15b ('with their conscience also bearing witness with them, and their conflicting thoughts accusing or perhaps excusing them ...')? One possible answer might run as follows, and this answer, I think, considerably strengthens my case.

Paul has just stated that those who do not have the law will be judged without the law, while those who have the law will be judged by means of the law. But at once he faces an exception; and the fact that this *is* an exception demonstrates more clearly than before that we must indeed be dealing with Christian Gentiles at this point. If those who are a 'law to themselves', because 'the law' (presumably the Jewish law) is written on their hearts, are non-Christians, then Paul has been talking nonsense in v. 12 when he suggested that Gentiles, not having the law, would be judged without the law. But if they are Christians, then they are in a sense neither fish nor fowl. They are not simply lawless Gentiles; but the Jewish law, which is now in some sense or other written on their hearts, and which in some sense they 'do', nevertheless has a sufficiently ambiguous relation to them for them still to be concerned that the eventual issue might be in doubt. Hence, as judgment day approaches, they may well find inner conflict as they reflect on their situation. They would not have this inner conflict were they not Christians. The situation would then be the simply one of v. 12.

We might supplement the argument further by pointing out that the warning of 2.13 ('it is not the hearers of the law who are righteous before God, but the doers of the law who shall be justified') anticipates almost exactly the charge of 2.23 ('you who boast in the law, do you dishonour God by breaking the law?') But there is another argument which strongly supports the conclusion that the people here described, as towards the end of the chapter, are indeed Christian Gentiles – and acutal ones, not merely hypothetical figures. This is v. 15a: they show that the work of the law is written on their hearts.

It has been pointed out often enough that this is a direct allusion to Jeremiah 31.33:

This is the covenant that I will make with the house of Israel after those days, says the Lord: I will put my law within them, and I will write it on their hearts; and I will be their God, and they shall be my people.

This, however, has not always been thought of particular relevance, since, for all sorts of reasons too complex to unravel in an exegetical paper, Paul has been thought to have little or nothing to do with covenantal theology, within which of course the Jeremiah passage so clearly belongs. But again the rest of the chapter comes to our help.

We have seen that the context of 2.17–29 is inescapably covenantal and exilic. Israel is in exile, longing for the renewal of the covenant, and seeking to grasp at a covenant membership that would be for Jews and Jews only. Paul asserts, on the basis of his whole theology, that in fact the covenant has already been renewed in Christ, and that Gentiles have found themselves among its beneficiaries; so that they, in some surprising and paradoxical sense yet to be explained, 'keep the statutes of the law'. In the present passage, they show that the law is 'written on their hearts'. I find it next to impossible that Paul could have written this phrase, with its overtones of Jeremiah's new covenant promise, simply to refer to pagans who happen by accident to share some of Israel's moral teaching. More likely by a million miles that he is hinting quietly, and proleptically, at what he will say far more fully later on: that Gentile Christians belong within the new covenant. In short, if 2.25–9 is an anticipation of fuller statements, within the letter, of Paul's belief that Christian Gentiles do indeed fulfill the law even though they do not possess it, 2.13–14 looks as though it is a still earlier statement of very nearly the same point.

Very nearly; but not quite. Paul does not just repeat points ten verses later for the sake of emphasis. The sequence of thought that runs between the two halves of chapter 2 now comes into play, and we must stand back a little and observe how it functions.

The presuppositions of all Paul's thought, as of more or less all serious Jewish thought, is that in some way or other Israel is the solution of the creator god, YHWH, to the problem of the world. The problem of the world is highlighted, if not even constituted, by gentile idolatry and sin. But Israel is herself sinful; so said all the prophets, and, in case there had been any doubt on the matter, Babylon settled it once for all. The nation that should have been the solution became part of the problem. The trouble with Israel was that she too was in Adam. The physician succumbed to the disease. What Israel now needed (as Isaiah 40–55 already saw) was a physician's physician, one who could do for Israel, and hence for the world, what neither could do for themselves or for each other.

The sequence of thought of Romans 2 catches this theological outline more or less exactly. The general opening in 2.1ff. is to be taken as exactly that, a general opening, not as a covert way of attacking Israel before the open assault in 2.17. It addresses all humans, Jew and Gentile alike, who might consider themselves exempt from the strictures of Romans 1.18–32. The turn in the argument at 2.17 thus functions like the well-known turn at Amos 2.6: the people who thought to escape the charge levelled against everyone else find the spotlight turned, revealingly and uncomfortably, upon themselves. The chapter then works like this: (a) (2.1–11) the general statement of coming judgment upon all humans, Jew and Gentile alike; (b) (2.12–16) Torah will not affect the fairness of this judgment, since those who have it will be judged by it, and those who do not, will not. However, there is a strange category of people who 'do the things of the law', in a sense yet to be explained, even though by birth they do not possess it; they will find themselves surprisingly vindicated at the judgment. (c) (2.17–24) Surely Israel is the solution to this problem of universal sin? Is she not the creator's means of bringing light into his dark world? Yes; but, alas, Israel has so far brought only darkness. The nation that was to lighten the pagan world has herself succumbed to pagan darkness, and the Torah, so far from alleviating the problem, instead intensified it. (d) (2.25–29) Nevertheless, YHWH is renewing the covenant, and the Torah is finding a strange new fulfilment. There is now in existence an Israel created by the Spirit, finding its validation from the creator god himself.

Conclusion

What then shall we say about Paul and the Law in Romans 2? Is Paul inconsistent? By no means. The charge of inconsistency falls to the ground once the actual sequence of thought, and the underlying theology, are allowed to come into view. Part of the trouble, I think, in recent Pauline scholarship is that a false polarisation has occurred, between the attackers of an assumed (but not always well understood) older orthodoxy and the would-be defenders of orthodoxy against assumed (but not always well understood) detractors. I would like to urge my colleagues on either side of this great divide, and in the sundry other positions that are currently taken up, to consider Romans 2 not just as a difficult passage to be fitted in somewhere and somehow in a scheme of Pauline theology – or even in an exegesis of Romans, though frankly it has not always received its proper due in that context either – but as a potential jumping-off point for fresh work on Paul.

In particular, Romans 2 introduces us to Paul's covenant theology. We should not be surprised by this, as though the apostle of justification by faith would be compromised for a single moment by continuing to think Jewishly. Nor should we imagine that his theology is the mere unthinking reflex of a religious or psychological experience. What we observe here, as elsewhere in his writings, is the apostle wrestling with the implications of his basic conviction: that in Jesus Christ, and by the Spirit, the creator god had acted to redeem his people and so to redeem the whole world. His charge against Israel was not that of 'legalism', or 'self-righteousness' in the older sense. But nor was it a mere random firing of shots into the air in the hope of hitting some target somewhere. It was a measured, careful critique, built upon the prophetic critiques, and in any case not expecting rebuttal: almost no Jew, certainly not Paul himself before his conversion, would have denied that Israel as she stood remained in need of redemption.

And what about the law in all of this? Pulling the 'law' threads of the discussion together into a quasi-systematic form, we might deduce the following:

1. The law, νόμος in Paul, is the Jewish law. Gentiles do not possess it by birth.

2. The law defines Israel over against the nations, and moreover indicates that Israel is designed by the creator god as a light to the nations.

3. The law sets the standard by which Israel will be judged; Gentiles will be judged without reference to it. However, there is one class of Gentiles who in a sense will be judged with reference to the Torah. This class consists of Gentile Christians; though by birth they do not possess the Torah, they are now in the strange position of 'doing the law', since the Spirit has written the 'work of Torah' on their hearts.

4. Israel boasts in her possession of the law; it sets her apart from the nations.

5. The boast is not made good, because that could be so only if Israel kept the law perfectly; and this is not the case. Israel is still in exile, still 'in her sins'. She is still guilty of lawbreaking.

6. The category of Gentiles mentioned above in connection with the final judgment is invoked again, this time to demonstrate how far ethnic Israel is from being affirmed as she stands. The covenant *has* already been renewed; its beneficiaries now 'fulfill the law', even though, in the case of Gentile Christians, they do not possess it. This 'fulfillment' seems to be of a different order from the fulfillments thought of within Judaism. Nor is it simply the (Lutheran) *tertius usus legis*. It is without precedent, for the simple reason that it has not happened before, and the manner of covenant renewal was not anticipated. As Paul says in Romans 8, 'what the law could not do ... God has done'.

7. The way is now clear for ch. 3, with its exposition of the cross, and of justification by faith in the *present* as its direct result. Paul will go on, later in the letter (ch. 8), to declare that there is no κατάκριμα for those who are ἐν Χριστῷ. But this is no more than a recapitulation, and a filling out, of what has already been said in principle in ch. 2. It is greatly to the detriment of the doctrine of justification by faith that exegetes have frequently not taken the trouble to notice what Romans 2 is actually about, as opposed to what it is usually supposed to be about.

Romans 2 thus takes its place both within the developing actual argument of the letter – as opposed to the imagined argument in which Paul simply sets out a systematic *ordo salutis* – and within a potential systematic account of Paul's whole theology, not least his theological reflections on the law. Thus equipped, exegesis should be able to proceed beyond the sterile 'either/or' of some recent debates, and move cheerfully toward the creative 'both/and' which reflects, in terms of method, the intricate but perfectly balanced theology which Paul bequeathed to his readers. Whatever we want to do with Paul's theology when we finally discover it, let us at least do justice to a mind, and a letter, that continue to instruct even as they fascinate, and to educate even as they inspire.

Three Dramatic Roles

The Law in Romans 3–4

by

RICHARD B. HAYS

Like the stone steps of an ancient university building, the topic of "Paul and the Law" has been worn smooth by the passing of generations of scholars. I suspect that few of our remarks in this conference will be surprising or original. I take it, therefore, that the aim of our conversation is to consolidate the results of recent study and to identify the areas of consensus as well as the major loci for continuing debate. My contribution to this cooperative venture is to attend particularly to Paul's statements about the Law in Romans 3–4 and to offer some synthetic judgments about the state of the question.

For the purposes of our discussion, I propose three basic theses concerning the role of the Law within Paul's argument in Romans 3–4. Paul contends that: (*A*) The Law defines the identity of the Jewish people. (*B*) The Law pronounces condemnation on all humanity. (*C*) The Law is an oracular witness that prefigures the righteousness of God disclosed in Jesus Christ. What I have to say about the first two of these theses is fairly straightforward and, I expect, relatively noncontroversial. The third thesis, however, may open up some issues that will require more detailed examination and debate.

A. The Law Defines the Identity of the Jewish People

In the first instance, the term ὁ νόμος refers in Paul's usage to the Law given by Moses to Israel (Rom 9:4, 10:5). By prescribing distinctive standards of conduct, the Law simultaneously accomplishes two things: it positively discloses the will of God, and it marks off the elect people from other nations. Let us consider each of these points in turn.

First of all, the will of God is revealed in the Law, and the people of Israel are called to obey it unconditionally (cf. Deut 30:11–14) as an expression of their covenant relation to God. To be a member of God's people is to find oneself obligated to adhere to the norms articulated in the Mosaic Torah. That this covenant obligation was understood, within the context of Judaism, not as a burden but as a privilege[1] is clearly recognized in Paul's diatribal address to an imagined Jewish interlocutor who "boasts in the law" (Rom 2:23):

But if you call yourself a Jew and rely on the Law and boast of your relation to God (καυχᾶσαι ἐν θεῷ) and know his will and determine what matters (τὰ διαφέροντα) because you are instructed in the Law, and if you are sure that you are a guide to the blind, a light to those who are in darkness, a corrector of the foolish, a teacher of children, having in the Law the embodiment of knowledge and truth, you, then, who teach others, will you not teach yourself? ... You that boast in the law (ἐν νόμῳ καυχᾶσαι), do you dishonor God by breaking the Law? (Rom 2:17–21a,23).

Knowing the will of God is, to be sure, not an unproblematic condition. Paul's argument challenges the Jewish reader to beware of a complacent sense of security that comes from having a special relation to God through the Law: it is only the *doers* of the Law who are to be justified (2:13).[2] The mere knowledge of the Law is of no value unless it is accompanied by obedience (cf. 2:25–29). Nonetheless, Paul never disputes the twin premises that the will of God is authentically revealed in the Law and that the Jew therefore possesses, through the Law, a privileged knowledge of what God requires (cf. 7:7–12, 9:1–5). This claim underlies Paul's apparently surprising assertion in 3:2 that "the advantage of the Jew" is "much in every way." Even if "some were unfaithful," Israel – unlike pagans who are able to recognize God only through the created world (1:19–20) – has been given the benefit of knowing God's revealed will *expressis verbis*.

Secondly, the Law functions to set apart a particular people for God, a people who are to serve as "a light to those in darkness" (2:19, echoing Isa 49:6). Thus, one of the most salient features of the Law is its role as the creator of an *identity* for a particular people. That is why Paul can refer to the Jewish people by using expressions such as οἱ ἐν τῷ νόμῳ (3:19) and οἱ ἐκ νόμου (4:14). Their identity is grounded in the Law; it provides the distinctive characteristics, the identity markers, that define the boundary between Israel and the Gentiles. James D.G. Dunn has made a signal contribution to our understanding of Paul's thought on the Law by highlighting this identity marking function;[3] he interprets "the works of the law" (3:20,28; cf. 4:2–6) as a reference to

---

[1] The work of E.P. Sanders (*Paul and Palestinian Judaism* [Philadelphia: Fortress, 1977]) has impressed this point upon Pauline scholarship. One hopes that the impression will prove indelible.

[2] The well-known problems surrounding the relation of Romans 2 to the theology of justification expressed elsewhere in Paul cannot be pursued here. See, e.g., E.P. Sanders, *Paul, the Law, and the Jewish People* (Philadelphia: Fortress, 1983), 123–35; K.R. Snodgrass, "Justification by Grace – to the Doers: An Analysis of the Place of Romans 2 in the Theology of Paul," *NTS* 32 (1986) 72–93. The essay of N.T. Wright in the present volume offers an important proposal that may shed new light on these difficulties.

[3] See, e.g., "Works of the Law and the Curse of the Law (Galatians 3:10–14)," *NTS* 31 (1985) 523–42; *Romans 1–8* (WBC 38A; Dallas: Word, 1988) 153–55, 158–60; "Yet Once

"the social function of the Law as marking out the people of the law in their distinctiveness."[4] Circumcision, dietary observance, and sabbath keeping are the practices that most explicitly set the Jewish people apart from the rest of the world; thus, these practices symbolize the more comprehensive body of "works of the Law" that establish Jewish identity. This insight is critical to the interpretation of Romans 3–4, for it helps us understand that Paul's critique of "works of the Law" is not focused, as the Reformation supposed, on human efforts to achieve God's approval through "works righteousness." Instead, his critique of "boasting" targets the problem of ethnocentric exclusivism.

Michael Winger, in a recent study of the meaning of νόμος in Paul's letters, offers the following general definition of "Jewish νόμος":

Those words given to and possessed by the Jewish people, which guide and control those who accept them and according to which those who accept them are judged.[5]

Or, as he rephrases his definition more succinctly, "Νόμος is what Jews do."[6] If indeed Νόμος is to be identified with the practices that constitute Jewish ethnic particularity – "what Jews do" – then it is not difficult to understand why Paul resists the imposition of nomistic practices upon Gentiles who have come to trust in Jesus Christ.

Only when this understanding of νόμος is kept clearly in view does Paul's line of argument in Rom 3:27–31 come clearly into focus. Boasting – i.e., Jewish ethnic pride in the Law (2:17,23) – is excluded (3:27) by the gospel that declares that "there is no distinction" betweeen Jew and Gentile, for all are justified by God's grace as a gift (3:22b–24). But such boasting can hardly be excluded by the Law "of works," which is itself the basis for Jewish distinctiveness. Paul therefore asserts, in a deft rhetorical play on words, that boasting is excluded διὰ νόμου πίστεως (3:27). The precise meaning of νόμος πίστεως is difficult to determine because the phrase, coined spontaneously by Paul here in counterpoint to νόμος τῶν ἔργων, does not appear elsewhere in his writings.[7] If, however, νόμος τῶν ἔργων means something like "Torah construed through the hermeneutical filter of distinctively Jewish practices," then its opposite, νόμος πίστεως, must mean "Torah construed through the hermeneutical filter of πίστις," the Law as read through the eyes

---

More – 'The Works of the Law': A Response," *JSNT* 46 (1992) 100–04. Cf. also F. Watson, *Paul, Judaism, and the Gentiles* (SNTSMS 56; Cambridge: Cambridge University Press, 1986).

[4] Dunn, *Romans 1–8*, 159. For more extensive discussion see pp. lxiii–lxxii.

[5] Michael Winger, *By What Law? The Meaning of Νόμος in the Letters of Paul* (SBLDS 128; Atlanta: Scholars Press, 1992), 104, italics in original.

[6] Ibid., 109.

[7] Cf., however, analogous formulations such as ὁ νόμος τοῦ πνεύματος τῆς ζωῆς Χριστῷ Ἰησοῦ (Rom 8:2) and ὁ νόμος τοῦ Χριστοῦ (Gal 6:2).

of faith.[8] (A striking example of this sort of reading is given in Rom 10:6–13.) To interpret the word νόμος in this formulation as having merely the generic meaning of "principle" or "rule" is to underinterpret Paul's theologically-laden language and to disregard the fact that he has been consistently using νόμος to refer to Israel's Law.[9] The "Law" that excludes boasting is precisely the Law that Paul has already called as witness to humanity's universal implication in sin (3:10–20) and as witness to God's saving righteousness (3:21–22). In other words, the Law *read as Paul has already claimed it should be read* is the νόμος πίστεως.

The rhetorical questions in 3:29 confirm unmistakably that the phrase "works of the Law" must designate the distinctive markers of Jewish ethnic identity: "Or is God the God of Jews only? Is he not the God of Gentiles also?" If righteousness were attainable only through works of the Law (as embodied in circumcision and *kashrut*), then God would be – Paul suggests – the God of the Jews only, a tribal deity concerned only with a single people. But, Paul insists, it is not so. His argument against this view is based on a fundamental tenet of Israel's confession, articulated in the *Shema*: God is one. Paul concludes from this that God's way of dealing with Jews and Gentiles alike must finally be the same: "Since God is one, who will justify the circumcision on the ground of faith, he will also justify the uncircumcision through faith" (3:30).[10] Thus, the very fact that the Mosaic Law serves to identify Israel as a distinctive people disqualifies it from serving as the basis of God's more universal setting-right (*Rechtfertigung*) of all peoples.

This theological claim inevitably raises an objection that Paul anticipates in 3:31: "Do we then abolish the Law through this faith?" Almost everything that

---

[8] See C.E.B. Cranfield (*A Critical and Exegetical Commentary on the Epistle to the Romans* [ICC; Edinburgh: T. & T. Clark, 1975], 1:219–20), H. Hübner (*Law in Paul's Thought* [Edinburgh: T. & T. Clark, 1984], 210), and Dunn (*Romans 1–8*, 185–87), all of whom hold that νόμος πίστεως refers to the Mosaic law newly construed hermeneutically from the perspective of Christian faith. F. Thielman (*Paul and the Law* [Downers Grove, IL: IVP, 1994], 183) suggests that "the law of faith" is an expression equivalent to "the new covenant." This comes close to C.K. Barrett's suggestion that "here and elsewhere for Paul law (νόμος) means something like 'religious system'" (*The Epistle to the Romans* [HNTC; New York: Harper & Row, 1957]).

[9] This position taken here represents a change of mind for me. The draft of this essay originally presented at the symposium was much more receptive to interpreting νόμος πίστεως as "principle of faith," but I was persuaded by the group's subsequent discussion to adopt the view articulated in this paragraph. I would like to record my particular gratitude to Prof. Otfried Hofius for a helpful conversation on this issue.

[10] My translation of the passage places a full stop at the end of v. 29, takes εἴπερ as the beginning of a new sentence, and reads καὶ ἀκροβυστίαν διὰ τῆς πίστεως as an elliptical clause requiring the verb δικαιώσει to be understood from the previous clause. This makes it clear that the justification of the uncircumcised through faith is a conclusion drawn from the premises that God is one and that God justifies the circumcised ἐκ πίστεως. For a fuller defense of this reading see R.B. Hays, "Have We Found Abraham to Be Our Forefather according to the Flesh?" *NovT* 27 (1985) 76–98.

Paul has said up to this point would lead us to expect him to say, "Yes we do abolish the Law, and good riddance!" Instead, however, he introduces a dialectical reversal that has kept the heads of Christian thinkers spinning from his time to ours: "By no means! On the contrary we uphold the Law" (3:31). In what sense does the gospel uphold the Law? His discussion of Abraham in Chapter 4 seeks to show that the νόμος πίστεως is consistent with the Law – now understood to mean, however, not the Mosaic covenant, but Scripture taken as a *narrative* whole. This is the hermeneutical transmutation that allows Paul to claim continuity between Law and gospel. The story of Abraham, read through the lens of Gen 15:6, serves to reinforce the claims that Paul has made about justification through faith; indeed, it clarifies that God justifies the ungodly (4:3–8). Furthermore, God reckoned Abraham righteous *prior to* his circumcision: therefore, he stands symbolically as the "father" of uncircumcised believers as well as of circumcised believers who walk in the footsteps of his faith (4:9–12). All this demonstrates three points crucial to Paul's argument: (1) that the inheritance promised to Abraham is to be received not through adherence to the practices of the Law but solely through God's grace (4:13–17); (2) that the promise is for "the whole seed" of Abraham (παντὶ τῷ σπέρματι, 4:16), not just for the Jewish people; and (3) that the gospel is the narrative completion, rather than the nullification of Law (= Scripture).[11] The implications of this hermeneutical shift must be left for consideration in the third part of this essay.

B. The Law Pronounces Condemnation

The second major function of the Law in Romans 3–4 is to pronounce judgment upon the unrighteousness of all human beings. Jews and Greeks alike are under the power of sin (ὑφ ἁμαρτίαν, 3:9), and the Law discloses their true condition through its emphatic proclamation of judgment: "There is no one who is righteous, not even one …" The catena of citations in 3:10–18 establishes that all humanity has turned away from God into disobedience and bloodshed.[12] (Interestingly, the emphasis in the catena lies upon deceptive speech and violence rather than upon the sexual offenses that were highlighted in Rom 1:24–27.) Consequently, the whole world is "accountable to God," standing under God's righteous sentence of judgment (3:19–20, cf. 3:3–7).

---

[11] For further elaboration of my reading of the argument, see Hays, "Have We Found Abraham?"

[12] For discussion of the composition of the catena, see L.E. Keck, "The Function of Romans 3:10–18 – Observations and Suggestions" in J. Jervall and W.A. Meeks (eds.), *God's Christ and His People*, FS N.A. Dahl (Oslo-Bergen-Tromsö: Universitetsforlaget, 1977), 141–57.

Even here, however, Paul has introduced a distinctive hermeneutical "spin" on the texts that he cites. As Dunn notes, the five Psalm citations in the catena (Ps 13:2-3, 5:10, 139:4, 9:28, 35:2, all LXX) are originally condemnations of Israel's enemies or of "the unrighteous" as distinguished from "the righteous." Paul has prefaced these with a universal indictment of human unrighteousness from Eccl 7:20 and interspersed a powerful passage from Isa 59:7–8 that prophetically decries Israel's unfaithfulness.[13] The result of this composite citation is to convert the Psalm passages also into condemnations of Jews as well as Gentiles. Dunn sums up the effect:

… it is hard to doubt that Paul intended the Psalm citations as a turning of the tables on Jewish overconfidence in their nation's favored status before God. The very descriptions which the psalmist used for those outside God's favor and righteousness can be seen in the light of the Ecclesiastes and Isaiah passages as a self-description and self-condemnation.[14]

Thus, the words of Scripture must be read in the spirit of humility demanded by Paul in Rom 2:1: "Therefore you have no excuse, whoever you are, when you judge others; for in passing judgment on another, you condemn yourself, because you, the judge, are doing the very same things."

Paul's hermeneutical warrant for reading these words of Scripture as addressed to Jews, not just to those outside the Law, is explained in 3:19: "Now we know that whatever the Law says, it speaks to those who are within the Law (τοῖς ἐν τῷ νόμῳ)." Although the citations are from Psalms, Ecclesiastes, and Isaiah, Paul treats these words as expressions of what "the Law says" (3:19), thereby demonstrating that he can sometimes treat the term νόμος as referring to Scripture as a whole, i.e., as a virtual synonym of γραφή.[15] (As we have already seen, this semantic linkage will be crucial for his argument in 3:31ff.) By reading these passages as the voice of "the Law," Paul establishes that the Law has the function of declaring condemnation on the whole world, "in order that every mouth might be stopped."[16] There can be no protest against God's justice, for the hypothetical protest (3:3–7) is answered decisively by appeal to the Law's indictment of human sin. Thus, θεοῦ δικαιοσύνη (3:5) is confirmed.

The case is rounded off by one more appeal to Scripture in 3:20: "For 'no human being will be justified in his sight' by works of the Law, for through the Law comes knowledge of sin." Here he is quoting Ps 143:2 (142:2 LXX), in its original context not a word of condemnation but of contrite appeal:

Do not enter into judgment with your servant,
for no one living is righteous before you.

---

[13] Dunn, *Romans 1–8*, 149–51.
[14] Ibid., 151.
[15] See also Gal 4:21, 1 Cor 14:21.
[16] (Cf. Gal 3:22a: "The Scripture locked all things up under sin …").

To sharpen his point, Paul adds the words ἐξ ἔργων νόμου, not found in the psalm text. Theologically speaking, the addition is consonant with the emphasis of the psalm, which appeals to God's covenant faithfulness (ἀλήθεια) and righteousness (δικαιοσύνη) as the ground of the psalmist's hope (Ps 142:1 LXX). The prospect of vindication depends not upon human observance of the Law (or: not upon the practices of Jewish ethnic particularity) but upon God's gracious fidelity to his covenant promise. Thus, the use of Psalm 143 anticipates the next turn in Paul's argument, his declaration that the answer to the human plight rests in "the righteousness of God."[17]

For the moment, however, Paul's point in 3:20 is that "through the Law comes the knowledge of sin." This claim is explicated in 7:7–12, but it is perhaps a mistake to read the full psychological complexity of that discussion back into 3:20. In the immediate context, at the conclusion of the unit of thought in 3:9–20, "the knowledge of sin" seems to mean simply the awareness of standing under God's judgment – an awareness forced upon us by the Law's relentless condemnation.

That is perhaps also what Paul means by declaring enigmatically that "the Law brings wrath" (4:15): it announces "God's decree" (τὸ δικαίωμα τοῦ θεοῦ, 1:32), God's sentence of death upon a human race in rebellion against God (1:18-32). Alternatively, the Law may bring wrath in the sense of creating the conditions necessary for culpability, i.e. the knowledge of good and evil (cf. 5:13b: "sin is not reckoned when there is no law"). Either way, the Law, being associated with wrath and condemnation, is set in juxtaposition to faith and to the *promise* given to Abraham (4:13–17). The provocative rhetorical force of this move should not be overlooked. Against the common Jewish view that the Law is a secure foundation, a source of life and hope for the elect community,[18] Paul highlights its negative functions, its power to curse and condemn. Those who boast in the Law are confronted with the warning that the Law is not so easily domesticated, *nicht verfügbar*. Those who rely on the Law will find that it recoils upon them and calls them to account in unexpected ways. (One recalls Gal 4:21: "Tell me, you who are so eager to be under the Law, do you not hear the Law?")

Paul was not unacquainted with a positive view of the Law. Rom 2:17–24 and Phil 3:4–6 demonstrate that he knew perfectly well how the Law was typically seen in contemporary Judaism. He has chosen here in Romans, however, to focus on its awesome capacity to pronounce judgment and to bring condemnation by demanding a righteousness that it has no power to produce (cf. 8:3–4). It is important to see such statements about Law both in the wider

---

[17] For elaboration of this argument, see R.B. Hays, "Psalm 143 and the Logic of Romans 3," *JBL* 99 (1980) 107–15.

[18] See Hermann Lichtenberger's essay in the present volume, "Das Tora-Verständnis im Judentum zur Zeit des Paulus."

context of the letter and in relation to the letter's contingent argumentative purpose.[19] Paul is not stating a systematic doctrine of the Law; rather, in a deliberately provocative manner, *he is seeking to destabilize an entrenched position that associates the Law with the privileged status of the elect Jewish people*. Consequently, he focuses with considerable rhetorical power on Scriptural texts that demonstrate that the whole world is accountable to God and that "all have sinned and fall short of the glory of God" (3:23). At the same time, it must be emphasized that Paul is not merely employing cheap rhetorical tricks to discredit the Law; rather, his revisionary statements about its destructive power are a direct theological consequence of reading Scripture freshly through a new hermeneutical filter shaped by the cross and by the Gentile mission.

C. The Law Is an Oracular Witness

And yet, Paul's statements about the role of the Law are by no means entirely negative, even in Romans 3–4. Three passages in the text suggest a function of the Law distinguishable from the two functions we have already considered (defining a way of life for the Jewish people and pronouncing judgment on the world).

(1) In 3:21 Paul affirms that although the righteousness of God has been disclosed apart from the Law (i.e., through Christ), it is nevertheless attested by the Law and the prophets (μαρτυρομένη ὑπὸ τοῦ νόμου καὶ τῶν προφητῶν).

(2) When Paul insists that through faith "we uphold the Law" (3:31) and then supports that claim by appealing to the story of Abraham, the "Law" that is being upheld seems to be not only the *Shema* (3:30a) but also the Pentateuchal narrative, construed as a prefiguration of the gospel.

(3) In 3:2, Paul insists that the Jewish people do have an "advantage" (τὸ περισσὸν) because they were "entrusted with the oracles of God (τὰ λογία τοῦ θεοῦ)." The term νόμος is not actually used here, but the context makes it clear that Scripture is meant.

These three passages share in common a view of the Law as proleptic, prefiguring the economy of salvation that is revealed in the gospel. This claim is explicit in the first and second of these texts, implicit in the third. Let us begin with the clearer instances before turning to reflect about Paul's unusual reference in 3:2 to "the oracles of God."

---

[19] Thielman (*Paul and the Law*) helpfully adopts the method of examining Paul's statements about the Law in each letter individually, seeking to demonstrate how Paul's handling of the issue is related to the contingent circumstances addressed.

(1) In what way is δικαιοσύνη θεοῦ attested by the Law and the prophets? Our earlier discussion has suggested one answer: Psalm 142 LXX, quoted in Rom 3:20, contains two references to God's δικαιοσύνη as the focus of the Psalmist's hope for deliverance. Especially noteworthy is Ps 142:11b LXX: ἐν τῇ δικαιοσύνῃ σου ἐξάζεις ἐκ θλίψεως τὴν ψυχήν μου ("By your righteousness you will rescue my life from affliction.") This subtext provides a metaleptic link between the plight evoked in 3:20 and the solution proclaimed in 3:21.[20] Paul quotes v. 2 of the Psalm to declare that no one will be justified before God, but echoes recollecting God's righteousness ripple out from the citiation and provide the new theme of the following sentence.

Of course, the idea of God's saving righteousness is hardly restricted to one OT Psalm. Passages such as Ps 97:2-3 LXX and Isa 51:4–5 provide equally important background for Paul's thought. Let us consider the latter text as an example:

Hear me, hear, my people,
And kings, give ear to me.
For the Law (νόμος) will go forth from me
And my judgment will go forth as a light to the Gentiles (ἐθνῶν).
My righteousness (ἡ δικαιοσύνη μου) draws near quickly,
And my salvation (τὸ σωτήριόν μου) will go forth as a light,
And in my arm will Gentiles (ἔθνη) hope.

It requires no great leap of the imagination to see how such a text stands behind Paul's declaration that the gospel is

the power of God for salvation (εἰς σωτηρίαν) to everyone who trusts, to the Jew first and also to the Greek. For in it the righteousness of God (δικαιοσύνη θεοῦ) is revealed through faith for faith (Rom 1:16–17).

Consequently, to say that the Law and the prophets bear witness to δικαιοσύνη θεοῦ is simply to say that the promise of God's righteousness as a saving power for all nations is already explicitly announced in OT texts such as the ones just cited. (In passing, we should note that this simple observation of the announcement of God's saving righteousness in the Psalms and in Isaiah ought to put an end to the old Bultmann-Käsemann debate over δικαιοσύνη θεοῦ: Käsemann was right to say that God's righteousness is God's eschatological saving power but wrong to dissociate it from God's covenant-faithfulness to Israel. It was also unnecessary to argue, as Käsemann did, that δικαιοσύνη θεοῦ was a *terminus technicus* in Jewish apocalyptic.[21] One need not ferret it out of Qumran texts; it is already explicitly present in OT texts from which Paul quotes extensively in this letter.)

---

[20] See R.B. Hays, *Echoes of Scripture in the Letters of Paul* (New Haven: Yale University Press, 1989), 51–53.

[21] E. Käsemann, "Gottesgerechtigkeit bei Paulus," *ZTK* 58 (1961) 367–78.

Apart from such specific references to God's righteousness, the Law (= Scripture) also bears witness more generally, in Paul's understanding, to the gospel.[22] In the salutation of Romans, Paul declares that "the gospel of God" was "promised beforehand through his prophets in holy writings concerning his Son, who was descended from David according to the flesh" (Rom 1:2). English translations usually treat the prepositional phrase περὶ τοῦ υἱοῦ αὐτοῦ as a modifier of εὐαγγέλιον, but this is an artificial expedient designed to spare Paul the embarrassment of having claimed that the Scriptures are "about" Jesus Christ. In fact, however, anyone hearing Paul's sentence read aloud in Greek would naturally hear περὶ τοῦ υἱοῦ αὐτοῦ as modifying γραφαῖς ἁγίαις. Hence: "holy scriptures concerning his Son ..." The formula may, of course, be pre-Pauline, but there is no reason to suppose that Paul did not believe, along with other early Christians, that the OT pointed to Jesus. Indeed, elsewhere he asserts it as a matter of the first importance that the death and resurrection of Jesus occurred "according to the Scriptures" (1 Cor 15:3–4), and in a passage such as Rom 15:3 he assumes that Christ is the speaker in Psalm 69, without feeling the need to supply any supporting argument for this extraordinary assertion.[23]

The conclusion that follows from such observations is that the whole question of Paul's reading of Scripture as a witness to Jesus Christ demands careful attention.[24] The participial phrase μαρτυρομένη ὑπὸ τοῦ νόμου καὶ τῶν προφητῶν is not explicated fully at Rom 3:22, but it may be a clue pointing to a hermeneutical substructure that is fundamental to Paul's interpretation of the Law. If so, the meaning of Rom 10:4 ("Christ is the τέλος of the law") would need to be considered afresh.

(2) Paul's reading of the story of Abraham seeks to "uphold the Law" by showing that the gospel of righteousness through faith is prefigured in the Law, i.e. in the Genesis narrative. Obviously, such a construal of the Law is possible only in light of a profound hermeneutical shift. This shift has at least two important dimensions.

First of all, Paul shifts from a reading of Law as *commandment* to a reading of Law as *narrative of promise*. As James A. Sanders has characterized this

---

[22] Cf. D.-A. Koch, *Die Schrift als Zeuge des Evangeliums: Untersuchungen zur Verwendung und zum Verständnis der Schrift bei Paulus* (BHT 69; Tübingen: J.C.B. Mohr [Paul Siebeck], 1986).

[23] On Paul's reading of the Psalms as utterances of Christ, see R.B. Hays, "Christ Prays the Psalms: Paul's Use of an Early Christian Exegetical Convention," in A.J. Malherbe and W.A. Meeks (eds.), *The Future of Christology* (Minneapolis: Fortress, 1993), 122–36.

[24] This *pace* my own earlier dictum that Paul's hermeneutic is "ecclesiocentric" rather than "christocentric" (*Echoes*, 84–121). For qualifying remarks to this position, see R.B. Hays, "On the Rebound: A Response to Critiques of *Echoes of Scripture in the Letters of Paul*," in C.A. Evans and J.A. Sanders (eds.) *Paul and the Scriptures of Israel* (JSNTSup 83; Sheffield: JSOT Press, 1992), 72–96, esp. pp. 77–78.

shift, Paul reads Torah not as *halakah* but as *haggadah*.[25] As I have stated the matter on an earlier occasion:

Paul finds the continuity between Torah and Gospel through a hermeneutic that reads Scripture primarily as a *narrative* of divine election and promise. God is the protagonist in the story, the one who has formed and sustained Israel from Abraham onward ..., and God's righteousness is the ground of the narrative unity between Law and gospel ... God's act in Jesus Christ illuminates, Paul contends, a previously uncomprehended narrative unity in Scripture. That is the burden of the argument in Romans 3 and 4: God has shown forth his righteousness in a new way in Christ, apart from Law, but the Law and the Prophets bear witness that this unforeseen act of grace is the supremely fitting climactic action of the same God whose character and purposes are disclosed in the narrative of his past dealings with Israel ... Moses and the Law of Sinai are assigned a temporary supporting role, not the lead, in the drama of God's redemptive purpose. Thus, the Torah is neither superseded nor nullified but transformed into a witness of the gospel.[26]

By moving the Abraham story into the hermeneutical center of attention, Paul argues that the Law is first of all the vehicle of God's covenant promise, a promise that extends to all nations, far beyond the more limited scope of the nation defined by the Sinai covenant.

Secondly, the promise expressed in Scripture's narrative is a word addressed immediately to the church of Paul's own time. Paul repeatedly assumes that the word of Scripture is addressed directly to himself and his readers, as he explains in a pair of important hermeneutical maxims:

These things happened to them τυπικῶς, and they were written down for our instruction, upon whom the ends of the ages have met (1 Cor 10:11).

For whatever was pre-written was written for our instruction, so that by steadfastness and by the encouragement of the Scriptures we might have hope (Rom 15:4).

Paul's point is not just that Scripture is profitable for doctrinal instruction, as in 2 Tim 3:16–17. Rather, he regards Scripture as a living voice speaking directly to the community.[27]

This is the sort of hermeneutic that is at work in Paul's reading of the Abraham story. The story is not merely an example of how God deals with human beings; instead, it is a word of promise addressed directly to Paul's readers, who are themselves Abraham's seed:

Now the words ἐλογίσθη αὐτῷ were not written for his sake alone, but also for our sake to whom it [righteousness] is going to be reckoned, to those who trust in the one who raised Jesus our Lord from the dead (Rom 4:23–24).

---

[25] J.A. Sanders, "Torah and Christ," *Int* 29 (1975) 372–90.

[26] Hays, *Echoes*, 157.

[27] For extended discussion, see Hays, *Echoes*, 116–17, 165–68; H. Hübner, *Gottes Ich und Israel: Zum Schriftgebrauch des Paulus in Römer 9–11* (FRLANT 136; Göttingen: Vandenhoeck & Ruprecht, 1984).

Thus the "Law" – the Abraham story – must be read as pointing foward to realities that can be discerned only retrospectively from within the community of faith – the community that the Law always aimed to bring into being. From within the community of faith, the Law *qua* narrative is seen to *prefigure* the gospel and the church.

(3) Finally, we must consider the meaning of Rom 3:2, in which Paul, using an expression unparalleled elsewhere in his letters, refers to τὰ λογία τοῦ θεοῦ. The expression does occur in the OT, often in contexts where obedience to or defiance of God's word is emphasized: for example, Psalm 107:10–11:

Some sat in darkness and in gloom,
prisoners in misery and in irons,
for they had rebelled against the words of God (LXX: τὰ λογία τοῦ θεοῦ),
and spurned the counsel of the Most High.

Thus, even though the expression τὰ λογία τοῦ θεοῦ is unusual in Paul, it is consonant with his general fondness for OT diction, and it fits nicely into the immediate context of Romans 3:1–3, where Israel's unfaithfulness is being emphasized.[28]

However, the word λογία in general Greek usage referred to the utterances of an oracle. (Philo frequently uses the term as a description of the content of Scripture, thereby stressing its divinely inspired character; he uses this language to refer not only to direct utterances of God but also to other passages in the narrative. See, for example, *Abr.* 62; *Mos.* 1.57 [used in synonymous parallelism with χρησμοί, as also in *Virt.* 63]; *Mos.* 2.176; *Mig.* 85, 166).[29] This connotative nuance cannot have escaped Paul and his readers. Dunn's comment on the passage highlights the implications of Paul's particular word choice here:

... for a gentile readership the word "oracle" would evoke the thought of inspired utterances preserved from the past, often mysterious and puzzling in character, awaiting some key to unlock their meaning. Paul may well imply then that the Jews had been entrusted with the stewardship of safeguarding and preserving these oracles of God until the coming of the key, that is, the gospel of Christ Jesus, which unlocked the mystery of what had always been God's purpose but which had remained hidden hitherto until this time of the End (cf. 11:25–27; 16:25–26).[30]

---

[28] Cf. also the use of τὸ λογίον τοῦ ἁγίου Ἰσραηλ in Isa 5:24 LXX, in synonymous parallelism to τὸν νόμον κυρίου σαβαωθ.

[29] For discussion of Philo's fondness for describing Scriptural passages as "oracles," see H. Burkhardt, *Die Inspiration heiliger Schriften bei Philo von Alexandrien* (Giessen/Basel: Brunnen Verlag, 1988), 111–25, especially on λογία pp. 119–22. See also Y. Amir, "Authority and Interpretation of Scripture in the Writings of Philo," in M.J. Mulder (ed.), *Mikra: Text, Translation, Reading and Interpretation of the Hebrew Bible in Ancient Judaism and Early Christianity* (Compendium Rerum Iudaicarum ad Novum Testamentum; Assen/Maastricht: Van Gorcum, 1990 and Minneapolis: Fortress, 1990), 421–53, especially pp. 429–32.

[30] Dunn, *Romans 1–8*, 138-39.

In light of our foregoing observations about Law/Scripture as a proleptic pre-figuration of the gospel, Dunn's reading is richly suggestive as an exegesis of Rom 3:2. I would add only one further point: the statement that the Jewish people had been *"entrusted* with the oracles of God (ἐπιστεύθησαν τὰ λογία τοῦ θεοῦ)" also adumbrates Paul's later reflections in Romans 9–11 on the dialectical mystery of the relation between the Jewish people and Gentile belivers. The Jews are entrusted with the oracular utterances of Scripture pre-cisely *for the Gentiles*, who will receive these oracles as words spoken di-rectly to and for them.[31]

One function of the Law, then – perhaps its most important function for Paul – is to point forward to the coming of Christ and to God's intent to call Jews and Gentiles together into a community that simultaneously confirms the fidelity of God and glorifies God for his mercy (cf. Rom 15:7–8). Readers of the Law who understand *that* meaning of the Law have truly understood the τέλος of the Law; readers who do not understand this prefiguative, oracular function of the Law remain ignorant of "the righteousness that comes from God" (Rom 10:3–4).

Conclusion

It remains to ask how the three functions of the Law that we have seen in Ro-mans 3–4 fit together – if at all. The answer, I would suggest, is complex; the three functions are not complementary aspects of a single systematic doctrine. Rather, we see within Romans Paul's movement from one hermeneutical per-spective to another. The Law originally had the primary function of *defining the identity of God's elect people*, the Jews. Within that hermeneutical per-spective, the Law was understood primarily as *commandment*. Because Paul became convinced, however, that the death and resurrection of Jesus was an apocalyptic event that had brought the old world order to an end, he moved to an entirely new hermeneutical perspective, within which the Law functioned primarily as *promise and narrative prefiguration of the gospel*. In between these two hermeneutical worlds stands the function of the Law as *pronounc-ing condemnation on the world*. Such a view (Law as word of condemnation) corresponds neither to Judaism's account of the purpose of the Law nor to Paul's distinctively Christian position that sees the Law as a positive fore-shadowing of the righteousness of God in Jesus Christ. Perhaps then we should see Paul's account of the condemning function of the Law as *a transitional rhetorical move* in an argument designed to deconstruct Jewish "boasting" in

---

[31] In our discussion of this passage at the symposium, this point was brought out with particular clarity by N.T. Wright.

the Law by showing how the Law itself undercuts confidence in anything other than God's radical grace.

If that is correct, then we should see Paul's account of the functions of the Law as narratively ordered in a three-act drama. In Act I, the Law defines the will of God and shapes the identity of a people who are summoned to live in accordance with God's revealed will. In Act II, it becomes clear that even the covenant people cannot stand before the radical demand of God's holiness. All fall short, and the Law pronounces sentence of condemnation upon them, as well as upon the rest of the world. In Act III, however, God acts for the salvation of the world through the death and resurrection of Jesus. In light of this event, everything is redefined and the Law assumes an entirely new role as witness and herald of God's saving righteousness. In each act, the Law is God's servant, playing a different role – serving, as it were, as Ariel to God's Prospero. (And perhaps – like Ariel – finally being dismissed to join "the elements" when his service is completed.)[32] Ὁ νόμος is always the same collection of texts, but the import of those texts shifts dramatically in accordance with the hermeneutical perspective at each stage of the unfolding drama.

---

[32] W. Shakespeare, *The Tempest*, Act V, scene i; cf. Gal 4:9.

The Adam-Christ Antithesis and the Law

Reflections on Romans 5:12-21*

by

OTFRIED HOFIUS

Both in form and content the passage Rom. 5:12-21 gains its distinctive profile from the antithesis of Adam and Christ in which Paul contrasts the sin of Adam and its consequences with the saving act of Christ and its consequences. The discussion, which stresses the universal relevance of these acts, refers twice expressly to the νόμος, i.e., to the Torah of Sinai proclaimed by Moses. The first reference is in the parenthesis of vv. 13-14a, the second is in the emphatic conclusion of vv. 20f. The question which we are to discuss is how we are to define more precisely the relation between the Sinai Torah and the Adam-Christ antithesis. Verses 13 and 14a and 20f. can be suitably understood only in relation to their context, and this points us to the way that we shall follow in our reflections. First, we shall give a structural analysis as a foundation. Then, we shall offer a commentated translation of vv. 12-21. Third, we define the place of the text in the flow of the epistle. Fourth, we shall look more closely at the antithesis itself. Fifth, we shall do a detailed interpretation of vv. 13 and 14a. Sixth, we shall do the same for v. 20f. Finally, a crisply formulated conclusion will bring our discussion to an end.[1]

---

* I owe some important references and suggestions to my assistant Hans-Christian Kammler.

1. The following works will be quoted only by the name of the author. (1) Commentaries: C. K. Barrett, *A Commentary on the Epistle to the Romans* (BNTC), London 1962; C. E. B. Cranfield, *The Epistle to the Romans I-VIII* (ICC), 3rd ed. Edinburgh 1980; J. D. G. Dunn, *Romans 1-8* (WBC 38A), Dallas 1988; E. Gaugler, *Der Brief an die Römer I: Cc. 1-8,* Zurich 1958; E. Käsemann, *An die Römer* (HNT 8a), 4th ed. Tübingen 1980; O. Kuss, *Der Römerbrief I: Rom. 1:1-6:11,* 2nd

1. Structural Analysis of Romans 5:12-21

As concerns structure and argumentation, plain linguistic signals tell us that
Romans 5:12-21 is a carefully fashioned construct. The expression διὰ τοῦτο in
v. 12a introduces the whole complex and ties it to what precedes in Rom. 5:1-
11. In the discussions that follow διὰ τοῦτο we may discern very clearly six
stages of thought: (1) in v. 12, (2) in vv. 13 and 14a, (3) in v. 14b, (4) in vv. 15-
17, (5) in vv. 18-19, and (6) in v. 20f. We can detect these stages in a form of the
Greek text that corresponds to our structural analysis and that will also bring
out the contrast between Adam and Christ.[2]

Διὰ τοῦτο

I 12a   ὥσπερ δι' ἑνὸς ἀνθρώπου
        ἡ ἁμαρτία εἰς τὸν κόσμον εἰσῆλθεν
        καὶ διὰ τῆς ἁμαρτίας ὁ θάνατος,

---

ed. Regensburg 1963; H. Lietzmann, *An die Römer* (HNT 8), 3rd ed. Tübingen 1928; O. Michel, *Der
Brief an die Römer* (KEK 4), 15/15th ed. Göttingen 1978; A. Nygren, *Der Römerbrief,* 4th ed.
Göttingen 1965; R. Pesch, *Römerbrief* (NeB.NT), Würzburg 1983; A. Schlatter, *Gottes
Gerechtigkeit. Ein Kommentar zum Römerbrief,* Stuttgart 1935, 2nd ed. 1952; H. Schlier, *Der
Römerbrief* (HThK 6), Freiburg, Basel, and Vienna 1977; H. W. Schmidt, *Der Brief des Paulus an
die Römer* (ThHK), 2nd ed. Berlin 1966; W. Schmithals, *Der Römerbrief,* Gütersloh 1988;
P. Stuhlmacher, *Der Brief an die Römer* (NTD 6), Göttingen 1989; U. Wilckens, *Der Brief an die
Romer I: Röm. 1–5* (EKK VI/1), Zurich, etc., 1978; D. Zeller, *Der Brief an die Römer* (RNT),
Regensburg 1985. (2) Monographs and essays: K. Barth, *Christus und Adam nach Rom. 5. Ein
Beitrag zur Frage nach dem Menschen und der Menschheit,* 2nd ed. in *Rudolf Bultmann. Ein
Versuch, ihn zu verstehen* and *Christus und Adam,* etc., *Zwei theologische Studien,* Zurich 1964, 67-
122; G. Bornkamm, "Paulinische Anakoluthe," *Das Ende des Gesetzes. Paulusstudien* (BEvTh 16),
Munich 1952, 76-92; E. Brandenburger, *Adam und Christus. Exegetisch-religionsgeschichtliche
Untersuchung zu Rom. 5:12-21* (1 Cor. 15) (WMANT 7), Neukirchen 1962; R. Bultmann, "Adam
und Christus nach Rom. 5," *Exegetica. Aufsätze zur Erforschung des NT,* Tübingen 1967, 424-444;
G. Friedrich, "Ἁμαρτία οὐκ ἐλλογεῖται Rom. 5:13," *Auf das Wort kommt es an. Gesammelte
Aufsätze,* Göttingen 1978, 123-131; E. Jüngel, "Das Gesetz zwischen Adam und Christus. Eine
theologische Studie zu Rom. 5:12-21," *Unterwegs zur Sache. Theologische Bemerkungen* (BEvTh
61), Munich 1972, 145-172; U. Luz, *Das Geschichtsverständnis des Paulus* (BEvTh 49), Munich
1968; P. von der Osten-Sacken, *Rom. 8 als Beispiel paulinischer Soteriologie* (FRLANT 112),
Göttingen 1975; *Das Bauersche Griechisch-deutsche Wörterbuch zum NT,* Bauer for 5th ed. (1958)
and Bauer/Aland for the 6th ed. (1988).

2. My punctuation differs from the Nestle/Aland text (27th ed.) as follows. At v. 12 a dash replaces the semicolon. At v. 13 I have a semicolon for the comma. At v. 14 a semicolon comes after
the second Adam. At v. 16 I use a semicolon instead of a period after δικαίωμα. At v. 17 a comma
comes before the apposition Ἰησοῦ Χριστοῦ (cf. n. 62). On the brackets at v. 16 cf. n. 7.

12b καὶ οὕτως εἰς πάντας ἀνθρώπους
    ὁ θάνατος διῆλθεν,
    ἐφ' ᾧ πάντες ἥμαρτον —

II 13 ἄχρι γὰρ νόμου ἁμαρτία ἦν ἐν κόσμῳ·
    ἁμαρτία δὲ οὐκ ἐλλογεῖται μὴ ὄντος νόμου

14a ἀλλὰ ἐβασίλευσεν ὁ θάνατος
    ἀπὸ Ἀδὰμ μέχρι Μωϋσέως
    καὶ ἐπὶ τοὺς μὴ ἁμαρτήσαντας
    ἐπὶ τῷ ὁμοιώματι
    τῆς παραβάσεως Ἀδάμ

III 14b ὅς ἐστιν τύπος τοῦ μέλλοντος.

IV 15   Ἀλλ'

15a *οὐχ ὡς τὸ παράπτωμα,*   *οὕτως καὶ τὸ χάρισμα·*

15b *εἰ γὰρ τῷ τοῦ ἑνὸς*   *πολλῷ μᾶλλον* ἡ χάρις τοῦ θεοῦ
    παραπτώματι   καὶ ἡ δωρεὰ ἐν χάριτι τῇ τοῦ ἑνὸς
                      ἀνθρώπου Ἰησοῦ Χριστοῦ

    οἱ πολλοὶ ἀπέθανον,   εἰς τοὺς πολλοὺς ἐπερίσσευσεν.

16a καὶ *οὐχ ὡς δι' ἑνὸς*   [*οὕτως καὶ*] τὸ δώρημα·
    ἁμαρτήσαντος

16b τὸ *μὲν* γὰρ κρίμα   τὸ *δὲ* χάρισμα
    ἐξ ἑνὸς   ἐκ πολλῶν παρπτωμάτων
    εἰς κατάκριμα,   εἰς δικαίωμα·

17 *εἰ γὰρ τῷ τοῦ ἑνὸς*   *πολλῷ μᾶλλον* οἱ τὴν περισσείαν
    παραπτώματι   τῆς χάριτος καὶ τῆς δωρεᾶς
                      τῆς δικαιοσύνης λαμβάνοντες

    ὁ θάνατος ἐβασίλευσεν   ἐν ζωῇ βασιλεύσουσιν
    διὰ τοῦ ἑνός,   διὰ τοῦ ἑνός, Ἰησοῦ Χριστοῦ.

V 18   Ἄρα οὖν

    ὡς δι' ἑνὸς παραπτώματος   *οὕτως καὶ δι' ἑνὸς δικαιώματος*
    εἰς πάντας ἀνθρώπους   εἰς πάντας ἀνθρώπους
    εἰς κατάκριμα,   εἰς δικαίωσιν ζωῆς.

19 *ὥσπερ γὰρ διὰ τῆς παρακοῆς*   *οὕτως καὶ διὰ τῆς ὑπακοῆς*
    τοῦ ἑνὸς ἀνθρώπου   τοῦ ἑνὸς

ἁμαρτωλοὶ κατεστάθησαν   δίκαιοι κατασταθήσονται
οἱ πολλοί,   οἱ πολλοί.

VI 20   νόμος δὲ παρεισῆλθεν,   οὗ δὲ ἐπλεόνασεν ἡ ἁμαρτία,
ἵνα πλεονάσῃ τὸ παράπτωμα·   ὑπερεπερίσσευσεν ἡ χάρις,

21   ἵνα
ὥσπερ ἐβασίλευσεν ἡ ἁμαρτία   οὕτως καὶ ἡ χάρις βασιλεύσῃ
ἐν τῷ θανάτῳ,   διὰ δικαιοσύνης εἰς ζωὴν αἰώνιον

διὰ Ἰησοῦ Χριστοῦ τοῦ κυρίου ἡμῶν.

Now that we can see the six structural stages, the train of thought will become
more apparent.

1. Verse 12 introduces the contrast between Adam and Christ that Paul has in
   view. The comparative conjunction ὥσπερ marks the new approach. As in the
   similar structure in vv. 18, 19, and 21, it awaits further development in a corresponding οὕτως καί. But linguistically and materially Paul interrupts his
   thinking after the ὥσπερ clause (anacoluthon).[3]
2. The reason for the break is that Paul finds cause to interject in vv. 13 and 14a
   an explanation of what was said in v. 12b.[4] This explanation has as its theme
   the relation between the nexus of sin and death and the Sinai Torah as it applies to the fact that there was no Torah between Adam and Moses.
3. The catchword Adam occurs twice in v. 14a, and the second occurrence enables Paul in v. 14b to make the basic and controlling statement on which the
   antithesis of this whole passage rests: ὅς ἐστιν τύπος τοῦ μέλλοντος. The relative clause stands for an independent and weighty principal sentence:[5] *He* is
   the anti-type of the future (Adam).[6] Now Paul can take up again the antithesis
   that he began but did not complete in v. 12, though it will not be until vv. 18f
   that he develops the antithetical correspondence that he has in view.

---

3. Barrett (109f.) offers an incorrect translation of v. 12: "As through one man sin entered the
world (and through sin came that man's death), so also death came to all men, because they all
sinned." For καὶ οὕτως does not mean "so also." οὕτως καί has that sense (v. 15a, 18b, 19b, 21b).

4. The γάρ of v. 13a introduces an explanation, not a reason, as is rightly noted by Wilckens 314
n. 1035.

5. On relative clauses cf. BDR 293,3c; E. G. Hoffman and H. von Siebenthal, *Griechische
Grammatik zum NT,* Riehen 1985 §§ 142g, 289g. For further examples in Paul cf. Rom. 2:29; 3:8;
9:24; Gal. 2:10.

6. Lietzmann 62 and Barrett 109, 112, rightly construe v. 14b as an independent statement.

4. In vv. 15-17 Paul first stresses the dissimilarity between Adam and Christ. The section as a whole stands under the sign of the adversative ἀλλά (v. 15a). Its arrangement consists of two steps (v. 15 and vv. 16f.) These are related materially as synthetic parallelism. They are introduced by the contrasting οὐχ ὡς . . . , οὕτως καί . . . (v. 15a, v. 16a),[7] comparing the act of Adam and its consequences on the one hand and the act of Christ and its consequences on the other. A γάρ that follows these two statements gives the reason for these consequences. Verse 15a rests on the argument from the lesser to the greater in 15b (εἰ . . . , πολλῷ μᾶλλον),[8] a real *comparatio*.[9] The saying in 16b forms the first basis (. . . μέν . . . , . . . δέ . . .)[10] and the argument from the lesser to the greater in v. 17[11] forms the second basis. This formally corresponds to v. 15b. It may be defined as a *comparatio*. It accompanies and supplements v. 16b.[12] Verses 16b and 17 firmly link the two reasons by contrasting the judgment that brings death with the pardon that brings life. The emphases differ, however, for judgment and pardon are to the fore in v. 16b, death and life in v. 17.

5. Verses 15-17 have emphatically shown that we are totally unable to compare what was done by Adam with what was done by Christ. Verse 18f. then demonstrates the antithetical correspondence between their acts and their consequences. They thus carry forward the comparison that was begun in v. 11, but broken off for material reasons.[13] The expression ἄρα οὖν, which refers back to vv. 15-17, is the sign under which vv. 18f. as a whole stand. It indicates

---

7. In v. 16 the grammatically indispensable οὕτως καί is omitted (ellipsis).

8. The secondary literature frequently reads εἰ γάρ . . . , πολλῷ μᾶλλον both here and at v. 17 (Bornkamm 82, Jüngel 164f.). In fact the γάρ relates not just to the εἰ saying but to the whole argument from v. 15b to v. 17.

9. On *comparatio* cf. H. Lausberg, *Elemente der literarischen Rhetorik,* 8th ed. Munich 1984, §78. The *comparatio* corresponds to the *locus a minore ad maius.* It is a transitory schema whereby a significant historical, literary, or fictional example is then excelled by the subject under discussion.

10. The γάρ again relates to the whole saying, not to the μέν.

11. On the arrangement of the γάρ see n. 8.

12. On giving a saying a twofold basis cf. R. Kühner and B. Gerth, *Ausführliche Grammatik der griechischen Sprache,* Zweiter Teil: Satzlehre, Vol. II, Hannover and Leipzig (3rd ed.), reprinted Hanover 1976, which says that two sentences with γάρ often follow a single preceding sentence. Examples may be found in J. D. Denniston, *The Greek Particle,* Oxford, 2nd ed. 1954, reprinted 1981, 64f. The analysis of Bornkamm 86 (cf. 82) takes a different view, finding elucidation in vv. 16a and 17, and the basis in v. 16b. Jüngel 167 finds the basis of v. 16b in v. 17. In my view these readings are not convincing.

13. What is said in relation to Adam in v. 18 corresponds exactly to what is said in v. 12; v. 18a to what is said there about death, and v. 19a to what is said there about sin.

that the comparison is under the proviso of the πολλῷ μᾶλλον. Two basically incommensurable magnitudes are now being compared.[14] The comparison involves two steps (v. 18: ὡς . . . , οὕτως καί . . . ; v. 19: ὥσπερ . . . , οὕτως καί . . .). The second "supports and elucidates" the first.[15] Materially, as between v. 15 and v. 16f., we find a relation of synthetic parallelism.

6. Verses 20f. bring the argument to a conclusion. In v. 20a, with a clear reference back to v. 13 and v. 14a, Paul first speaks about the Sinaitic Torah. He mentions very briefly its function and effect. He is referring to the law as that which fully discloses the power of sin. His point, then, in v. 20b is that the grace set forth in Christ is overwhelmingly stronger. He then develops the soteriological statement of v. 20b and explicates it in the concluding saying of v. 21, which takes up and gathers together the corresponding sayings in vv. 15-17 and vv. 18f., laying all the stress upon the triumph of grace over the power of sin and death.

As regards the more detailed structural analysis of vv. 20f., the antithetical correspondence of v. 21a and v. 21b (ὥσπερ . . . , οὕτως καί . . .) is plain to see. Defining the structure of v. 20, however, is difficult. Bornkamm's view[16] is that v. 20a (νόμος δὲ παρεισῆλθεν, ἵνα πλεονάσῃ τὸ παράπτωμα) relates neither to the Adam side nor to the Christ side but must be seen as a parenthesis outside the antithesis. It is only with v. 20b that we find the two sides once again, with the words οὗ δὲ ἐπλεόνασεν ἡ ἁμαρτία referring to the Adam side and the words ὑπερεπερίσσευσεν ἡ χάρις to the Christ side. Jüngel obviously accepts the verdict of Bornkamm when he notes that the thesis of v. 20a is formally completely outside the correspondence structure of vv. 15-17, but that this is taken up again in v. 20b and v. 21.[17] I myself, however, do not think that the analysis of v. 20 by Bornkamm and Jüngel is correct. As I view it, the contrast between what Adam does and what Christ does is consistently carried through in v. 20; v. 20a relates to Adam and v. 20b to Christ. If the adverbial clause οὗ δὲ ἐπλεόνασεν ἡ ἁμαρτία seems as a whole to relate to the Christ side, this does not in any way form an objection to my analysis. Verse 20b corresponds to the hamartiological expression ἐκ πολλῶν παραπτωμάτων in v. 16b, which relates to the Christ side, and the whole sentence οὗ δὲ ἐπλεόνασεν ἡ ἁμαρτία,

---

14. Bornkamm 87.
15. Käsemann 149 (ET 157).
16. Bornkamm 82, and cf. Brandenburger 247.
17. Jüngel 170.

ὑπερεπερίσσευσεν ἡ χάρις in v. 20b corresponds materially to τὸ δὲ χάρισμα ἐκ πολλῶν παραπτωμάτων εἰς δικαίωμα in v. 16b. In both cases the negative reality of sin is expressly mentioned with reference to Christ, for it has been vanquished by Christ's saving action. The real stress is on the positive soteriological statements τὸ δὲ χάρισμα . . . εἰς δικαίωμα in v. 16b and ὑπερεπερίσσευσεν ἡ χάρις in v. 20b.

2. Commentated Translation of 5:12-21

On the basis of the structural analysis, the text of 5:12-21 may now be translated in a way that seeks so far as possible both to discern the flow of the argument and to present the meaning of the individual statements.[18] We may mention first some linguistic phenomena to which the translation must do justice.

1. Not only in v. 16,[19] but elsewhere, too, we find brevity of diction and ellipses which call for appropriate material definition, i.e., one that can be gained only from the context.
2. Homoioteleuton obviously plays an important role in the choice of substantives (παράπτωμα — χάρισμα in v. 15, δώρημα — κρίμα — κατάκριμα — χάρισμα — δικαίωμα in v. 16, and παράπτωμα — δικαίωμα in v. 18).[20] In seeking the precise meaning of the words we must certainly take account of the fact that they are selected for rhetorical reasons.
3. Regarding the genitives πολλῶν in v. 16b and ἑνός in v. 18a and 18b the linguistic question arises whether they are to be understood adjectivally as a neutral attribute of the genitive substantive that follows, or substantively as a masculine *genitivus auctoris*.[21] Here again the decision must depend upon the context.

Since we are not offering an express exegesis of 5:12-21 in the present essay, the English text will be accompanied by footnotes that will justify the translation or provide brief commentaries upon it. The sections that follow will more

---

18. We have selected an arrangement which separates the translation from the structural analysis of the Greek text.

19. Barrett 114 notes that "the verse is full of obscurities."

20. Cf. Rom. 11:12: παράπτωμα — ἥττημα — πλήρωμα.

21. In the case of ἑνός the ambiguity is partly due to the fact that it occurs with an article in v. 15bα, v. 17a and b (cf. n. 62), and v. 19b, and without an article in v. 16bα and v. 18a and b.

closely discuss and interpret the text, and in particular vv. 13 and 14a and vv. 20f.

Therefore:[22]

I 12a   Just as through *one* man,
           sin[23] came into the world,[24]
           and through sin death,[25]

   12b   and so death came to *all*,[26]
           for[27] *all* have sinned[28] —

II 13a   even before the law was given[29] sin was already[30] in the world;[31]

   13b   sin was not yet[32] imputed[33] (to the sinner),
           so long as there was no law.[34]

---

22. On διὰ τοῦτο as an introduction to the whole passage cf. Section 3.

23. Sin is here personified as a *power* (cf. Rom. 3:9, 20; 5:21; 6:1f., 6f., 10-14, 16-18, 20, 22f.; 7:7-9, 11, 13f., 17, 20, 23; 8:2f., 10, and cf. 1 Cor. 15:56).

24. κόσμος denotes the world of God's creation. εἰσέρχεσθαι εἰς τὸν κόσμον (cf. Wis. 2:24; 14:14) means came into existence or came on the scene, cf. for material A. Schlatter, *Die Sprache und das Heimat des vierten Evangelisten* (BFChTh VI 4), Gütersloh 1902, 48 (on John 3:19), cf. also jTa῾an III, 12, 67a 13 (on the flood) and TargQoh 3,14; 4,2 (on punishment).

25. Death is also personified as *power,* cf. v. 14a; 17a; Rom. 6:9; 7:5; 1 Cor. 15:26, 54-56.

26. For διέρχεσθαι εἰς as "came to," "reached" cf. Josephus *Antiquitates Judaicae* XIV, 414.

27. For ἐφ' ᾧ = ἐπὶ τούτῳ ὅτι, "for" or "because," as in 2 Cor. 5:4; Phil. 3:12; cf. BDR § 235 n. 3; 294 n. 6.

28. πάντες ἥμαρτον, cf. 3:23, referring to actual sins.

29. This is what the expression ἄχρι νόμου means. Bauer/Aland 259 s.v. ἄχρι 1.a correctly translate it "until the time the law was given." This is the period ἀπὸ Ἀδὰμ μέχρι Μωϋσέως (v. 14a), the time before the παρεισέρχεσθαι of the νόμος (v. 20a.). The term νόμος is used metonymically for νομοθεσία. On the omission of the article cf. BDR § 258,2, which notes that Paul has not used it for either ἁμαρτία or νόμος (cf. ibid. n. 3). In v. 13a and b and v. 20a νόμος without the article denotes the law of Sinai.

30. For γάρ cf. n. 4.

31. Unlike the use in v. 12, ἁμαρτία (cf. ἁμαρτάνειν in 12b) means actual sin (cf. Rom. 5:20b; 14:23; 4:8 - Ps. 31:2 LXX) and κόσμος is more narrowly the human world (cf. Rom. 3:6, 19; 1 Cor. 1:21; 4:9, 13; 6:2; 2 Cor. 5:19).

32. The particle δέ in v. 13b means "of course," "at any rate," cf. Denniston (n. 12), 165. My rendering of δέ as "yet" is based on H. Menge, *Das Neue Testament,* 11th ed. Stuttgart 1949, 236.

33. On οὐκ ἐλλογεῖται cf. nn. 188ff.

34. We might use "if" or "because" for "so long as." I give reasons for my rendering in n. 183.

14a Nevertheless[35] death reigned[36] from Adam to Moses[37] even over those who did not sin by transgression as Adam did.[38]

III 14b *He* is the antitype of the coming (Adam).[39]

IV 15 However:

15a Not like the trespass (of Adam) is (Christ's) gift of grace.[40]

15b For

15bα if through the trespass of *one* many have died,[41]

15bβ in incomparable fashion the grace of God, and therewith[42] the gift[43] (that is given)[44] through the grace of the *one* man Jesus Christ, have abounded immeasurably to many.[45]

16a And not like what was done[46] by *one* sinner[47] is[48] the gift (brought by *one* man Jesus Christ).[49]

---

35. Cf. Bauer/Aland 74 s.v. ἀλλά 2.

36. In this verse and v. 21 the aor. ἐβασίλευσεν has a complexive sense in contrast to the ingressive sense in v. 17.

37. In the expression ἀπὸ Ἀδὰμ μέχρι Μωϋσέως the prepositions ἀπό and μέχρι have an exclusive sense. The reference is to the time between Adam and Moses.

38. Literally this means "those who did not sin in the likeness of Adam's transgression," cf. Bauer/Aland 1150 s.v. ὁμοίωμα. 1. We get the point of v. 14a if we translate it thus: "Nevertheless, death reigned from Adam to Moses even over those who did not sin by transgressing an express commandment of God as Adam did."

39. On this saying and the term τύπος cf. nn. 99ff.

40. On χάρισμα cf. n. 142.

41. οἱ πολλοί in v. 15bα and β and v. 19a and b is the equivalent of πάντες ἄνθρωποι in v. 12b and v. 18a and b. The words οἱ πολλοὶ ἀπέθανον correspond to the statement in v. 12b: εἰς πάντας ἀνθρώπους ὁ θάνατος διῆλθεν. That all have died means that they have all fallen victim to death, cf. ἐγὼ δὲ ἀπέθανον in Rom. 7:10.

42. The καί does not make ἡ χάρις τοῦ θεοῦ a second factor. It introduces the decisive implication.

43. ἡ δωρεά in v. 15bβ, 17b equals τὸ δώρημα in v. 16a.

44. Not just the words ἐν χάριτι but the whole expression ἐν χάριτι τῇ τοῦ ἑνὸς ἀνθρώπου Ἰησοῦ Χριστοῦ must be seen as a more precise attributive definition of ἡ δωρεά. For details cf. nn. 154ff.

45. Verse 17b explains v. 15bβ.

46. For an understanding of this concise statement cf. v. 16b and also v. 12 and v. 17a.

47. The participle ἁμαρτήσας is chosen rather than the noun ἁμαρτωλός because the concrete reference is to the *one* sinful act of Adam in Genesis 3.

48. Cf. n. 7.

49. For τὸ δώρημα cf. δωρεά in v. 15b. The brief statement finds its basis here.

16b   For

16bα the judgment[50] (of God) upon *one*[51]
      (has led) to the condemnation (of many),[52]

16bβ but the gracious act[53] (of *one*) (leads) from the trespasses of
      many[54] to the pardon[55] (of these many).

17   Indeed,[56]

17a   if through the trespass of the *one*
      death gained dominion (over all) through that *one,*[57]

17b   so incomparably will those who receive the superabundant
      fullness[58] of grace and[59] the gift of righteousness[60]

---

50. Here κρίμα has the general sense of "judicial decision," "verdict," "judgment."

51. We must not supplement ἐξ ἑνός with a παραπτώματος like Lietzmann 62f.; Barrett 109, 114f.; Schmidt 96, 101, etc. The expression, like δι' ἑνὸς ἁμαρτήσαντος in v. 16a, or διὰ τοῦ ἑνός in v. 17a, refers to the *one* man Adam. The preposition ἐκ does not give the reason, but like the parallel structure in v. 16bα and bβ names the starting point (cf. Käsemann 131, ET 140; Wilckens 324; Stuhlmacher 77). The "upon *one*" thus stands metonymically for "upon *one* trespass."

52. Here and in v. 18a κατάκριμα means condemnation to death (cf. Rom. 8:1 and cf. κατάκρισις at 2 Cor. 3:9). On the basis of v. 16bβ a πολλῶν must be added (cf. Wilckens 324; Stuhlmacher 81).

53. On τὸ χάρισμα cf. v. 15a.

54. ἐκ πολλῶν παραπτωμάτων: (a) On purely linguistic grounds πολλῶν might be an adjective ("many trespasses") or a noun ("trespasses of many"). But ἐξ ἑνός in v. 16b counts against the adjectival use advocated, e.g., by Lietzmann 62; Barrett 109, 114f.; Kuss 224; Michel 185; Zeller 113, and in favour of its use as a noun, supported, e.g., by Bornkamm 86; Käsemann 131 (ET 140); Schmithals 166. As a noun πολλῶν corresponds syntactically to ἑνός in δι' ἑνὸς παραπτώματος (v. 18a) and δι' ἑνὸς δικαιώματος (v. 18b). (b) πολλοί without art. catches up the οἱ πολλοί of v. 15b (cf. v. 19) and has the same meaning as "all." On πολλοί without art. cf. J. Jeremias TDNT VI (1968), 541, 543. (c) In v. 16b the preposition ἐκ is not causal. Its nuance is different from that in v. 16b. It denotes the sphere from which Christ's saving work has liberated those who had fallen victim to κατάκριμα (cf. Kasemann 145, ET 154).

55. The use of δικαίωσις in v. 18b, which mans the justification for life that was accomplished by the death and resurrection of Jesus Christ and that is now proclaimed in the word of the gospel. But in v. 16bβ it is chosen for purely rhetorical reasons because it corresponds to its antonym κατάκριμα in v. 16bα.

56. The saying in v. 16a lies behind what is said in both v. 16b and v. 17 (cf. the structural analysis ad loc.).

57. Wilckens 325 admirably emphasized that Adam's sin had consequences for all. On the aorist ἐβασίλευσεν cf. n. 36.

58. περισσεία catches up ἐπερίσσευσεν (v. 15bβ) and with v. 17b explains what is said there.

59. On καί cf. n. 42.

60. Here and in v. 21b δικαιοσύνη corresponds to the δικαιοῦσθαι of Rom. 3:24, 28; 4:2; 5:1, 9 (cf. Gal. 2:16f.; 3:24; 1 Cor. 6:11). It is participation in the salvation based upon God's redeeming

reign in (eternal) life[61] through the *one,* Jesus Christ.[62]

V 18   Therefore (thus):

18a   just as through the trespass of *one*[63]
       condemnation (to death) has come upon all,[64]

18b   so through the righteous act of *one*[65]
       justification for life[66] (has come) for all.

19   For

19a   just as through the disobedience of *one* man
       many became sinners,[67]

19b   so through the obedience of *one* (man)[68]
       many become righteous.[69]

---

power and action which consists essentially of forgiveness and justification for life (cf. Rom. 4:1-8; 2 Cor. 5:19, 21). 2 Cor. 3:9 contrasts δικαιοσύνη with κατάκρισις. On the Pauline doctrine of δικαιοσύνη cf. O. Hofius, "'Rechtfertigung des Gottlosen' als Thema biblischer Theologie," *Paulusstudien* (WUNT 51), 2nd ed. Tübingen, 125f.

61. As in 18b, ζωή here means ζωὴ αἰώνιος (cf. v. 21b and 6:22f.) and βασιλεύσουσιν is thus a true eschatological future. ἐν ζωῇ might have a causal sense: "in the power of eternal life," cf. M. Zerwick, *Analysis philologica Novi Testamenti Graeci* (SPIB 107), 4th ed. Rome 1984, 344 ad loc.

62. At v. 17b we should read . . . διὰ τοῦ ἑνός, Ἰησοῦ Χριστοῦ. ἑνός is not an attributive adjective but a substantive to which Ἰησοῦ Χριστοῦ is in apposition.

63. In δι' ἑνὸς παραπτώματος (v. 18a) and δι' ἑνὸς δικαιώματος (v. 18b) ἑνός is not a neutral attribute for παραπτώματος or δικαιώματος but a masculine and thus a *genitivus auctoris.* This rests on the contrasting "one" and "all" of v. 18a and b and the parallel expessions διὰ τῆς παρακοῆς τοῦ ἑνὸς ἀνθρώπου and διὰ τῆς ὑπακοῆς τοῦ ἑνός in v. 19a and b.

64. Regarding κατάκριμα in v. 18a J. J. Wettstein, *Novum Testamentum Graecum,* II, Amsterdam 1752 (Graz, 1962, 49), rightly adds θανάτου.

65. Unlike in v. 16b β, δικαίωμα means here Christ's redemptive act; cf. nn. 145ff., and for the grammatical structure n. 63.

66. δικαίωσις ζωῆς is the antithesis of κατάκριμα (θανάτου) in v. 18a. The genitive expresses the goal (cf. BDR § 166,1 with n. 1). The noun δικαίωσις (cf. Rom. 4:25) conveys here the sense of δικαιοῦν ("to pardon or justify") (Bauer/Aland 397 s.v. 3). ζωή equals ζωὴ αἰώνιος (cf. n. 61 on 17).

67. On the passive of καθίστημι or καθιστάνω in the sense "to become something" cf. Bauer/Aland 792 s.v. 3 (with examples).

68. We need to add ἀνθρώπου in 19b (elipsis).

69. For the future κατασταθήσονται cf. n. 161. Paul calls δίκαιος the one who has received δικαιοσύνη (v. 17b).

VI 20a   The law then came in[70]
        so that the trespass might become great.[71]

  20b   But when sin[72] increased
        grace entered the stage with more than abundant fullness.

  21   so that

  21a   even as sin[73] reigned
        through death,[74]

  22b   so grace will reign
        through (the gift) of justification for eternal life[75] —
                    through Jesus Christ, our Lord.

3. Romans 5:12-21 in the Context of Romans

If we are to judge the place of the section Rom. 5:12-21 in the context of the epistle, whether in thought or substance, we must properly define the introductory διὰ τοῦτο. The majority of commentators seek to attach the usual meaning to this expression, and thus to see it as a conjunction which opens up all that follows ("therefore," "thus," "hence"). On this view whatever is said in 5:12-21 has to be seen as based upon all that precedes, whether it be 5:10,[76] 5:11,[77] 5:1-11,[78] 3:21–5:11,[79] or 1:18–5:11.[80] H. Schlier, however, raised an objection

---

70. On παρεισέρχεσθαι cf. nn. 208ff.

71. We do best to render the general sing. τὸ παράπτωμα as the trespass of humanity as a whole. The verb means "to increase," "to grow," "to become great" (cf. Rom. 6:1; 2 Cor. 4:15; 2 Thess. 1:3; with ἁμαρτία Sir. 23:3 LXX). It does not relate here only to quantity (cf. section 6). Because of the different nuances I choose to translate it "become geat."

72. Since this catches up the τὸ παράπτωμα of v. 20a, the stress should be upon the active character of sin.

73. ἁμαρτία is again seen as a *power*, as in v. 12a.

74. ἐν τῷ θανάτῳ = in order that, standing under God's κατάκριμα, they should all come to death (cf. Rom. 6:16f., 20f., 23; 7:13). Death here is depicted as something that happens.

75. διὰ δικαιοσύνης εἰς ζωὴν αἰώνιον means "in order that they might receive the gift of justification that results in eternal life" (cf. Rom. 5:9). The gift is mentioned in v. 15b and v. 17b (ἡ δωρεὰ τῆς δικαιοσύνης) and materially δικαιοσύνη εἰς ζωὴν αἰώνιον corresponds to δικαίωσις ζωῆς in v. 18b.

76. Schmidt 97.

77. Brandenburger 258.

78. Schlatter 185, von der Osten-Sacken 169, Michel 186 n. 1, Cranfield 271f., Wilckens 314.

79. E. Kühl, *Der Brief des Paulus an die Römer,* Leipzig 1913, 174.

80. Dunn 271f.

against these proposals, stating that "therefore" "in the strict sense made hardly any sense."[81] Regarding 5:1-11, the sayings in vv. 12-21, which depict the universal redemption of all humanity, can hardly be regarded as a deduction from what is said in vv. 1-11 about "our" redemption, i.e., that of Christians.[82] Materially, indeed, we should have to understand 12-21 as "the *presupposition* of 1-11."[83] Schlier thus understands διὰ τοῦτο as "to continue." We have here a transitional particle. The idea is that of "it must now be considered."[84] Gaugler, too, expressly contends against the view that with the διὰ τοῦτο Paul is drawing conclusions from what he has said before. In his view Paul is seeking "to give the *reasons*" for the section that has just ended (1-11).[85] Käsemann is of the same opinion. As he puts it, διὰ τοῦτο marks the beginning of a new line of arguments which "also substantiates vv. 10f." or the whole of 1-11.[86]

To achieve a well-grounded assessment of διὰ τοῦτο in view of these controversial opinions, we have to consider the material and argumentative connection between 5:1-12 and the preceding presentations in the epistle. In 5:1-11 Paul was definitely speaking about "us" — Christians — and in vv. 6ff. he expressly expounded the ὑπὲρ ἡμῶν (v. 8) of the saving work of Jesus Christ. We might summarize the apostle's statements as follows. Even then (κατὰ καιρόν, v. 6), even when we were those who had become subject to death (v. 6),[87] without God (ἐχθροί, v. 10), Christ died for us just as we were (vv. 6-8). He justified

---

81. Schlier 159 with examples.

82. This problem does not arise only if we apply what is said about the work of Christ, in contrast to that of Adam, to Christians alone, thus linking it up with the "we" of 1-11. But the wording of the text speaks decisively against this interpretation (cf. v. 18b and v. 19b).

83. Schlier (italics mine). Jüngel 152 tries to link deduction and presupposition when he states that in 5:12ff. Paul deduces from the problem of Christian existence dealt with in 5:1ff. a consequence that relates to all humanity, which is also the basis of what he says in 1ff.

84. Schlier ad loc., cf. Lietzmann 61, Barrett 110, Bultmann 433.

85. Gaugler 124f. (italics mine). The Peshitta understood what Paul was saying in this way, for it does not use *miṭṭol hānā'* ("thus") here, as elsewhere in Paul (Rom. 1:26; 4:16; 13:6; 1 Cor. 4:17; 11:10, 30; 2 Cor. 4:1; 7:13; 13:10; 1 Thess. 2:13; 3:5, 7; 2 Thess. 2:11) but instead uses *gêr* ("for").

86. Käsemann 138 (ET 146).

87. The noun ἀσθενής in v. 6, which occurs with ἀσεβής (v. 6), ἁμαρτωλός (v. 8), and ἐχθρός (v. 10), does not find adequate rendering if it is translated "weak" or "incapable" or "impotent." In my view it means "belonging to the sphere of death," "marked for death," "subject to death." We must compare it with the expressions ἐν φθορᾷ and ἐν ἀσθενείᾳ in 1 Cor. 15:42b-44a or with 2 Cor. 13:4, where ἀσθένεια denotes the weakness of our mortal nature. I might also refer to the ἄνθρωπος ἀσθενὴς καί ὀλιγοχρόνιος of Wis. 9:5 or to Ps. 6:3 LXX, where the petitioner, seeing that he stands under the wrath of God (v. 2), and knowing that he belongs already to the sphere of death (v. 6), confesses concerning himself: ἀσθενής εἰμι. Cf. also Heb. 7:28 with 7:23.

us. He reconciled us to God (vv. 9f.). He definitively ensured that we should be saved at the last judgment and that we should share in the δόξα of God, i.e., in eternal life.[88]

The "we" of whom Paul speaks, as the ἀσθενεῖς, ἀσεβεῖς, ἁμαρτωλοί and ἐχθροί they were, all belong to the πάντες whose total lostness Paul indicated in the first part of Romans (1:18–3:20), the πάντες who were also redeemed according to 3:23f.: πάντες . . . ἥμαρτον καὶ ὑστεροῦνται τῆς δόξης τοῦ θεοῦ, δικαιούμενοι δωρεὰν τῇ αὐτοῦ χάριτι διὰ τῆς ἀπολυτρώσεως τῆς ἐν Χριστῷ Ἰησοῦ. The thesis of 3:23 (πάντες . . . ἥμαρτον καὶ ὑστεροῦνται τῆς δόξης τοῦ θεοῦ) had already been expressly unfolded in 1:18–3:20 and was now given a broader basis.[89] The basis of the saying πάντες . . . δικαιούμενοι δωρεὰν τῇ αὐτοῦ χάριτι διὰ τῆς ἀπολυτρώσεως τῆς ἐν Χριστῷ Ἰησοῦ (3:24), however, had not yet been given, and *without* it the material reason had not yet been explicitly stated for the unheard of claims of 5:1-11. The underlying statement had to be made in what followed 5:1-11.[90] It had to be shown that the redemption accomplished in Christ Jesus (3;24) really applied to all, that the universal lostness of 1:18–3:20 had been universally overcome by the salvation achieved in Christ, so that the grace of God would comprehensively win the victory over the contaminating power of sin and death. The διὰ τοῦτο signalizes the transition to this presentation, which is quite indispensable to the context of the argument of the epistle. The διὰ τοῦτο leads us from the expression of a full assurance of salvation (5:1-11), couched in the language of a personal confession, to a theological exposition that provides the presupposition, the basis, and the validity of such assurance (5:12-21).[91] The words διὰ τοῦτο do not introduce an implication of 5:1-11. They form the opening of a section that gives the true reason for what was said there.[92]

Regarding the specific statements of 5;12-21, we must mention two com-

---

88. The two conclusions *a maiore ad minus* in vv. 8f. and 10 clearly state the fact that the decision regarding participation in the future, eschatological salvation was irrevocably made in the crucifixion of Christ.

89. Cf. the emphatic πάντες (vv. 9, 12), πᾶν στόμα and πᾶς ὁ κόσμος (v. 19), and πᾶσα σάρξ (v. 20) in the summary given in 3:9-20.

90. Cf. Käsemann, who rightly objects vigorously against the exegetes who isolate 5:12-21 from the flow of Romans as an "erratic block" or an "excursus" (132, ET 141).

91. Rom. 5:12-21 is related to 5:1-11 as 2 Cor. 5:19a and b (ὡς ὅτι θεὸς ἦν ἐν Χριστῷ κόσμον καταλλάσσων, μὴ λογιζόμενος αὐτοῖς τὰ παραπτώματα αὐτῶν) is to 2 Cor. 5:18b (τοῦ καταλλάξαντος ἑαυτῷ διὰ Χριστοῦ).

92. Hence the διὰ τοῦτο of 5:12 corresponds materially to the ὡς ὅτι of 2 Cor. 5:19.

plexes. The first supplements and deepens what was said in 1:18–3:20, showing that the fall of Adam is the final historical cause of the fact that humanity as a whole has now come under the sway of sin and death. The second — and here the emphasis lies — points to the universality of the salvation effected in Christ, developing it, and providing the basis of what had already been stated in 3:23f. (πάντες . . . δικαιούμενοι κτλ). There can be no doubt that the decision made through Christ in 5:12-21 *also* corresponds to what was said about this death in 5:6ff. Paul has this death in mind when he speaks about the grace (v. 15a, v. 16b), the righteous act (v. 18b), and the obedience (v. 19b) of Christ. Only a view that in fact isolates 5:12-21 can argue that we get no echo of a theology of the cross or of an atonement in the antithesis of Adam and Christ.[93] If we note how closely 5:1-11 and 12-21 are materially interwoven, there can be no evading the conclusion that what is said about "the one, Jesus Christ," carries a consistent reference to the crucified and risen Lord.[94]

4. The Antithesis of Adam and Christ

This antithesis is the main theme of Rom. 5:12-21. Its presupposition may be found in the statement regarding Adam in v. 14b: ὅς ἐστιν τύπος τοῦ μέλλοντος. When Paul uses the terms Ἀδάμ and ὁ μέλλων (Ἀδάμ) here, we are reminded of the ὁ πρῶτος ἄνθρωπος and the ὁ δεύτερος ἄνθπωπος (or ὁ ἔσχατος Ἀδάμ) of 1 Cor. 15:45ff.[95] As regards the general argument of Rom. 5:12-21 it should be noted that the confrontation of Adam and Christ is given linguistic expression. Concerning Adam we find εἷς ἄνθρωπος in v. 12a, εἷς ἁμαρτήσας in v. 16a, ὁ εἷς ἄνθρωπος in v. 19a, ὁ εἷς in v. 15bα and v. 17a, and εἷς in v. 16bα and v. 18a, while for Christ the corresponding terms ὁ εἷς ἄνθρωπος in v. 15bβ and v. 19b,[96] ὁ εἷς in v. 17b, and εἷς in v. 18b are used.

We have mentioned in the structural analysis that there is a contrast between the act of Adam and the act of Christ in their relevance and consequences for all people. The universal aspect of both acts is fully emphasized (πάντες ἄνθρωποι in v. 12bα, v. 18a and b, πάντες in v. 12bβ, and [οἱ] πολλοί in v. 15bα and

---

93. Cf. Schmithals 172.

94. von der Osten-Sacken 163 offers good reasons for this view.

95. I will not discuss the background in religious history here except to note that the thesis of a Gnostic basis for the Adam-Christ typology is unproved and unprovable.

96. ἄνθρωπος is elided in v. 19b, cf. n. 68.

v. 16bβ, v. 19a and b). The antithesis that uncovers this universality, as we have already noted, takes up materially the statement in Rom. 3:23f: πάντες . . . ἥμαρτον καὶ ὑστεροῦνται τῆς δόξης τοῦ θεοῦ, δικαιούμενοι δωρεὰν τῇ αὐτοῦ χάριτι διὰ τῆς ἀπολυτρώσεως τῆς ἐν Χριστῷ Ἰησοῦ. Both the statements relating to Adam and those relating to Christ stand under the sign of Rom. 3:22b: οὐ γάρ ἐστιν διαστολή (sc. Ἰουδαίου τε καὶ Ἕλληνος [cf. 10:12a]. They are of equal concern to both Jews and Gentiles. They are valid for all, whether or not they know the Sinaitic Torah.

The antithesis of Adam and Christ in 5:12-21 involves two entities that are beyond comparison.[97] The fact that their deeds are incomparable, along with their consequences, has its basis in the fact that the persons themselves are radically incomparable. Adam represents the human race in its confrontation with God. As such he acts *in the presence* of God. Christ, however, is the one and only person who, as the "Son of God" in origin and essence (5:10), stands *at the side* of God, and *in* whom, therefore, God himself acts in relation to all others.[98] In Adam we find a human action, in Christ a divine action that is based upon the unity of the Crucified with God. For this reason the grace of God as such is also the grace of this one man Jesus Christ (v. 15bβ). Again, what Adam did affects only himself and all others with him. Everyone else is marked and constituted by what Adam did *for himself alone.* The act of Christ, however, does not concern himself. It concerns sinners exclusively. Sinners are retrieved by what Christ did *for them.* Regarding the fact that there can be no comparing Adam and Christ, Calvin finely observed (on 14b) that the statement that Adam is a τύπος of Christ can be regarded as a possible and meaningful statement only because the likeness goes along with the greatest possible contrasts.[99] The likeness is simply that both Adam and Christ do things that affect the destiny of all of us. Their deeds have universal significance and consequences.[100] Both Adam and Christ universally define the πάντες or the πολλοί, Adam the old Adamic humanity, Christ the new humanity of those who are in Christ. *To this degree, but only* to this degree, there is correspondence between Adam and Christ in

---

97. Bornkamm 87f.

98. Cf. Wilcken's important discussion (36f.). On 327 Wilcken says that Christ as the origin of righteousness for all does not *represent us before God* as Adam did, but *represents God before us.* Barth 80, also finely states that we are *against* the one God but Christ is the one God *for* us.

99. Ioannis Calvini in Novum Testamentum Commentarii, ed. A. Tholuck, Vol. V: *Epistola Pauli ad Romanos,* 4th ed. 1864, 88.

100. Bornkamm 83.

spite of the antithesis. The correspondence must be defined as one of antithesis. Christ is the antitype of Adam.[101] Antitype must be our translation of the τύπος of v. 14b even though this meaning is not attested elsewhere. It is materially necessary.[102] We must reject the renderings and interpretations that depict Adam as the prefiguration,[103] pre-presentation,[104] prototype,[105] promise,[106] or forerunner[107] of Christ.

Factually what we have just said has given us something that is essential if we are to interpret Rom. 5:12-21 properly. As Paul saw it, Adam was a real figure of history, the protoplast, the first human.[108] The apostle did not view Adam as no more than an exemplary figure from whom we can read what we all are. He put him at the beginning of the human story as the progenitor of the race. A decision was made by his historical act that affects all his descendants, the whole of Adamic humanity. We are told this in the first verse of the section.

Verse 12a refers only to Adam: δι' ἑνὸς ἀνθρώπου ἡ ἁμαρτία εἰς τὸν κόσμον εἰσῆλθεν καὶ διὰ τῆς ἁμαρτίας ὁ θάνατος. Paul had in view the sayings in the primal story of Gen. 2:4b–3:24, and it is important that we should inquire into the way he understood the OT text.

If sin came into the world through the one man Adam, the reference is to the unheard of act of the protoplast that is later called the παράπτωμα (v. 15aα, v. 15bα, v. 17a, v. 18a) or the παρακοή (v. 19a) of the one. The word παράπτωμα means "fault" or "failing" or "trespass" or "sin," but not "transgression," and certainly not "fall."[109] It is not a synonym of παράβασις (v. 14a), but, as we learn from v. 20, it is a synonym of ἁμαρτία (v. 13a, v. 20), i.e., of sin as

---

101. Ibid. 85, cf. Wilcken 321.

102. Barth, *Römerbrief,* 1st ed. Bern 1919, 133; *Christus und Adam* 75 (ET 74); Nygren 161; Wilckens 306; Stuhlmacher 77 and 81.

103. Bultmann 431.

104. L. Goppelt, art. τύπος κτλ., TDNT VIII (1972), 252: "advance presentation."

105. Barth, *Römerbrief,* 2nd ed. Munich 1922, 150 and 154 (ET 171, 176).

106. Schlatter 189, and cf. Barth, *Römerbrief,* 2nd ed. 154 (ET 176).

107. Schlatter 193.

108. Cf. Luz 201; Käsemann 133, ET 142.

109. Käsemann 145 (ET 153) on 15a does not think that παράπτωμα and χάρισμα are concrete acts. As he sees it, "the connection between action and result is emphasized." That is why he uses "fall" and "grace" in translating v. 15 (131, ET 140). He then uses "transgression" for παράπτωμα at v. 17a, v. 18a, v. 20a. H. Conzelmann, art. χάρισμα, TDNT IX (1974), 404, n. 18 states (as I see it incorrectly) that "παράπτωμα is the totality, the act of Adam and its effect. Χάρισμα is to be taken similarly."

an *act* in the sense of ἁμαρτανειν (v. 12b).[110] As Paul sees it, Adam's παράπτωμα is the trespass against God of which we read in Genesis 3. He has this concrete act in mind when he refers to Adam's παράπτωμα in v. 19a. An adequate explanation for the choice of this term may be found in Gen. 3:11b and 17. Adam's trespass or disobedience or act of sin introduced sin into the world as a power (ἁμαρτία in v. 12a, v. 21a), and it now holds sway in the world.

As we read on in v. 12a we learn that θάνατος is the result of ἁμαρτία. θάνατος has come into the world. This does not mean physical death or creaturely mortality. The context already tells us this.[111] The meaning is that death is the consequence of sin.[112] Sin as such means that Adam comes under God's sentence of condemnation (κατάκριμα, v. 16bα, v. 18a) i.e., eschatological condemnation. The death that comes into the world through Adam's sin is the eschatological death of separation from God.[113] The antithesis of death in 5:12-21 is not physical life but ζωὴ αἰώνιος (5:5, 17, 18, 21, cf. 6:22f.).[114]

As Paul more precisely defines what Adam did in the words καὶ διὰ τῆς ἁμαρτίας ὁ θάνατος, and when we compare such texts as Rom. 3:23 and 1 Cor. 15:42-49, using them for elucidation, we can see how he interpreted the story of paradise and the fall in Genesis 3. We cannot do more than offer a short sketch of the essentials. Genesis 2:7 describes the creation of Adam: καὶ ἔπλασεν ὁ θεὸς τὸν ἄνθρωπον χοῦν ἀπὸ τῆς γῆς καὶ ἐνεφύσησεν εἰς τὸ πρόσωπον αὐτοῦ πνοὴν ζωῆς, καὶ ἐγένετο ὁ ἄνθρωπος εἰς ψυχὴν ζῶσαν. Adopting this passage in 1 Cor. 15:42ff., Paul interprets it as follows. The πρῶτος ἄνθρωπος Ἀδάμ was ἐκ γῆς (47a) and as such χοϊκός (vv. 47a, 48a, 49a). He became a ψυχὴ ζῶσα (v. 45a), one who had been given by God the breath of life.[115] He was a σῶμα ψυχικόν, an ensouled body (v. 44a). Created from the earth and granted the breath of life, Adam possessed creaturely, physical life but not thus far eternal life. It can be said of his creation according to Gen. 2:7: σπείρεται ἐν φθορᾷ, ἐν

---

110. In v. 16bβ and v. 20a the term παράπτωμα is thus used for the sinful acts of the act that derives from Adam.

111. Note the material correspondence of v. 15bα, v. 16bα, and v. 17a.

112. Romans 6:23a states this metaphorically when it describes sin as the owner or ruler: τὰ . . . ὀψώνια τῆς ἁμαρτίας θάνατος.

113. Von den Osten-Sacken 165; cf. also Schmidt 98; Zeller 115, 117; Stuhlmacher 80.

114. Rightly emphasized by Schmidt 98 and Zeller 115.

115. The expression ψυχὴ ζῶσα in 1 Cor. 15:45a (= Gen. 2:7) must be taken as metonymy. It means bearer of a living soul.

ἀτιμίᾳ, and ἐν ἀσθενείᾳ, *not* σπείρεται ἐν ἀφθαρσίᾳ, ἐν δόξῃ, and ἐν δυνάμει (vv. 42b, 43).[116] 2. According to Gen. 2:8-17 Adam is placed by God in the garden of Eden, and in the midst of the garden is the tree of life (v. 9). He may eat of all the trees, but the tree of the knowledge of good and evil is forbidden him (v. 16f.). He can and should eat *even of* the tree of life (ξύλον τῆς ζωῆς)! As Paul sees it, Adam might not have been created as an immortal being. But nor was he created as a mortal being in the sense that dying "naturally" would put an end to his life.[117] He was made ἐκ γῆς and was thus "earthy," but his destiny and goal was that he should receive ζωὴ αἰώνιος and with this the δόξα τοῦ θεοῦ. Creation according to Paul's interpretation of Gen. 2:7 was not yet complete. It was meant to go further, but sin intervened.[118] Genesis 3 then tells about the sin of Adam and its consequences. The result of the fall was expulsion from paradise (vv. 22-24). Adam could no longer eat of the tree of life and attain to eternal life (μήποτε ἐκτείνῃ τὴν χεῖρα καὶ λάβῃ τοῦ ξύλου τῆς ζωῆς καὶ φάγῃ καὶ ζήσεται εἰς τὸν αἰῶνα, v. 22b). Paul sees here an actualization of the threat of death according to Gen. 2:17b: ᾗ δ' ἄν ἡμέρᾳ φάγητε ἀπ' αὐτοῦ, θανάτῳ ἀποθανεῖσθε. The consequence of sin is the death that is passed over Adam, the death which is as such the fulfillment of the κρίμα of God, that has the character of κατάκριμα. This death is quite distinct from natural death. In the apostle's view the amazing fall prevented God from bringing his plans for creation to completion. Burchard put this well when he said that through his sin Adam remained a ruin of creation.[119]

If Adam himself and Adam alone was spoken of in 12a, the reference in v. 12b is to the whole of Adamic humanity as the consequences of the act of Adam for all his descendants are described: καὶ οὕτως εἰς πάντας ἀνθρώπους ὁ θάνατος διῆλθεν, ἐφ' ᾧ πάντες ἥμαρτον. This statement is parallel to that in 3:23: πάντες ἥμαρτον καὶ ὑστεροῦνται τῆς δόξης τοῦ θεοῦ. The δόξα τοῦ θεοῦ here is the eternal life that God the Creator had destined for Adam and that the protoplast had then forfeited through his sin. It is then said of all his descendants that all of them have sinned as those that belong to this ancestor, and

---

116. For relating the fourfold σπείρεται of 1 Cor. 15:42b-44a to creation (and not to burial) cf. C. Wolff, *Der erste Brief des Paulus an die Korinther* II: Auslegung der Kapitel 8-16 (ThHk, VII/2), Berlin 1982, 198f.

117. C. Burchard, "1 Korinther 15:39-41," ZNW 75, 1984, 233-58, Burchard notes concerning 1 Cor. 15:45 (244, n. 43) that Adam was not created for mortality.

118. Burchard, loc. cit.

119. Ibid., 252.

that they, too, have forfeited the glory of God. The reference is not to the loss of a possession. ὑστερεῖσθαί τινος does not mean to lose something or to have lost it. It means "to be deprived of," "not to have it."[120] Paul stresses, therefore, that a child of Adam, as *homo peccator,* does not have the glory that was planned for the first man at his creation. A corresponding statement is when the apostle also declares that this δόξα will be imparted to us at the eschatological resurrection on the basis of the crucifixion and resurrection of Jesus Christ.[121] The resurrection does not restore the *status integritatis* that Adam had in paradise. Instead, it is the first realization of the original purpose God had in creation, a purpose which had been left unfulfilled through the παράβασις of Adam.

The words ἐφ' ᾧ πάντες ἥμαρτον are often taken to mean that alongside the fate announced in v. 12a Paul also mentions the personal guilt of individuals as the cause, in this way emphasizing that we are all responsible for our falling into sin.[122] I do not myself think that this is the meaning, not least because it does not accord with the καὶ οὕτως that ties v. 12a and v. 12b together.[123] The adverb οὕτως has to have a modal sense (in this way), pointing back to what was said in v. 12a. What the statement is saying is that as a result of the fact that sin came into the world through Adam, and death through sin, death now applies to all of us, for we all stand inescapably under the sign of this fact, and therefore we all have sinned.[124] This means that even the πάντες ἥμαρτον is the unavoidable result of Adam's trespass, and death also follows for all. Paul himself will expressly say this a few verses later when describing the consequences of the παράπτωμα or παρακοή of Adam, for through the disobedience of the *one* the many (i.e., all) have become sinners (v. 19a); or through the trespass of *one* condemnation to death has come upon all (v. 18a,

---

120. The renderings of 3:23 are incorrect that point to the loss of the glory of God, or to deprivation of it.

121. Romans 5:2; 8:17f.; 1 Cor. 2:7; 15:43; 2 Cor. 3:18; Phil. 3:20; 1 Thess. 2:12.

122. Cf. e.g., Bornkamm 84, 89; Brandenburger 175ff.; Bultmann 433f.; Jüngel 154f.; Schlier 162f.; Stuhlmacher 80.

123. The chiastic structure of v. 12 is also an argument. The words εἰς πάντας ἀνθρώπους ὁ θάνατος διῆλθεν (B) and ἐφ' ᾧ πάντες ἥμαρτον (A) simply reverse the order connecting sin in the world as cause and the dominion of death in the world as a consequence, as compared with δι' ἑνὸς ἀνθρώπου ἁμαρτία εἰς τὸν κόσμον εἰσῆλθεν (A) and καὶ διὰ τῆς ἁμαρτίας ὁ θάνατος (B).

124. Cf. B. Weiss, *Die paulinische Briefe und der Hebräerbrief,* 2nd ed. Leipzig 1902, 58; A. Jülicher, *Der Brief an die Römer* (SNT 2), 3rd ed. Göttingen 1917, 258f.; Schmithals 175; Käsemann 140f. (ET 148f.).

cf. v. 16bα); or through the trespass of *one* death has gained dominion over all through that *one* (v. 17a); or in consequence of the trespass of one many (i.e., all) have died (v. 15bα).[125] In v. 12b Paul states that death is the punishment for every individual sin,[126] but he also says that through the παράπτωμα or παρακοή of Adam a definitive decision was made already that we would all sin and therefore all fall victim to death. It is not at all the case that each individual repeats what Adam did.[127] The transition from *posse non peccare to non posse non peccare* was made only *once* by Adam. Individuals cannot make the same transition. Viewing things thus, Paul has Genesis 3 in mind. All the descendants of Adam begin their lives outside paradise. They stand already under the shadow of the sin of Adam and their own sin. The statement of Bultmann that sin came into the world through sinning[128] applies strictly only to Adam, the first man. Afterward there is only the destiny of sinning, the factual subjection of all to sin and death as the consequence of individual sin.[129] It was only because Paul saw here a definitive destiny that he could argue that *all of us* without distinction are sinners.[130] Since Adam, and because of Adam, falling into sin has become an inescapable destiny, and sinning means becoming guilty and being guilty before God. This is not just because a free will is given to each individual, and *posse non peccare* is open to all of us. Sin is guilt before God precisely because *by nature* and *objectively* it is ἀσέβεια (Rom. 1:18) and ἔχθρα εἰς θεόν (8:7). It is a fundamental "No" that we address to God when we ought to give to our Creator praise and thanksgiving and obedience and service (1:21).[131] We are no longer defined for a life from God and for God.[132]

---

125. Pesch 53 rightly observes that the sin that came into the world through Adam worked itself out in the sins of all and caused death for all.

126. Schmithals 175.

127. Paul does not share the view of SyrBar 54:19 that Adam alone was the reason why he fell, and that each of us has to become Adam.

128. Bultmann 432, also *Theologie des Neuen Testaments,* 4th ed. Tübingen 1961, 251 (ET I, 186).

129. Schmithals 175.

130. Cf. Schmithals, loc. cit. Weber 317 reverses the flow of 5:12 by saying that when all sinned the dominion of sin was established in the world.

131. Käsemann 141 (ET 149) rightly stress that for Paul sin is "an offense against the deity of God and therefore against the first commandment."

132. For the insight that we are under the destiny of sin from our mother's womb, i.e., from the very first, and yet that sin is our own sin and guilt before God cf. Ps. 51 (esp. 3–5)!

In view of what precedes we can no longer think that Paul adopted a mythical conception of history that can speak of an inherited curse and inherited death, or construe the expression ἐφ' ᾧ πάντες ἥμαρτον as introducing this idea.[133] Verse 12bβ neither breaks into nor corrects what is said in v. 12a and bα. Paul is here emphasizing as sharply as possible that by our own conduct we confirm the fact that we are in a world that is always marked by sin and death. We lie under its lasting curse.[134] This judgment of the apostle rests upon his knowledge of the crucified Christ who died for *all,* for this knowledge makes it clear, clear *beyond all doubt,* how deeply and inescapably all Adamic humanity has fallen.[135]

Looking back upon the way we understand Rom. 5:12, we have to state that from the very first, from Adam, death has the character of an eschatological condemnation. We must stress in advance the fact that it is not given this character only by the law,[136] for v. 14a points to its reign of terror (v. 17a) even in the time between Adam and Moses when there was no law.[137] It is not the law that makes death the result of sin. The law does not first qualify sin and death in a negative way eschatologically. It merely validates the fact that death *is already* the result of sin and that sin and death are phenomena that give a negative qualification eschatologically. In short, the law *tells* us what *is* previously the case. If we ask how a negative qualification eschatologically comes through sin and death, we find the answer in 16bα. The judgment of God (κρίμα) imposes condemnation (κατάκριμα) to death. This κρίμα is not a verdict based solely upon the Torah.[138] The orientation to Genesis 2f. makes it unquestionably clear that Paul has the judgment pronounced upon Adam in mind,[139] the threat of

---

133. Bornkamm 84, and cf. 90, where he says that the law and gospel shatter the mythical conception of 5:12-21 even at the first verse. Bornkamm followed the lead of his teacher R. Bultmann, cf. Bultmann's art. θάνατος in TDNT III,15 and *Theologie des NT* 251ff. (ET 186).

134. Käsemann 141 (ET 149).

135. We must reject the emphatic view of Wilckens 315ff. that the church's doctrine of original sin misunderstands Rom. 5:12-21. No doubt the Old Latin and Vulgate were wrong to translate ἐφ' ᾧ (12b) by *in quo,* and to base faulty theological arguments upon this rendering, yet it is still the case that the doctrine of original sin does appropriately represent what Rom. 5:12 has to say about the fateful character of sin and death.

136. Jüngel 155ff. and Wilckens 318ff. take a different view.

137. It contradicts the clear wording of v. 14a and the whole flow of the text when Wilckens 319 declares that death cannot really have dominion (v. 14) apart from the law.

138. *Contra* Wilckens 324 (and n. 1084), and cf. Jüngel 167.

139. Michel 190, Cranfield 286, Küasemann 146 (ET 154), Stuhlmacher 81.

death in Gen. 2:17b, and its execution in Gen. 3:17-19[140] and 3:22-24 when Adam and his descendants were forbidden access to ζωὴ αἰώνιος.[141]

We have thus far discussed what Paul says about the act of *Adam* and its consequences. We shall now turn to what the apostle says in vv. 15ff. about the act of *Christ* and its consequences.

Paul describes the *act* of Christ, in antithesis to τὸ παράπτωμα of v. 15aα and bα, v. 17a, and v. 18a, as τὸ χάρισμα (v. 15aβ, v. 16bβ) and τὸ δικαίωμα (v. 18b), and then in antithesis to the ἡ παρακοή of v. 19a as ἡ ὑπακοή (b. 19b). The fact that it is in antithesis to παράπτωμα shows that χάρισμα must have here the sense of "act of grace."[142] For rhetorical purposes it is obviously selected in place of χάρις,[143] and this was possible because one of its meanings is "demonstration of grace."[144]

Like χάρισμα, δικαίωμα is plainly chosen because of its likeness to παράπτωμα. It can hardly have the sense of an "act of justification,"[145] or an "act that makes righteous."[146] It's meaning is a "righteous act[147] or deed."[148] The parallel ὑπακοή (v. 9b) shows what is meant in v. 18b. As παρακοή in v. 19a concretely denotes the disobedient *act* of Adam of which we read in Genesis 3, so ὑπακοή in v. 19b focuses on the obedient *act* of Christ, namely, his crucifixion. We need not turn to Phil. 2:8 in elucidation: "The ὑπακοή of Christ is not for Paul a single act but characterizes his total way and work."[149] The fact that Christ died for us even when we were ungodly, sinners, and enemies of God (5:6ff.), in his death taking to himself the κατάκριμα that weighed upon us all (8:3, cf. Gal. 3:13; 2 Cor. 5:21) is called an act of obedience because Christ willed and did what the saving will of his

---

140. We recall here the judgment passed upon Adam in Gen. 3:19: "Dust thou art and to dust thou shalt return" (γῆ εἶ καὶ εἰς γῆν ἀπελεύσῃ).

141. Paul takes up what the author meant to say, for if we link Gen. 3:24 with v. 22 we see that the judgment of God removes from Adam all possibility of gaining eternal life.

142. Cf. Bornkamm 85; Barrett 113 ("act of grace"). But most commentators decide for "gift of grace" (as in Rom. 6:23; 11:29; OrSib 2,54; Did. 1,5; Ignatius Eph. 17,2).

143. For this meaning of χάρις cf. Bauer/Aland 1751f. s.v. 3.

144. Sir. 7:33 S; Philo *Legum allegoriae* III,78 (δωρεὰ . . . καὶ εὐεργεσία καὶ χάρισμα, "gift, benefit, and proof of [God's] grace"); 2 Cor. 1:11.

145. Käsemann 131 (ET 140); Wilckens 306.

146. Bornkamm 88; Wilckens 326.

147. Brandenburger 232; Kuss 224, 238; Barth 77; Schlier 158, 173; Michel 185, 191.

148. Stuhlmacher 78, 82; Dunn 270, 283, 297 ("righteous act or deed"). For this sense cf. Bar. 2:19; Rev. 15:4; Barn. 1,2 (plur.), and Aristotle *Ars Rhetorica* 1359a,25; 1373b,1 (τὸ δικαίωμα as the antonym of τὸ ἀδίκημα).

149. Bornkamm 88 and materially Cranfield 291, Michel 191.

Father had decreed. The ὑπακοή of Christ was not obedience to the law[150] either in the sense of a representative fulfillment[151] or in the sense of an individual, archetypical fulfillment.[152] It is not correct, of course, to describe this ὑπακοή as obedience to the justifying grace of God.[153] For this ὑπακοή is itself the act of a voluntary self-offering to death that affects salvation. It enacts the grace of God (v. 15bβ, v. 17b) and offers proof of the love of God (5:8).

The consequences of this act are described in v. 15bβ: ἡ χάρις τοῦ θεοῦ καὶ (and therewith) ἡ δωρεὰ ἐν χάριτι τῇ τοῦ ἑνὸς ἀνθρώπου Ἰησοῦ Χριστοῦ εἰς τοὺς πολλοὺς ἐπερίσσευσεν. For a proper understanding of the words ἡ δωρεὰ κτλ. the insight is important that not just the expression ἐν χάριτι but the whole phrase ἐν χάριτι τῇ τοῦ ἑνὸς ἀνθρώπου Ἰησοῦ Χριστοῦ defines ἡ δωρεά much more precisely. It is thus inappropriate to see in ἡ δωρεὰ ἐν χάριτι a substitute for ἡ δωρεὰ τῆς χάριτος,[154] and there are no true examples of the use of the ἐν alone in Greek as a genitive.[155, 156] The widespread rendering "the gift of grace (or gracious gift) of the one man Jesus Christ" is therefore inaccurate.[157] The meaning is either "the gift that consists of the grace (the demonstration of grace) of the one man Jesus Christ," or "the gift that is granted through the grace of the one man Jesus Christ." In my view the latter is more probable. For like the grace of God the grace of Jesus Christ is the source of the gift of salvation.[158] Indeed, the grace of God *is* as such the grace of our Lord Jesus Christ (2 Cor. 8:9).[159] The overwhelming fullness and power of the grace referred to in v. 15b lies in the fact that it reverses what Adam

---

150. Rightly stressed in Wilckens 326ff.; Pesch 54; Schmithals 170.

151. So Lietzmann 64: "The representative fulfillment of the demands of the law."

152. So Cranfield 291 and von den Osten-Sacken 167, 171f, though with divergent explanations.

153. Wilckens 328 quoting Pesch 54.

154. Lietzmann 63; Brandenburger 220 n. 3 quoting Bauer; Wilckens 322 n. 1077 (referring to Brandenburger) Cf. Michel 189, n. 10.

155. Bauer 518 s.v. IV.4.b; Bauer/Aland 526 loc. cit. But cf. Bauer 417 and Bauer/Aland 423 s.v. δωρεά : the "gift that is granted in grace."

156. Bauer 518 mentions Philo *Mechanicus* 75,29 (τὸ ἐν τῷ κυλίνδρῳ χοίλασμα) and EpArist 31 (ἡ ἐν αὐτοῖς θεωρία), and Bauer/Aland refer to Tatian *Or.* 18,1 (πᾶν τὸ ἐν αὐτῇ εἶδος). But these are not to the point, for the translations should run "the hole in the cylinder," "the view expressed in the books," and "the phenomenon belonging to medicine." If ἐν as a preposition replaces a genitive we have to see a Hebraism here.

157. Cranfield 285 rightly claims that this translation would need a nominative art., not a dative, after χάριτι.

158. Kuss 235.

159. For the fact that the grace of God and the grace of Christ are one cf. 2 Cor. 6:1 and 8:9; Gal. 2:21 and 1:6. The love of God and the love of Christ are also the same for Paul, cf. Rom. 5:8, 39 on the one side and 2 Cor. 5:14; Gal. 2:20 on the other; cf. also Rom. 8:35, 39.

inaugurated, overpowering the reality of sin and death and breaking their corrupting and destructive might.[160] The gift itself consists of δικαιοσύνη (v. 17b, v. 21b),
or of the δικαίωσις ζωῆς that is identical with the δικαίωμα of 16b (v. 18b). It is justification, a redeeming pardon that sets those who are forgiven under the promise
of eternal life (v. 17b, v. 18b, v. 21b). The redeeming act of Christ (v. 19a) has as its
consequence that the many who became sinners through Adam (v. 19a) have now
become righteous. The future δίκαιοι κατασταθήσονται (unlike the βασιλεύσουσιν
of v. 17b) is not a true eschatological future but a logical future as seen from the
standpoint of Adam).[161] The justification of the wicked that is based upon the
death and resurrection of Christ is *already* a reality, unlike ζωὴ αἰώνιος or participation in the δόξα τοῦ θεοῦ. Along these lines v. 17b expresses the fact of a righteousness *already* given, and a participation in eternal life that is *still awaited,* in
the phrase οἱ τὴν περισσείαν τῆς χάριτος καὶ τῆς δωρεᾶς τῆς δικαιοσύνης
λαμβάνοντες ἐν ζωῇ βασιλεύσουσιν διὰ τοῦ ἑνός, Ἰησοῦ Χριστοῦ. When Paul, with
the gift of justification in view, refers to the περισσεία τῆς χάριτος, he is thinking
of the deductions from major to minor in Rom. 5:8f., 10. Similarly the participle
λαμβάνοντες catches up the ἐλάβομεν of v. 11 (δι' οὗ νῦν τὴν καταλλαγὴν
ἐλάβομεν). The participle in no way limits the universality of the statements in vv.
15f., as though the πάντες refers only to those who receive the gift of grace. In a
critical debate with Kuss Wilckens has rightly stressed this point.[162] The same objection is also made against Bultmann's observation regarding v. 17b that while
logically Christ should grant life to all, that is not Paul's meaning, for he presupposes that we all have to decide whether or not we belong to the λαμβάνοντες
when the word of proclamation reaches us. Adam brought death to us all with no
possibility of escape, but Christ has provided this *possibility* for all.[163] Bornkamm,
too, introduces a thought that is alien to the text when in his interpretation of v. 17b
he notes that the reign of grace mentioned in v. 21b presupposes acceptance of the

---

160. "What was done" is meant in v. 16! Lietzmann misses the point of the verse when he takes
it to mean that the condemnation was the reaction to *one* sin that grace has shown to be incalculable
and unending in its intensity. Dubious, too, are the observations of Bornkamm 86, Brandenburger
226, and Zeller 119 relative to v. 16.

161. So, e.g., Cranfield 291 and Wilckens 328. The statements in v. 17b, v. 18b, and v. 21b support a logical future, and cf. Rom. 5:1, 9. Gal. 5:5 offers no support for an eschatological future, for
ἐλπὶς δικαιοσύνης does not mean "hoped for righteousness" but "the hope that is guaranteed by the
righteousness (already given)."

162. Wilckens 325 contra Kuss 237.

163. Bultmann 437, cf. *Theologie des NT,* 253.

offer of grace.[164] In fact statements of this kind undermine the argument of 5:12-21, namely, the thought that basically grace is of overpowering strength. For how can we seriously regard something as overpowering when it is merely an offer that has to be accepted,[165] and that can thus prove to be effective only when it is accepted? In this connection we have to ask on what grounds Adamic people, who have fallen victim to sin and death, can have any dealings with an offer of grace and can therefore enter into a positive relation with God. The idea that in the encounter with the word of proclamation they are set anew in the state of the *posse non peccare* enjoyed by Adam before the fall is one that Paul himself never for one moment entertained. The opinions quoted above presuppose that the expressions πάντες ἄνθρωποι and οἱ πολλοί in the Adam-Christ antithesis of 5:12-21 are used ambiguously. In relation to Adam the "all" unequivocally means "all" the descendants of Adam, but in relation to Christ the "all" means only those who are the recipients of grace, i.e., "all" Christians.

Can this interpretation be supported exegetically? One might, of course, quote 1 Cor. 15:22f. Here in relation to Christ the πάντες of v. 22b is taken up and given further definition by the οἱ τοῦ Χριστοῦ of v. 23b. But a restrictive defining of this kind is not found in Rom. 5:12-21. On the contrary, ἐπίγειοι and καταχθόνιοι [Phil. 2:10] of the second strophe of the hymn to Christ in Phil. 2:6-11)[166] cannot be simply rejected.[167] Should we ask how the πάντες relative to Christ connects with the πάντες οἱ πιστεύοντες of Rom. 3:22 (cf. 1:16; 10:4), we must note that Paul conceives of faith strictly as the work and gift of *God*. Hence the οἱ πιστεύοντες in no sense implies a reference to a condition that we must fulfill.[168] In principle there are two possibilities of answering the question posed above. If the use of πάντες in Rom. 5:12-21 is non-equivocal, even the

---

164. Bornkamm 87.

165. Bornkamm ad loc. admits that the grace of Christ is an overpowering reality, but it is so only when it is grasped. Unlike sin, it does not work naturally or by force, like a spell or a curse, even though it is aimed at the world, at all who are in the world. Bornkamm is right when he argues that the working of grace is basically different from that of sin, but this does not permit him to reject the concept of irresistible grace. *Irresistible* is defined by *grace*. We have thus to speak of the compelling grace and love of God which savingly overcomes our ungodly rejections. We must rightly assert this relative to the irrelevant comparisons which are to be found in H. G. Pöhlmann, *Abriß der Dogmatik. Ein Kompendium,* 4th ed. 1985, Gütersloh, 261ff.

166. Cf. O. Hofius, *Der Christushymnus Philipper 2:6-11, Untersuchungen zu Gestalt und Aussage eines urchristlichen Psalms* (WUNT 17), Tübingen, 2nd ed. 1991, 18ff., 122ff.

167. Cf. also the πάντες of Rom. 11:32 and the universal statement in 2 Cor. 5:19.

168. For fuller support cf. my essay "Wort und Glaube bei Paulus," *Paulusstudien,* 148-174.

words πάντες οἱ πιστεύοντες must be given a universal sense. If the use is equivocal, then those words are particularizing and exclusive. Relative to Christ, the πάντες must always be defined as those who in the power of the death and resurrection of Christ have been led by the decision made on their behalf to faith in Christ as their Savior.

5. The Statement in Romans 5:13 and 14a

As our structural analysis has shown, vv. 13 and 14a are an explanatory note linking up with v. 12b, which tells us that death has come to *all* because *all* have sinned. Paul needs to make it clear, with reference to the time without the Torah between Adam and Moses, why he can talk in this way. In his earlier discussion of sin,[169] and of death as its ineluctable consequence,[170] he had always related the two very strictly to the Sinaitic Torah. The great attack in the first part of Romans (1:18–3:20) had been upon our human ungodliness and unrighteousness (1:18), and 3:9-20 makes it unmistakably clear that the basis of this complaint is the Torah (v. 20).[171] In the context of the accusation it is stressed that by the norm of the Torah only the ποιηταὶ νόμου will be accounted righteous at the last judgment (2:13). According to the Targum on Isaiah, which Paul endorsed, a doer of the Torah is a righteous person who has never sinned and who has kept the Torah with a perfect heart.[172] Paul, however, believes without fail that there has never been, and never will be, a ποιητὴς νόμου in the humanity deriving from Adam.[173] We all of us stand in the shadow of Adam. None of us can go back before Adam. This means, however, that judged by the Torah we all without exception prove to be παραβάται νόμου,[174] and as such we are guilty before God and righteously condemned (3:19f.).

---

169. The predominant theme of 1:18–3:20, and cf. also 3:22b, 23; 3:25; 4:6ff., 25; 5:6ff.

170. We read that death is the consequence of sin not only in 1:32 but materially also in 2:5ff, 12 and especially 3:23. Regarding καὶ ὑστεροῦνται τῆς δόξης τοῦ θεοῦ in 3:23, Jüngel 155 has the excellent comment that if the δόξα τοῦ θεοῦ is lacking, then ζωή is also lacking, and those who lack ζωή receive death as the wages of sin.

171. Note that in c. 2 νόμος is used 16 times for the Torah of Sinai (vv. 12-15, 17f, 20, 23, 25f.).

172. Cf. O. Hofius, "'Rechtfertigung des Gottlosen' als Thema biblischer Theologie," *Paulusstudien* 127.

173. Loc. cit.

174. The term παραβάτης νόμου occurs in Rom. 2:25, 27, cf. Gal. 2:18.

The term παράβασις τοῦ νόμου (2:23) means objectively transgression of the will of God expressly declared and written down in the Torah. It is an objective trespassing over the boundary that is expressly drawn by the holy, just, and good commandments of God.[175] We can speak of παράβασις only when there is an express commandment of God and the boundary is expressly indicated. This is the condition for describing and characterizing sin as a "transgression." But if by nature sin is ἀσέβεια (1:18) and ἔχθρα εἰς θεόν (8:7), if it is a fundamental rejection of God and his will, then the Torah of Sinai defines the sin as παράβασις because it rejects the God who *speaks* in the law and the will of God that is there *declared*. In the second part of Romans (3:21–4:25), which deals with God's redeeming act in Jesus Christ, the Torah is one of the themes, for in the very first sentence Paul describes this act as one that has taken place χωρὶς νόμου (3:21).[176] This tells us first that the act of God is independent of the law. It took place without the law's participation. But the main point is that the accusation brought by the Torah, and the condemnation that it shows to be valid, are both put to silence where Jesus Christ intervenes for sinners with his atoning death.[177] In the redeeming act of God there has taken place in Jesus Christ that which was totally impossible according to the law and "under the law," namely, the justification of those that the law calls the ungodly (4:5, cf. 5:6). In regard to this event Rom. 4:7 quotes Ps. 31:1 LXX: "Blessed are those whose lawless acts are forgiven and whose sins are covered." The words ἀνομίαι and ἁμαρτίαι are parallel here, making it clear once again that sin is viewed as transgression of the Torah.[178] Similarly 4:15b says that the Torah that accuses sinners, and places them inescapably under the wrath of God,[179] has now been silenced by the saving act of God, for there is now no παράβασις, it has been forgiven.[180]

In the first two parts of Romans, Paul always relates sin and death to the Torah.

---

175. It is not important whether the transgression is conscious or not.

176. χωρὶς νόμου in 3:21 corresponds to χωρὶς ἔργων νόμου in 3:28 and χωρὶς ἔργων in 4:6.

177. The χωρὶς νόμου of 3:21 is an exact antithesis of the διὰ νόμου of 3:20b.

178. Cf. also of 3:20b; 6:15, 23, where the ἁμαρτία of vv. 16ff., 20, 22f. is as such ἀνομία (v. 19).

179. The phrase ὁ νόμος ὀργὴν κατεργάζεται ("the law brings only wrath") in 4:15a tells us that when we have to do with the Torah, because this causes transgression, we inevitably have to do with the eschatological wrath of God, and with this alone. If we are to understand the antithetical statement of 4:15, we must note structurally that each half of the verse contains one of the points that Paul is making: v. 15a: νόμος [παράβασις] → ὀργή, v. 15b: οὐ νόμος → οὐδὲ παράβασις → [οὐδὲ ὀργή]. For ὀργή as God's eschatological wrath cf. 1:18; 2:5; 3:5; 5:9.

180. If we see the verse strictly in the context of c. 4, with special reference to vv. 5ff., this is the point of 4:15b: οὗ δὲ οὐκ ἔστιν νόμος οὐδὲ παράβασις. Cf. Kuss 188f., and Wilckens 271.

This being so, we might get the impression, as Paul himself obviously did, that the combination of sin and death will be present only when the Torah is also present. Yet this is not the case, as the apostle makes clear in his explanatory note (5:13, 14). For he also stresses the reality and universality of sin (v. 13a) and its consequence, namely, death (v. 14a), in the time before the law. The dominion of sin and death inaugurated by Adam is thus independent of the Torah. It is a reality already present; the Mosaic law proclaims it. The note in v. 13 and v. 14a expresses implicitly what Paul will later develop emphatically in chapter 7. The Sinaitic Torah is the cause neither of sin (7:7) nor of death (7:13).[181] Yet it is plain, too, that the nature of sin and death are not decided by the relation to the Torah. The saying in v. 14a, then, distinguishes sin in the time without the law from the sin of Adam only by reason of the fact that it its not the transgression of a concretely issued commandment of God. Sin again becomes transgression with the lawgiving at Sinai. Objectively, the law now shows it to be a rejection of the *declared* will of God and, therefore, of *God himself,* as the one who gave the Torah. The Sinaitic Torah defines and characterizes the prior sin of Adam as παράβασις and, therefore, a mortal offense (cf. Rom. 1:32). But the nature of sin is not hereby constituted. When sin is shown by nature to be ἀσέβεια and ἔχθρα εἰς θεόν this throws light on it with revealing clarity and powerfully demonstrates how absolutely it is worthy of punishment. Similarly death is from the very first defined as the death of judgment and the curse. The fact that it is thus defined finds clear and valid expression in the Torah.

To this state of affairs there corresponds something that is dealt with in v. 13b: ἁμαρτία δὲ οὐκ ἐλλογεῖται μὴ ὄντος νόμου. This saying is difficult and its exegesis has given rise to highly controversial interpretations. Its formulation in the present separates it off from its context (ἦν in v. 13a, ἐβασίλευσεν in v. 14a). To understand it properly it is essential that we pay attention to the chiastic structure of v. 13 which finds forceful emphasis in the epiphora on the outer side (νόμου) and the anaphora (ἁμαρτία) on the inner side:

13a A   ἄχρι γὰρ νόμου
     B   ἁμαρτία ἦν ἐν κόσμῳ,
13b B   ἁμαρτία δὲ οὐκ ἐλλογεῖται
     A   μὴ ὄντος νόμου.

---

181. Cf. Bornkamm 84, who states that death and sin were there before the law. The law did not bring them into being.

The structure shows that the words ἁμαρτία δὲ οὐκ ἐλλογεῖται relate directly to the phrase ἁμαρτία ἦν ἐν κόσμῳ and that the adverbial definition μὴ ὄντος νόμου corresponds directly to the expression ἄχρι νόμου. This makes it clear that what is said in v. 13b relates precisely to the period that is spoken of in v. 13a and then again in v. 14, namely, to the historical time when there was no law between Adam and Moses.[182] The *genitivus absolutus* μὴ ὄντος νόμου is neither conditional nor causal. It corresponds to ἄχρι νόμου and must be defined temporally: "so long as there is no law."[183] Hence, v. 13b, though put in the present tense, must not be seen in relation to Jewish statutes,[184] nor as a thesis that Paul himself formulated using Rabbinic legal ideas,[185] nor simply as a general principle,[186] nor as a parallel to Rom. 4:15b, which has been mistakenly equated with it and used as a comparison.[187] Paul chooses the present tense in v. 13b because, with the time between Adam and Moses in view, he is making a basic and universally valid statement which could also be seen as a characteristic of the Torah itself.

But what does ἁμαρτία οὐκ ἐλλογεῖται mean? The more precise interpretations vary,[188] but all the exegetes agree that the verb ἐλλογεῖν in Rom. 5:13b is the equivalent of the word *imputare* in ecclesiastical Latin, so that the verse is to the effect that where there is no law sin is not imputed, or reckoned, or charged to the account, by God and with God. But some then think that sin *as such* is not imputed,[189] others that sin *as transgression* is not imputed.[190] The thesis advanced by G. Friedrich[191] — and before him by H. Preisker![192] — has found broad agreement, namely, that the OT and Jewish idea of heavenly book-

---

182. This was finely seen by the transmitters of the text to whom we owe the reading ἐνελογεῖτο, attested by ℵ* it vg^cl sy.

183. For the genitive absolute as "so long as" cf. Rom. 7:3; ζῶντος τοῦ ἀνδρός, "so long as the husband is alive," also Heb. 9:8; 2 Esdr. 17:3; Job 27:3 LXX; 1 Kgs. 22:4 and 25:7 LXX.

184. Brandenburger 195f. has convincingly refuted this view.

185. *Contra* Brandenburger 195f.; Zeller 117.

186. *Contra* Friedrich 129; Luz 198f.

187. On Rom. 4:15b cf. n. 180.

188. Cf. the references in Friedrich 124ff.; Brandenburger 194ff.; Luz 198ff.

189. Cf. Barth 98, who says that ἁμαρτία ἐλλογεῖται means "literally" that sin is not noted, registered, charged to the account as such.

190. Cf. Pesch 53, who says that sin can be charged as transgression only when the law exists.

191. Friedrich 127f.

192. Preisker, art. ἐλλογέω, TDNT II, 517, n. 5. Brandenburger 197 n. 6, von den Osten-Sacken 166 n. 24, Wilckens 319 n. 1061 were wrong to point to Friedrich as the first to advance this view.

keeping lies behind this ἐλλογεῖσθαι of sin. All our human sins were listed in these books.[193] But linguistically ἐλλογεῖν very definitely does *not* mean "charged to our account."[194] The true meaning[195] is that of "taking into account." The construction used is ἐλλογεῖν τινί τι. Paul uses the same construction in Philemon when he says: "If he has wronged you or owes you anything, charge it to "If he has wronged you or owes you anything, charge it to me" (τοῦτο ἐμοὶ ἐλλόγα).[196] As this verse from Philemon makes clear, the word ἐλλογεῖν does not have to do with private or public bookkeeping, i.e., the process whereby we note down and keep a record of the fact that others owe us something, and of what they owe us.[197] On the contrary, the verb tells us of an act that is directed outwards to the debtor. The debtor is shown the account, he or she is told very plainly what is owed, and the sum must be met.[198] Thus the figurative meaning in v. 13b is this. The passive ἐλλογεῖται in no way points to an activity in the heavenly world.[199] Materially God is the subject, but what is clearly at issue is the one addressed. It is an expression *ad hominem*. We need to add as an object τῷ ἁμαρτήσαντι (or τοῖς ἁμαρτήσασιν) which the author leaves out for the sake of brevity. Verse 13b tells us of the days without the law between Adam and Moses, when sin was not imputed to the sinner so long as there was no law. The basic implication is the fact that the account is presented to the sinner in and with the Torah. But this means that the Torah first brings to

---

193. Brandenburger 197ff.; von den Osten-Sacken 166 n. 24; Schlier 164f.; Michel 187, n. 6; Wilckens 319; Käsemann 141 (ET 149); Zeller 117; Schmithals 177; Dunn 274; Stuhlmacher 81.

194. *Contra* M. Dibelius and H. Greeven, *An die Kolosser, Epheser, an Philemon* (HNT 12), 3rd ed. 1955, Tübingen 106; E. Lohse, *Die Briefe an die Kolosser und an Philemon* (KEK IX,2), 14th ed. 1968, Göttingen 284, n. 2; Luz 199, n. 243; Bauer 500 s.v. ἐλλογέω (rightly corrected in Bauer and Aland 509 s.v.).

195. Cf. A. Deissmann, *Licht vom Osten,* 4th ed. 1923, Tübingen 66; J. H. Moulton and G. Milligan, *The Vocabulary of the Greek Testament Illustrated from the Papyri and Other Non-Literary Sources,* Grand Rapids 1976, 204b s.v. ἐλλογάω (έω); F. Preisigke and E. Kiessling, *Wörterbuch der griechischen Papyruskunden,* Berlin I, 1925, 471 s.v. ἐλλογέω; IV, 1944, 771 ad loc.; Preisker, TDNT II, 517. For materials cf. Moulton and Milligan, op. cit.; Dibelius and Greeven 106; Lohse (see n. 194) 284, n. 2; T. Nägeli, *Der Wortschatz des Apostels Paulus. Beitrag zur sprachgeschichtlichen Erforschung des NT,* Göttingen 1905, 48.

196. "Write on my account" is an incorrect translation (Dibelius and Greeven, op. cit.).

197. *Not* "as of an entry made in a ledger" (Sanday and Headlam, *The Epistle to the Romans* [ICC], 5th ed. Edinburgh 1992, 135).

198. Cf. the synonym ἐλλογίζω in Clement of Alexandria *Stromateis* III,I,31,1 (quoted from Isidorus Gnosticus). G. W. H. Lampe, *A Patristic Greek Lexicon,* Oxford 1978, 452a has "set down against" as the traditional use (κόλασις — punishment — is recognized).

199. Cf. Friedrich's thesis (124).

expression and to knowledge that which has already been the reality for all of us from the days of Adam, namely, that we are sinners, and that under the condemnation of God, death is the consequence of our sins. This is all brought to our knowledge and given just and valid expression by the Torah. The Torah tells us in black and white what the ousting of Adam from paradise (Gen. 2:16f.) has previously told in the form of a threat, namely, that death is the wages of sin (Rom. 6:23a). The Torah given to Israel at Sinai thus holds before us the judgment of God, the condemnation and death sentence passed upon us all. Romans 5:13b speaks of the *usus elenchticus legis* in the sense of an *objective* conviction of sin.[200] The saying ἁμαρτία οὐκ ἐλλογεῖται μὴ ὄντος νόμου thus corresponds to what is said in Rom. 3:20b: διὰ . . . νόμου ἐπίγνωσις ἁμαρτίας: The Torah brings sin to our knowledge by documenting and activating the accusation of God in such sort that all of us, both Jews and Gentiles, are ὑφ' ἁμαρτίαν (3:9). We are thus told without ambiguity how we stand before a just and holy God (3:19).[201]

In the explanatory note of vv. 13 and 14a regarding the time without the law between Adam and Moses, a firm assessment of the Torah is thus presupposed. The Torah does not initiate the combination of sin and death. It finds it already there. But it shows that it is really there. It brings it to inevitable expression. It objectively clarifies that *each of us* is *homo peccator,* the one who has fallen victim to death as the κατάκριμα imposed by God.[202] Without the law we cannot know the fact that we are sinners standing under the divine sentence and justly condemned to eternal death.

This interpretation implicitly rejects all other interpretations of these difficult and controverted verses.[203] In this context we can hardly refer to these or

---

200. That Rom 5:13b is a statement *ad hominem* dealing dogmatically with the *usus elenchticus legis* is something that in spite of all its problems in detail both Augustine and Luther were rightly convinced of, cf. Luther's *Vorlesung über den Römerbrief* 1515/1516, Lateinisch-Deutsche Ausgabe, Darmstadt 1960, I 348ff. on 5:13 (ET *Luther's Works* 25, 302f.). The undifferentiated reference in Friedrich 123f. does not do justice to Luther and other Reformers, and Schmithals 176 very briefly and superficially calls the interpretation of the Reformers totally erroneous.

201. Cf. also Rom. 1:32, for it is only God's νόμος that shows us that it is his righteous decree that sinners deserve eternal death.

202. Similarly 2 Corinthians 3 calls the "ministry" of Moses a διακονία τῆς κατακρίσεως and διακονία τοῦ θανάτου (vv. 9, 7).

203. This interpretation does *not* result in the contradictions and inconsistencies noted in Bultmann 433.

comment upon them.[204] But in relation to the place and function of the Torah we must at least refer very briefly to the interpretation of Jüngel and Wilckens, for this has far-reaching consequences. Jüngel gathers from the verb ἐλλογεῖσθαι in v. 13b that it is the function of the nomos eschatologically to qualify ἁμαρτία (negatively) as παράβασις.[205] He then proceeds in detail[206] to state that without the law sin cannot have eschatological validity as sin. The law is there for the sake of transgressions, i.e., to give sin eschatological validity (Gal. 3:19). By its very nature the law gives this validity to what is there already, i.e., to sin from the days of Adam. It is thus indispensable to the correspondence between Adam and Christ. For on the basis of Paul's doctrine of justification this correspondence can be for him only an eschatological one. Relative to this correspondence, the Christ side is from the very first eschatological. Not, however, the side belonging to Adam. But the law gives it this qualification by giving eschatological validity to the sin that was already there. It does this to the Adam side by *negatively* qualifying this side *eschatologically* by the linking of sin and death.

Wilcken's interpretation follows much the same line as that of Jüngle. The law for the first time gives eschatologically forensic power to the ὀργή that is visited upon sin. This applies to every sinner as such. An eschatological documenting of sins thus applies retrospectively to all those who lived between Adam and Christ.[207]

The main objection to both these interpretations is that they take the verb ἐλλογεῖσθαι in v. 13b to mean "imputed *by* God and *with* God," a sense which is philologically untenable. A further objection is that the nexus of sin and death is clearly given a negative eschatological qualification by the κρίμα of God passed upon Adam. *From the very outset,* however, the Adam side of the antithesis has this qualification. It does not need the law to acquire it.

---

204. I point again to the references given in n. 188. We might add to these by mentioning Käsemann's interpretation (141, ET 149f.), which rests on an unhappy exegesis of Rom. 1:24ff. According to Käsemann vv. 13 and 14a tell us that under the law we can expect "judgment . . . on the last day," but during the time before the law "punishment falls on committed sin according to the nexus of act and consequence described in 1:24ff when the world is 'handed over' by the wrath of God to general corruption."

205. Jüngel 157.

206. Ibid. 158f.

207. Wilckens 319f.

6. The Statement in Romans 5:20 and 21

The Torah had already been under discussion in vv. 13 and 14a and now it is referred to again in vv. 20 and 21 at the end of the section. These verses speak about its function and operation. An unexpressed question is the occasion. Paul had expressly raised this question in Gal. 3:19. If salvation comes only through Christ, what is the point of the law?

Verse 20a speaks expressly about the Torah: νόμος δὲ παρεισῆλθεν, ἵνα πλεονάσῃ τὸ παράπτωμα. Our structural analysis has shown us that within the contrast of Adam and Christ this verse belongs to the Adam side of the equation. A material analysis of the content will confirm this result.

We must first look into the meaning of the words νόμος δὲ παρεισῆλθεν. We must state emphatically that the verb παρεισέρχεσθαι does *not* mean "come or enter between."[208] There is no grammatical support for the view of Bultmann that the law is an entity that stands between Adam and Christ,[209] or for the view of Schlatter that the law came between sin and righteousness, between death and life, between Adam and Christ.[210] Nor does the verb offer linguistic support for the far-reaching thesis of Jüngel that according to v. 20 the function of the law is to give a higher potency to sin, giving it eschatological validity, and that in this way it is a theologically necessary intervention between Adam and Christ[211] if there is to be correspondence between them.[212]

On such views the verb παρέρχεσθαι, which means "to come (alongside),"[213] in a questionable way has the negative force of "to intervene" or "intrude." Commentators say that it does so secretly,[214] that it sneaks in[215] or slips

---

208. Contra Barth's *Römerbrief* 1st ed. 144; 2nd ed. 161 (ET 182ff.); *Christus und Adam* 102 (ET 85); Schlatter 193; Bornkamm 88; Brandenburger 249ff.; Nygren 166f.; Schmidt 96, 102; Stuhlmacher 78, 82, etc. We find this error in Calvin 92 on 5:20a when he says that the law intervenes, and cf. Theodoret of Cyrrhus, *Interpretatio Epistolae ad Romanos, ad loc.* (MPG 82, 104 B): τοῦ δὲ Ἀβραὰμ καὶ τοῦ Χριστοῦ μέσος παρεισῆλθεν ὁ νόμος.

209. Bultmann 439.

210. Schlatter 193, and Bornkamm 88, who also states that the law has intervened between sin and righteousness, death and life, Adam and Christ. Cf. Nygren 166; Jüngel 171.

211. Jüngel 171.

212. Ibid. 171f., cf. 159.

213. Epicurus, Frgm. 281 (351,11 Usener): Plutarch, *De sollertia animalium* 964 C.

214. Polybius II,55.3; Plutarch, *De genio Socratis* 596 A; Lucian, *Gallus* 28; *Dialogi Meretricii* 12,3.

215. Plutarch, *Coriolanus* 23,1; *De sollertia animalium* 980B.

in,[216] that it enters cunningly.[217] The word, however, simply means "to pene-trate,"[218] "to arrive,"[219] "to enter,"[220] "to arrive in addition."[221] The accent is not negative. A fully neutral use may be seen in Philo's *De ebrietate* 157 when he states that among the unhappy effects of ἄγνοια for the soul is that it causes no light or word to enter (μήτε φῶς μήτε λόγον παρεισελθεῖν ἐῶσα).[222] We find a similar neutral, not negative, use in Rom. 5:20a.[223] The saying νόμος δὲ παρεισῆλθεν has in mind what is said in v. 12a: ἡ ἁμαρτία εἰς τὸν κόσμον εἰσῆλθεν καὶ διὰ τῆς ἁμαρτίας ὁ θάνατος. It is to the effect that the law "is added."[224] We might put it thus: The law comes into the world subsequent to sin and death,[225] or: The law has also entered the world from outside. Either way the meaning is that the law has been added to the nexus of sin and death that was initiated with and by Adam.[226] This is not a derogatory judgment.[227] By no means is the law a "subsidiary factor" in the divine plan of salvation.[228] What is clear is that the Sinaitic Torah very certainly belongs to the side of sin and death, and therefore to that of Adam.

---

216 Galatians 2:4; Philo, *De Abrahamo* 96; Plutarch, *Publicola* 17,2; Cicero 28,2; Ps.-Lucian, *Asinus* 15. Perhaps TestJud 16,2 has the sense "to slip in," though cf. n. 221.

217. Polybius I,7,3.

218. Philo, *De opificio mundi* 150; Diodorus Siculus XVIII, 105,1; cf. παρεισπορεύεσθαι in 2 Macc. 8:1.

219. Polybius I,8,4; Plutarch, *Lucullus* 9,8; Diodorus Siculus XII,27, 2.

220. Philo, *De ebrietate* 157; Clement of Alexandria, *Paedagogus* II,III, 38,5; *Stromateis* III,II,7,3.

221. The sense of addition is found in Clement's *Stromateis* I,II, 20,3 and perhaps in TestJud 16,2: παρεισέρχεται ἡ ἀναισχυντία, "shamelessness is added (to drunkenness)."

222. M. Adler in Philo von Alexandria, *Die Werke in deutscher Übersetzung* V, Berlin, 2nd ed. 1962, 57 has the rendering: "Ignorance forbids the entry of light and the word."

223. Typically different from Gal. 2:4!

224. So such older lexicons as C. A. Wahl, *Novi Testamenti philologica*, Editio minor, Leipzig 1831, 252b s.v. ("insuper accedo") J. H. Thayer, *A Greek-English Lexicon of the NT,* Edinburgh 4th ed. 1961, 487b s.v. ("to enter in addition, come in besides"), S. C. Schirlitz and T. Eger, *Griechisch-deutsches Wörterbuch zum NT,* Giessen 6th ed. 1908, 318a s.v. ("noch ausserdem dazukommen"), H. Ebeling, *Griechisch-deutsches Wörterbuch zum NT,* Hanover 3rd ed. 1929, 320a s.v. ("komme [daneben] ausserdem dazu"). One might compare προσετέθη in Gal. 3:19 with παρεισῆλθεν in Rom. 5:20a.

225. One may compare Clement's *Stromateis* II,II, 7,3: τό τε ἐμὸν καὶ τὸ σόν φησι διὰ τῶν νόμων παρεισελθεῖν, "He (Epiphanius) maintained that the terms 'my' and 'thy' were brought into the world by laws."

226. Cf. T. Beza, *Testamentum Novum,* Geneva 4th ed. 1588, II,39: The law came in later, i.e., to add to the guilt of those who are contaminated by the one sin.

227. Rightly stressed by Wilckens 328f. and Cranfield 291f.

228. Cf. Lietzmann 65.

The phrase ἵνα πλεονάσῃ τὸ παράπτωμα tells us what the aim and goal of this addition of the law is.[229] Exegetes have debated the meaning of this phrase. We must surely see first that it is a function of the law to reveal the full extent of our human failure, our sin. But what is the more precise meaning? Bultmann suggested that he law provokes us to sin by making us seek our own righteousness through observing it. It kindles in us καυχᾶσθαι, our basic human sin.[230] Wilckens is right to refute this interpretation.[231] His own view is in keeping with the way he interprets vv. 13 and 14a. But it, too, is unconvincing. As he sees it, Paul was saying that through the law sin achieves its full power, the power to destroy eternally.[232]

If we are to understand the meaning of the words ἵνα πλεονάσῃ τὸ παράπτωμα, we must first recognize that here the verb πλεονάζειν expresses both a quantitative and a qualitative enhancement of sin. This means that the clause in v. 20a is to be understood along the lines of Romans 7. The law compels sin to demonstrate its full power and greatness by arousing within us the sleeping sinful passion (Rom. 7:5) and by kindling the latent ἐπιθυμία directed against God (Rom. 7:7ff.).[233] The Torah plainly tells us to do this or not to do that. Sin rises up against it, sharply rejecting the divine command or prohibition. In opposition to the νόμος τοῦ θεοῦ it sets up its own νόμος, forces it upon us, demands our subjection, and thus makes us disobedient to God (Rom. 7:17ff.). Our reaction against the Torah makes it plain that we are the slaves and playthings of sin. We have fallen hopeless victims to it, and this fully demonstrates the reality of what began with Adam.

This reaction is the theme of Rom. 1:32: οἵτινες τὸ δικαίωμα τοῦ θεοῦ ἐπιγνόντες ὅτι οἱ τὰ ποιαῦτα πράσοοντες ἄξιοι θανάτου εἰσίν, οὐ μόνον αὐτὰ ποιοῦσιν ἀλλὰ καί συνευδοκοῦσιν τοῖς πράσσουσιν. Here we see the concrete reality of the sin that takes place in the presence of the Torah, in which we may know its legal demand and legal definition. Paul offers a basic theological for-

---

229. The conjunction ἵνα has a final and not a consecutive sense, cf. Chrysostom, *Commentarius in Epistolam ad Romanos, ad loc.* (MPG 60, 478). Luther misunderstood it (*Works* 25,307).

230. Bultmann 439, also Brandenburger 252f.; Jüngel 171, n. 88.

231. Wilckens 329 n. 1104.

232. Ibid. 329, and cf. Jüngel 171 with his claim that the function of the law is to give the sin that is already there its full potency, and to give it eschatological validity.

233. Cf. the two ἵνα clauses in Rom. 7:13. We might also adduce 1 Cor. 15:56b: ἡ δὲ δύναμις τῆς ἁμαρτίας ὁ νόμος. The reference is to the thing that makes sin so strong and powerful because it reveals its full power and dreadfulness, namely, the law.

mula in Rom. 8:7: τὸ φρόνημα τῆς σαρκὸς ἔχθρα εἰς θεόν, τῷ γὰρ νόμῳ τοῦ θεοῦ οὐχ ὑποτάσσεται, οὐδὲ γὰρ δύναται. By the concrete disobedience which is the necessary reaction of the σάρκινος ἄνθρωπος (7:14) against God's law, it is plain that we who come from Adam are inescapably in contradiction with the will of God. We are thus ungodly, enemies of God.

The statement in 5:20a expresses two things. For one thing it is now evident, as in vv. 13 and 14a, that the Torah precedes the reality of sin and death. It is not caused by them. For another, the placing of the law on the side of Adam and the definition of its goal (ἵνα πλεονάσῃ τὸ παράπτωμα) make it abundantly clear that the Sinaitic Torah is of no help whatsoever when we face the nexus of sin and death. It cannot be a protection against sin. It cannot dam it up. It certainly cannot control it or break its power.[234] Above all, it cannot open up the way of life for sinners, or give them life (Gal. 3:21b).[235] Making this statement, Paul is in fundamental opposition to the way that older Judaism understood the Torah, namely, as a means of resisting sin, its function being to guard against it,[236] and to open up for those upon whom the fall of Adam had brought the sentence of death the possibility of deliverance, the way of life[237] Paul does *not* say this and cannot say it, for his knowledge of Christ and the atoning event of his crucifixion and resurrection is the only basis for the conquering of sin and for the winning of access to eternal life.

Paul adds to his statement in v. 20a the saying: οὗ δὲ ἐπλεόνασεν ἡ ἁμαρτία, ὑπερεπερίσσευσεν ἡ χάρις (v. 20b). This is a strong reference to God's saving work in Jesus Christ, namely, to the victory of grace over sin achieved in the Christ event.[238] Relative to the adverb that introduces the saying, there is even less of a case than in Rom. 4:15b or 2 Cor. 3:17b that the οὗ denotes the condi-

---

234. Schmidt 97 rightly observes that the law is not the power that can set a limit to the dominion of sin.

235. Schmidt is also right when he claims that the law is not seen as a power to give life (102). Cf. Luther's quotation of Augustine (*Works* 25, 307) and his own comment that "the law did not come in to take away sin or to make alive."

236. Cf. LevR 1,10 on 1:1 and the material in Billerbeck IV/1,476f.

237. Cf. 4 Esr. 7:21ff, 88ff. 127ff.; 9:7ff., 30ff.; 14:22; SyrBar 85:3ff. On the Torah as the law of life, granting it or opening up the way to it, cf. Sir. 17:11; 45:5; Bar. 3:9; 4:1; PsSol. 14:2; 4 Esr. 14:30; SyrBar 38:2; TargPsJon Deut. 30:19f.; also the Rabbinic materials in Billerbeck III, 129ff., 237, 277f.

238. We cannot agree with Schmithals (179) when he says that the greater sin became, so much the greater became grace, nor with Schlier (177), who says that the more sin gained power, so much the more did grace gain power.

tion rather than the place.[239] The saying does not speak of the condition for the ὑπερπερισσεύειν of grace but of our lost *situation,* whose full hopelessness has been displayed by the law, but into which grace comes in victoriously. The statement is about ourselves. We have become inescapably the victims of sin and death. The law has unmasked us as sinners. We are under righteous condemnation. But God in his far more powerful grace, which conquers sin and death, has turned to us in Jesus Christ. No final link is made here between the enhancing of sin by the law (v. 20a) and the emergence of a much more mighty grace (v. 20b).[240] Not with a single syllable does Paul assert that the law is in the service of grace by increasing the guilt of sin,[241] or that it has the divinely appointed (ἵνα) task of negatively preparing the way for grace by increasing sin,[242] or that through that increase it contributes to the superabundant measure of grace, to its περισσεία,[243] or that as an instrument of death it forms the presupposition on which the grace of God can be imparted to us,[244] or that it is a temporary but materially necessary transitional stage which has the function of eschatologically preparing the way that leads from Adam and sin to Christ and his grace.[245] Such interpretations overlook the fact, or do not take it seriously enough, that the sole purpose of the ἵνα clause in v. 20 is to tell us what was the goal of the νόμος, the goal of the legislation that God gave at Sinai. The reference of the divine purpose expressed in the ἵνα clause in v. 21 is exclusively to the statement in v. 20b. It tells us very strictly what is the purpose that lies behind the ὑπερπερισσεύειν of grace.[246]

If the interpretations cited above must be seen as *eisegesis,* the same is even

---

239. So Bauer/Aland 1193 s.v. 1b. Nor does the saying quoted fit the passage mentioned for Josephus (*Antiquitates Judaicae* II,272).

240. Galatians 3:24 also is not to be seen as a final clause. The context of 3:19–4:7 and vv. 19 and 23-25 leave us in no doubt that we are to take εἰς Χριστόν in a temporal sense ("up to the coming of Christ") and that the saying ἐκ πίστεως δικαιωθῶμεν expounds the words εἰς Χριστόν ("for we are to be justified by faith").

241. Schlatter 193, who falsely claims both that the law stands in the service of grace and that Adam was a forerunner of Christ.

242. Bornkamm 89, and cf. Schmidt 103.

243. Schlier 177.

244. Von der Osten-Sacken 173, and cf. Wilckens 329 (see n. 248).

245. Balz 87 (see n. 208).

246. Wilckens 329f. is mistaken when he claims that sin *was meant* to gain full dominion over the world through death, but in the same way grace was meant to achieve its *far superior* dominion. This interpretation rests upon a ἵνα clause that is not found in Paul's text.

more true of the claim supported by many expositors that according to vv. 20f. the law had a soteriological function or significance.[247] Hence we cannot agree with Wilckens that the "more" of grace cancels the "more" of sin. On his view grace acquires its "more" because of sin. Sin is the presupposition on which grace achieves its dominion. In virtue of its radical function on the side of Adam, sin thus has a direct *soteriological* significance.[248] The οὗ at the beginning of v. 20b offers no adequate basis for an interpretation that ascribes to the law a fundamental significance in the emerging of grace to its superior dominion. It is only on a premise that we have already rejected as untenable, namely, that the law alone gives eschatological validity to sin, or gives a negative eschatological qualification to the nexus of sin and death, that Wilckens can say that the *place* of sin, i.e., the *world* (v. 12), becomes such only through the coming of the law, but only, of course, that *as such* it may mark the place for the rule of the grace which with its far mightier power fully takes over the place of sin.[249] Wilckens has here adopted the interpretation of Jüngel. On the premises mentioned above, and assuming that the law is a theologically necessary transitional stage between Adam and Christ, Jüngel reaches the conclusion that the history of sin and death inaugurated with Adam was made the *place* of the new history.[250] For *where* sin became greater because the law intervened, grace became even greater. The οὗ that now replaces ὥσπερ is defined by the law. This substitution brings to light the hermeneutical function of the law based upon its eschatological function. By giving a new potency to sin, the law makes the *history* of sin the *place* for this history of overcoming grace. The history of sin and death can be vanquished only in this history, which thus becomes the *place* of the new history of the grace of God, achieving *permanence* as the place of the new history of the grace of God. Thus far Jüngel.[251] But this interpretation stands or falls with its exegetical presuppositions. In this regard we have to ask whether the adverb οὗ, used in a transferred or improper sense, is not considerably over-interpreted. The formulation οὗ, (ἐκεῖ)[252] . . . is not the expression of

---

247. E.g., Schlier 177; Wilckens 329; Pesch 54; von der Osten-Sacken 173f. (with special emphasis).

248. Wilckens ad loc.

249. Loc. cit. Note the final clause ("only, of course, that") for which there is no basis in Paul's text.

250. Jüngel 171.

251. Loc. cit.

252. On the ellipsed ἐκεῖ cf. Rom. 4:15; 2 Cor. 3:17; Prov. 14:4 LXX; Job 39:30 LXX.

reflections on the "place" of the grace that conquers sin. With it we hear of the unheard of transformation that comes with Christ's gracious act and that completely replaces all that was there before.[253]

7. Conclusion

If we finally try to formulate our findings, we must state that the emphasis in the discussions of Rom. 5:12-21 lies on the contrast between the side of Adam and that of Christ. The universal corruption wrought by Adam is described on the one hand, the universal salvation accomplished by Christ on the other. What is said about the νόμος in vv. 13 and 14a and vv. 20 and 21 does not form part of the main statement, and it is certainly not a hermeneutical key to an understanding of the Adam-Christ antithesis. The sayings about the law are rather necessary observations that define the relation of the Torah to the two sides of the antithesis. The Sinaitic Torah finds its place exclusively on the side of Adam and Adamic humanity. It does not belong to the side of Christ, and it is in no sense something that comes between Adam and Christ. The underlying antithesis of vv. 12-21 thus implies a precise differentiation of the Sinaitic Torah from Christ.

With powerful legal validity the law makes known the fact that human sin stands under the κατάκριμα of God that results in the death of the sinner. The nexus of sin and death is thus *eo ipso* given a negative eschatological qualification. But by making this known, the Torah makes it objectively clear how it stands with the Adamic humanity that derives from Adam and with each individual who stands under the shadow of Adam. It discloses the fact that the history of sin and death that the παράπτωμα of Adam inaugurated is a history that stands under the sign of the κατάκριμα of God. Hence it assigns the judgment of condemnation and death to each individual sinner; this is a reality for all of them.

What we have here, then, is the primal purpose of the Torah according to God's institution. It has no power to guard against sin. Nor can it open up to sinners the way of salvation. By the event of his sin-bearing death and by his resurrection, *Christ* vanquished the history of sin and death that Adam had inaugurated, that stood under the κατάκριμα of God, and that had been shown to

---

253. Cf. the way ἐν τῷ τόπῳ οὗ . . . ἐκεῖ . . . is used in Rom. 9:26 (= Hos. 2:1 LXX).

be such by the Torah. If however, the history of Adam had to be vanquished, the Torah, too, was necessarily concerned, for its task and function stood in relation to this history. In their own way, then, the discussions in 5:12-21 state what Paul would then expressly formulate in Rom. 10:4: "Christ is the *end* of the law for the salvation of those that believe."[254]

---

254. The significance of the Torah for believers in Christ is something I have discussed in relation to Rom. 10:4 in my essay "Das Gesetz des Mose und das Gesetz Christi," *Paulusstudien* (see n. 60) 50-74, esp. 65f.

Hermeneutics of Romans 7

by

HANS HÜBNER

By way of preliminaries I should refer to the exegetical presuppositions upon which my hermeneutical discussion rests. My starting point is that Romans 7 and 8 confront us with two contradictory lifestyles. Romans 8 depicts the life of the justified to which 8:9 refers: πνεῦμα θεοῦ οἰκεῖ ἐν ὑμῖν. Romans 7, however, describes the pitiable state of the nonjustified as seen by those who are already justified.[1] Only those in whom the Spirit of God dwells can truly understand what it means to have ἁμαρτία dwelling in one rather than the Spirit. No contrast can be more radical than that of Rom. 7:17, 20: ἡ ἐνοικοῦσα ἐν ἐμοὶ ἁμαρτία and ἐνοικοῦν ἐν ἐμοὶ πνεῦμα θεοῦ, or that of Rom. 8:6: τὸ φρόνημα τῆς σαρκὸς θάνατος and τὸ φρόνημα τοῦ πνεύματος ζωή. Death and life — here is an absolute antithesis, unsurpassable, ontologically total.

Upon this premise my hermeneutical discussion of Romans 7 is based. The theme that I will now expound, and that will, I hope, become the subject of a fruitful theological discussion, goes to the theological depths of the chapter, with a special reference to 7:14ff. I will first advance as a thesis something of which Romans 7 will be an illustration. The thesis is that the NT is substantially a hermeneutical book. We see this from two standpoints.

1. The NT seeks to be understood, be it noted, in a way that those who un-

---

1. This is the view of most commentators, including J. A. Fitzmyer, *Romans. A New Translation with Introduction and Commentary* (AncB 33), New York 1993, 465. For a different standpoint cf. J. D. G. Dunn, *Romans 1–8* (Word Biblical Commentary 38A), Dallas, 1988, 377. Cf. also J. Lambrecht, *The Wretched "I" and Its Liberation. Paul in Romans 7 and 8* (LThPM 14), Louvain 1992 and my understanding of Rom. 7:7ff. in H. Hübner, *Das Gesetz bei Paulus. Ein Beitrag zum Werden der paulinischen Theologie* (FRLANT 119), Göttingen, 3rd ed. 1982, 62ff (ET *Law in Paul's Thought*, Edinburgh 1984, 69ff.), and my *Biblische Theologie des NT* II: *Die Theologie des Paulus und ihre neutestamentliche Wirkungsgeschichte,* Göttingen 1993, 291ff.

derstand it accept its message as existentially applicable to them. There can be
no understanding of the NT kerygma without faith. Trying to understand the
NT without faith means that those who supposedly understand it do not truly
grasp the content of the Christian book of revelation. At the very best they see
only the terminology and not the reality.[2]

2. The NT does not *seek* only to be understood. It states very expressly that it
wills to be understood. It does not present the kerygma alone. At decisive points
it also expressly reflects on understanding with faith, and on faith with understanding.

The NT authors know very well the phenomenon of unbelief. This is particularly evident in John's Gospel. John 8:43 tells us this unmistakably: οὐ δύνασθε
ἀκούειν τὸν λόγον μου. The Jewish listeners in John 8 regarded the ἀλήθεια as a
lie. Dreadfully blinded, they thought that the incarnate God was possessed by
the devil. A hermeneutical line — or perhaps we should say an anti-
hermeneutical line — should be drawn from John 9 to Romans 7.

But nuances are needed. It is too simple to speak directly of anti-hermeneu-
tics. Perhaps we should refer to a singular intermingling of hermeneutical and
anti-hermeneutical elements. In this setting I need not mention the material
course of the statements in Romans 7. We all know these down to the last details, and we are all well aware of the puzzling exegetical problems and the associated discussions. When, therefore, I refer to individual sayings of the apostle, I would ask you to place them in the sequence of his argument and to reflect
upon it.

Now to the point! The section Rom. 7:7ff. introduces many verbs of understanding, etc., that stand out even on a cursory reading. They may be listed as
follows: 7:7: οὐκ ἔγνων, οὐχ ᾔδειν; 7:13: ἵνα φανῇ; 7:14: οἴδαμεν; 7:15: οὐ
γινώσκω; 7:16: σύμφημι; 7:18: οἶδα; 7:21: εὑρίσκω; 7:22: συνήδομαι; 7:23:
βλέπω. Romans 7 has to do with understanding or not understanding, which in
this context means life or death. So serious, then, is all hermeneutics or anti-
hermeneutics. It means life or death! There is no middle ground!

But why, then, do I speak of an intermingling of hermeneutics and anti-
hermeneutics? What is meant becomes clear when we contrast ὄδαμεν in v. 14
with οὐ γινώσκω in the next verse. In v. 14 we have a theological and confessional assessment of the νόμος. It is πνευματικός. It belongs to the side of

---

2. A typical opposing view is that of K. Berger, *Theologie des Urchristentums. Theologie des NT*
(UTB), Tübingen and Basel, 1994.

God. It is an outward expression of his will. In it the God who gives his commands eventuates himself. Belonging in this way to God, the pneumatic *nomos* stands opposed to carnal humanity, that has sold itself to *hamartia*. But we humans who are victims are not aware of this miserable slavery that dishonors us. This comes out well in v. 15: "*For* (γάρ) what I want to do I do not do." This tells us of individuals under the law who do not know their true situation. A classical formulation may be found in Käsemann's Romans: "What sin really is, and the nature of its dominion, escape the category of what may be experienced even in standing under the law. . . . They are brought to light only by the gospel."[3]

In modern terms, οὐ γινώσκω stands on a meta-level. We can speak if it only retrospectively.[4] It is the terrible tragedy of the people of 7:14ff., who are so caught in the illusion of existence under the law that they do not truly see what they are doing or what its effects are. We might interpret ὃ γὰρ κατεργάζομαι as referring to the consequences of my deeds. A paraphrase of 7:15 would then be: "I do not perceive the results of what I am doing."[5] The point theologically: "I do not see the fatal direction of what I do. I do not see that through *hamartia* the carnal action that I do as *sarx* will bring about the same result as the *hamartia* itself, which dwells in me according to 7:13: ἀλλὰ ἡ ἁμαρτία, ἵνα φανῇ ἁμαρτία, διὰ τοῦ ἀγαθοῦ μοι κατεργαζομένη θάνατον. . . ." Bultmann is right when he makes the much disputed point that it should be clear what the meaning of ὃ γὰρ κατεργάζομαι οὐ γινώσκω (v. 15) is, namely, that we do not know that our "δονεύειν ἐν παλαιότητι γράμματος leads to death. . . ."[6]

Thus far what I have said about Romans 7 is not fundamentally new. Nevertheless, I have developed it at length, because from one angle — yet to be indicated — it has to be placed in a broader hermeneutical horizon — a horizon, that in my view, has been considerably neglected. My present investigation will take us much beyond what I said about Romans 7 in my biblical theology, vol-

---

3. E. Käsemann, *An die Römer* (HNTa), Tübingen, 4th ed. 1992, ET 200.

4. But cf. C. E. B. Cranfield, *The Epistle to the Romans* I (ICC), Edinburgh 1975, 358f., who has "I do not approve" rather than "I do not know" for οὐ γινώσκω. The use of "approve" for γινώσκω is not good Greek nor is it Pauline. Again, Romans 7 and Romans 8 are absolute antitheses. Cranfield overlooks the different dimensions of time that overlap in Romans 7.

5. Liddell and Scott, 924, have "effect by labour," "achieve" for κατεργάζομαι. κατεργάζεσθαι is not identical with ποιεῖν or πράσσειν. In 7:16ff. Paul uses ποιεῖν and πράσσειν for the doing of the law, but he has the results in mind in 7:15.

6. R. Bultmann, "Römer 7 und die Anthropologie des Paulus," *Exegetica. Aufsätze zur Erforschung des NT,* Tübingen 1967, 206.

ume 2.[7] For in this chapter of Romans we find not only verbs of knowing but also verbs of willing, and these, too, have a dominating role in the arguments of Paul. Now, it is true that exegetical discussion has not neglected the significance of the much utilized θέλειν. There has, in fact, been much inquiry into the relation of the controverted ἐγώ to the θέλειν sayings. But while this has been intensively discussed, it has not been discussed from a strictly hermeneutical angle.[8] My present task is to put the hermeneutical question of the meaning of the three terms, ἐγώ, γινώσκω and θέλω.

But first let us look at the history of philosophy, or more narrowly the history of Voluntarism. In 1974 the classical philologist, Albrecht Dihle, gave a lecture at the University of California in Berkeley on the theme "Theory of Will in Classical Antiquity."[9] A German translation was published in 1985.[10] In this work Dihle handled in depth a view taken by many historians of philosophy that the concept of the will was developed by Augustine as a means of theological and philosophical analysis such as we find in the earlier Scholasticism and then right on through Schopenhauer and Nietzsche in all kinds of different connections.[11] That is right in principle. From all appearances, however, the term Voluntarism was coined in the 19th century by the sociologist Friedrich Tönnies. In the 2nd edition of RGG, R. Seeberg had an article on Voluntarism in which he defined it as the primacy of the will and its associated affects in the functions of the spiritual and intellectual life. Seeberg, too, stresses the importance of Augustine and his view that by our very *nature* we are will.[12] God, too, is life and will as the Spirit who determines all things.[13] If we regard Augustine,

---

7. H. Hübner, *Biblische Theologie des NT,* II, 291ff.

8. Except in a neglected and hence disregarded work by Hans Jonas, "Philosophische Meditation über Paulus, Römerbrief Kapitel 7," *Zeit und Geschichte, FS Rudolf Bultmann,* ed. E. Dinkler, Tübingen 1964, 557-570. Jonas reflects on the relation between cogito me cogitare and volo me velle. Hermeneutically the will is for him the basic form of being (561). He had earlier dealt with Romans 7 in his work *Augustin und das paulinische Freiheitsproblem Eine philosophische Studie zum pelegianischen Streit* (FRLANT 27), Göttingen 1930, 2nd ed. 1965.

9. Published in 1982 by the University of California Press as Vol. 49 of the Sather Classical Lectures.

10. *Die Vorstellung vom Willen in der Antike,* Göttingen 1985.

11. Ibid.

12. R. Seeberg, art. "Voluntarismus," 2nd ed. RGG V, 1710.

13. Ibid. 711. H. Blankertz, art. "Voluntarismus," 3rd ed. RGG VI, 1491f. views Augustine as the high point of a development that began with the Hellenistic phase of Graeco-Roman philosophy. In connection with practical wisdom this dealt with questions of fate and freedom, trying to understand Roman law as a truth deriving from our attitude to the human will, and to take seriously as a challenge to ancient metaphysics the distinctive position of Christianity.

whose theological importance we cannot overestimate, as the first theoretical advocate of Voluntarism, we have also to document the fact that in both the OT and the NT God and ourselves are to be essentially understood in terms of the will.

I will illustrate from Psalms 40 (39 LXX). We read in v. 8: *la 'asôt-rəṣônəḵā 'ælohaj ḥapāṣtî*, which, freely translated, means: "In what is pleasing to you, my God, do I take pleasure" But 39:9a stresses this in a way that makes it a factual expression of what later systematic reflection would think of as voluntarism: τοῦ ποιῆσαι τὸ θέλημά σου, ὁ θεός μου ἐβουλήθην: "I willed, my God, to do thy will." 39:9b then formulates as follows the unity of the divine will and the human: καὶ τὸν νόμον σου ἐν μέσῳ τῆς κοιλίας μου. The one who prays has the law of God in his or her inward part. This reminds us of salvation in Ezekiel 36 and 37. Thus we read in Ezek. 36:26f.: καὶ δώσω ὑμῖν καρδίαν καινὴν καὶ πνεῦμα καινὸν δώσω ἐν ὑμῖν καὶ ἀφελῶ τὴν καρδίαν τὴν λιθίνην ἐκ τῆς σαρκὸς ὑμῶν καὶ δώσω ὑμῖν καρδίαν σαρκίνην. καὶ τὸ πνεῦμά μου δώσω ἐν ὑμῖν καὶ. ποιήσω ἵνα ἐν τοῖς δικαιώμασί μου πορεύησθε καὶ τὰ κρίματά μου φυλάξησθε καὶ ποιήσητε. These two chapters in Ezekiel form the OT background of Romans 8, especially 8:2-11.[14] The concept of voluntarism as it developed from Augustine through the Franciscan Scholastics Duns Scotus and William Ockham to its modern advocates, especially Schopenhauer and Nietzsche, has now become an inalienable part of our own intellectual and philosophico-historical background. We can no longer isolate ourselves from the influence of the concept. We are compelled to read the biblical sayings that do in fact express voluntarism against this background. The history of the way the biblical texts operate[15] is a history to which *we* belong. We cannot ignore this fact. If we do, we will read the most important statements of scripture very uncritically, and we will consequently distort them. The history, while it is not a criterion of biblical truth, is one of the tools that we need for investigation of the Bible. It is only one tool, but it is an indispensable tool. Augustine, Duns Scouts, and other commentators and theologians cannot — and must not — be left out of account when it is our purpose to discover the original, relevant, and meaningful intention of the biblical passages relating to θέλειν, θέλημα, or βούλεσθαι.

---

14. H. Hübner, "Der Heilige Geist in der Heiligen Schrift," KuD 36, 1990, 189ff.; also *Biblische Theologie des NT* II, 298ff., and cf. J. D. G. Dunn, *Romans 1–8,* Word Biblical Commentary 38a, Dallas 1988, 417.

15. H. G. Gadamer, *Wahrheit und Methode. Grundzüge einer philosophischen Hermeneutik,* Tübingen, 3rd ed. 1973, 284ff.

Back to Romans 7 and to what Paul has to say about the *I* and its willing! As
we have seen, the *I* is looking back to the period prior to conversion. It is well-
aware of what it willed. It willed the good, the ἀγαθόν. It willed what God
willed. It willed what the νόμος πνευματικός willed. Truly this was an ideal situation. Luther seemed to speak about it in his discussion of the *conformitas in
voluntate* between God and us in Romans 8.[16] Nevertheless, this conformity
does not apply to the one who knows himself to be in the presence of God. The
I may will what is right and good, but because of the weakness of its σάρξ it
cannot achieve the good.[17] What is depicted in Rom. 7:15 is our *basic inability*
to understand what we do, to *understand ourselves.* This is in fact a misunderstanding of the divine law and its original purpose. Everything is summed up in
the word "purpose." Purpose means planned volition aiming at an intended
goal. Knowing and willing are very closely linked in it. Of help here is the
knowledge that is bound up with voluntarism in, for example, Duns Scotus. The
best account of Duns Scotus was that given by Seeberg, and I will now quote
from it. According to Seeberg there is a firm connection between the will and
the reason. The natural power of the will is granted the possibility of orienting
itself to concepts. But then an intellectual act must precede the act of will (Sent.
I d 17 q4,4). This act might be natural or the knowledge might be necessarily
determined by its object. But the will moves freely (*Quaest. in metaph.* IX q
15,6). The intellect, of course, must certainly influence the will insofar as it
presents objects to it. The primacy of the will is expressed here, for it relates to
the intellect as the end does to the means or as form does to matter (IV d 49 q ex
lat 18).[18] The voluntarism of Duns Scotus is not absolute. Nevertheless, the
Scottish theologian viewed what was primary in the soul, its *essentia,* as that
which would attain to God in the *fruitio.* This was the legacy of Augustine. And
the *fruitio* was an affair of the will, which could not be distinguished in fact
from the essence of the soul.[19]

One might say that the human will, closely linked to knowledge, offers peo-

---

16. *Luther's Works* 25, esp. 353ff., 370ff. Cf. H. Hübner, *Rechtfertigung und Heiligung in
Luthers Römerbriefvorlesung. Ein systematischer Entwurf* (GlLeh 7), Witten 1965, 155ff., c.IV,5, in
which grace is described, not as ontic exaltation, but as *conformitas in voluntate.*

17. Cf. Ovid *Metamorphoses* 7,20f.

18. R. Seeberg, *Lehrbuch der Dogmengeschichte* III: *Die Dogmenbildung des Mittelalters,
Darmstadt,* 6th ed. 1959, 643f. Modern works on Scotus include H. Mühlen, *Sein und Person nach
Johannes Duns Scotus,* Werl 1954 and W. Dettloff, art. "Duns Scotus/Scotismus I," TRE 9, 218-231.

19. TRE 9,221 (Dettloff).

ple their personal orientation according to the ideas of Voluntarism. An individual *is* what he or she *wills*. The formulation of Rom. 7, and of many other passages in scripture, is that the human ἐγώ reveals itself in the θέλειν. It is essential, however, that our θέλειν, our being as those who express themselves ontologically (M. Heidegger), should be given an ontic concrete form. By its very nature θέλειν always has to have a goal. In the case of Romans 7, the perversion of the ego (vv. 14ff.) is that it unknowingly works against its own intentions. Unwittingly the ego does not do what it wills to do. It thus falls short of its true life. It unwittingly fails to do what is in accord with the will of God and his law, and it thus misses its own proper life (v. 10: ἡ ἐντολὴ ἡ εἰς ζωήν). The classical formulation of Bultmann is that the dominion of sin means that our action works against its own proper intention.[20]

It has already been said that the God who reveals himself as "God for us" has to be seen and understood in terms of his own θέλειν. If God is essentially will, creative, judging, and redeeming will, so are we as those who are made in his image (Gen. 1:26). The image of God means that we have knowledge, but in a highly essential way it means that *(like God!)* we *are* will. God as absolutely holy will has created a counterpart that participates in his essential being as will. In serious *meditation,* which is for us an indispensable task in these hectic days, we need to consider, to become aware of the inner gravity of what it means that *God as holy will has created us as willing beings.* In this sense, in the light of our significance for God, the primal mystery, we can see that we ourselves are a mystery. Only through such meditation will we also see what it means that the *I* of Romans 7 can still believe that there is a *conformitas in voluntate* between God and us when in reality God's will and ours are pointed in very different direction. According to Romans 7 the direction of the human will is distorted. The word we should use is *per-vertere.* If we *are* will, and if the will *is* perverted, the terrible consequence according to Romans 7 is that we are people of perversion. We are such as those who know, and we are such as those who will.

Those who stand as *sarx* under the dominion of *hamartia* are totally oriented to *hamartia* and *thanatos.* As such we exist in the unity of a false knowledge and an evil will and are unknowingly in enmity against God (cf. Rom. 5:10: ἐχθροὶ ὄντες). This is the disaster of illusions about ourselves in which our

---

20. *Theologie des NT* in the 9th edition revised and supplemented by O. Merk, Tübingen 1984, 246.

knowledge and will are both led astray by *hamartia,* and a hermeneutic of the Word of God has been made impossible. Incapable of this hermeneutic, in a fatal ignorance of self, we do not perceive our anti-hermeneutic, so that the holy and pneumatic law of God, which has already thrown light on *hamartia,* is made into an instrument of death (7:10: αὕτη εἰς θάνατον). Paul uses the adjective ταλαίπωρος for these caricatures of humanity, for the people of the law (7:24). In fact, looking back as a believer, the apostle can let this unhappy and tormented *I* cry out: ταλαίπωρος ἐγὼ ἄνθρωπος! If 7:25b is a gloss, as many suppose,[21] this lamenting ἐγώ is the final ἐγώ in this disastrous chapter (Romans 7).

Our conclusion is that we should not relate hermeneutics only to an understanding of the act of knowledge. Hermeneutics must also include willing as one of its themes. We must supplement a hermeneutics of knowing by one of willing. We usually do this unreflectingly, but express reflection is also needed. As regards Romans 7, hermeneutical reflection on both γινώσκειν and θέλειν will reveal to us the seriousness, the tragic seriousness, the full weight of the disaster that finds expression there. When we turn to Romans 8, similar reflection will show us the significance of the existence of φρονεῖν τὰ τοῦ πνεύματος. We *are* in fact our φρονεῖν. Those who have spoken about the darkness of chapter 7 are allowed to open up the joyous prospect of chapter 8. The hermeneutic of chapter 8 will help us to look back on the ego's anti-hermeneutic in chapter 7 as merely belonging to a disastrous past.

---

21. R. Bultmann, "Glossen im Römerbrief," *Exegetica,* 278ff.

Paul and the Law in Romans 9–11

by

STEPHEN WESTERHOLM

Among the few untapped areas for dissertations in our field must be reckoned the classification of various biblical personalities according to the four temperaments of popular physiology: was Noah, or Jacob, or Zephaniah a sanguine, phlegmatic, choleric, or melancholic? The many intriguing possibilities cannot be pursued here. Still, perhaps one observation, uncontroversial yet significant for our purposes, may be allowed: whether Jeremiah is properly classified a melancholic or a choleric would require further investigation; but he may be excluded at once from the ranks of the sanguine. Indeed, one of the problems besetting the proverbially weeping prophet throughout his career was the need to distinguish true prophets from false. And the thesis is at least arguable, perhaps even defensible, that much of what Jeremiah said on the subject can be summed up in the dictum, "No true prophet can be a sanguine."

The more remarkable, then, that even so *un*sanguineous a personality as Jeremiah found himself investing in Judean real estate at a time when experts declared all the land worth having to be in Egypt – and proclaiming the purchase a sign of good things to come (Jer 32:1–44). In fact, however, the same convictions that led Jeremiah to announce doom for his contemporaries all but required such a message of hope for the future. They are, indeed, assumptions on which the Hebrew Bible as a whole appears to be united.

The first conviction, most explicit in wisdom and psalmic materials but assumed throughout, is that creation received its order from a God of awesome goodness, and, hence, that that order is to be celebrated with uninhibited delight, with music and dance and boisterous praise, as itself awesomely good. The second conviction, explicit in wisdom, psalmic, historical and prophetic materials alike, is that the *dis*order that disfigures creation owes much to the insistence of human beings on ordering their own affairs independently of, and in conflict with, the wisdom inherent in the divine scheme of things: a course of action seen as quintessentially foolish, wicked, and baneful. In the Hebrew scriptures, disorder is, with a remarkable degree of consistency, explained not in tragic terms as the surfacing of tensions or flaws inherent in the nature of the cosmos, but in moral and religious terms, as the result of culpa-

ble creaturely unfaithfulness toward a Creator (who, for Israel, is also Re-
deemer) and a created order (perfectly expressed, Israel came to believe, in
the Torah) that are themselves good. The third conviction, likewise apparent
in all parts of the Hebrew scriptures, is that the awesome goodness of God
necessarily expresses itself in awesome and unfailing opposition toward
whatever mars the goodness of his handiwork. At times it may seem as though
the moral order itself is said to reject and punish those who defy it.[1] But, in the
context of the Hebrew scriptures, it would be wrong to isolate the assertion of
the moral order from the will of its Creator.[2] His goodness is thought, to be
sure, to demand that his judgments be just, and even that he show himself
longsuffering in their execution, but never entails an obligation of tolerance
toward those who scorn and disfigure what is good. In addition to these three
convictions comes a fourth, found in prophetic (and apocalyptic) literature in
surprising juxtaposition with outpourings of gloom and doom, yet almost demanded once involvement in history is posited of the God whose irrepressible
goodness is backed up with an irresistible right arm. Such a God, inevitably,
will see to it in some way that the baneful effects of creaturely unfaithfulness
are one day reversed and goodness prevails, at least in the case of God's own
people, though the perspective is at times expanded, even universalized. In
some way: the scripts are many, though the basic plot is a constant. Even a
Jeremiah, in the midst of a national disaster fully warranted (he believed) by
his people's unfaithfulness, was sure that soil in their promised land would
one day be a blessed commodity.

Like the other authors of early Christian writings that found their way into
our New Testament, the apostle Paul shared the four convictions listed above
as well as a fifth, more specifically Christian: namely, that Jesus of Nazareth
has a decisive role to play in the reversal of creation's disorder and the ultimate triumph of God.[3] Again, the scripts are many, though the basic plot is a
constant. A nuanced summary of Romans would need to note how the letter
addresses particular concerns and issues of the mid-first century church. But
Paul felt constrained to deal with those concerns in the context of a wide-rang-
ing discussion of the nature and implications of the Christian gospel.[4] As a

---

[1] Cf. the well-known article of Klaus Koch, "Gibt es ein Vergeltungsdogma im Alten
Testament?" in *ZTK* 52 (1955) 1–42.

[2] Cf. Lennart Boström, *The God of the Sages: The Portrayal of God in the Book of Prov-
erbs* (Stockholm: Almqvist & Wiksell International, 1990) 90–140.

[3] Cf. James D.G. Dunn, *Unity and Diversity in the New Testament: An Inquiry Into the
Character of Earliest Christianity* (Philadelphia: Westminster, 1977) 369–372;; E.E.
Lemcio, "The Unifying Kerygma of the New Testament, I and II," in *JSNT* 33 (1988) 3–17
and 38 (1990) 3–11; and note the description of "normative Christianity" in Arland
Hultgren, *The Rise of Normative Christianity* (Minneapolis: Fortress, 1994), esp. 84–103.

[4] Hence the impression, shared by many, that the summary of "the gospel" in Rom 1:16–
17 is a statement of theme for the chapters that follow. The more "systematic" character of

result, those interpreters are not wrong who see the epistle's theme as the triumph of God: in effect, Romans amounts to the Pauline script of the plot sketched above, accounting both for the disfigurement of creation and for the divine reversal of that disfigurement through Jesus Christ. A nuanced statement might also want to distinguish what is traditional and Jewish from what is Christian or even Pauline innovation. We must be content here to note that Paul traces all human *sins* (plural) to the fundamental sin of refusing to acknowledge God the Creator and give him his due;[5] that God's wrath is seen in the abandoning of humankind to the viciousness and ugliness inherent in its rejection of God and the good;[6] that the word "flesh" captures for Paul this basic human orientation of rebellion and disobedience, shared by all who are "in Adam," and representing a departure from, a "falling short of," the "glory" God designed for humankind;[7] that God's law, though providing Israel with a privileged reminder of God's claim on human obedience and a true statement of his "holy and righteous and good" demands, can, in its encounter with rebellious "flesh," only aggravate, not transform, the situation;[8] hence, in their transgression of the law, even the covenant people of God prove denizens of the old, Adamic order, and find themselves united with idolatrous, immoral Gentiles in the human dilemma of guilt, moral impotence, bondage to sin, and death.[9] So far the disfigurement. The divine triumph is achieved, the divine δικαιοσύνη demonstrated and effective,[10] in the death and resurrection of Jesus, understood both as expiating the bane of sin[11] and as making possible the translation of the old, disfigured order into a new one of righteousness, freedom, and life as believers baptized into Jesus share his "death to sin" and new "life to God."[12] If redemption is not yet complete, if Christian existence for the present is still tied to mortal bodies, temptations of the flesh, and sundry forms of suffering,[13] nonetheless the presence of the divine Spirit gives a foretaste of coming glory, and God's demonstrated love for his people grounds a

---

Romans is perhaps to be explained, in part, by Paul's sense of obligation, as "apostle to the Gentiles," to see to it that the church in Rome rightly understands the nature and implications of the Christian gospel. Cf. L. Ann Jervis, *The Purpose of Romans: A Comparative Letter Structure Investigation* (Sheffield: Sheffield Academic Press, 1991) 161–164; Mark A. Seifrid, *Justification by Faith: The Origin and Development of a Central Pauline Theme* (Leiden: Brill, 1992) 207.

[5] 1:19–21, 28.
[6] 1:18–32.
[7] 7:14–8:8; 5:12–19; 3:23.
[8] 2:17–18; 3:2; 5:20; 7:5–25.
[9] 2:23–24; 3:19–20, 22–23; 7:5, 14–25.
[10] 1:17; 3:21–26; 10:3.
[11] 3:24–25.
[12] 5:12–6:11.
[13] 6:12–13; 8:10, 13, 18–25, 35–36.

hope that cannot d.sappoint.[14] So far the reversal of the disfigurement, though it is worth underlining Paul's insistence, again paralleled in the prophets, that the triumph is exclusively God's own, an expression of the divine will to redeem rather than a reflection of the merits of the redeemed.[15] If, as Paul repeatedly insists, the result of *sin* is that humanity is left without excuse before God,[16] he is equally insistent that, as a result of the divine triumph, humanity is left without a boast.[17] Jeremiah, who rated the human capacity to overcome its evil bent no better than leopard skills in spot-removal, would not have disagreed.[18]

An arm-chair theologian, having finished the mighty hymn that closes Romans 8, would have been loathe to reopen the discussion and risk spoiling the effect. Romans 9–11 proves once again that Paul's thinking was incorrigibly theological, but, equally, that his theological reflections were too rooted in first century reality to warrant the designation "armchair." The mid-first century reality for Paul was that, on the whole, his fellow-Jews had so far failed to show the "obedience of faith" requisite to participation in the divine triumph he has just portrayed. Apart from the personal anguish this caused the apostle (9:1–3; 10:1), Paul felt constrained to explain how the Christian gospel could represent a triumph for the God of Abraham in spite of appearances suggest-

---

[14] 8:23; 5:5–11; 8:15–17, 32.

[15] 1:1, 16–17; 3:21–26, 30; 4:5; 5:6–8; 8:3–4. In the Hebrew scriptures, prayers for God's aid for his people at times invoke their "righteousness" as a motivation for the intervention (e.g., Job 31:1–40; Ps 7:2–18 [ET 1–17]; 26:1–12; 44:18–25 [ET 17–24]). Still, a not uncommon motif finds the one praying declaring that no grounds can be found in the behaviour of his people that would warrant action by God on their behalf – indeed, the opposite is often affirmed to be the case – but pleading nonetheless that God will find it consistent with his own goodness or mercy or faithfulness to deal favourably with his people (note esp. Dan 9:4–19; also Jer 14:7–9, 19–22; Mic 7:18–20; Ps 79:8–9; 106:6–47, etc.). The motif is paralleled in the claim of passages like Ezek 20:5–44; 36:16–32 that Israel's restoration owes nothing to the character or deeds of the people and everything to the divine disposition (cf. also 16:53–63; Isa 43:22–44:5; and note Deut 9:4–7). The (inevitable) link, in discussions of divine deliverance, between reminders of human turpitude (seen, after all, as the root cause of the dilemma from which deliverance is required) and an insistence that God's salvific acts are rooted in his character and will alone is of course paralleled in Paul (e.g., Rom 3:19–24; 4:5–8; 5:6–8).

Perhaps it should be said here that the point in referring to parallels from the Hebrew scriptures is not to imply direct dependence of Paul on the passages cited; rather, by way of response to those who claim that sixteenth century spectacles are needed to interpret Paul as I do, I hope to show that the categories of thought and concerns I see in Paul were natural to ancient Jews intent on affirming the ultimate triumph of God's goodness while attributing current ills to the corruption of the human heart.

[16] 1:20; 2:1; cf. 3:19.

[17] 3:27–28; 4:2. Cf. 1 Cor 1:27–31; Gal 6:14.

[18] Jer 13:23; 17:9; 9:22–23 (ET 9:23–24). Cf. Frank Thielman, *From Plight to Solution: A Jewish Framework for Understanding Paul's View of the Law in Galatians and Romans* (Leiden: Brill, 1989) 28–45.

ing that the Jewish people were not on the winning side, and what this said about the divine commitment to Israel (cf. 9:6; 11:1).

Paul's explanation is two-fold. First, nothing in the present situation, disheartening though it may be, requires us to think that God has proved unfaithful to his commitment to Israel. Quite the contrary. God has *never* been bound to include every physical descendant of Abraham in the community of blessing. The present limiting of that community (as far as Jews are concerned) to a remnant has both precedent and prophetic sanction; at the same time the very existence of a remnant provides evidence of God's continuing commitment to the people of Israel. As for *unbelieving* Israel, its *present* condition may be viewed from two perspectives: on the one hand, it should be seen in the light of God's prerogative to harden human hearts; on the other hand, Israel has proved again, this time in its response to God's "righteousness" in Christ, a "disobedient and contrary people" (10:21). Still (and here we move to the second part of Paul's answer), if the present, disheartening situation does not require us to think that God's commitment to Israel has failed, the future will witness its faithful fulfilment. Israel's "hardening" represents not simply a divine prerogative but, mysteriously, a part of his benevolent purpose.[19] In what is essentially a Christianized restatement of the prophetic hope that, beyond the present crisis, God will one day reverse concurrently the apostasy and the fortunes of his people, Paul affirms that, when the hardening has served its function, Israel's present "ungodliness" will be banished, its unbelief will be abandoned; "and so," in the end, no mere remnant but "Israel as a whole will be saved" (11:23, 25–26).[20]

Such a summary, though, I believe, correct in what it says, does leave unaddressed a number of issues critical to an understanding of this section in

---

[19] On the nature of the divine purpose, see now Terence L. Donaldson, "'Riches for the Gentiles' (Rom 11:12): Israel's Rejection and Paul's Gentile Mission," in *JBL* 112 (1993) 81–98, here 92–98.

[20] Israel's current "unbelief" (11:20, 23), "ungodliness" (11:26), and "disobedience" (11:31) are clearly epitomized for Paul in their lack of response to the proclamation of God's righteousness in Christ (cf. especially 10:3, 14–21). If for no other reason than that Paul sees Israel's salvation as requiring an abandoning of their "unbelief" (11:23) and a banishing of their "ungodliness" (11:26), it is clear that he does not envisage such salvation apart from faith in Jesus Christ. Cf. Ferdinand Hahn, "Zum Verständnis von Römer 11.26a: '... und so wird ganz Israel gerettet werden,'" in *Paul and Paulinism*, ed. M.D. Hooker and S.G. Wilson (London: SPCK 1982) 221–236; E.P. Sanders, *Paul, the Law, and the Jewish People* (Philadelphia: Fortress, 1983) 194–195; Heikki Räisänen, "Paul, God, and Israel: Romans 9–11 in Recent Research," in *The Social World of Formative Christianity and Judaism*, ed. Jacob Neusner, Peder Borgen, Ernest S. Frerichs, and Richard Horsley (Philadelphia: Fortress, 1988) 178–206, here 189–192 (also Räisänen's "Römer 9–11: Analyse eines geistigen Ringens," in *ANRW* II, 25, 4 [1987] 2891–2939, here 2917–2918); Bruce W. Longenecker, "Different Answers to Different Issues: Israel, the Gentiles and Salvation History in Romans 9–11," in *JSNT* 36 (1989) 95–123, here 98–101.

Romans. Detailed treatment is of course not possible here. The following addenda must suffice.

1. Paul's overarching theme remains, in Romans 9–11 as in chapters 1–8, the triumph of God's goodness in a creation corrupted by sin. But in clarifying God's dealings with Israel in the later chapters, he shows how divine goodness "divides and conquers" Adamic humanity by dealing now with Jews, now with the Gentile nations, with the ultimate goal of showing mercy to all (11:30–32). Just as God once, to achieve his redemptive purposes, favoured Israel as his people to the (temporary) exclusion of the Gentile nations, so now Israel finds itself (largely, but temporarily) excluded while Gentiles are called to salvation. Such is the divine scheme as Paul expounds it in Romans 11. But before he elaborates the larger divine agenda, he must first account for the present condition of Israel: does not the exclusion of Israel, apparent from its rejection of the gospel, entail the failure of God's commitment to Abraham and his "seed"?

2. And, of course, for Paul the notion that the divine "word" might have failed is unthinkable (9:6). It should be noted that the "word of God" whose viability is affirmed in 9:6a must refer to the divine commitment to the Jewish people evidenced in the immediately preceding verses. That Paul's fellow-Jews, many of whom do not believe in Jesus the Christ, nonetheless belong to a people who possess divine promises has thus just been affirmed.[21] That the lack of Christian faith on the part of many Jews throws into question the viability of the promises made to Israel is of course precisely the point behind the suggestion that the "word of God" might have failed. Paul's declaration to the contrary must therefore mean that the promises made to the Jewish people remain in place.[22] And the insistence that a largely unbelieving people remain the objects of a valid divine commitment already contains within itself the presuppositions demanding a transformation such as that envisaged in 11:25–26.

3. In the meantime, however, how is Paul to maintain God's faithfulness to Israel while acknowledging that few of his contemporary Jews belong to the community of God as it is presently constituted? His initial answer, in effect, is that there is nothing new in the current situation; that, on the contrary, the Israel that has enjoyed God's favour and blessing has always been made up, not of *all* Abraham's descendants, but of a selection from among them. Thus

---

[21] Note that the antecedent of the οἵτινες (9:4) to whom the privileges (including the divine "promises") are said to belong is Paul's "brothers by race, according to the flesh": those for whom he could have wished himself accursed (9:3).

[22] The parallel between 9:6 and 3:3–4 should be noted. In both, the unbelief of "some" Jews leads to the question whether God's faithfulness (3:3) or promise (9:6) to his people remains firm. In both, Paul asserts unequivocally that it does. But only in the later text does Paul follow up the assertion with a detailed explanation.

"not *all* who are *of* Israel are Israel, nor are *all* the children the (promised) seed of Abraham" (9:6b–7a). And, Paul continues, if this is so, if not every physical descendant is included in the community of blessing, then it follows that what effectively constitutes the community of blessing is the divine promise to Abraham's descendants, not physical descent *per se* (9:8). This, it should be noted, is not to deny that divine promises have been made to physical descendants of Abraham: in verses 3–4, Paul has just declared that his fellow-Jews "according to the flesh" *are* the recipients of such promises. The point of verse 8 is only to insist that God's promise, not their physical descent, remains the basis of their entitlement and that God is therefore free to select the effective objects of the promise among the descendants.[23] This claim is said to be confirmed on the one hand by the examples of Isaac and Jacob, whose share in the blessing of Abraham's children is realized by their being, not simply his descendants, but descendants of whom divine promises were explicitly made; and, on the other hand, by the exclusion of Ishmael and Esau, in spite of their physical descent. The argument of these verses is thus not that the blessings promised to Abraham's children apply to a spiritual Israel not descended from Abraham; rather, and more to the point, such blessings are not necessarily the lot of all Abraham's descendants, so that the contemporary exclusion of many Jews does not in itself invalidate the divine promise.

4. The principle on which Paul builds his argument is, in itself, unexceptionable Jewish theology.[24] The cited examples of Ishmael and Esau are obvious enough. Jewish tradition saw many Jews as effectively excluded from the blessings promised to Israel. *M. Sanhedrin* 10, after declaring that "All Israelites have a share in the world to come," promptly proceeds to list a number of "Israelites" not among the "all Israelites" who possess such a share (a list, it should be noted, that includes whole generations).[25] And remnant theology –

---

[23] Cf. C.E.B. Cranfield, *A Critical and Exegetical Commentary on the Epistle to the Romans*, Vol 2 (Edinburgh: T. & T. Clark, 1979) 475; Ulrich Wilckens, *Der Brief an die Römer*, Vol 2 (Cologne: Benziger; Neukirchen-Vluyn: Neukirchener Verlag, 1980) 193 n855; James D.G. Dunn, *Romans 9–16* (Dallas: Word, 1988) 539–540; also Johannes Munck, *Christ and Israel: An Interpretation of Romans 9–11* (Philadelphia: Fortress, 1967) 35–36.

[24] Cf. E. Elizabeth Johnson, *The Function of Apocalyptic and Wisdom Traditions in Romans 9–11* (Atlanta: Scholars Press, 1989) 148–149.

[25] Note, further, that *any* theology by which some physical Israelites are excluded from the community of God's blessing is bound to hold some equivalent to Paul's claim in v 8 that physical descent from Abraham is not, in and of itself, decisive. The belief, for example, that, though God has committed himself to ethnic Israel, even ethnic Jews must not prove apostate as the wilderness generation did if they are to enjoy divine favour, could be expressed (in a paraphrase of Paul), "It is not the physical descendants of Abraham who enjoy God's favour, but those who show themselves faithful to God." The "dialectic negation" (cf. H. Kruse, "Die 'dialektische Negation' als semitisches Idiom," in *VT* 4 [1954] 385–400) of such a statement is not meant as a denial that God's favour is directed toward physical descendants of Abraham. The point is rather that, to qualify as a recipient of that favour, *not only* physical descent is required, *but also*, and as an ultimately decisive factor, faithfulness

by which the majority of Jews at given points in history are declared faithless
and bound for judgment while the community of survivors, prior to a dramatic
turning to God in the "last days," is effectively limited to a minority of Israelites – was no Pauline innovation.[26] Furthermore, this very conventional claim
does represent a basis for the affirmation in 6a: the unbelief of much of contemporary Jewry does not mean that God's commitment to Israel has failed
since God's promised blessing to Abraham's descendants need not include
every Jew, or even (the majority of) every generation of Jews.

5. It follows that we misread the truism of 9:6b if we construe it as a disen-
franchisement of ethnic Israel from the divine promise, thus in effect eliminating the πάντες from both verses 6 and 7, and taking the conventional "Not *all*
who are of Israel are Israel" to mean "Ethnic Israel has nothing to do with
spiritual Israel (apart, perhaps, from a minor, and purely coincidental, overlapping of citizens)."[27] Paul's traditional claim that the Israel of God's blessing, though made up of Jews, is not coterminous with ethnic Israel is thus
turned into a radical claim that the two are essentially unrelated entities. Not
only does such a reading distort Paul's words and argument at this point, but it
ignores the preceding five verses, in which the divine covenants and promises
are explicitly said to belong to Israel "according to the flesh," and gives "Israel" in 9:6b a "spiritual" sense that it bears nowhere else in these chapters (cf.
9:27, 31; 10:19, 21; 11:2, 7, 25–26).[28]

6. Paul's initial refutation of the suggestion that the unbelief of Jews entails
the failure of God's commitment to Israel thus takes the form of a reminder
that not all Jews are included in the Israel *of promise*. The argument then pro-

---

to God. A Pauline comparison is furnished by Rom 4:12, according to which ethnic (circumcised) Jews *are* allowed to be the children of Abraham as promised, provided that they *also*
share Abraham's faith. But, in a context such as that of Romans 9 in which divine sovereignty is stressed, the "dialectic negation" takes the form, "It is not the children of the flesh
who are the children of God but the children of the promise who are reckoned as seed" (9:8):
i.e., it is the divine promise made to Abraham's seed, not physical descent *per se*, that effectively constitutes the community of blessing.

[26] Cf. Ronald E. Clements, "'A Remnant Chosen by Grace' (Romans 11:5): The Old Testament Background and Origin of the Remnant Concept," in *Pauline Studies*, ed. Donald A.
Hagner and Murray J. Harris (Grand Rapids: Eerdmans, 1980) 106–121.

[27] So, e.g., Erich Dinkler, "The Historical and the Eschatological Israel in Romans Chapters 9–11: A Contribution to the Problem of Predestination and Individual Responsibility,"
in *JR* 36 (1956) 109–127, here 114–117; Francis Watson, *Paul, Judaism and the Gentiles: A
Sociological Approach* (Cambridge: University Press, 1986) 162–163.

[28] It is true that Gentiles, formerly not God's people, are later said to be, like Jews, the
objects of a divine call (9:24). But these Gentile believers are not here designated a kind of
spiritual "Israel"; they are portrayed alongside the remnant of believing Jews (9:24–29)
through whom God's commitment to ethnic Israel is said to be maintained (cf. 11:1–5). Cf.
Rom 15:8–12, where the "promises" made to the "forefathers" are fulfilled by Christ's service "*of the circumcision* (= Jews)." Gentiles, though also given cause to glorify God, are not
involved in the fulfilment of the promises made to the patriarchs of Israel here in view. Cf.
also 15:27.

ceeds by defining more fully, and justifying, the character of God's promissory activity: God's election is rooted, Paul insists, in his own sovereign purpose, not in any consideration of the deeds of those he does or does not choose: "Not of works, but of him who calls" (9:12).

We may well ponder why Paul introduces the latter point here.[29] That he considers it significant is clear, since the verses that follow both reiterate it by observing that everything depends on the will of the God who shows mercy, not on human "willing" or "running" (9:16), and defend it by insisting on God's prerogative to show mercy or harden as he chooses (9:17–23). Certainly Paul is not polemicizing against human beings' *doing* anything, against their "willing" or "running" *per se*. What they do may be "good or bad" (9:11); human "willing" and "running" are not criticized, but merely declared irrelevant in the inscrutable selection of the objects of divine mercy. No doubt we should see here a preparation for the argument of chapter 11, since belief in the ultimate triumph of God's benevolence in spite of universal human disobedience might well be thought to require the prior conviction that God carries out his own purposes regardless of human deeds. Such was Paul's view of humanity in the "flesh" that, were God to wait for appropriate human activity to warrant the granting of his favour, he would wait in vain.

But clearly there is more at stake. *Some* connection must exist between the ruling out of any role for human "works" in 9:12 and the claim that Israel wrongly pursues a path of "works" in 9:32. The parallel is, to be sure, not complete. In 9:11–12, it is not certain specific "works" that are excluded from consideration in God's election; rather, by definition, *no* human activity[30] can be a factor if God's "election" is to remain rooted in his sovereign purpose alone. On the other hand, when Paul refers to the "works" wrongly pursued by Israel in 9:32, there is no doubt that he has specific "works" in mind: those required by the Mosaic law, perhaps especially the boundary-defining "works" for which Jews displayed particular zeal.[31] But it is at least tempting to suspect that Paul introduced the exclusion of "works" (in general) in 9:12 with a view to the later claim that Israel's pursuit of a path involving particular human "works" was misguided. And the question is at least worth posing

---

[29] Cf. the comments in William Sanday and Arthur C. Headlam, *A Critical and Exegetical Commentary on the Epistle to the Romans*, 5th edition (Edinburgh: T. & T. Clark, 1902) 243–244, on the completeness of Paul's argument without the "new thought" of 9:11–12.

[30] Dunn (*Romans* [see n. 23 above], 542) quite properly notes that the stress in 9:11 is on the exclusion of consideration for "*anything*" done, but fails to follow up on this observation when he limits the "works" excluded in 9:12 to "works of the law" (543). Cf. C.E.B. Cranfield, "'The Works of the Law' in the Epistle to the Romans," in *JSNT* 43 (1991) 89–101, here 97.

[31] Cf. James D.G. Dunn, "Yet Once More – 'The Works of the Law': A Response," in *JSNT* 46 (1992) 99–117, here 100–104; Bruce W. Longenecker, *Eschatology and the Covenant: A Comparison of 4 Ezra and Romans 1–11* (Sheffield: Academic Press, 1991) 217.

whether part of the thinking behind Paul's claim that Israel's pursuit of (specific) "works" was misguided is to be found in his reason for thinking "works" in general are excluded in 9:11–12: God achieves his purposes without reference to human activity. We will return to the question below.

7. After claiming that not every Israelite belongs to God's Israel, that God chooses his people according to his own sovereign will, and that human activity is not a factor in the selection, Paul proceeds to argue that it is God's prerogative to "show mercy" or "harden" as he pleases (9:14–23).

Two observations are in order. First, though Paul here portrays divine activity without explicit reference to unbelieving Israel, in this context his point in speaking of divine election and hardening must be to demonstrate not only that Israel's unbelief does not frustrate God's purposes, but that it can be explained as an outworking of those very purposes. Clearly, while Paul denies that God's decision to display mercy toward some while hardening others is a *response* to human deeds (9:11–18), he does think that the divine decision *takes effect* in the coming to faith of believers[32] and the persistent unbelief of others.[33] That God's role in the matter does not, for Paul, remove Israel's responsibility for their unbelief is apparent from Rom 10:21 – as well, of course, as from the fact that divine sovereignty and human responsibility were traditionally held together in Jewish thought.[34]

Second, though Paul's account of divine election and hardening is meant to account for the response of contemporary Israel to the gospel, it does not follow that he thought, even while writing Romans 9, that Israel was permanently excluded from the sphere of God's blessing. His own continued prayers for Israel's salvation (10:1) and his hope that his mission would lead to the

---

[32] Thus, for Paul, believers are always those who have been "called" or "chosen" by God (1 Thes 1:4, 1 Cor 1:21 ["those who believe"] and 1:24 ["those who are called"]; Rom 1:6–8, etc.

[33] We may compare the Genesis story in which the cruelty of Joseph's brothers was seen both as a genuine expression of personal hatred for which they were responsible *and* as an element in God's salvific plan (Gen 37:4, 18; 42:21; 44:16; 45:5, 7–8; 50:20). Similarly, Paul saw Israel's unbelief both as a culpable expression of the people's inveterate resistance to God's purposes *and* as a designed element in the accomplishment of those purposes.

[34] I.e., Paul – and other Jews – obviously believed that God is capable of sovereignly ordering the affairs of humankind in such a way that humans remain responsible for their actions. Cf. Joseph A. Fitzmyer, *Romans* (New York: Doubleday, 1993) 108; Räisänen, "Research" (see n. 20 above), 186; "Analyse" (see n. 20 above), 2910–2911. It is true that biblical passages that speak of God's ordering of human affairs, if understood mechanistically and pressed to what might appear to be their logical conclusion, would violate the second "conviction" listed above as characteristic of the biblical writings as a whole: creaturely unfaithfulness is the cause of creation's disorder. But this does not happen: even where the divine sovereignty is most in view, a sense of humanity's responsibility for its faithlessness toward God is retained. – That mechanical conceptions of causation are the product of the "scientific age" is argued by Oliver O'Donovan, *On the Thirty-Nine Articles: A Conversation with Tudor Christianity* (Carlisle: Paternoster, 1986) 65–75.

salvation of "some" (11:13–14) show at least that he continued to envisage the possible salvation of individual Jews. And his stated conviction in 9:4–5 that God remains committed to the people of Israel implicitly demands, as we have seen, some scheme for their ultimate salvation. Nor can we read earlier affirmations in Romans about God's redemption of Adamic humanity as conceivably allowing the designed exclusion of the Jewish people (e.g., 5:12–21). A sufficient justification for the language of election and hardening in Romans 9 is furnished, as we have seen, by Paul's need to show that the unbelief of contemporary Israel, far from frustrating God's purposes, in fact finds a place within them. Romans 9 declares that the unbelief is (from one perspective) the result of divine activity and justified by the prerogatives of a Creator; it leaves to chapter 11 the elaboration of the divine purpose and scheme behind God's "hardening" activity.[35]

8. The argument of Rom 11:1–10 returns to the issue raised in 9:6a. God's commitment to Israel is again said to stand firm in spite of the current unbelief of many Jews. In 9:6–13, this is affirmed negatively: God is not bound to every physical descendant of Abraham and thus, by implication, those Jews who do not now believe need not be a part of the Israel of God's blessing. In 11:1–6, the positive point is made that those Jews who do believe, however few they may be, are enough to show that God's commitment remains in place.[36] Furthermore, unbelieving Jews are here explicitly said to be "hardened" by God.

9. That being said, Paul immediately proceeds to claim that Israel's current "blindness" will one day be removed, its "ungodliness" will be banished, and "Israel as a whole will be saved." Such a dénouement, though reserved for chapter 11, cannot be said to entail the retraction of all that Paul said in chapters 9 and 10. Israel was seen throughout as the recipient of the divine promise. That promise was declared to stand firm in spite of present appearances: the unbelief of some represents no failure of the promise, which did not require the blessing of every individual Jew in any case, and which is proved to remain in place by the existence of a remnant. Nor does the ultimate, blessed dénouement render pointless Paul's anguish over the recalcitrance of contemporary Israel any more than the sanguine hopes of prophets of old kept them from lamenting the behaviour and fate of their fellowcountrymen. If Paul's account of contemporary Israel's unbelief in chapters 9 and 10 did not declare that unbelief to be permanent, it is also true that his expectation of a divine

---

[35] Note that the conditional form of 9:22–23 gives the verses the force, not of an assertion that God is determined to act in the way described, but of a claim that it is his prerogative to do so (i.e., the introductory "What if …?" implies some such apodosis as "Do you then, as a mere creature, have any right to object?"). Even so, the verses refer to God's "patient bearing" of those "fitted for destruction" without speaking of (God's prerogative to carry out) their actual destruction. Cf. Cranfield, *Romans* (see n. 23 above), 495–496.

[36] The notion of a remnant was of course introduced already in 9:27–29; it is here given positive significance.

intervention on behalf of "Israel as a whole" does not require that each individual Israelite would share in the blessing.[37] In addition to the obvious parallel in *m. Sanh.* 10:1–4, we might compare Ezek 20:33–44, where the prophet, though expressing the common prophetic hope that God will one day intervene to end the apostasy of contemporary Israel and bless them with his favour, nonetheless speaks of persistent rebels who will be excluded from the land (20:38).[38]

10. In short, Paul presumes throughout these chapters that God is committed to the blessing of (ethnic) Israel. He believes that that commitment does not require the blessing of every individual Israelite – or, indeed, of whole generations of Israelites. He is convinced that the unbelief of much of contemporary Israel places them, for the moment at least, outside the sphere of divine blessing. It follows that, if they abandon their unbelief, they will experience the divine blessing. His statements in chapter 11 to the effect that such an abandoning of unbelief will one day take place on the part of πᾶς Ἰσραηλ merely represents the final, glorious fulfilment of a promise that Paul affirms as still in place throughout chapters 9 and 10 without setting aside the affirmation of the earlier chapters that those who resist the "righteousness of God" must not be thought to frustrate the fulfilment of God's word.

We turn now to consider the passage within these chapters in which Paul speaks about the law (9:30–10:13). Though he sums up his own larger argument in the words "God has consigned all to disobedience, that he may have mercy upon all" (11:32), it must be conceded that Paul does not consider *Gentile* disobedience to require further demonstration. Romans 9:6–29, taken together with 11:1–10, treat *God's* role in the consignment of Israel to disobedience, whereas 9:30–10:21 explain wherein Israel's disobedience lay. It is in this latter section that the subject of the law is introduced.

The opening "What shall we say then?" (9:30) suggests that the consideration or dilemma about to be stated is rooted in something that has just been said.[39] The immediately preceding verses make the claim that Gentiles, formerly "not [God's] people," are now among the "vessels of [his] mercy," joining a mere remnant of Israel. This development is now given paradoxical expression: "Gentiles not pursuing righteousness have obtained righteousness, that is, the righteousness based on faith. But Israel, pursuing a law of righteousness, did not attain to the law." In both cases, the relation between human

---

[37] Cf. Traugott Holtz, "The Judgment on the Jews and the Salvation of All Israel: 1 Thes 2,15–16 and Rom 11,25–26," in *BETL* 87 (1990) 284–294, here 288–293. The point of affirming salvation for πᾶς Ἰσραηλ lies not in declaring the destiny of each individual Jew, but in declaring that, though at present only a "remnant" believes and a (large) "part" of Israel has been hardened (11:1–7, 25), in the future Israel *as a whole* will be saved.

[38] Cf. also Ezek 11:21, in the context of Ezek 11:17–21.

[39] Cf. 4:1; 6:1; 7:7; 8:31; 9:14; and note 3:1, 9.

"pursuit" and attainment is declared, with deliberate paradox, to be negative. What is the point behind the paradox?

In the case of Gentile Christians, Paul is saying that, while they had not pursued good standing with the God of Israel (i.e., by being circumcised and submitting to Israel's law), they had obtained such standing by faith (in Christ). Israel, conversely, though intently pursuing a law that offered good relations with God, failed to reach the goal of the law. That goal could only be attained, Paul declares, not by "works," but by "faith" (in Christ) (9:32). Their refusal to "believe in him" (9:33) proves to be their downfall; Christ is the "stone" on which they "stumbled," their "rock of offence."

So much is clear. But if we conclude that that is *all* that Paul is saying, then (a) we reduce the programmatic paradox of 9:30–31 to a mere curiosity; (b) we fail to see the relation between the exclusion of "works" in 9:12 and that in 9:32; and (c) we fail to see the point of the contrast between the "righteousness of the law" and that "of faith" in 10:5–13.

(a) The first century reality confronting Paul was that Gentiles were filling an increasing number of church pews while the Jews as a whole remained outside. To that reality Paul gives careful and programmatic formulation in a pardox meant to convey, like other Pauline paradoxes, the unfathomable ways of the Almighty, who chooses to make something of human nothings while persistently bringing to nothing whatever, humanly speaking, promises to be something. The same God who "has made foolish the wisdom of the world," who "has chosen the weak things of the world to shame the strong," the "things that are not to bring to nought the things that are" (1 Cor 1:20, 27–28; cf. 2 Cor 4:10–11; 12:9–10; Rom 4:17), has purposed, according to our passage, to grant righteousness to those who did *not* pursue it – while those who did, fall short. The point of the passage is not simply that righteousness is found in Christ, not Moses, so that Gentiles who pursued it in Christ obtained it while Jews who pursued it in Moses did not. That is not the stuff of paradox, nor does it correspond to Paul's language. It is not that Israel is found to be "barking up the wrong tree," but that the prey is granted, paradoxically, not to the zealous "barkers" but to the indifferent passersby. The relation between human "pursuit" and the obtaining of divine favour is affirmed, paradoxically but necessarily, to be negative.[40] The programmatic nature of the paradox is further apparent from the repetition of its first half (9:30) in 10:20, of its second half (9:31) in 11:7.

(b) The paradox is prefaced, as noted above, with "What shall we say then?" It must, in other words, bear some relation to the preceding argument. And so it does, when given its proper force. After initially claiming that true

---

[40] Cf. T. David Gordon,"Why Israel Did Not Obtain Torah-Righteousness: A Translation Note on Rom 9:32," in *WTJ* 54 (1992) 163–166, here 165.

Israel is defined by the divine call, Paul devotes the next stage of his argument
to an insistence that that call has its roots solely in the divine purpose, repeatedly excluding any consideration of human activity, and insisting on God's
prerogative to deal with his creatures as *he* chooses: "I will have mercy on
whom I have mercy, and I will have compassion on whom I have compassion"
(9:15; cf. v 18). If that is borne in mind, it should come as no surprise (though
the formulation is pointedly paradoxic) to learn that human "pursuit" bears no
relation to the obtaining of divine favour.[41] That Gentiles indifferent to relations with Israel's God have obtained standing with him by faith (9:30) illustrates perfectly the independence of God's call from any consideration of human "works" (9:11–12). Conversely, we should not be surprised to learn that
Israel's pursuit of a path to righteousness involving their performance of
"works" is thought misguided. To be sure, the "works" performed by Israel
are those prescribed by the Mosaic law; but nothing in this passage suggests
that Israel is pursuing the wrong *kind* of "works."[42] What is emphatically excluded is consideration of *any* human "work" in the granting of divine favour
(9:12): an exclusion which naturally includes the particular "works" enjoined
by Moses.[43]

This relation between the exclusion of "works" in 9:12 and that in 9:32 is
confirmed by the third occurrence of the phrase in 11:5–7. If Israel as a whole
has failed to submit to God's righteousness (so 10:3), a "remnant" at least has
found it. But, Paul insists, in the nature of the case, it is a remnant "according
to an election of grace. But if it is by grace, it is no longer by works, for otherwise grace would no longer be grace. What then? What Israel seeks, it did not
attain, but the election [of grace] attained it." Here the "works" that are ex-

---

[41] Note that the same metaphor of a race with its goal lies behind the (fruitless) "running"
in 9:16 and the (fruitless) "pursuing" in 9:30–31. – It should be added that Paul does not
appear to be criticizing the notion of a "pursuit" *per se*, any more than 9:12 is an attack on
"works," or 1 Cor 1:26–29 is an attack on the "strong" or the "nobly born." He does observe
that neither human "running" (Rom 9:16) nor "pursuit" (9:31) nor "strength" nor "noble
birth" is a factor when God constitutes his people – indeed, God is pleased to make his own
those with no such apparent credentials. Of course, a "pursuit" of "works" accompanied by
a refusal to "submit to God's righteousness" based on "faith" *is* seen as culpable (9:32; 10:3,
18–21).

[42] Cf. Johnson, *Function* (see n. 24 above), 155.

[43] Cf. Douglas J. Moo, "'Law,' 'Works of the Law,' and Legalism in Paul," in *WTJ* 45
(1983) 73–100, here 94–97. – In fact, as we have seen, the whole passage (9:6–23), while
preparing for the claim that God has hardened Israel in 11:7–10, does so by treating *in general terms* God's mode of operation: he shows mercy and hardens according to his own sovereign purposes without regard to the "works" of people. In such a *general* treatment (in
which Paul prepares for claims specifically about Israel), it is natural that "works" in *general* are discounted (as preparation for the claim that Israel's "works" in compliance with
the Mosaic law cannot secure status with God). The issue can of course be raised whether
Jews did not see their own election as a matter of grace, their "works" as a mere response to
God's goodness; moreover, did not Paul require "works" of his own converts? We will consider below why Paul sees the matter in a different light.

cluded as a factor in the "election" of the "remnant" are clearly the "works" that a "remnant" of *Israelites* might be expected to perform, and those which (hardened) "Israel" did carry out in the fruitless "search" of 11:7; like those in 9:32, they are the "works" prescribed by the Mosaic law. But Paul's reason for excluding them in 11:6, and, hence, the reason why he thinks their pursuit is bound to fail (11:7), is that of 9:11–12: any consideration of human "works" is incompatible by definition with divine election, which is necessarily rooted in God's purposes and "grace" alone. The remnant owe their place in God's favour to divine election (11:5, 7); the "election" is one of divine "grace" (11:5); an election of "grace" operates without reference to human works (11:6); therefore Israel's "search," necessarily involving works (cf. 9:31–32), can only lead to failure. To repeat: the "works" in view may be those demanded by Israel's "particularism"; but it is not because of the *kind* of "works" they are (i.e., that they are expressions of Israel's particularism, or, for that matter, that they are done in a spirit of self-assertion or self-righteousness) that they are excluded, but because the assigning of a role to human works of *any* kind would mean that God's purposes were not being achieved through his own gracious election: and it is through gracious election, which programmatically excludes consideration of human endeavour, that God has determined to act.

(c) Paul thus sees Israel's pursuit of righteousness through the fulfilment of the law's "works" as a doomed enterprise, in part at least because it is at cross-purposes with the divine *modus operandi* of granting favour by grace alone. It follows that Paul must depict the "righteousness of faith" in such a way as to show that it, unlike Israel's pursuit of righteousness through the law, is consistent with the free operation of divine grace.

Such a depiction of faith has of course already been offered in Romans 4. In what is essentially another statement of the principle of 9:11–12; 11:6, we are told in 4:4 that what is granted to "the one who works (τῷ δὲ ἐργαζομένῳ)" cannot be awarded "by grace (κατὰ χάριν)," but must be reckoned as such a person's "due." Again, it is no doubt the case that Paul has in mind the "works" of the Mosaic law when he excludes any consideration of "works": the first century issue with which he was confronted was whether or not Gentile Christians should comply with specific requirements of the Mosaic law, not whether "good works" of a general sort might be thought to merit God's salvation. But, again, such "works" are said to be excluded, *not* because they represent a particular kind of work, but because consideration of *any* human "work" (including the performance of deeds prescribed by the Mosaic law) in the granting of righteousness necessarily involves a recognition of human deserts that is incompatible with the sovereign gift of divine grace.[44] Con-

---

[44] I.e., Paul attempts to resolve the first-century dilemma by showing which of the potential courses of action is compatible with a correct understanding of the character and ways of

versely, divine grace *is* operative in the case of one who "does not work but believes on him who justifies the ungodly" (4:5). Hence the juxtaposition of μὴ ἐργαζομένῳ with πιστεύοντι in this context has the force, not simply of denying that the believer need perform the particular works enjoined in the law, but of characterizing faith in God as compatible with – indeed, as finding its essence in – an abandoning of the thought that one might contribute anything to the process of "justification" and receiving it from the God in whom one believes as a gift of "grace" – as, indeed, it must be when the "justified" are the "ungodly" (4:5).[45]

Such faith, Paul claims, was shown by Abraham, who in this respect is the prototype of Christian believers. Why, we may wonder, does Paul not consider such "faith" itself as a human contribution to the process of justification? The answer is apparent. Paul's point is not that Abraham or Christians are people characterized by a human attitude called "faith"; rather, as admiration is evoked by beauty, so "faith" is thought of by Paul as necessarily a *response* elicited by the proclamation of what God has done (so in the case of Christian faith) or (as in the case of Abraham; cf. Rom 4:18–22) what he is about to do: "faith comes from hearing, and hearing through the word of Christ" (10:17).[46] Indeed, in 1 Thes 2:13, the "word of God" is thought to actively effect the response of faith; and it is apparent everywhere that Paul believes God's "call" or "election" is the necessary precondition of Christian faith.[47] As a trust in God evoked – even created – by the proclamation that God himself, of his own initiative and grace, has done (or will do) all that is necessary, "faith" is thought compatible with the complete gratuity of God's

---

God. The same theological consideration is invoked to resolve a different first century problem in 1 Cor 1:26–31. It is affirmed more "abstractly" in Eph 2:8–9; cf. Tit 3:4–7.

[45] As noted above, there is an inevitable link, in Paul as in the Hebrew scriptures, between the insistence on human sinfulness and the gratuity of divine salvation (cf. Rom 3:23–24; 5:15–17; 2 Cor 5:18–6:1).

[46] For "faith" as a response to proclamation, cf. also 1 Cor 2:4–5; 15:11, 14; Gal 3:2, 5. "Darum ist der Glaube nicht das Mittel, das der Mensch anwenden muss, um gerechtfertigt zu werden. Er ist nicht die subjektive Voraussetzung für das Heilsgeschehen, sondern die Konsequenz des am Menschen erfolgten Tuns Gottes. Er ermöglicht nicht das Wirken Gottes, sondern das Wirken Gottes ermöglicht den Glauben des Menschen. Darum kann der Glaube nicht die Bedingung sein, die der Mensch erfüllen muß, wenn er errettet werden will, sondern die Verkündigung von dem durch Gott den Menschen in Christus bereiteten Heil ist die Bedingung für die Ermöglichung des Glaubens" (Gerhard Friedrich, "Glaube und Verkündigung bei Paulus," in *Glaube im Neuen Testament*, ed. Ferdinand Hahn and Hans Klein [Neukirchen-Vluyn: Neukirchener Verlag, 1982] 93–113, here 109–110). Cf. also Otfried Hofius, "Wort Gottes und Glaube bei Paulus," in *Paulus und das antike Judentum*, ed. Martin Hengel and Ulrich Heckel (Tübingen: Mohr, 1991) 379–408.

[47] See n. 32 above. Cf. 2 Cor 4:6, where the divine illumination which results in faith is compared with the creation of light in Gen 1:3. Paul's own "Damascus" experience was, he would have believed, precisely of that character, and forbade his assuming any credit for his own coming to "faith."

salvific activity,[48] whereas the regarding of his blessing as in any way contingent on the independent performance of human "works" is not.

A similar understanding of "faith" is implicit in 9:30–32. After insisting that God "calls" people without reference to their works (9:6–23), Paul notes that good standing with God *is* obtained *by* "*faith*" on the part of those who do *not* "pursue" it, while Jews involved in the "pursuit" miss the path of "faith" (9:30–32). The "faith" in question is obviously and necessarily faith *in Christ*: faith has for Paul the character of response, and saving faith is response to the proclamation of God's salvation in Christ. Christ is the "stone" over which Jews "stumble" through unbelief; he is the agent of God's righteousness. But in this passage, as in Romans 4, it is part of the essence of faith in Christ that it accepts the "gift" (so Rom 5:17; cf. 3:24) of divine righteousness apart from human "pursuit" in a way compatible with God's eternal purpose of constituting his people through his call and grace alone.[49]

Finally, when the "righteousness of the law" is contrasted with that "of faith" in 10:5–13, the point of the contrast is the same. The law requires "doing"[50] as the path to life: "the one who does these things will live by them." The righteousness of faith, by contrast, is immediately distanced from human endeavour. After all, no human can have any part either in bringing Christ down from heaven or in bringing him back from the dead (10:6–7). No, the path of faith has been made accessible to people, brought "near" to them (10:8) without their pursuing it; it has been "put at their fingertips," we might say, though Deuteronomy's "in your mouth and in your heart" (Deut 30:14, cited in 10:8)[51] allows the desired connection to the *oral* confession that Jesus is Lord and the *inner* conviction that God raised him from the dead.[52]

---

[48] Note that Phil 1:29 sees "faith" itself as a gift of God's grace. The compatability of "faith" and "grace" in Paul's thought is also apparent in Gal 5:4–5; Rom 3:21–30; 5:1–2; and esp. 4:16: διὰ τοῦτο ἐκ πίστεως, ἵνα κατὰ χάριν ... Cf. also the classic statement in Eph 2:8–9. On the relationship between "grace" and "faith" in Paul, see Darrel J. Doughty, "The Priority of ΧΑΡΙΣ," in *NTS* 19 (1972–1973) 163–180.

[49] Cf. Timo Laato, *Paulus und das Judentum: Anthropologische Erwägungen* (Åbo: Åbo Academy Press, 1991) 250–251 for the insistence that the "christological" explanation of Israel's shortcoming in 9:30–10:3 complements rather than rules out an "anthropocentric" explanation.

[50] The essence of the "righteousness of the law" must be found in the words ὁ ποιήσας, since it can hardly rest in the unspecified αὐτά/αὐτοῖς (or variants thereof).

[51] An incidental confirmation that Paul's point here is that "the righteousness of faith" does not involve human endeavour is provided by his omission, in quoting Deut 30:14, of the notion that the word is "near ... *to do it*" (LXX αὐτὸ ποιεῖν). Cf. C. Thomas Rhyne, "*Nomos Dikaiosynes* and the Meaning of Romans 10:4," in *CBQ* 47 (1985) 486–499, here 496–497; Johnson, *Function* (see n. 24 above), 158.

[52] On the appropriateness of using this passage in Deuteronomy as a characterization of the "righteousness of faith," see James D.G. Dunn, "'Righteousness from the Law' and 'Righteousness from Faith': Paul's Interpretation of Scripture in Romans 10:1–10," in *Tradition and Interpretation in the New Testament*, ed. Gerald F. Hawthorne with Otto Betz (Grand Rapids: Eerdmans; Tübingen: Mohr, 1987) 216–228.

It appears, then, that the argument of these chapters requires us to see in Israel's misguided pursuit of "works" rather than "faith" not simply a zealous pursuit of a particularistic path oblivious to recent christological developments, but a failure to perceive that God's favour in Christ is bestowed, as it has always been bestowed, gratuitously, not in recognition of human endeavour, and that it can be enjoyed only by those who respond to the gift with faith. Similarly, in 10:3, Israel's attempt to establish "their own righteousness" rather than submit to God's righteousness means more than that they adhered to a covenant that embraced their own nation in a peculiar way rather than the divine righteousness that embraces all peoples on identical terms.[53] Unless we are to isolate completely Paul's explanation of Israel's misunderstanding in 9:32 from his statement of their ignorance in 10:3, the latter claim too must mean that they attribute to their "own," human endeavours to fulfill God's demands a significance that the "righteousness of God"[54] will not allow.

It remains to address Paul's perception of the role played by the Mosaic law in Israel's purported misunderstanding. Is the essence of the law understood as (a) its demand for "works," so that Israel's misunderstanding is rooted in the nature of the law itself? Or is the law understood as essentially (b) a preparation for faith, so that Israel's misunderstanding is rooted in its own distortion of the law? The answer appears to be: "(c) both of the above." According to 9:31, Israel's "pursuit" has "the law of righteousness" as its goal. The Mosaic code is clearly intended. That it is defined by the genitive δικαιοσύνης perhaps reflects Paul's earlier allowance that its commands are "righteous" (7:12). Note, too, that Paul can speak of the "righteousness based on the law" in 10:5: the "law of righteousness" (9:31) is thus the one that spells out a path to righteousness in the terms, "The one who does these things will live by them" (Rom 10:5, citing Lev 18:5). But a path described in these terms is clearly being *contrasted* with the path of faith[55] whereby divine salvation is

---

[53] So, e.g., N.T. Wright, *The Climax of the Covenant: Christ and the Law in Pauline Theology* (Minneapolis: Fortress, 1992) 241; Sanders, *Paul* (see n. 20 above), 38.

[54] We need not decide here whether the "righteousness of God" in 10:3 refers to his salvific activity in Christ (i.e., τοῦ θεοῦ as subjective genitive; cf. 3:25–26) or his "gift of righteousness" to those who believe (i.e., τοῦ θεοῦ as objective genitive; cf. 5:17; 2 Cor 5:21; Phil 3:9). The opposing arguments, here as in 1:17; 3:21–22, are finely balanced.

[55] That the "righteousness of faith" in 10:6–13 is contrasted, not identified, with the "righteousness of the law" in 10:5 is all but demanded by the structure of 10:5–6: "When Paul sets righteousness ἐκ πίστεως alongside righteousness ἐκ something else, with δέ as the linking word, he obviously intends his readers to understand a contrast between the two phrases (4:16; 9:30, 32; as well as Gal 2:16 and 3:21–22)" (Dunn, *Romans* [see n. 23 above], 602). Such an interpretation is confirmed by (a) the contrast elsewhere in Romans of the law and its "works" with faith (e.g., 3:21–22, 28; 4:13, 14, 16); (b) the parallel *contrast* of the *same* two "righteousnesses" in Phil 3:9; (c) the use in Gal 3:12 of the same Leviticus text cited in Rom 10:5 to establish that "the law is not of faith." To suggest that Paul identifies the "righteousness of the law" in Rom 10:5 with that of "faith" in 10:6 thus requires us to

made available apart from human endeavour (10:6–13); the essence of the "righteousness of the law" is thus portrayed in 10:5 as its demand for deeds in compliance with its prescriptions (cf. 2:13). Hence, Israel's "pursuit" of the "law of righteousness" can only refer to Israel's efforts at securing their good standing with God by proving faithful to the prescriptions of Torah. And yet, Paul claims, the efforts have proved fruitless (9:31b) – indeed, they are misguided (9:32). How does Paul envisage the shortcomings of Israel's "pursuit"?

It would be wrong to forget at this point all that Paul has said in the first eight chapters of the epistle. Israel was given the law, but because of their transgressions, they have been left standing, with Gentiles, culpable before God (Romans 2–3). The law's demands may be "holy and righteous and good," but when they encounter a "flesh" that is rebellious against God, they can only aggravate the rebellion (Romans 7). The mindset of the "flesh" is at enmity with God; it does not, and cannot, submit to his law (8:7). In these chapters Paul provides an "anthropological" explanation for the self-critical tradition by which Israel viewed its past as a litany of stubborn, stiff-necked rebellion in the face of divine favour. Given his support for that tradition, it is obvious that Paul did not think Israel had ever measured up to the law. The law's promise of life (2:13; 10:5; cf. 7:10) had been frustrated by its "weakness," its inability to overcome the "flesh" (8:3). Israel's transgressions of the law are seen as keeping them from securing the good standing with God promised to them as his people *if* they complied with his commands. When the law and Israel's history under its regime are regarded in these terms, then it is clear that the coming of Christ and his death "for our sins" must be thought to mark a divinely declared and emphatic end (τέλος) to the possibility, proclaimed in the law itself, that righteousness could be secured through its "works" (10:4–5; cf. 3:20–22).[56]

---

believe "that, whereas he quotes Lev. 18:5, without elaborating on it, as a self-evident demonstration that 'the law does *not* rest on faith' in Gal. 3:12, he quotes the same verse, without elaboration, as a self-evident demonstration that the law *does* rest on faith in Rom. 10:5" (Stephen Westerholm, *Israel's Law and the Church's Faith: Paul and His Recent Interpreters* [Grand Rapids: Eerdmans, 1988] 128). Cf. also J.S. Vos, "Die hermeneutische Antinomie bei Paulus (Galater 3.11–12; Römer 10.5–10)," in *NTS* 38 (1992) 254–270, here 258–260.

[56] That τέλος in 10:4 can mean "end" has been amply demonstrated by Dunn, *Romans* (see n. 23 above), 589–591; cf. Heikki Räisänen, *Paul and the Law* (Philadelphia: Fortress, 1986 [1983]) 53–56. That the Sinaitic covenant and, with it, the Mosaic law, though divinely given and "glorious," have now served their divine purpose and are (at least for those in Christ) no longer valid is, I believe, maintained consistently by Paul, who contrasts not only the "old" covenant with the "new," but also the time (and path) of the "law" with that of "faith" (cf. 2 Cor 3:6–14; Gal 3:19–25; Rom 3:21–22; 7:6). (For the limited polemical purpose of statements about Christian "fulfilment" of the law, see my "On Fulfilling the Whole Law [Gal. 5:14]," in *SEÅ* 51–52 [1986–1987] 229–237; also *Law* [see n. 54 above], 201–205. Rom 3:31 perhaps refers to the law as a witness to the "righteousness of faith"; or it may simply be an affirmation that Paul rather than his opponents proclaims what God really

So much seems clear. Curiously, however, in spite of his agreement in 10:5 (and elsewhere) that the law demands "works," Paul declares in 9:32 that Israel's attempts to measure up to the law by means of its "works" are misguided; only by "faith" can their goal be achieved. How are we to understand this latter claim?

In fact, of course, the Christian Paul could not believe that God had ever intended the law to serve as the true path to righteousness (cf. Gal 3:21). Such a divine intention would reduce Christ to God's "Plan B," a notion unacceptable both for its displacement of the centrality of Christ and for its implication that God's "Plan A" had met with unexpected failure. Moreover, the notion that God could ever recognize human deeds in compliance with the law as a factor in securing his favour would run counter to Paul's depiction of the divine mode of operation in 9:6–23. In God's plan, then, the law must have been intended to serve some role preparatory to the revelation of his righteousness in Christ. God's design for the law must have been, in part, to go on record as demanding what is "holy and righteous and good," but also (indeed, even more) to demonstrate the rebellious character of humanity in Adam through the shortcomings of the most privileged segment of Adamic humanity (3:19–20). Paradoxically, then, the righteousness demanded *by* the law can only be attained *apart from* the law, by faith in Christ. But since the law had a divine role to play until Christ came, since it demonstrated the culpability of humanity from which Christ brought redemption, it can be said to have been pointing all along to Christ. And given Paul's use of the metaphor of a race for Israel's "pursuit" of the "law of righteousness," it is just possible that, with τέλος in 10:4, Paul intends to designate Christ as the "goal" as well as the "end" of the law's promise of righteousness to those who keep its demands.[57] Finally, since the law's true purpose is found, not in the impossible fulfilment of its demands by the "flesh," but in preparing the path to faith, Israel can only measure up to the law itself, not "by works," but "by faith" (9:31–32).

But what, we may ask in conclusion, induced Paul to contrast "faith" and "works" in this way, and to portray non-Christian Jews in a fruitless pursuit of righteousness through "works"?[58] And why did he not see his own insistence

---

intended in giving the law [cf. 3:20; 4:15; 5:20] and in that sense *he* "establishes" it.) The ending of the (temporary) institution of the Sinaitic covenant does not, however, mean for Paul the setting aside of God's (prior) promise to Abraham and his "seed" – though only in Romans does he insist that the historical people of Israel constituted by the promise remain its effective object.

[57] Where a Greek term or phrase appearing in different contexts must be rendered in quite different ways in English, it is normally unwise to suggest that the term or phrase can have both meanings in a single context. But "goal" and "end" are not necessarily unrelated meanings. Cf. C.K. Barrett, *Essays on Paul* (London: SPCK, 1982) 146–147.

[58] On this matter, cf. the helpful comments of Heikki Räisänen, "Der Bruch des Paulus mit Israels Bund," in *The Law in the Bible and in its Environment*, ed. Timo Veijola (Hel-

on proper Christian behaviour as subject to the same condemnation of "works"?

For the Christian Paul, reflecting on humanity's (now self-evident) need of redemption through a crucified and resurrected Messiah, it seemed clear that God's decisive salvific intervention could not possibly be one that left untransformed the character of human "flesh." And, however privileged Israel may have been; indeed, however much they might owe their favoured status to God's grace and redemption, the record of their history in sacred scripture would, to his mind, demonstrate that they remained "flesh";[59] their "redemption" from Egypt and the subsequent gift of the law had not altered Israel's all too human recalcitrance toward God and his will.[60] The picture is not altered if we insist that Israel's efforts at fulfilling the law were merely required to *maintain* a standing with God granted by divine favour, or that nothing more than a modicum of intended obedience was demanded. If "flesh" is defined by its fundamental hostility toward God, good standing with him can neither be gained nor maintained by a path that requires any such "works" of "flesh" (cf. Rom 8:7–8). What is required is a new order of humanity; a second, but obedient, Adam; a new creation or, if you will, the redemption of the old. In any case, these are all job descriptions such that no human need apply, even for an assistant's role: when God "cooked up" creation, he kept the recipe to himself.

But, of course, for Paul, God *has* acted, there *is* a new creation for those who are in Christ; a second, obedient Adam *has* overcome the dilemma created by the disobedience of the first. And it is all, Paul insists, God's doing. To be sure, the proclamation of what God has done should evoke trust in those who hear it, as beauty evokes admiration. Without such faith, humanity remains in its "fleshly" refusal to acknowledge God and give him his due. But the transformation (6:1–11), the reconciliation of God's enemies (5:6–11), the justification of the ungodly (3:21–26; 4:5), is entirely God's doing: both Paul's depiction of the human dilemma and a religious vision, like Isaiah's, that sees God as the only effective Actor on the stage of history and the only worthy recipient of praise,[61] led Paul to this insistence.

---

sinki: Finnish Exegetical Society; Göttingen: Vandenhoeck & Ruprecht, 1990) 156–172, here 169–171.

[59] Cf. Phil 3:3–6, in which the privileges and practices of Judaism are considered to belong to the realm of the "flesh"; also the insistence in Gal 3:3 that for Gentile believers to be circumcised is to return to the realm of the "flesh"; and of course Rom 7:14–25; 8:3. It is not without significance that Paul claims no σάρξ can be "justified by the works of the law" (Gal 2:16; Rom 3:20; cf. Thielman, *Plight* [see n. 18 above], 63–65).

[60] Again, the notion that Israel's untransformed recalcitrance proved disastrous for its relation with God in terms of the Sinaitic covenant, though exploited by Paul, was hardly a Pauline innovation; it is thematic, e.g., in the Deuteronomistic history, as in Jeremiah and Ezekiel.

[61] Rom 9:6–29; 11:25–36; 1 Cor 1:18–31. Cf. Isa 2:11, 17, 22; 29:14–16; 31:3, etc.

That being said, Paul shares, in addition to the five we have listed, a sixth conviction with the other early Christian authors represented in our New Testament: the divine transformation achieved in Jesus Christ must have moral consequences in the lives of his followers.[62] Only God can transform the "flesh" – but a transformation *is*, necessarily, a transformation: if service of God and of righteousness does not mark the citizens of the new age, then how does it differ from the old? Paul does not hesitate to demand righteous behaviour of Christians – though it is worth noting that he frequently qualifies statements of Christian activity with reminders that the true agent is the divine spirit within.[63] If righteous, God-pleasing behaviour is only possible by those whom God has translated into a new order of humanity and in whom God's spirit (or Christ, or the Spirit of Christ) resides, such deeds are themselves an effect, an expression, of God's transforming grace (1 Cor 15:10; 2 Cor 1:12; 12:9; cf. Phil 1:6; 2:13); necessary, to be sure, but hardly subject to the exclusion of human "works" intended to ensure that no "fleshly" endeavour is given a role in the securing of divine favour. The "works" which Paul discounts are those of the unredeemed "flesh"; the righteous behaviour that he requires is the "fruit" of the Spirit borne in those who have responded to God's demonstration of righteousness with faith.

Conclusions: Recent scholarship is correct in its insistence that first century "Judaism" must be understood in its own terms; and Sanders' "covenantal nomism"[64] finely captures the essence of at least much of the first century Jewish religious scene. We do not, however, do full justice to Paul's argument in Rom 9:30–10:13 (and elsewhere) when we confine Paul's perception of the shortcomings of (non-Christian) Jewish religiosity to christological obtuseness or nationalistic particularism. Jewish convictions about God's goodness and sovereignty over the affairs of humankind found expression long before Paul in the notions that God accomplishes his (ultimately benevolent) purposes independently of human designs or activity and that, given the recalcitrance of the human heart, divine deliverance must be rooted in divine goodness and faithfulness, not in the merits of the delivered. Such notions are the very pith of the Pauline gospel and, at the same time, a crucial element in his argument in Romans that "flesh" cannot be "justified" by human observance of the law. To deny Paul's contrast between "faith" and "works," or to confine its scope to a polemic against Jewish particularism, is thus to fail to appreciate both the theocentric focus of Paul's religious view and the radicalness with which he views the human dilemma and the divine redemption. On the one

---

[62] Cf. Hultgren, *Rise*, 95–97.

[63] Rom 8:9, 13–14; Gal 5:18, 22, 25; cf. Rom 15:18; Gal 2:20; Phil 2:13.

[64] E.P. Sanders, *Paul and Palestinian Judaism* (Philadelphia: Fortress, 1977) 75, 426–428.

hand, God must be the one "from whom, through whom, and for whom are all things" (Rom 11:36). On the other, "flesh" cannot be made good by giving it commands to keep, however righteous those demands in themselves might be. The old, corrupted order must give way to that of righteousness. Such was the divine triumph accomplished in Christ.

Or so, at least, runs the radical Pauline script of the sanguine prophetic hope for divine renewal.

Faith, Works and Election in Romans 9

A Response to Stephen Westerholm

by

HEIKKI RÄISÄNEN

In Romans 9–11 Paul explains how the gospel can be taken to represent a triumph for God, even though most of the Jewish people appear to be on the losing side.[1] The issue of law comes up in the section on Israel's disobedience (9:30–10:21).

In his closely argued paper, Stephen Westerholm acknowledges that "faith" means in 9:30–33 faith in Christ – not, e.g., an attitude of humble trust toward the old law.[2] On this point we are in agreement. For Westerholm, however, the main point in Paul's contrast between 'faith' and 'works' is *not* Israel's lack of Christological faith (in contrast to those Gentiles who have believed and been included in God's people)[3]; even less could that be said to be its only point.[4] Such interpretations, he says, fail "to appreciate both the theocentric focus of Paul's religious view and the radicalness with which he views the human dilemma and the divine redemption" (p. 236). For the latter point little evidence is found in Romans 9–11; a debate on it would have to be carried out over

---

[1] For a full discussion see my articles Römer 9–11: Analyse eines geistigen Ringens, ANRW II.25.4, 1987, 2891–2939; Paul, God and Israel. Romans 9–11 in Recent Research, in The Social World of Formative Christianity and Judaism, FS H.C. Kee (ed. J. Neusner et al.), Philadelphia 1988, 178–206; Romans 9–11 and the "History of Early Christian Religion", in Texts and Contexts: Biblical Texts in their Textual and Situational Contexts, FS L.Hartman (ed. T. Fornberg – D. Hellholm), Oslo 1995, 743–765.

[2] For the latter view cf. C.E.B. Cranfield, A Critical and Exegetical Commentary on the Epistle to the Romans II (ICC), Edinburgh 1979, 510.

[3] This is my position in Paul and the Law (WUNT 29), Tübingen 1987 (2nd ed.), 174: "the main reason for the Jews' unbelief is a Christological one".

[4] Thus E.P. Sanders, Paul, the Law and the Jewish People, Philadelphia 1983, 37: "Israel's failure is not that they do not obey the law in the correct way, but that they do not have faith in Christ." A similar result is reached in the course of a fresh analysis by W. Reinbold, Paulus und das Gesetz: Zur Exegese von Röm 9,30–33, BZ 38, 1994, 263: "Paul reflects here on the different reaction of Gentiles and Israel to the Gospel"; 264: "Auf Röm 9,30–33 kann sich die gemeinhin mit dem Namen von E.P. Sanders verbundene Position mit Recht berufen." See now also H. Boers, The Justification of the Gentiles, Peabody 1994, 136, cf. 75–76 and passim.

Romans 1–8 which oversteps the limits of the present discussion. In these remarks I shall concentrate on the issue of "theocentric focus".

According to Westerholm, Paul establishes in 9:30f a "programmatic paradox" which is explained by referring back to 9:11–12.15.18. The problem is
not that Israel is pursuing the wrong kind of "works" or conducting her works
in the wrong spirit; rather, consideration of *any* human "work" or "pursuit" is
emphatically excluded in the granting of divine favour (p. 229). The same
idea is expressed in 11:5–7.

I. 9:6–18 does not speak of faith

Paul does indeed suggest a link between 9:6ff and 9:30ff, since he inserts the
words "not because of works" into 9:12: Rebecca received the divine message
concerning her sons when "they were not yet born and had done nothing either
good or bad, in order that God's purpose of election might continue, *not because of works but because of him who calls*".

However, this combination, though Pauline, is awkward; one has to ask
whether it really reflects the main line of Paul's thought. The word 'works'
occurs in both places, 9:30ff and 9:6ff (as it does in 11:6). By contrast, 'faith'
is *not* mentioned in 9:6–23, the section on election.[5] The opposite of 'works'
in 9:12 is, rather, "he who calls". What is worse, a mention of 'faith' would not
fit into that passage at all; it would damage it. Where *any* human activity is
excluded, there even faith disappears from the picture, and rightly so.[6]

One does well to distinguish between Paul's inmost aim – what he "really"
has in mind – and his way of arguing his case. Undoubtedly Paul has Jewish
Christians in mind all the time when he speaks of God's merciful election.

---

[5] It is not mentioned in 11:1–10 either.

[6] The antithesis "through faith"/"by works (of the law)" belongs to the context of justification; there two mutually exclusive human attitudes are confronted with each other. "In
Röm 9,12 hingegen geht es um den Gegensatz Gott – Mensch. Und dass der Glaube hier
nicht genannt ist, entspringt der Gesamtanlage von Röm 9–11." H. Hübner, Gottes Ich und
Israel (FRLANT 136), Göttingen 1984, 25. Cf. O. Kuss, Der Römerbrief III, Regensburg
1978, 709 (quoting W. Beyschlag): "... ein 'nicht aufgrund von Werken, sondern aufgrund
des Berufenden'" is "etwas wesentlich Anderes als ein 'nicht aufgrund von Werken, sondern
aufgrund von Glauben". "Indem der Apostel jenes schreibt und nicht dieses, macht er einen
wesentlich anderen Gegensatz als den, welcher den ersten Hauptteil seines Briefes – Röm
1–8 – bedingt, den Gegensatz nicht zwischen diesem und jenem menschlichen Verhalten zu
Gott, sondern zwischen menschlicher und göttlicher Aktivität in Dingen unseres Heils. Mit
anderen Worten: er schliesst damit nicht bloss die werktätige, sondern *jede* menschliche Initiative bei der Aufnahme ins Reich Gottes aus und lässt nur die göttliche stehen ..." (my
emphasis). These authors differ from Westerholm in that according to them "faith" must be
counted as *some kind of "human activity"*; by contrast, Westerholm argues that, for Paul,
faith is "thought compatible with the complete gratuity of God's salvific activity" (pp. 230–1);
see below.

The shape of his argument prevents him, however, from spelling this out; otherwise the argument which rests on God's total sovereignty would be undermined. Paul's omission of any mention of faith here may indicate that somehow he sensed the tension. In 9:6ff Paul speaks as if humans are saved simply by God's free, indeed arbitrary[7] action: their destinies are decreed by God even before they are born.

Actually Romans 9:6ff is a singular passage in Paul. Compared with the general tenor of his letters, Paul goes here "too far", as the argument leaves no room for faith. The same is true of the (in itself quite different) passage 11:25–36 where the argument would logically lead "too far" in the opposite direction: to the idea of ἀποκατάστασις (which was actually found there by many older commentators[8]).

The difference between the roughly parallel statements Gal 3:22 and Rom 11:32b is instructive. The former belongs to a context where "justification by faith" is set forth: Scripture has consigned all under sin in order that what was promised might be given to *"those who believe"*. The latter is about God's sovereign mercy: God has consigned all men to disobedience, that he may have "mercy upon *all*". It is difficult to emphasize human faith and divine omnipotence simultaneously.

II. Secondary lines of thought

It seems to me that what Westerholm regards as the basis of Paul's theological thought is actually a secondary device. Similar devices, i.e. statements about divine hardening, double predestination or the like, occur in the Old Testament, in Qumran, in Mark, in John and in the Koran.[9] In all these cases the idea of divine hardening, leading astray or predestination *ad malum* is employed to make sense of the negative social experience of the individual or of the group (the message in question is being rejected by the majority).[10]

For Paul, the problem posed by the "unbelief" of Israel was of such magnitude[11] that "normal" solutions – such as the talk of Israel's disobedience in not

---

[7] Verse 9:14 shows that Paul is not insensitive to this issue. Predestination *to damnation* is envisaged in 9:6–18.

[8] E.g. by H. Weinel, Biblische Theologie des Neuen Testaments, Tübingen 1928 (4th ed.), 315.

[9] Cf. Ex 7:3, 9:12 etc.; Isa 6:9–10; Mark 4:11f.34; John 6:37.44, 6:64f., 10:26, 11:52, 12:37–40; 1 QS 3:13–4:26; Koran Sura 7:179/178, 11:119/120 etc.

[10] Cf. H. Räisänen, The Idea of Divine Hardening, Helsinki 1976 (2nd ed.); E.P. Sanders, Paul and Palestinian Judaism, London 1977, 257–70 (on Qumran).

[11] Expressions like "not all Jews" (Westerholm p. 222, cf. p. 219) or "many Jews" (p. 221) tend to obscure the seriousness of Paul's problem which was not that less than 100 per cent of the Jews believed in Christ, but that (shall we say) 99 per cent did not.

accepting the message about Jesus, 10:14–21 – could not fully satisfy him. In wrestling with the problem he resorts in 9:6–18 (temporarily!) to the extreme idea of double predestination, although it does not fit his "normal" thought.

A rival explanation is the idea that the blindness of the unbelievers is to be traced back to Satan, the "god of this aeon" (2 Cor 4:4). This idea fits the context of 2 Corinthians, but were it introduced into Romans 9, it would utterly destroy the argument there. This should warn interpreters of making Paul's theological thought more systematic or consistent than it is.

Paul's attempt to link Israel's failure (as depicted in 9:30–33) with 9:11–12 seems, then, somewhat tortured. Nevertheless, Paul forged the link. The question is, How central is this to his theology? I repeat what I have written in concession to those who criticize Sanders's position on Paul's view of "works of the law": "It may be too much to exclude all overtones of the idea of anthropocentric legalism ...[12] Paul may have seen some tendency toward smugness and self-righteousness in the Jewish way. But if so, this was a by-product, not the underlying error."[13] One should distinguish "between the 'target' of Paul's argument (he argues 'against privileged status') and the way he actually conducts his argument (alluding to a 'by works' soteriology on the part of the Jews and Judaizers)".[14] Paul does speak at times as if God's grace were unknown in Judaism and as if everything was built on men's "works". This, however, is a secondary consequence of Paul's exclusively Christ-centred soteriology.[15] This dynamics, I think, has been at work in the writing of Romans 9 as well.

In my view, this assessment comes quite close to the thoughts of Westerholm himself in his fine book on Paul, where he writes:

"It is because Paul believes the coming of the new covenant implies the inadequacy of the old that he characterizes the one as resting on divine grace, the other on human works."[16] "Forced to explain (as his opponents were not) both the law's inadequacy and the distinction between the path of faith and that of the law, Paul characterized the law and the gospel in terms crucial to his case, but foreign to the understanding of his opponents." That is, he gave 'grace' "an exclusive sense (eliminating any role by 'works' ...) and 'faith' a narrower definition (it 'does not work' ...) than was normal in Jewish writings".[17]

This, however, led to an anomaly in Paul's view of 'faith'.

---

[12] This was written with regard to Rom 4, but it applies to 9:30–33 as well.

[13] Paul and the Law 176.

[14] Paul and the Law xxviii; Paul's Call Experience and His Later View of the Law, in Jesus, Paul and Torah (JSNTS 43), Sheffield 1992, 37 (cf. 46).

[15] H. Räisänen, Der Bruch des Paulus mit Israels Bund, in T. Veijola (ed.), The Law in the Bible and in its Environment, Helsinki-Göttingen 1990, 170f.

[16] S. Westerholm, Israel's Law and the Church's Faith: Paul and His Recent Interpreters, Grand Rapids 1988, 163; cf. 147–50.

[17] Westerholm, op.cit. 150.

III. Paul's view of faith

Westerholm (p. 230) raises a reasonable question: why does Paul not consider "faith" itself to be a human contribution to the process of justification? He answers by simply paraphrasing Paul: faith is "thought compatible with the complete gratuity of God's salvific activity" (pp. 230–1).[18] Of course! But if we allow ourselves to put critical questions to Paul's thinking, it is hard to avoid the impression that this Pauline view is at odds with Paul's own depiction, say, of Abraham's faith in Rom 4:18–23. However much Paul may wish to stress the gratuity of Abraham's faith in 4:4–5, in verses 18–23, as Francis Watson puts it,

"Abraham's faith is seen as a steadfast and heroic trust in God to fulfil his promises, despite unfavourable outward circumstances. According to v. 22, it was because Abraham had this kind of faith that righteousness was reckoned to him. 4:18ff is thus incompatible with the view that for Paul salvation is by grace alone. Grace is presupposed here in the form of promise, but a strenuous human response, encompassing one's whole life, is required."[19]

The repeated emphasis on the extraordinary strength of Abraham's faith in the passage ("he believed against all hope", "did not weaken in faith", "no distrust made him waver", "grew strong in his faith", "fully convinced") hardly suggests the analogy of admiration which is simply "evoked by beauty" (Westerholm p. 230).

How strenuous an activity a "faith decision" actually entailed for a Gentile is also spelt out by Watson.

"The decision of faith means the decision to abandon many of the norms and beliefs of one's previous social environment, and to adopt new norms and beliefs within a new social environment ... Faith for Paul is thus essentially active ... He is therefore able quite consistently to say that certain prohibited forms of conduct prevent people from entering the kingdom of God (Gal. 5:20f), and he is able to make salvation dependent on satisfactory conduct ... (Gal. 6:7f)."[20]

Westerholm refers to 1 Thes 2:13 where "the 'word of God' is thought to actively effect the response of faith" (p. 230). Yet what Paul actually says is that the word of God accepted by the Thessalonians is (now) working (or is effective) in them. "Where the word of God is welcomed with obedient faith,

---

[18] Westerholm's remark (p. 232) that "God's favour in Christ is bestowed, as it has always been bestowed, gratuitously, not in recognition of human endeavour", is intriguing. For if God's favour has *always* been bestowed in this way, why was it necessary at all to send Christ?

[19] F. Watson, Paul, Judaism and the Gentiles (SNTSMS 56), Cambridge 1986, 140.

[20] Watson, op.cit. 64f.

there the power of God is at work."[21] Actually the Thessalonians might have regarded Paul's gospel as "the word of men"; fortunately they did not behave in this way, but "accepted" it as the word of God. Ernest Best captures the nuance in pointing out that ἐδέξασθε is "practically synonymous with *received* but perhaps lays more stress on the action of the hearers".[22] A certain "co-operation" on man's part can hardly be denied in this case either.[23] Indeed the only effective way to exclude *all* human efforts in the event of salvation would be a doctrine of double predestination.

IV. Indifferent sympathizers?

If Paul really intends to separate faith from human activity in 9:30ff, this would reflect forced reasoning on his part.[24] If we follow Westerholm's "paradoxical" reading of the passage, the stage for the "race" is set in a curious way. For on what basis could Paul claim that Gentiles (meaning Gentile Christians!) "did not pursue righteousness" in their pre-Christian state? In most cases they surely did just that, both in moral terms[25] and, most of all, in sympathizing with Jews! How could Paul suggest that they had been "indifferent passersby" or "indifferent to relations with Israel's God" (p. 228), if they had in fact largely been sympathizers in contact with synagogues? Christian preaching was actually drawing people primarily "because of their prior attraction to Judaism."[26] If the "not pursuing" is to make any sense at all,[27] it

---

[21] L. Morris, The First and Second Epistles to the Thessalonians (NIC), Grand Rapids 1989 (1959), 88.

[22] E. Best, The First and Second Epistles to the Thessalonians (BNTC), London 1977, 111.

[23] Cf. E. von Dobschütz, Die Thessalonicher-Briefe (KEK), Göttingen 1974 (1909), 104: "an sich ganz synonym, müssen die Verben hier nach der rezeptiven ... und der aktiven Seite unterschieden werden: (ohne eignes Zutun) bekommen und (in freier Entscheidung) annehmen ..." Becoming a Christian thus entails both a "receptive" and an "active" aspect.

[24] In Rom 10:9–10 "the confession of the mouth" is added to "faith of the heart", as if that did not imply any human activity, endeavour or decision. Does a confession of the mouth really follow from faith as "admiration is evoked by beauty"? Moreover, in 10:9 faith has a clear intellectual content, defined in the ὅτι-clause. Is there no human activity involved in accepting a "scandal"? Why is "response" not regarded as an activity?

[25] Of course there were *some* (but, even in a place like Corinth, only some!) exceptions to this, as Paul's careful wording in 1 Cor 6:11 ("and such were some of you") makes clear.

[26] R.L. Fox, Pagans and Christians, New York 1989, 318. Cf. with regard to Paul's own activity M. Hengel, Die Stellung des Apostels Paulus zum Gesetz in den unbekannten Jahren zwischen Damaskus und Antiochien, in this volume, pp. 30–2, 43; M. Reiser, Hat Paulus Heiden bekehrt? BZ 39, 1995, 76–91. Reiser's conclusion (91): "Die Heiden, die Paulus bekehrt hat, waren längst nicht mehr Heiden, wie wir sie uns gewöhnlich vorstellen. Nicht nur das Judenchristentum, auch das Heidenchristentum kommt aus der Synagoge."

[27] If the notion of Gentiles responding to God in the only acceptable way by "not pursuing righteousness" were a leading idea in Paul's thought, it would logically follow that, in

must mean "outside of Israel's covenant", i.e. outside the sphere of Torah. But then Sanders is right: the "paradox" *is* about full observance of the Torah after all.[28]

V. Continuity with the Old Testament?

Playing down Paul's originality – and along with it the problematic nature of much of what he says –, Westerholm emphasizes Paul's continuity with the Old Testament[29]: "remnant theology – by which the majority of Jews at given points in history are declared faithless ... – was no Pauline innovation", but a "very conventional claim", even a "truism" (p. 222). But in Rom 9:6ff it is *not* the case that some (Jews) are *declared* faithless.[30] The notion of a *chosen* remnant (11:5) is very peculiar, if "chosen" is allowed to mean what 9:6ff implies: that humans are elected *before their birth*. Some, then, are *predestined* to be faithless. By contrast, the Old Testament typically speaks of a remnant which has *"proved* faithful".[31] To be sure, the existence of a remnant is the result of God's action, but this is related to the doings of men. The normal Old Testament pattern is this: the people transgress against Yahweh's will and anger him; Yahweh destroys the godless people; Yahweh spares a remnant.[32]

Typically, Paul's interpretation of the Elijah passage (Rom 11:4f) differs from its original message. In the Old Testament story Elijah himself has been "very zealous (!) for the Lord" (1 Kings 19:10.14), and the seven thousand faithful ones are those who, in the midst of general apostasy, have not lapsed into Baalism, thus displaying a remarkable human effort (or so one would think).

Westerholm underlines Paul's continuity with the Old Testament in another way, too (p. 236): "Jewish convictions about God's goodness and sovereignty over the affairs of humankind found expression long before Paul in the no-

---

order to find a right relationship with God, Israel too ought to have been an "indifferent passerby". Israel ought not to have cared about God's will revealed in the Torah; she ought to have been a people just like Gentiles! It is scarcely thinkable that Paul *really* thought so. Is not the "paradox" of 9:30–31 simply an attempt to account for what has actually happened (Gentiles have been more responsive to the Christian message than Jews)?

[28] Cf. J.D.G. Dunn, Romans 9–16 (Word Biblical Commentary 38B, Dallas 1988, 580: Paul is speaking "of a righteousness which can be pursued only within the covenant".

[29] Compare the similar move in the course of interpreting Rom 2–3 in Westerholm, Israel's Law 158–59, and my rejoinder in Bib. 71, 1990, 272.

[30] This *is* the case, of course, in 9:30ff and 11:17–24.

[31] Cf. R.E. Clements, "A Remnant Chosen by Grace" (Romans 11:5): The Old Testament Background and Origin of he Remnant Concept", in Pauline Studies (ed. D.A. Hagner & M.J. Harris, Grand Rapids 1980), 106. Westerholm (p. 222 n. 26) appeals to Clements' article.

[32] A. Laato, Who Is Immanuel? The Rise and the Foundering of Isaiah's Messianic Expectations (Åbo 1988), 88–94.

tions that God accomplishes his (ultimately benevolent) purposes independently of human designs or activity ..." He sees an analogy between Paul and Isaiah: both see "God as the only effective Actor on the stage of history" (p. 235). But this comparison misleading, due to the fact that Paul's understanding of divine "deliverance" is rather spiritualized, or "dematerialized", in comparison with Old Testament expectations.[33] Isaiah speaks of eschatological reversals in *nature and history*. The latter must needs be acts of God alone; no human could possibly help to bring about theophanic earthquakes.[34] Isaiah 2, for instance, depicts the terrors of the Day of the Lord on which the *pride* of haughty men will be brought low. (According to Westerholm, Israel's alleged pride is *not* the issue in Rom 9:30ff.) Quite properly, it is in an apocalyptic context that this text is alluded to in the New Testament (Rev 6:12ff); the closest counterpart in Paul's letters would be the destruction of the "powers" in 1 Cor 15:24ff. The two "redemptions" should not be "assimilated" (although this is routinely done in Christian theology).[35] Where the issue is that of men responding in faith to God's grace in Christ, some kind of responsive co-operation by humans can be seriously discussed – in fact it must be presupposed.

VI. Conclusion

Pace Westerholm, it still seems to me that the inclusion of the Gentiles in God's people without such "works of the law" as circumcision *is* the main point in Rom 9:30ff (and in other places where Paul contrasts faith with works). At least it is the *starting* point for his discussions of the matter. The "theocentric focus" of Rom 9:6ff is untypical in that it borders on the idea of double predestination. No wonder it yields to other solutions to the problem of Israel when Paul develops his argument in Romans 10 and 11.

---

[33] Cf. A. Chester, Jewish Messianic Expectations and Mediatorial Figures and Pauline Christology, in M. Hengel – U. Heckel (eds.), Paulus und das antike Judentum (WUNT 58, Tübingen 1991), 66–71.

[34] Thus e.g. Isa 2:11ff (referred to by Westerholm p. 235 n. 61).

[35] For "assimilation" as a device used by New Testament writers cf. K. Syreeni, The Making of the Sermon on the Mount 1, Helsinki 1987, 119, 219; H. Räisänen, The Redemption of Israel: A Salvation-Historical Problem in Luke-Acts, in P. Luomanen (ed.), Luke-Acts: Scandinavian Perspectives, Helsinki-Göttingen 1991, 107.

Response to Heikki Räisänen

by

STEPHEN WESTERHOLM

Professor Räisänen and I appear to be in substantial agreement[1] on what Paul is saying in Romans 9. We dispute how seriously he means what he says.

1. It seems clear to us both that Paul links his claims about Israel's shortcomings in Rom 9:31–32 with the preceding argument by repeating its exclusion of "works." In Räisänen's opinion, however, the link is awkward and can hardly reflect a point of importance in Paul's thought. Whereas "works" are contrasted with election in 9:6–26, the contrast is with "faith" in 9:32; and (Räisänen insists) language of divine election and that requiring human "faith" are not really compatible. Along a similar line, Räisänen grants that, while Paul regards the necessity of faith as consonant with the complete gratuity of God's salvific activity, such a view is both untenable and peripheral in Paul, given the strenuous activity involved in the "faith" of Abraham and that of Gentile converts to Christianity.

The logic of Räisänen's argument may well seem self-evident. But it is patently not the logic of Paul, who routinely combines language of divine election and human faith[2] and who, while frequently depicting the activity (indeed, the "strenuous" activity) shown by faith, can nonetheless speak of the believer as "one who does not work" (Rom 4:5) and of the "justification" received by faith as an utter "gift" of God's grace (Rom 3:22–26; cf. 5:15–17;

---

[1] Not complete agreement, however; I still do not think, for reasons given in my paper, that we can rightly speak of "double predestination" in Romans 9. Furthermore, Professor Räisänen believes he differs from me in thinking that the inclusion of Gentiles in God's people without such "works of the law" as circumcision is the "main point" in Rom 9:30ff. Since, however, he allows that Paul does here express a view of God's salvific activity as excluding human contribution, the difference between us, at the primary level of interpretation, is one of emphasis.

[2] I suggest in my paper that Paul thinks divine election *takes effect* in the coming to faith of believers. For the combination of "faith" and "election" language in Paul, see n. 32 of my paper. That the two notions do not necessarily exclude each other seems apparent when we reflect on the extent to which even human parents can shape and determine their offspring's *choices*. – Note, further, the typically Pauline reflex in Gal 4:9: Paul begins a statement that might suggest that the conversion of the Galatians represented a decision or activity of their own; but he immediately restates it from what is, for him, the truer perspective whereby God is seen as the acting force.

Phil 3:9) – a "grace" that, by definition, excludes human "works" (Rom 11:6). Given the persistence of the theme, the primary task of the Pauline scholar must surely be to ask what it is about Paul's perception of the life of faith that makes such claims self-evident to him. Part of his point, I propose in my paper, is that the divine spirit that indwells believers (or, more simply, God, the grace of God, or Christ) must be seen as the effective agent of what they accomplish;[3] part, I also propose, is that in his view faith is never the natural characteristic of a human being but always a response evoked by (what the respondent, thanks to divine illumination,[4] perceives as) an overwhelming demonstration of divine goodness. Obviously such a response can be a very active, even strenuous one (the more strenuous, the better!), as Paul's own response indubitably was; yet, from one perspective (and I believe it was Paul's), the intensity of the response simply testifies to the impact of the experience of grace that elicits it. If these explanations of Paul's language are deemed inadequate, then further examination of his understanding of "faith" would seem to be in order. I remain inclined to think that, given the frequency with which the theme appears in Paul, the difficulties to which Professor Räisänen draws attention are rooted in the gap between Pauline horizons and our own rather than in Paul's resorting to a way of speaking at variance with "what he 'really' [had] in mind."[5]

2. Räisänen sees the paradox of Rom 9:30–31, not as an expression of a central theme in Pauline thought, but simply as an *ad hoc* "attempt to account for what has actually happened." Paul, he claims, could not have seriously meant that Gentile Christians had *not* pursued righteousness in their pre-Christian state, nor thought that Israel ought to have displayed indifference toward Torah. The seriousness of Paul's statement, however, is supported (as I argue in my paper) both by abundant evidence from the argument of Romans 9–11 and by numerous other formulations in Paul, all suggesting something programmatic about the paradox by which God "chooses to make something of human nothings while persistently bringing to nothing whatever, humanly speaking, promises to be something." The objections raised by Räisänen do

---

[3] Cf. especially Gal 2:20; also Rom 15:18; 1 Cor 15:10; 2 Cor 4:7; 12:9; Phil 1:6; 2:13; 4:13; 1 Thes 5:24, etc. The obvious relation between this insistence and Paul's notion of the impotence of the "flesh" to please God (cf. Rom 7:7–8:8) would seem to compel the recognition that we are dealing with fundamental aspects of his thought.

[4] So 2 Cor 4:6.

[5] Räisänen wonders why, if Paul thought God had *always* bestowed his favour gratuitously, it was necessary to send Christ. Paul's answer, no doubt, would be that, though "justification" is always received by humans as a "gift" (Rom 3:24), it is only effective "through the redemption that is in Christ Jesus, whom God put forward as an expiation by his blood" (Rom 3:24–25). That redemption is seen as applicable to all of Adamic humanity, though, in the pre-Christian period, only a measure of its blessings could be (proleptically) experienced (so I read Rom 3:25–26).

not seem sufficient to call this principle in question. Paul frequently alludes to the pre-Christian state of his converts; but he never intimates that their antecedent piety(!) was a factor in their entrance into the people of God. His conviction to the contrary (adopted, to be sure, on dogmatic, theological grounds) clearly found enough confirmation in the pre-conversion idolatry and immorality of some believers to warrant the exclusion of human piety as a factor in divine election. As to Israel, Paul speaks of their zeal for God (shown in their devotion to Torah) as positive though insufficient (Rom 10:2). The reference rules out any suggestion that Israel should have been indifferent toward Torah. Yet Paul does seem to think (here, no doubt, with empirical support!) that such zeal, though in itself positive, can have the negative effect of blinding Jews to the coming, and the nature, of God's righteousness in Christ. Again, then, the point of the paradox was confirmed in Paul's eyes: human piety is not a factor when God elects his people.

3. Räisänen discounts the claim that Paul's divinely *chosen* "remnant" can parallel "remnants" referred to in Old Testament passages: in Paul, *God* is responsible for the remnant's existence; in the Old Testament texts, "remnants" are made up of the few who *themselves* prove faithful while others transgress. Again, however, Räisänen is imposing on the texts his own insistence on assigning responsibility for human actions to God *or* to people. According to the ancient writers (Paul and the Old Testament alike), humans bear responsibility for what they do even when God has designed their activities to serve his purposes.

Finally, I would of course grant that not every reference to Isaiah cited in my footnote is analogous on all counts to Paul's view of redemption. The passages in Isaiah do stress, as does Paul, that, in the end, human pretensions will be shattered and God alone exalted. In any case, there is ample Old Testament support[6] – Ezek 36:16–32 is merely the most explicit passage – for the notion that, given the recalcitrance of the human heart, divine deliverance must be rooted in divine goodness and faithfulness, not in the merits of the delivered.

There is, in short, every reason to believe that Paul's exclusion of a role by human "works" in the constituting of God's redeemed people is both intentional and programmatic.

---

[6] See the references in n. 15 of my paper, where a reason for drawing attention to such parallels is given.

Paul's Jewish Background
in View of His Law Teaching in 1Cor 7

by

PETER J. TOMSON

In this paper I shall be confronting the main thesis of my book, i.e., that Paul's letters evince significant traces of Jewish law or halakha,[1] with recent discussions about his doctrine of justification. In doing so, I am making one of my earlier presuppositions operational, namely that in the context of ancient Judaism, law and thought operated on different levels which do not always interfere, though they sometimes do. Viewed in another way, this is articulating the widest context of my quest, namely Paul's supposed Jewish background, both in relation to his practical instruction and to his justification doctrine.

I. Paul's Relation to His Jewish Background

The end of historical criticism, in the double sense of its *telos*, is to explain historical persons and phenomena within their contemporary framework. For religious personalities, this includes not only the languages spoken and the literatures read – let alone the political, social and economical forces at work – but also the festivals and other ceremonies celebrated, the prayers said, the holy scriptures read out and the comments on them, and furthermore that multitude of customs and beliefs which make the stuff of a religious life. The *telos* implies a limitation: the insuperable boundary between human reason and divine reality, the secret of revelation which passes all understanding. There was a time when this delimitation was thought to encroach on the power of scholarly reason, but one may today take it as the maturation of critical epistemology, which allows quiet assurance about the things that are within reach of

---

[1] *Paul and the Jewish Law; Halakha in the Letters of the Apostle to the Gentiles* (CRINT III/1) Assen / Maastricht – Minneapolis 1990, pp62–68, cf 265–9. On the origins and modern use of the term *halakha* see my article, 'La Première Epître aux Corinthiens comme document de la tradition Apostolique de halakha', in R. Bieringer (ed.) *The Corinthian Correspondence* (BETL 125) Leuven, due 1996.

human reason.[2] Or with the famous words in which Ludwig Wittgenstein summed up both the power and the poverty of philosophy and science, i.e. their *telos*: 'Wovon man nicht sprechen kann, darüber muß man schweigen.'[3]

Hence if explaining Paul within the framework of Greek and Hebrew speaking Judaism – traveling up and down between Jerusalem and the diaspora and living some sort of a Jewish life while freely communicating with Greeks – is no more than seeing his actual person in a mirror dimly, it is also true that our hopes of once coming face to face with him and with his unutterable vision need in no way inhibit our mobility in finding out his cultural roots. Even with this delimitation, an important and difficult question remains: in what terms can we describe the radical change that took place in his life?

Historical criticism, traditionally close to German Protestantism, has long cherished the hypothesis that the *initium* of Paul's characteristic theology lay not in his Jewish background, but in its Hellenistic surroundings.[4] In other words, his post-conversion faith in the justifying grace of God excluded Judaism and its Law, and must perforce stem from Hellenism or Hellenistic Christianity. This allowed clear-cut terms in which to describe Paul's conversion: the radical difference between his pre-Christian and his Christian[5] life would have coincided with the equally decisive boundary between Judaism and Hellenism. The single voice of dissent at the time against this consensus, that of Albert Schweitzer who located the background of Paul's Christ mysti-

---

[2] One may think here of K. Popper, who in his *Logik der Forschung*, (1935) Tübingen 1984[8], demarcated the domain of assured knowledge rationally by means of the principle of falsifiability, or the fundamental empirical correctibility of scientific pronouncements ('Falsifizierbarkeit als Abgrenzungskriterium', no 6, pp14–17).

[3] L. Wittgenstein, *Tractatus logico-philosophicus*, London 1961, 7th (final) thesis. His semantic rationalism has an agnostic-mystical corollary: 'Es gibt allerdings Unaussprechliches. Dies *zeigt* sich, es ist das Mystische' (ib 6.522); '"Gott kannst du nicht mit einem Andern reden hören, sondern nur, wenn du der Angeredete bist." – Das ist eine grammatische Bemerkung' (*Zettel,* ed G.E.M. Anscombe – G.H. von Wright, Berkeley – Los Angeles 1970, no. 717 – significantly, again the final item!). This aspect of Wittgenstein is explored by Russell Nieli, *Wittgenstein: From Mysticism to Ordinary Language; A Study of Viennese Positivism & the Thought of Ludwig Wittgenstein*, Albany (State U of NY Press) 1987.

[4] Notably W. Bousset (*Kyrios Christos; Geschichte des Christusglaubens von den Anfangen des Christentums bis Irenäus*, 2nd ed Göttingen 1921) and W. Reitzenstein (*Die hellenistischen Mysterienreligionen*, 3rd ed Stuttgart 1927) and, under their influence, R. Bultmann, *Theologie des Neuen Testaments*, 5th ed Tübingen 1965, programmatically: 'Die Theologie des Paulus ist der Predigt Jesu gegenüber eine neue Bildung, und das demonstriert nichts anderes als eben dieses, daß Paulus seine Stellung innerhalb des hellenistischen Christentums hat. Die so oft und so leidenschaftlich verhandelte Frage: Jesus und Paulus ist im Grunde die Frage: Jesus und das hellenistische Christentum' (p190). For selective overviews of Pauline study, with interesting convergencies, see Westerholm and Seifried (below n10), and my book, 9–19.

[5] Paul does not yet use the name 'Christian' but speaks of 'believers', whether Jews or gentiles.

cism in Jewish apocalypticism,[6] was noted but long remained without response.[7] Nowadays Schweitzer is getting more attention, but it tends to focus on his negative corollary, i.e. that justification by faith was erroneously made into the essence of Paul by the Reformers.[8] This has even inspired the idea of 'de-lutheranizing Paul',[9] a slogan which could not but provoke protest.[10] Avoiding that unfruitful dilemma, others began to look for the roots of justification theology within Judaism itself; we shall come back to that.[11] Schweitzer had emphasized both aspects: positively, the background of Paul's teaching was fully within Judaism, and negatively, justification without the Law was not the centre of his thought.[12]

In his Durham-Tübingen paper of 1988, *Der vorchristliche Paulus*, Martin Hengel has joined the debate, taking his point of departure in the positive as-

---

[6] A. Schweitzer, *Geschichte der paulinischen Forschung von der Reformation bis auf der Gegenwart*, Tübingen 1911; id, *Die Mystik des Apostels Paulus,* (1930) repr with 'Einführung' by W.G. Kümmel, Tübingen 1981. One major flaw (probably unavoidable at the time) is Schweitzer's schematic opposition between Judaism and Hellenism; see next n.

[7] R. Bultmann, 'Zur Geschichte der Paulus-Forschung', (*TR* n.s. 1 [1929] 26–59), repr in K.H. Rengstorf – U. Luck (eds), *Das Paulusbild in der neueren deutschen Forschung*, Darmstadt 1982, 304–37. It was W.D. Davies who programmatically followed Schweitzer's lead, while correcting his exaggerated 'anti-Hellenism', in his *Paul and Rabbinic Judaism,* (1948) 3rd ed London 1971; cf his 1960 SBL paper, 'Paul and Judaism since Schweitzer', ib vii–xv. In turn, Davies influenced K. Stendahl ('Paul and the Introspective Conscience of the West' [1963] repr in id, *Paul Among Jews and Gentiles, and Other Essays*, Philadelphia / London 1977, 78–96). But it was not until E.P. Sanders gathered up these influences into his *Paul and Palestinian Judaism; A Comparison of Patterns of Religion*, Philadelphia / London 1977, triggering the recent discussion (see also n12).

[8] Conversely, this must be the reason why Käsemann and Stuhlmacher stress the importance of apocalypticism *without referring to Schweitzer*, and *explicitly* rejecting his criticism of Reformation exegesis: E. Käsemann, 'Gottesgerechtigkeit bei Paulus', *ZTK* 58 (1961) 367–78; P. Stuhlmacher, *Gerechtigkeit Gottes bei Paulus*, Göttingen 1965.

[9] The phrase is F. Watson's: *Paul, Judaism and the Gentiles; A Sociological Approach* (SNTS MonSer 56) Cambridge 1986, taking his inspiration from Stendahl's brilliant article (above n7).

[10] Cf already E. Käsemann's vehement reaction against Stendahl, in his *Paulinische Perspektiven*, Tübingen 1972, and Stendahl's reply, ib (see previous n) 129–32. For recent arguments for justification as a central Pauline theme see S. Westerholm, *Israel's Law and the Church's Faith; Paul and His Recent Interpreters*, Grands Rapids 1988; and M.A. Seifrid, *Justification by Faith; The Origin and Development of a Central Pauline Theme*, Leiden 1992. Westerholm, countering Watson's 'de-lutheranizing Paul' on the basis of a fresh reading of Luther, does not steer clear of Reformation exegesis by restricting his reading mainly to Romans and Galatians. The same methodological drawback is found in Seifrid (Romans mainly), but it is partly corrected by studying the theme of justification both in Jewish sources and in Paul (see below).

[11] Käsemann and Stuhlmacher, see above n8. On Dahl and Flusser see below.

[12] In this respect, Sanders' milestone work (above n7) still fell back behind Schweitzer. While the first part impressively corrects the 'Lutheran' bias on Judaism, the second fails to view Paul's background as an actual part of that Judaism. Cf J.D.G. Dunn's criticism, 'The New Perspective on Paul', *BJRL* 65/2 (1982) 95–122 (also in id, *Jesus, Paul and the Law; Studies in Mark and Galatians*, London 1990, 183–214).

pect and describing the pre-Christian Paul as a Jew in all respects, even if his garb was Greek. Without mentioning Schweitzer, Hengel emphasizes: '... Die griechische Bildung ist bei [Paulus] von der jüdischen nicht zu trennen. *Er bleibt auch im griechischen Gewand ganz und gar Jude.*'[13] As so many Jews then and now, Paul was bi- or trilingual, both a *hellênistês* and a *hebraios*.[14] Nor was this cultural plurality restricted to the linguistic sphere: Paul, or Saul, may even have been a teacher of Tora and commandments in one or more of the Hellenists' synagogues in Jerusalem.[15] So much for the mythological watershed between Judaism and Hellenism. But what does does this mean for the radical difference between the pre-Christian and the Christian Paul? Hengel is emphatic: 'Die Kenntnis des *Juden* Saulus ist eine Voraussetzung zum Verständnis des *Christen* Paulus.'[16] Correcting the current misunderstanding that 'Paul' became his name at his conversion and summarizes his Christian existence, Hengel points out that it may well have been his family's patronal name, which he preferred to use when acting as a missionary in pagan surroundings (Acts 13:9).[17] Similarly, Paul's affirmation that he 'knows Christ no longer according to the flesh' (2Cor 5:16) does not preclude continuity with his own prior knowledge of the historical Jesus.[18] The question is, what continuity does it imply between Paul the Christian and the Jew?

Here, Hengel resolutely joins the opposition to Schweitzer's famous second point and squarely rejects his criticism of Reformation exegesis. The radical change which took place in Paul's life signified that *theologia crucis* and Pharisaic law observance were mutually exclusive, and justification by faith, far from being a 'subsidiary crater', was the very heart of Paul's theology: 'Der jüdische Lehrer wird zum Heidenmissionar, an die Stelle des "Eifers für das Gesetz" tritt die Verkündigung des gesetzesfreien Evangelium. ... Auch

---

[13] M. Hengel, 'Der vorchristliche Paulus', in M. Hengel – U. Heckel, *Paulus und das antike Judentum* (Tübingen-Durham-Symposium im Gedenken an den 50. Todestag A. Schlatters) Tübingen 1991, [177–293], 186, his emphasis. Cf his criticism on Bultmann and Reitzenstein (ib 188 n37) for their exclusively Hellenistic explanation. Strikingly similar things have been said long ago by A. Deissmann, *Paulus; eine kultur- und religionsgeschichtliche Skizze*, Tübingen 1911, 59–77, 'Der Jude Paulus'; esp. p67: 'Paulus ist Jude geblieben auch als Christ, trotz seiner leidenschaftlichen Polemik gegen das Gesetz ... man kann Paulus ... ruhig den großen Judenchristen der Urzeit nennen.'

[14] ib 220, 232f.

[15] ib 260–5, giving due weight to the expression from the inscription of Theodotos son of Vettenus indicating the aim of the Hellenist synagogue he founded in Jerusalem: *eis anagnôsin tou nomou kai eis didachên entolôn*. This milieu suggests the existence of halakha formulated in Greek, a phenomenon I postulated on other grounds, ib (above n1) 143f, 220, 263f. And see below, n48.

[16] ib 178, italics in original.

[17] ib 200. And see already the acute observations by Stendahl, ib (above n7) 11.

[18] ib 266. Cf the admirable article of C. Wolff, 'True Apostolic Knowledge of Christ: Exegetical Reflections on 2 Corinthians 5:14ff.', in A.J.M. Wedderburn (ed) *Paul and Jesus; Collected Essays* (JSNT Sup 37) Sheffield 1989, 81–98.

wenn heute gerne das Gegenteil behauptet wird, das eigentliche Wesen der paulinischen Theologie, das sola gratia geschenkte Heil, hat niemand besser als Augustinus und Martin Luther verstanden.'[19] So if it was not the frontier between Judaism and Hellenism which Paul crossed during his conversion, it was the boundary between Judaism and some form of non-Jewish Christianity. Rejecting Schweitzer's negative corollary seems to implicate his positive emphasis on Paul's Jewish context.

I propose to step aside here and consider whether historical reason after all does not allow the possibility that 'Paul the Christian' did not deny but somehow re-integrated his Jewish past. If indeed for him Judaism and Jewish life were not summed up in 'knowing Christ according to the flesh', then why should the alternative to Pharisaism necessarily be to become a non-observant apostate?[20] Cannot we envisage other combinations of belief and behaviour within the context of Second Temple Judaism, certainly so since Paul's conversion story is couched in apocalyptic language which suggests a Jewish context even there?[21] Does he not affirm, in the letter unanimously acclaimed to be his most balanced, that the benefits of 'the covenants, the lawgiving, the worship and the promises' were irrevocably entrusted to his kinsmen, the Israelites, 'whose are the patriarchs and from whom is the Christ according to the flesh' (Rom 9:4f)? If the Apostle to the gentiles himself can say all this in one breath, then why should his conversion (the ultimate content of which forever remains beyond the confines of historical research) lose its value if we conceive it as formally having taken place *on Jewish terms and within Judaism*, or in his own words, within the irrevocable framework of 'the covenants and the lawgiving' (cf also Rom 11:29)?[22] Paul's soteriology seems to allow for

---

[19] ib 283–91, quote p290. Such Lutheran emphases have been a sostenuto in Hengel's work, see his *Die Zeloten; Untersuchungen zur jüdischen Freiheitsbewegung in der Zeit von Herodes I bis 70 n. Chr.*, Leiden 1976[2], on the role of Pharisaic law observance vis-à-vis Hellenistic universalism; and *Judaism and Hellenism; Studies in their Encounter in Palestine during the Early Hellenistic Period* 1–2 (ET of 2nd ed 1973) repr London 1981, beginning and end, with explicit reference to Paul's providential role. Deissmann's approach (above n13) is more uninhibited here.

[20] Thus also the emphasis of A.F. Segal, *Paul the Convert; The Apostolate and Apostasy of Saul the Pharisee*, New Haven/London 1990; cf p121 on 'Paul's own conversion from the surety of his Pharisaic observances to the freedom and uncertainties of his gentile Christianity'. And see below.

[21] Segal's insistence on the 'conversion' terminology, supported by Seifrid (above n10) 136–8, is certainly correct. But the calling to the Apostleship to the Gentiles remains an essential aspect, as emphasized by Stendahl ib (above n7) 7–23, 84f.

[22] This emphasis is made recently from different angles by F. Thielman, *From Plight to Solution; A Jewish Framework for Understanding Paul's View of the Law in Galatians and Romans*, (SuppNovTest 61) Leiden 1989; K.-W. Niebuhr, *Heidenapostel aus Israel; Die jüdische Identität des Paulus nach ihrer Darstellung in seinen Briefen* (WUNT 62) Tübingen 1992; B. Rosner, *Paul, Scripture and Ethics; A Study of 1 Corinthians 5–7* (AGAJUC 22) Leiden 1994. None of these most sympathetic studies, however, undertakes an actual comparison with ancient halakhic literature.

the continued value of these foundations of Jewish existence. This leads us to consider the social and religious function of Jewish law or halakha.

Overviewing the various movements that we know of in Second Temple Judaism, we find a common basis in the phenomenon of law observance, i.e. the drive towards practical implementation of the assignments incumbent upon the community of Israel, whatever the definition of the latter. Precisely this common basis permitted the thriving diversity of sects and movements. And it is reasonable that Jesus and his followers found their place among them, probably somewhere between Pharisaism and Essenism. Now one's definition of the community of Israel – which in Jewish terms would be closely related to one's soteriology – most likely also had an impact on the particular shape of one's law observance. Severity in observance would correspond with an exclusive view of the community of believers, and vice versa. Qumran presents us with the combination of the strictest possible Law observance and a most restrictive, apocalyptically motivated conception of election. Somewhere at the other end of the spectrum, Philo wholeheartedly embraced Greek language and thought without perceiving any contradiction with his unfailing devotion to the Law of Moses. Most likely, Hellenistic diaspora Jews maintained their own Law observance, their minority position being an incentive towards conservatism.[23] In Palestine, we further find the two schools of Pharisees, the Shammaites being the more conservative and rigid, and the Hillelites the more flexible and open towards outsiders, a difference which can be pointed out both in thought (i.e., midrash and aggada) and in halakha.[24] It would follow that the community of disciples of Jesus kept their own particular Jewish observance, probably even including some internal diversity corresponding to the various factions. In any case, being a Jew meant sympathizing with one of these movements by means of keeping the corresponding observance, and changing groups would mean changing observances.

How does Paul fit into this picture? I see no real necessity to assume that his conversion to Christ – his new-found gospel that, for Jew and gentile alike, salvation lays not in keeping the law but in faith in God who in resurrecting Christ brought the new era upon us – excluded his 'remaining in his calling as a Jew' and his 'keeping the commandments'. Nor do I consider Mark Seifrid's recent suggestion conclusive that Paul's moral teaching was based on his soteriology and that this deprived 'the Law and its associated *halakha*' of any significance.[25] Rather, I think that Samuel Belkin was right, back in 1935,

---

[23] See my book (above n1) 36–47 on the halakha in Philo and diaspora Judaism.

[24] See S. Safrai, 'The Decision According to the School of Hillel in Yavneh', in *Proceedings, World Congress of Jewish Studies* 7/3 (1981) 21–44 (in Hebr.); and for a summary id, 'Halakha', in id, *The Literature of the Sages. First Part: Oral Tora, Halakha, Mishna, Tosefta, Talmud, External Tractates* (CRINT II/3a), Assen – Philadelphia 1987, [121–209] 185–200.

[25] ib (above n10) p19 n62. Seifried allows for the potential significance of practical parenesis, but he does not seem to share my view that analysis of halakhic elements in Paul

when he wrote about the influences of Paul's Jewish background: '... We have to look for these influences not so much in Paul's theology as in his references to customs, practical morality, and in rules which he formulated for his converts in Asia Minor and Europe.'[26] As he was to do later in the case of Philo, Belkin went on to unearth a number of Jewish law elements from Paul's practical teaching. Similarly, not knowing Belkin's study, I proposed my analysis of halakha in Paul on the hypothesis that whatever the weight and implications of the justification theology, his practical teaching operates on a different level in which the law has retained a real significance. Precisely the example of Philo, the paragon of Hellenistic Judaism, is illuminating. Not for one moment did his mystical philosophizing impede his practical involvement in the Jewish community, and Jewish community life means halakha. Halakha and thought operate on different levels, and in a case like Philo's could display a very different dynamic.[27]

Hence the cumulative evidence that Paul based his practical instruction on elements of halakha can not be dismissed as a relic of his Jewish past gone out of use with his revelation of Christ. It must imply that rules functioning in some variety of Jewish community life informed his authoritative teaching as an Apostle. As I said, I now wish to balance this thesis by considering his doctrine of justification and his practical instruction simultaneously, each in their own right and in the hypothetical framework of contemporary Judaism. 1Cor 7 is most suitable to this aim, since it contains both a number of very prescriptive injunctions and an intriguing fragment of justification theology.

II. The Commandments in 1Cor 7 and Their Judeo-Christian Background

Reading First Corinthians for an analysis of Paul's law teaching is unusual, and this is because *the problem of the law is mostly perceived only as a theo-*

---

does not replace study of his theology and soteriology. I am insisting that, as in Judaism at large, law and thought operated on different levels. Surely, the divorce prohibition (see below) had an independent dynamic from justification by faith!

[26] 'The Problem of Paul's Background', *JBL* 54 (1935) 41–60, setting forth halakhot concerning circumcision, mixed marriage, 'spiritual' betrothals (see below), the *epitropos*, and slavery.

[27] See S. Belkin, *Philo and the Oral Law; The Philonic Interpretation of Biblical Law in Relation to the Palestinian Halakah*, Cambridge MA 1940; cf his *The Alexandrian Halakah in Apologetic Literature of the First Century C.E.* Philadelphia n.d. His point was reiterated on the basis of different material by Naomi G. Cohen, 'The Jewish Dimension of Philo's Judaism – An Elucidation of the Spec. Leg. IV 132–150', *JJS* 38 (1987) 164–86. The duality of thought and practice was admiringly described by none other than E.R. Goodenough, *An Introduction to Philo Judaeus* (1940) 2nd ed Oxford 1962; see my book p40–44.

logical problem. This perception derives from the Reformers,[28] as does the method of documenting it only from Romans and Galatians.[29] Yet the practical aspect of the law must have been very real to Paul and his readers, Jewish or gentile. Such issues as sex, marriage and divorce, idolatry or occultism, ritual and custom, and last but not least the participation of women in the liturgy, keep bothering and dividing Christian churches till the present day. They have an undeniable bearing on the law and its interpretation, and it is exactly to these issues that First Corinthians is largely devoted. The disregard of this remarkable letter is another symptom of the underrating of the law and its practical meaning typical of Protestant exegesis, which is seen also in the disregard for the practical teaching in Paul's letters in general[30] and for the positive statements about the law found in the major justification passages.[31] Roman Catholic exegesis tends to be less inhibited here, undoubtedly because of the interest in Apostolic continuity, Patristic exegesis, and canon law.[32]

Some have proposed to read the apparent 'legalism' of First Corinthians as an episode quickly to be replaced by the 'normal' Paul of justification by faith alone.[33] This endeavour breaks down, however, on the presence of three unmistakable allusions to the justification theme. One is a digression in the chapter under discussion (7:17–20); a second, expressing Paul's 'missionary stance' (9:19–23),[34] figures in a digression of the argument on idol offerings; and the third one has been described as a 'flash-like', habitual association

---

[28] Augustine thought that the Law had retained its practical meaning for Jesus and the Apostles, but this did not hold for his own time because of the absence of Jewish Christians. See my book (above n1) p184 and 224, and cf B. Blumenkranz, *Die Judenpredigt Augustins*, Paris 1947. On any count, the Church Fathers did perceive the practical aspect of the Law, see my book p1–3.

[29] Cf above n10. Westerholm's anxiety about the pendulum having swung too far towards the practical and social (ib 222f), though understandable, does not assess the relationship of the practical and theological *per se*. Again, Paul's Jewish frame of reference is of fundamental importance here.

[30] Notable corrections are W. Schrage, *Die konkreten Einzelgebote in der paulinischen Paränese*, Gütersloh 1961; J. Barclay, *Obeying the Truth; A Study of Paul's Ethics in Galatians*, Edinburgh 1988.

[31] See especially the quest of P. von der Osten-Sacken, *Evangelium und Tora; Aufsätze zu Paulus*, Munich 1987; id, *Die Heiligkeit der Tora; Studien zum Gesetz bei Paulus*, Munich 1989.

[32] E.g. Y. Congar, 'Die Kasuistik des Heiligen Paulus', in *FS F. Arnold*, 1958 (I gratefully owe this reference to P. von der Osten-Sacken, but have not yet been able to track it down); G. Schneider, 'Jesu Wort über die Ehescheidung in der Überlieferung des Neuen Testaments', in id, *Jesusüberlieferung und Christologie; Neutestamentliche Aufsätze 1970–1990*, Leiden 1992, 187–209.

[33] U. Wilckens, 'Zur Entwicklung des paulinischen Gesetzesverständnisses', *NTS* 28 (1982) 154–90; J.W. Drane, *Paul, Libertine or Legalist? A Study in the Theology of the Major Pauline Epistles*, London 1975.

[34] Cf G. Bornkamm, 'The Missionary Stance of Paul in I Cor. 9 and in Acts', in L. Keck – L. Martyn, *Studies in Luke-Acts in Honour of P. Schubert*, London 1966, 194–207, with habitual emphasis on justification as the essence of Paul.

within the resurrection chapter (15:54–56).[35] They are all brief evocations made in passing, which proves both that the idea existed in Paul's mind and that he saw no need to develop it. In other words, the author is the same as that of Romans and Galatians, but apparently addressing a different situation which mobilized other elements of his thought. If we do not recognize him as the authentic Paul, we might need to adjust our historical imagination.

A telling aspect of First Corinthians in this connection is its official character. A number of passages clearly respond to practical questions which the Corinthians had submitted in written form (7:1), in part reacting to a prior letter of Paul's (5:9).[36] In other words, we find Paul here in his authority of Apostle, patiently setting forth his answers to the specific questions of the Church of his foundation. The official, authoritative character is underscored by the repeated mention made of the sources of authority, that is, other than the most general and obvious source, Scripture. The phenomenon is most conspicuous in chapter 7.[37]

Let us now review the subject matter of the chapter. The opening phrase, *peri de hôn egrapsate,* indicates that at least the first subject was raised in the letter of the Corinthians, but the chapter has a formal unity which suggests that this was the case with all subjects. The recurrence of the phrase in v25, *peri de tôn parthenôn,* confirms this. There also seems to have been a single motivation for all questions. v5 mentions periods of devotion to 'prayer', and vv26–35, in more detail, uninhibited devotion to 'the things of the Lord' in view of the 'need' and the 'brevity' of the present time. The phrase in v14, 'the unbelieving man is sanctified in the woman' and vice versa, might somehow also relate to this. Hence the Corinthians had asked something like the following: Is it allowed, for the sake of devoting oneself to the Kingdom of God, to abstain from marital intercourse (vv1–7), to divorce or separate (vv10–16), or not to marry altogether (v8f, 25–40)?

Paul specifies his answer in six separate categories, a specification which in itself shows an intriguing aspect of casuistry[38] on the part of an author apparently well-versed in discussing legal problems. In reviewing them, I emphasize the elements expressing the formal status of Paul's teaching in each case.

---

[35] H. Räisänen, *Paul and the Law*, Tübingen 1983, 143, adding this to his arguments for Paul's inconsistency. See my book (above n1) p71 for the explanation from a targum tradition, which indeed may be assumed to be habitual for Paul.

[36] For the pre-history of 1Cor J.C. Hurd, *The Origin of I Corinthians*, London 1965, remains a classic, despite the criticism by Margareth Mitchell (below n49).

[37] See the 'formal sources' listed in my book (above n1) 82f.

[38] It was sure enough a Roman Catholic, Yves Congar to note this (above n32). And cf E.P. Sanders' hesitation in *Paul, the Law, and the Jewish People*, London – Philadelphia 1984, p119 n46: 1Cor 7 'is close to halakha'.

(1) vv1–7, temporary marital abstinence: Paul says '*by way of an advice, not a commandment*' (v6), that married partners may desist from intercourse only for a limited period and by mutual consent.

(2) v8f, '*I say* to the unmarried and widowed: it would be good if they remained as I also am, but if they cannot contain themselves, let them marry, for it is better to marry than to burn' (burn: of passion, or in hell?).

(3) v10f, 'To the married *I order, not I but the Lord*: the wife is not to depart from the husband – and if she did depart, she must remain single or return to her husband – and the husband is not to dismiss his wife' (v10f).

(4) vv12–16, 'To the others *I say, not the Lord* ...;' this apparently is the category of those married to an unbelieving partner by an informal marriage, the marriage by *usus* known in Hellenistic law,[39] in which exceptional case Paul allows divorce if the unbelieving partner wishes so (a ruling which under the name of *privilegium paulinum* became the loophole for dissolving marriages in Roman Catholic canon law: canon 1143).

Here follows a digression, namely the fragment of justification doctrine we shall deal with in a moment. Then Paul resumes:

(5) v25ff, 'Now about the virgins, *I have no commandment of the Lord, but I give my opinion* ...;' and after a longish parenetical passage about devotion to the Lord and worrying, Paul pronounces: 'he who marries his virgin does well, and who does not marry her does better' (v38). As Belkin suggested, the case may well have been that of unconsummated marriages.[40]

(6) Finally for widows, who were already included in category 2 but apparently require further specification, Paul gives a general rule followed by his own opinion: 'A woman is bound as long as her husband lives; but if the husband decease, she is free to be married to whom she wishes, if only in the Lord; but she is happier if she stays so, *in my opinion* ...' (v39f).

First, let me sum up some conclusions on the authority level.

(a) Paul keeps distinguishing between his own authority and that of 'the Lord', an insistence which may reflect the intention of the questions from Corinth.

(b) In view of the unmistakable synoptic parallels, 'the Lord' who in v10f 'commands' a prohibition of divorce is none other than Jesus.[41]

(c) Paul knew the commandments of Jesus and ascribed highest authority to them, which qualifies his statement that he does 'not know Christ according to the flesh' (2Cor 5:16).[42]

---

[39] See my book (above n1) 117–119.

[40] ib (above n26) 49–52; in halakhic terms: *eirusin beli kiddushin*. This supposes application of another halakhic category to the case of gentiles; for others see my book ib 120–122.

[41] Specifically Lk 16:18 and Mk 10:11f. Mt 5:32f and 19:9 reflect a 'shammaizing' mitigation of the absolute prohibition, see my book 108–116.

[42] But he did not know Mt 19:10–12 which attributes Jesus with a preference for celibacy!

(d) The only source of the Jesus tradition being his disciples, Paul had a fundamentally positive relationship with the Jerusalem Apostles, as he stated in Gal 2:1–10.[43]

(e) The ruling for widows, which contrasts with Paul's own opinion, is not attributed to 'the Lord' but anonymous; hence it must derive from the Christian community, which is supported by the curious, archaic expression *en Kyriôi*.

(f) Paul not only cites the practical teachings of Jesus but also those of the Apostolic church.

Now as I have set forth elsewhere, the commandments Paul gives all appear to have Jewish antecedents, source evidence for which in this case happens to be unusually rich and varied; I quickly resume my findings corresponding to the six categories in 1Cor 7 that were just enumerated.[44]

(1) The temporal limitation of marital abstention and the mutual right to intercourse closely resemble rabbinic principles.

(2) Celibacy, while exceptional by rabbinic terms, was the rule with the Essenes.

(3) Divorce being allowed by Pharisaic standards – either for any cause whatsoever according to the Hillelites or, in the Shammaite view, only on the grounds of unchastity – an absolute prohibition seems reflected in Qumran writings.

(4) The idea that marriage with an outsider lacks legal ground and needs no formal dissolution is fundamental to rabbinic law.[45]

(5) If Belkin's suggestion is acceptable, 'the virgins' here correspond to the legal possibility in ancient rabbinic law of non-consummated marriages.

(6) The last category contains three halakhic elements: death of the partner dissolves marriage even by Essene standards; the freedom to choose another partner once the marriage is legally dissolved is basic to rabbinic halakha; while a condition limiting that freedom (cf *monon en Kyriôi*) was a conservative option rejected by the Hillelite majority of rabbis.

One implication deserves closest attention in the present framework. If we imagine Paul in his former Pharisaic surroundings, he can only have embraced either the Shammaite or the Hillelite opinion on the grounds for divorce. An absolute prohibition of divorce was beyond the strictest Pharisaic option; we noted its Essene colouring. However Paul leaves no doubt as to where he got it from: he cites it explicitly in the name of Jesus. This means that Paul in this instance, rather than turning from Pharisaic legalism to some type of universalistic liberalism,[46] *switched from his Pharisaic opinion to a more severe one, that of the disciples of Jesus*. If we may extrapolate from the question of divorce, which apparently was of great significance in ancient Judaism and for that reason is so richly documented in the sources, we seem to

---

[43] This conclusion enhances the possibility that Gal 1:18 implies Paul received Apostolic tradition from Peter. See J.D.G. Dunn, '*Historêsai Kêfan*', in his *Jesus, Paul and the Law* (above n12), and, for philological objections, O. Hofius, 'Gal 1,18: *hisorêsai Kêfan*', in id, *Paulusstudien*, Tübingen 1989, 255–267.

[44] ib (above n1) 103–124.

[45] See also Belkin ib (above n26) 47f.

[46] Cf Segal above n20.

have grounds here to suppose that indeed Paul's conversion involved a transfer of adherence from his Pharisaic law tradition to that of Jesus and his disciples, which differed and in certain respects was more severe.[47]

This tradition could only have been known to him through the Jerusalem Apostles and, as I have proposed, may be identified as the Apostolic tradition of halakha. Apart from specific details, it was characterized by its source of highest authority, the law teachings of Jesus. In our chapter, the rule that the woman 'after the death of her husband is free to be married to whomever she wishes *if only in the Lord*', by its literary form a law and by its contents to be located somewhere between Pharisees and Essenes, is an astonishing example of this Apostolic halakha. While it is based on the divorce prohibition taught by Jesus, it clearly presupposes the community of 'the Lord' in non-believing (Jewish) surroundings. Another most important feature is that it apparently also circulated in Greek form early on.[48]

One interesting formal aspect of this law tradition seems to be the recurring introductory formula, *peri de* ... Not only is it found twice in our chapter but another four times elsewhere in the letter (7:1, 25; 8:1; 12:1; 16:1, 12). While the use of this formula to announce another subject known to the reader is common in classical and Hellenistic Greek, a more specific parallel is found in the Didache, where it occurs six times in the framework of casuistic instruction with an official and authoritative, 'apostolic' character.[49] This alone would suffice to hypothesize a Jewish-Christian, halakhic background of the term. In addition however, the halakhic letter found in Qumran, 4QMMT, provides us with a Hebrew parallel. While the document is rather badly damaged, the author seems to have been announcing a new halakhic subject some twenty times by means of the formula: *we-al* ..., or *we-af al* ... (*we-al zevah ha-goyim ... we-af al ha-mutsakot anahnu omrim* ..., etc.).[50] It appears that Paul uses terminology typical of Jewish casuistic teaching current both in

---

[47] Other Essene-like halakhic features of that tradition were the order bread-wine at communal meals (see D. Flusser, 'The Last Supper and the Essenes', *Immanuel* 2 [1973] 23–7; and my book 139–42) and, appartenly, the liturgical calendar (A. Jaubert, *La date de la Cène*, Paris 1957).

[48] Cf above n15. The milieu where the words of Jesus might have been translated into Greek was most interestingly described by M. Hengel, 'Zwischen Jesus und Paulus; Die "Hellenisten", die "Sieben" und Stephanus (Apg 6,1–15; 7,54–8,3)', *ZTK* 72 (1975) 151–206.

[49] Did 6:3; 7:1; 9:1, 3; 10:8; 11:3, each time introducing a new area of religious law. For the wider Greek usage see M.M. Mitchell, 'Concerning *PERI DE* in 1 Corinthians', *NovT* 31 (1989) 229–256. She does not take in the Didache, and directs her main argument against the view that the formula signals answers to *written* questions.

[50] For terminological analysis in relation to the ancient halakha see especially Y. Sussman, 'The History of Halakha in the Dead Sea Scrolls – A Preliminary to the Publication of 4QMMT', *Tarbiz* 59 (1990) 11–76 (in Hebrew); and cf L.H. Schiffman, '*Miqsat ma'aseh ha-Tora* and the Temple Scroll', *RdQ* 14 (1990) 435–457.

Greek and in Hebrew, and that we have here another trace of halakha formulated in Greek.

In sum, I really do not think it is pressing too far to compare First Corinthians with the phenomenon of written practical instruction or 'halakhic letters' which can be pointed out in the ancient Jewish sources, and which in Medieval Judaism, in changed circumstances, developed into the corpus of *Sheelot u-teshuvot* or *responsa* literature. The decisive difference is of course that First Corinthians addresses a community of gentiles, or rather gentile believers in Christ.[51] Yet this comparison may serve to make us once again aware of the remarkable phenomenon of a letter of the Apostle to the Gentiles using Jewish and Jewish-Christian terminology and rules.

III. The Fragment of Justification Doctrine, 1Cor 7:18–19

1Cor 7 may be called the most prescriptive, or if you wish legislative, Pauline chapter. But true to Paul, there is also this 'theological' digression in vv17–24, to which we now turn.[52] Let us first review its character and function. It has two sub-themes: the relative status of the circumcised and uncircumcised, and that of slaves and free men. These themes are connected by the key word 'calling', *klêsis, kalein*: 'Only, as the Lord alloted to everyone, everyone as God has called him, let him thus walk (17) ... Let everyone remain in the calling, in which he was called (20) ... Let everyone remain, brethren, in that in which he was called, before God (24).' For a better understanding we must read on a little, since the style of the digression returns after the introductory formula to the next main subject:[53] 'Now about the virgins'; and it is only then that a more elaborate motivation for all these injunctions is given. Paul thinks it well to be unmarried 'because of the present distress' (v26); anyhow, 'are you bound to a woman, do not seek freedom; are you free from a woman, do not seek a woman' (v27), for 'the appointed time has become very short' (v29). Hence the overall theme of the digression is the relativity of one's status or 'calling', and this flows over into the main subject of being unmarried.[54]

---

[51] Gentiles addressed: 1Cor 12:2 and chs 8–10; cf my book p58–62. On halakhic letters see my 'Halakhic Correspondence in Antiquity: Qumran, Paul and the Babylonian Talmud', in *Proceedings, Conference on the Question of the Letters of Paul from the Perspective of the Jewish Responsa Mode* (Cath. Theol. Union, Chicago, Nov. 15 & 18, 1991) limited photocopy edition, Chicago 1992, 63–83; and in Dutch, 'Halachische brieven uit de oudheid: Qumran, Paulus en de Talmoed', *NedTT* 46 (1992) 284–301.

[52] Cf other digressions, 6:1–11 within chs 5–6; 9:1–10:23 in chs 8–11; 12:12–13:13 in chs 12–14.

[53] It is also announced in 7:15, *keklêken humas ho theos*.

[54] The digression appears to be aimed mainly at the issue of *parthenoi* which must therefore have been prominent in the Corinthians' written inquiry.

Let us now take a look at the materials our passage takes in. The language about the 'appointed time' (*kairos*) and the 'present distress' is unmistakably apocalyptic,[55] and it is meant to illuminate the commandment to stay as you are. A first thing to conclude is that in Paul's thought practical commandments and apocalyptic thought can go hand in hand, as in fact we have it in the Qumran scrolls and a number of Pseudepigrapha.[56] Yet I do not think it correct to explain all of Paul's ethics from his apocalyptic motivation, as Schweitzer did. Apocalypticism is one strand of his thought, law is another, and a third one is general Hellenistic thought. The indifference of one's status as a slave or free man was a motif typical of popular Cynico-Stoic philosophy,[57] and the same goes for the social metaphor of the body which is indirectly associated with our passage.[58] In fact, the Cynical indifference towards social status fits remarkably well to the apocalypticist relativisation of this-wordly institutions. We should not miss this opportunity to note the combined presence of law, apocalypticism and popular Hellenistic philosophy, which invites a reconsideration of the relationships of Judaism, Christianity and Hellenism.

The composite character of the chapter extends to the content of the digression and its prolongation, as compared with the main argument. The phrase, 'are you bound to a woman, do not seek freedom' (v27), envisages the possibility of divorce and hence contradicts the absolute prohibition of the Lord in v10f. The same can be said of the famous *mallon chrêsai* addressed to slaves (v21), which, however one interprets it,[59] considers the option of individual manumission and equally runs against the grain of the main argument. Apparently the author takes his readers to be able to discern between rhetorical digressions and clear-cut commandments. Once again this makes Paul's explicit appeals here to authoritative commandments of the Lord stand out.

Now let us address the passage of our interest, v18f. It starts out using the key word 'call' of the digression, and then continues with a formula better known from other letters (I translate the frankly un-Victorian language literally): 'Was someone called when circumcised, let him not have it stretched back; was it having his foreskin that someone was called, let him not be circumcised; circumcision is nothing and the foreskin is nothing, but keeping

---

[55] Cf the 'shortening of time', Mk 13:20//Mt 24:22; Ps-Philo 19:13; 2Bar 20:1; 54:1; 83:1; 4Ezra 4:26f; PesRK 5:7 (Mandelbaum p88) = CantR 2:19.

[56] 1QS and CD (which I take to be one document); Jub; and cf Test12Patr.

[57] See F. Stanley Jones, *'Freiheit' in den Briefen des Apostels Paulus; Eine historische, exegetische, und religionsgeschichtliche Studie*, Göttingen 1987, 27–37.

[58] Via 1Cor 12:13. On the metaphor See J.J. Meuzelaar, *Der Leib des Messias*, Assen 1961, 149–155.

[59] The reading that Paul means that a slave should take the opportunity to get free deserves priority as the *lectio difficilior*, which is confirmed by the subtle message of Phlm, see my book p92–4. Cf S.S. Bartchy, *Mallon Chrêsai: First-Century Slavery and I Corinthians 7:21* (SBL Diss Ser 11) Missoula 1973.

God's commandments.' Obviously, this is another variant of the formula found in Galatians, Colossians and elsewhere in First Corinthians, which in its most quoted version reads: 'There is no longer Jew nor Greek, no longer slave nor free man, no longer male and female, for you are all one in Christ' (Gal 3:28). When one compares the form of all of its seven occurrences, the polarity of 'Jew and Greek', which equals 'circumcision and foreskin', appears to be basic.[60] This explains its relevance to Galatians, that passionate letter against forced circumcision for non-Jewish Christians, where it is used three times. In turn, this suggests a close relation to its main motif, justification by faith, which is confirmed by its context in each case.[61] Hence it is to this main theme of Pauline *theology* that this digression within a chapter of *practical* teaching refers us. In fact this is a clear instance of the interference of the 'theological' and the practical levels, of practical instruction and justification doctrine, but its coincidental character is equally obvious. The best way to describe it may be as an expression of the liveliness of Paul's mind, which never suffers itself being locked up in a single category or dimension.

As to the justification doctrine itself, I must be brief. The approach I find most adequate is that of Niels Dahl, who built on a more general theory of David Flusser.[62] Flusser noted back in 1958 that specific Pauline terminology which is lacking in the synoptic tradition finds clear parallels in the Qumran scrolls, and concluded that Paul here drew on a specific Jewish-Christian theological tradition. Thus we find in the scrolls the concepts of man's utter inability to make himself acceptable before God and of his justification by grace alone,[63] concepts of outstanding soteriological character which are also

---

[60] Rom 10:12 (3:29f); 1Cor 7:19; 12:13; Gal 3:28; 5:6; 6:15; Col 3:10f. Paul seems to vary it according to the needs of the context, adding 'barbarian and Scyth' in Col 3:11 (cf Rom 1:14), or reducing it to 'circumcision and foreskin' in Gal 5:6; 6:15 and to 'Jews and Greeks' in 1Cor 12:13 and Rom 10:12. The absence of the male-female polarity in 1Cor 7:18f and 12:13 is about as puzzling as its being there in Gal 3:28 *only*. Hence the more elaborate versions need not be the more original. Rather, the one constant item, that of Jew and Greek, seems basic.

[61] It concludes Gal 3 which classically sums up justification by faith; it opens ch 5 about freedom from the law; and in the personal postscript it sums up the letter's aim. To my mind, all of this indicates that Paul is the author of the 'rule' (*kanôn*, Gal 6:16!).

[62] N.A. Dahl, 'The Doctrine of Justification: Its Social Function and Implications', in id, *Studies in Paul; Theology for the Early Christian Mission*, Minneapolis 1977, 95–120; D. Flusser, 'The Dead Sea Sect and Pre-Pauline Christianity', in *Scripta Hierosolymitana* 4 (1958) 215–266 (also in his *Judaism and the Origins of Christianity,* Jerusalem 1988, 23–74), involving a revolutionary correction of Bultmann's view that this second stage of Christianity was rooted in the 'hellenistische Urgemeinde' (an idea adopted from W. Bousset's *Kyrios Christos*, Göttingen 1921²). Flusser advanced his own interpretation of Paul's special justification doctrine, rather more like Käsemann's and Bultmann's, in 'Paulinizm etsel Paulus', in D. Flusser, *Jewish Sources in Early Christianity; Studies and Essays*, Tel Aviv 1979, 359–80 (in Hebrew).

[63] See especially the Hodayot, 1QH 4:29–40; 9:14f; 13:16f; 16:11 – all closely related to Ps 143:2, a key text for Paul (see below).

found in Paul, here typically adapted to express the significance of Jesus' vicarious death and resurrection.[64] Dahl refined these observations as far as Paul is concerned. He first pointed out that a related, rather broad idea of justification by grace existed more widely in early Christian tradition, which was then adopted by Paul.[65] Secondly, Paul developed this idea in other places into a specific argument with a distinct social and polemical function. This is the case in Galatians and Romans, where the practical relationship of Jews and gentiles is involved and Paul defends the right of gentiles to remain Christians without becoming Jewish.[66] In this way Dahl is able to do justice to the general importance of salvific justification both in Paul and elsewhere, without neglecting the social significance of the specific justification doctrine. In other words, this doctrine may quietly be called a *Nebenkrater* or a *Kampfeslehre*, as long as one does not pretend that is all there is to say about justification as a soteriological concept, either in Paul or elsewhere.

At any rate, in Dahl's analysis the phrase 'there is no Jew nor Greek' is the practical corollary of Paul's specific justification doctrine. It is not intended to eradicate all social differences, as is not the case either with the formulae 'there is no slave nor free man, there is no male nor female'; Paul's practical instruction here and elsewhere makes that abundantly clear.[67] It does formulate the *practical consequence of the soteriological equality of Jewish and gentile Christians*, as against the separatist stance of the more extreme Jewish Christians at table in Antioch (Gal 2:11–14), or as Dahl put it: 'For Paul, the behavior of Peter and Barnabas constitutes their rejection of the doctrine of justification by faith.'[68] The question then is, what was Paul's own position on the law, or more precisely put: it being clear that he defends the soteriological equality of gentile and Jewish Christians, what did he think of the validity of the law for the latter? Dahl is not clear on this question.[69]

---

[64] Flusser ib (above n62) 222–7.

[65] Dahl ib (above n62) p100, referring to Lk 18:14 (*diakiousthai* is rather typical of Luke). And cf 1Tim 3:16 (*dikaiousthai* of Christ himself! cf Rom 1:4, equally pre-Pauline); 2Tim 4:8 (*dikaiosunês stephanos*); furthermore *dikaiosunê* in Matthew (3:17; 21:32), James (1:20; 3:18) and 1–2Peter, but also, authentically Pauline, in 2Cor 6:7, 14; 11:15!

[66] ib (above n62) p108–110, here following Stendahl ib (above n7) 2, 26. In fact, the case of Galatians is opposite to that in Romans, but on the same foundation, namely the relative right of Jewish and non-Jewish believers to 'stay as they are'. In Galatians this concerns non-Jewish, and in Romans, Jewish Christians. Dahl's failure to distinguish here betrays unclarity; see below n69.

[67] 1Cor 7:21–23; 11:2–16; 14:35–37; Col 3:18–25; and in Paul's tradition, Eph 5:22–24; 6:5–8; Tim 2:9–15; 6:1–2.

[68] ib (above n62) p109.

[69] p108, Paul 'completely rejects' the demand that gentile Christians keep (some of) the ceremonial commandments; p109, following Peter and Barnabas, 'in practice, the commandments of the Mosaic law would regain their validity'. The latter statement reflects the Christian tradition of radical law abolition. And cf n66 above.

For an answer, I return to our passage in First Corinthians, 'the circumcision is nothing and the foreskin is nothing, but keeping God's commandments' (1Cor 7:19). First let us note that the images of 'foreskin' and 'circumcision' are metonymies for being gentile or Jewish, and that in Antiquity, which knew of no 'secularized Jews', this either meant being non-Jewish or an observant Jew. Then if we may paraphrase, 'being a law-abiding Jew or living as a gentile mean nothing, but keeping God's commandments,' what can this mean? While von Harnack could not recognize here but a sign of Paul's 'Jewish constraints',[70] Schweitzer read more positively: Paul actually meant that Jewish Christians should keep the law. His rather schematic explanation was that, although in principle obsolete, the law obtains as long as the *status quo* of this vanishing world persists.[71] Rejecting that apocalyptic explanation, Davies suggested an even more positive reading on the basis of rabbinic material and of Paul's own explicit words about Israel's irrevocable election.[72] More soberly, Stendahl proposed to read Paul as addressing the relationship of actual Jews and gentiles, even *within the churches*.[73] As I noted, the criticism of Protestant exegesis by these scholars has drawn heavy fire, but their remarkable interpretation of this crucial verse has been curiously neglected. For Sanders and Räisänen it has remained 'one of the most amazing sentences' Paul ever wrote, 'surprising' in its 'Jewish' character.[74] Does indeed this enigmatic passage reflect Paul's continuous Jewish background?

Let us step aside again and review 1Cor 7 as a whole. As far as I see, the chapter as a whole indeed invites us to envisage how Paul's practical instruction and his justification doctrine could exist in his mind simultaneously and each in their own right. He does not seem to have felt any contradiction between appealing to commandments of Jesus or the law of Moses and stating that Jews and gentiles should each stick to their respective ways of life. Either

---

[70] A. von Harnack, *Beiträge zur Einleitung in das Neue Testament* IV: *Neue Untersuchungen zur Apostelgeschichte und zur Abfassungszeit der synoptischen Evangelien*, Leipzig 1911, 43f.

[71] ib (above n6) 178–99.

[72] ib (above n7) 69–85, referring also to W.L. Knox. Davies does not apply here his researches into the rabbinic tradition of the abolition of (certain) commandments in the Messianic age, cf his *Torah in the Messianic Age and/or the Age to Come* (JBL MonSer 7) Philadelphia 1952; id, *The Setting of the Sermon on the Mount*, Cambridge 1963, 109–190. See my book p94 n160 and 272 n11 for the material, and cf criticisms by P. Schäfer, 'Die Torah in der messianischen Zeit', *ZNW* 65 (1974) 27–42.

[73] ib (above n7), esp 1–6.

[74] Sanders ib (above n38) 161f; Räisänen ib (above n35) 67f. Instead, Sanders ib 171–179 explicitly reverts to the Patristic idea of the church as a non-Jewish 'third race'. Watson, (above n9), going for a 'de-lutheranized' Paul in the following of F.C. Baur's, turns Stendahl's solution upside down and ends up endorsing Sanders' position. Seifrid, ib (above n10) 20f rightly criticizes contradictions in Schweitzer's *status quo* solution but attempts no explanation of 1Cor 7:19f. To my mind, Stendahl's hermeneutics of *combined criticism of Reformation and Patristic exegesis* is still ahead of these positions.

way, commandments are involved, as is explicit in the remarkable phrase, 'keeping God's commandments'. In my view, Paul's appeal to the Apostolic law tradition with its commandments of Jesus and the affinity of the latter to halakhic traditions decide the case. According to Paul, Christians should keep commandments, Jewish Christians their Judeo-Christian commandments, and gentile Christians, at least such commandments as are given in First Corinthians. In that sense, being Jewish or being gentile means nothing, 'but keeping God's commandments'. The latter phrase, as I have shown elsewhere, alludes to Jewish wisdom motifs and signifies wholehearted devotion to basic commandments.[75]

Some more must be said about the commandments in First Corinthians, whose validity extends to gentile Christians. Taken together from the whole of the letter, these correspond to basic domains of ancient halakha: sex and marriage (chs 5–7), idolatry (chs 8–10) and ritual and liturgical customs (chs 11–14). These domains are among the universal commandments which according to a varying, ancient Jewish tradition are incumbent upon all mankind and which the later halakha subsumed under the heading of 'Noachide commandments'.[76] Hence First Corinthians as a whole indicates that Paul shared one, apparently rather mild, form of that tradition, containing what he called 'commandments of God' for Gentile Christians.

At this point, the words which Paul adds to the introduction of his digression deserve full attention: 'Thus I order in all churches' (1Cor 7:17). Since the first subject of the digression, the status of Jews and gentiles, is also the one constant element in the parallel forms of this saying elsewhere, it must have been basic in Paul's instruction in all his churches. I conclude that *the observance of distinct sets of commandments by Jewish and gentile Christians was the basic principle of Paul's missionary work*, and he laid it down in the rule, 'circumcision is nothing and the foreskin is nothing, but keeping God's commandments'.[77] And if this is so, the debate on Paul and the Apostolic Decree is reopened.[78]

This conclusion finds confirmation also in the main documents of the justification doctrine, Romans and Galatians. Rom 4 portrays Abraham as 'the father of all those who believe while having their foreskin, so that righteousness

---

[75] See my book p272.

[76] For its antiquity cf Jub 7:20. Sex and marriage correspond to *gilluy arayot* or *zenut*, in Greek *porneia*; idolatry to *avoda zara* or *eidôlolatreia*, and ritual and liturgical customs, which Paul seems to announce under the heading of *paradoseis* (11:2), may be thought subsumed under *avodat ha-Shem* (the worship of God); cf my book p50, 98f. See now especially M.N.A. Bockmuehl, 'The Noachide Commandments and New Testament Ethics; with Special Reference to Acts 15 and Pauline Halakhah', *RB* 102 (1995) 72–101.

[77] This considerably restricts the freedom to interpret the famous passage about Paul's own behaviour, 1Cor 9:19–23.

[78] For some intimations see my book, ch6.

is accounted to them as well, and the father of the circumcision, for those who
not only are of the circumcision but also follow the tracks of the faith which
our father Abraham had when still in the foreskin' (Rom 4:11f). Clearly, Jewish Christ-believers do *not only keep the law* but also are true to Abraham's
pre-circumcision faith; hence they do keep the law. In Galatians, one of Paul's
'learned' arguments against the judaizers is precisely that 'if you have your-
selves circumcised, Christ will be of no use' (5:2); this is what 'I, Paul, say to
you' – and we are reminded of his distinguishing between his own opinion and
the commandments of the Lord and the Apostolic tradition in 1Cor 7. As occurs there several times, he now continues and apparently quotes a formal
rule: 'Again, I testify to anyone who has himself circumcised, that he is
obliged to do the whole law' (5:3). As I have pointed out, this rule has convincing parallels both in rabbinic literature and, of all sources, in the letter of
James.[79] For Paul, there is no half-way judaizing; there is only believing in
Christ, either being a Jew and keeping the whole law, or living as a gentile,
keeping one's own share of God's commandments.

IV. Conclusion

Let us return to Paul's cultural context, and more specifically, to the question
what change his conversion had brought about in it. If the specific justification doctrine meant in practice that gentiles kept their minimum set of 'commandments of God' while Jewish Christians kept 'the whole law', Paul must
indeed be classified with some variant of law-observant Judaism. Now the
actual contents of the commandments he taught in 1Cor 7 allow us to be more
specific. In particular the divorce prohibition pinpoints Paul's law teaching in
a specific tradition, more radical than that of his Pharisaic past. His explicit
appeals to commandments of Jesus in this connection make it plausible that he
followed the Apostolic tradition in which Jesus was the highest authority.
Hence Paul's conversion meant that he changed from his Pharisaic observance to that of the followers of Jesus. It also entailed his calling to be the
Apostle to the gentiles, and that means the seeds of his special justification
doctrine were sown at the moment of his calling. When read as a special application of the general idea of justification by grace or faith, this doctrine does
not necessarily imply a shift beyond the boundaries of pluriform Second Temple Judaism either. Its practical corollary, the soteriological equality of Jew
and gentile, was put to the test in Antioch. The cleavage between Paul and
James which now became visible must not be underestimated but seems to
relate to a basically different *halakhic* approach.

---

[79] Jas 2:10; see my book, 88f.

All of this means that we must think in terms of super-imposition rather than exclusion, which in the history of culture is more likely to start with. Paul's novel conception of justification by faith, for gentiles *without* the law and for Jews *having* it, did not mean the abolition of law observance but its *integration into a universal soteriological context*. Precisely this is borne out in Rom 9–11, which starts out with Israel's priority and concludes in universal, apocalyptic terms (Rom 9:1–5; 11:25–33). On the halakhic level it is translated in the practical rule, 'to live Jewish or gentile does not mean anything'.

There is another level, moral philosophy. The indifference of social status and the idea of society as a body with different members belong to Hellenistic philosophy. This is the level where Paul developed his ecclesiological christology – or christological ecclesiology if you wish. The body is Christ, and his members, though different, are equal in value. Hence *there is no need for* a specific explanation, apocalyptic or other, of the idea that Jewish Christians should keep observing the law. Though it does not save them, it is there for them to keep, as ever. Law, apocalypticism, and christology go together within the wider ambience of oriental Hellenistic thought.

In this sense, I think, Paul's conversion did not burst the bounds of Judaism or of his personal observance *per se*. Nor did it leave him a regular Jew, had he ever been one. It burst the bounds of any language he knew, any human knowledge or description. Historical theologians must not try better.

'All Things to All People'

Paul and the Law in the Light of 1 Corinthians 9.19–23

by

STEPHEN C. BARTON

I. Introduction

'The trouble with Paul has always been to put him in his place.' This is the statement with which Edwin Judge began his seminal essay of 1972 on 'St Paul and Classical Society'.[1] It expresses a sentiment with which I suspect many of Paul's own contemporaries would have agreed. This would have been so not least with respect to Paul's attitude to and practice of the law. Paul's own testimony to his apostolic practice, in 1 Cor. 9.19–23, shows us why he has been so hard to pin down in this area as in many others: 'to the Jews I became as a Jew ... to those under the law I became as one under the law ... to those outside the law I became as one outside the law ... to the weak I became weak, I have become all things to all people, that I might by all means save some.'[2]

The aim of this essay is to analyse this text in its literary and historical context with a view to showing what light it throws on the question of 'Paul and the law'. As such it is an exercise in what C.F.D. Moule called, 'interpreting Paul by Paul'[3]: but we shall have to cast our net considerably wider also, as we shall see. What I shall attempt to show is that this text has a crucial role in helping us to recognize that Paul's stance in relation to the law has to be set in the context of the world of ancient politics and political rhetoric. That is to say, 'Paul and the law' is not just a theological issue to do with soteriology and christology, fundamental as those dimensions of his thought are. For in so far as Paul laboured to create and sustain a viable Christian ecclesial polity, his stance in relation to the law has to be seen in political and social terms as well. To put it

---

[1] E.A. Judge, 'St Paul and Classical Society', *Jahrbuch für Antike und Christentum*, 15 (1972), 19–36, at p. 19.

[2] Unless indicated otherwise, English translations are taken from the *New Revised Standard Version* of the Bible (1989).

[3] C.F.D. Moule, 'Interpreting Paul by Paul', in M.E. Glasswell and E.W. Fasholé-Luke, eds., *New Testament Christianity for Africa and the World* (London: SPCK, 1974), 78–90.

another way, Paul's soteriology and christology are linked inextricably with Paul's socio-political practice and with that of the Corinthians as well.

Of course, in using words like 'political' and 'social' of aspects of Paul's thought and practice, there is always the danger of reading Paul in ways which are anachronistic or which make him captive to the pragmatic interests of a particular school of interpretation, liberation theology, for example.[4] On the other hand, failure to attend to issues of social embodiment and the exercise of power in Paul and his churches faces the equal danger of reading Paul in ways which are narrowly 'idealist' and prone to make Paul captive to other kinds of pragmatic interests, those of the religiously or politically conservative, for example. There is no simple way out of such heremeneutical complexities, which are at the forefront of contemporary debates in biblical interpretation.[5] What is important, however, is to be aware of the issues, to attempt a reading which is sensitive historically and contextually, and to avoid claiming too much for one's own proposal.

II. 1 Cor. 9.19–23 in context

1. The literary context

The first argument which points us in the direction of ancient politics as an appropriate setting for interpreting our text comes from the immediate literary setting. Here, it is important to understand that 1 Cor. 9 is not at all so loosely related to what comes before and after about eating 'food sacrificed to idols' (εἰδωλόθυτα) that it ought to be treated separately as an editorial misplacement or an interruption. On the contrary, as Wendell Willis has argued,[6] 1 Cor. 9, which consists of Paul's account of his own behaviour as an apostle, is an integral part of his overall argument in 8.1–11.1, the aim of which is to persuade the 'strong' in Corinth voluntarily to limit their freedom to eat εἰδωλόθυτα for the sake of the 'weak'.

The underlying rationale of Paul's argument in 1 Cor. 9 is the *imitatio Pauli*. Just as Paul himself has refrained from exercising his authority (ἐξουσία) as an apostle to accept the financial support of the Corinthians, in order not to 'put an obstacle in the way of the gospel of Christ' (9.12), so the Corinthian strong are to refrain from exercising their authority in the matter of εἰδωλόθυτα. Paul's

---

[4] On the socio-pragmatic aspects of liberationist hermeneutics, see Anthony C. Thiselton, *New Horizons in Hermeneutics* (London: HarperCollins, 1992), ch. XII.

[5] See further, Francis Watson, ed., *The Open Text. New Directions For Biblical Studies?* (London: SCM, 1993).

[6] Wendell Willis, 'An Apostolic Apologia? The Form and Function of 1 Corinthians 9', *JSNT*, 24 (1985), 33–48; so too, Hans Conzelmann, *Commentary on 1 Corinthians* (Philadelphia: Fortress, 1975), 137–138.

positive example in chapter 9 is then balanced in chapter 10 by a powerful negative example from the scriptural story of Israel, designed to act as a deterrent against idolatry arising out of commensality at 'the table of demons'. But the conclusion of the argument in 10.31–11.1 returns to the principle of accommodation for the sake of the weak, set out so clearly in 1 Cor. 9.19–23, and culminates with the command: 'Be imitators of me, as I am of Christ' (11.1). In other words, rather than being an unrelated digression, 1 Cor. 9 is integral to Paul's argument, an argument which is carefully structured. In fact, as others have pointed out, chapter 9 functions in relation to chapters 8 and 10 in a similar way to the function of chapter 13, the famous 'digression' on the 'more excellent way' of ἀγάπη, in relation to chapters 12 and 14.[7]

Why is it important to note the intimate connection between 1 Cor. 9 and its immediate context in Paul's argument? The answer is that only by so doing shall we be able to recognize that Paul articulates his principle of accommodation, not in a general theoretical and 'theological' digression on the nature of apostleship as he understands it, but in the specific rhetorical context of an epistolary act of persuasion. In this act of persuasion, Paul is attempting to stave off the disintegration of the Christian community in Corinth. He does this by giving instruction related to the often-discussed philosophical-political *topoi* ἐλευθερία and ἐξουσία and by providing a practical policy on εἰδωλόθυτα, grounded in his own example, which will enable the strong and the weak to coexist for their mutual benefit.

In a word, Paul is engaged in 'politics'. He is engaged, as the 'father' of the community (cf. 4.14–21), in the strenuous task of nurturing its fragile existence in the face of external pressures and internal differences which threaten to blow it apart. The implication of this for 'Paul and the law' is that, when Paul says in this connection that he became τοῖς ὑπὸ νόμον ὡς ὑπὸ νόμον … τοῖς ἀνόμοις ὡς ἄνομος (9.21–22), the force of what he is saying is in some important sense political, concerned with laws and the law in so far as they build up or break down a people's common life. Such a perspective may be an important corrective to theological or religious interpretations of 'Paul and the law' which either neglect or have no room for the material, corporate and public dimensions of the question.

2. The rhetorical context

Paul's argument in 1 Cor. 9 ist part of a general argument which unites the whole letter. This has been skilfully demonstrated by Margaret Mitchell in her

---

[7] See further, Wendell Willis, 'An Apostolic Apologia?', 39 and nn. 53–55.

recent monograph, *Paul and the Rhetoric of Reconciliation*.[8] Prior to her
study, there was a widespread recognition that Paul's letter addresses the problem of disunity in the housechurches of Corinth, a problem which Paul identifies at the outset (1.10ff.). But a persistent tendency in interpretation was to
interpret the roots of the disunity purely in terms of *Religionsgeschichte*, and
great energy was expended on trying to identify the religious beliefs and identities of Paul's 'opponents' in Corinth, be they gnostics or Spirit-enthusiasts or
antinomians or Judaizers or whatever. None of this work is to be gainsaid. It is
undeniable, for example, that doctrines of σοφία and γνῶσις, together with
issues of socio-religious identity (including the interaction of Jews and Gentiles), played an important part in the conflicts in Corinth.[9]

The approach has at least two shortcomings, however. One is that it fails to
give a satisfactory explanation for the shape of the letter as a whole. It is common in the history of exegesis, for example, for a line to be drawn between
chapters 1–4 and 5–16, on the view that the former deal with the problem of
religiously-motivated party strife and the latter with a conglomeration of
loosely related pastoral and theological challenges facing the Corinthian community. Some interpreters even argue that chapters 1–4 are so different in content and tone that they belong to a different letter.[10]

The second shortcoming is that the *religionsgeschichtlich* approach overlooks the extent to which the language Paul uses, the topics he addresses, and
the stategies of persuasion he adopts, are heavily indebted to the world of ancient politics.[11] Instead of trying to achieve what has turned out to be the impossible task of correlating the conflicting religious parties in Corinth with the
various pastoral and theological issues Paul tackles, Mitchell argues strongly
that the common denominator which ties all the issues together is that they all
contribute to factionalism, and that it is factionalism itself (rather than particular factions) which Paul is attempting to combat from the beginning of 1 Corinthians to its end. Instead of talking of Paul's 'opponents' and trying end-
lessly to clarify their identities in terms which suit our own hermeneutical

---

[8] Margaret M. Mitchell, *Paul and the Rhetoric of Reconciliation. An Exegetical Investigation of the Language and Composition of 1 Corinthians* (Louisville: Westminster/John
Knox, 1993).

[9] Useful early surveys are C.K. Barrett, 'Christianity at Corinth', *BJRL*, 46 (1963–64),
269–297; and R. Scroggs, 'Paul: ΣΟΦΟΣ and ΠΝΕΥΜΑΤΙΚΟΣ', *NTS*, 14 (1967–68), 33–
55.

[10] For the most recent study of the subject, which argues, not that 1 Corinthians is a composite of two (or more) letters, but that it was written by Paul in two stages, represented by
chapters 1–4 and 5–16, see Martinus C. De Boer, 'The Composition of 1 Corinthians', *NTS*,
40 (1994), 229–245.

[11] Persuasive also on this score are L.L. Welborn, 'On the Discord in Corinth: 1 Corin-
thians 1–4 and Ancient Politics', *JBL*, 106 (1987), 85–111; and Peter Marshall, *Enmity in
Corinth: Social Conventions in Paul's Relations with the Corinthians* (Tübingen: J.C.B.
Mohr, 1987).

predispositions towards 'religion' and 'theology', what we should be attending to is Paul's sense of the threat to the church posed by the socio-political problem of factionalism *per se* and the strategies he commends in order to combat it. According to Mitchell, '1 Corinthians represents the fundamental problem of *practical ecclesiology* which Paul chose to treat by employing Greco-Roman political terms and concepts for the society and the interrelationships of its members. This means that Paul in 1 Corinthians presents a viewpoint on the church as *a real political body* (even the local church) to which some Greco-Roman political lore, especially the call for concord, is directly applicable.'[12]

How then, we may ask, does this reading of the text in the light of ancient political rhetoric affect the interpretation of 1 Cor. 9, especially vv. 19–23? In fact, this reading makes very good sense. In chapters 5–7, Paul addresses a range of issues widely recognized in the political manuals of antiquity to be of crucial importance to the stability and unity of society: namely, marriage rules and household order and the related questions of community discipline and how to seek redress.[13] His all-pervading concern here is to combat the disunity arising out of the moral and domestic discord in the church. As Paul says in 7.15, addressing the problem of divorce in a 'mixed marriage': 'It is to peace that God has called you.' One of the ways in which Paul strives for peace (εἰρήνη) – the widely recognized goal of any political leader in antiquity – is to resist a doctrine of freedom (along with its behavioural corollaries) which undermines the common good. He does so by redefining freedom so that it becomes no longer a slogan distinguishing one faction over against another but instead a basis for encouraging the good of the whole.

This deeply political concern to redefine freedom and to transcend differences which threaten the stability and very existence of the church runs right through to chapter 11 and beyond. As Henry Chadwick pointed out long ago, the oscillating character of Paul's argument in 1 Corinthians bears witness to the lengths Paul goes in trying to keep all the parties on side and his concern to move the competing factions towards unity.[14] At the linguistic level, a recent study by Dieter Lührmann highlights the frequency of ἐξουσία and ἐλευθερία and cognates in 5.1–11.1, an observation which supports the argument that the definition of freedom along with its behavioural corollaries is what dominates Paul's argument here.[15]

---

[12] Margaret M. Mitchell, *Paul*, 300 (author's emphasis).

[13] See further, O. Larry Yarbrough, *Not Like the Gentiles. Marriage Rules in the Letters of Paul* (Atlanta: Scholars Press, 1985).

[14] H. Chadwick, '"All Things To All Men" (I Cor. IX.22)', *NTS*, 1 (1954–55), 261–275.

[15] See D. Lührmann, 'Freundschaftsbrief trotz Spannung. Zu Gattung und Aufbau des Ersten Korintherbriefs', cited in Margaret M. Mitchell, *Paul*, 118 n. 324.

Paul's response to the controversy over the practice of the strong in eating εἰδωλόθυτα is likewise intelligible in political terms. Perhaps we can say that, having in the preceding section dealt with threats to unity arising from the domestic sphere of marriage rules and household ties, Paul now moves outwards to threats to unity arising from the more public realm involving Christian participation in the life of pagan cults, voluntary associations, festivals, the hospitality of 'outsiders' and the like. As in what he says about the domestic sphere, what he now says about the more public sphere is an attempt to mitigate the socially divisive consequences of the Corinthian believers' new self-understanding. Thus, he criticizes the factionalism inherent in a doctrine of γνῶσις which claims to be democratic (8.1) but which, in practice, is exclusivist and oligarchic. He also qualifies the freedom based upon this γνῶσις, both by showing its limits (8.2) and by subordinating γνῶσις to the community-sustaining virtue of ἀγάπη (8.3). For whereas knowledge 'puffs up' the privileged few who possess it and leads to the downfall of those who do not, love of a christomorphic kind (cf. 8.11) is a virtue which 'builds up' (οἰκοδομέω) the community – the use of the building metaphor here being another favourite of Paul's also indebted to ancient political rhetoric urging unity.[16]

The central admonition comes in 8.9: 'But take care that this liberty [ἐξουσία] of yours does not somehow become a stumbling block [πρόσκομμα] to the weak [τοῖς ἀσθενέσιν]'. Noticeable here is Paul's rhetorical ploy of addressing his advice to the strong, for they are obviously the most influential in the church and it is their behaviour which will do most to divide or unite. Significant also is the politically important advice to yield to the weak in matters of no abiding significance, for the sake of the common good. To cause 'offense' (πρόσκομμα) is a tactic of party politics. It is to act in ways which cause faction and undermine the unity of the people. Therefore, using repetition intended to be emphatic (cf. 8.9,13), Paul calls upon the strong to curb their eating habits for the sake of the weak. Underpinning all that Paul says, furthermore, is the continual reminder in one way and another that God is over all and that the strong are to practise their ἐξουσία in ways which conform to the rule of God and the lordship of Christ. To sin against a fellow-member in 'the body' – another metaphor with strong political connotations which Paul makes heavy use of subsequently (12.12–27) – is to sin against Christ (8.12).

In 8.13–9.27, Paul then appeals to his own apostolic autobiography. Here we have a case, familiar from ancient politics, of the leader leading by personal example. The strong are to limit their individual freedom for the sake of the common good because that is what Paul himself has done, and they are

---

[16] E.g. 3.9–17; 6.19; 8.1,10; 10.23; 14.3–5,12,17,26; etc. See further, Margret M. Mitchell, *Paul*, 99–111.

under obligation to imitate him as their apostle (9.1–2). In obeying Paul's instruction not to let their behaviour become a πρόσκομμα to the weak (8.9), they will be conforming to their leader's example of refraining from exercising his 'right' (to make his living by the gospel) lest in so doing he becomes an 'obstacle' (ἐγκοπή) in the way of the gospel (9.12). The recurring language of obstacle or offense in Paul's argument is noteworthy. It occurs again at the climax of this section, in 10.31–11.1, where Paul concludes: 'Give no offense [ἀπρόσκοποι] to Jews or to Greeks or to the church of God ...' (10.32). The terminology is significant because it comes from the realm of ancient party politics and refers to the hostile way factions relate to each other to the detriment of peaceful coexistence in the social body.[17]

Paul's autobiographical testimony is intended to show how to avoid faction and offense. In relation to the specific case of εἰδωλόθυτα, he makes the point emphatically and hyperbolically, in 8.13: 'Therefore, if food is a cause of my brother's falling [σκανδαλίζει τὸν ἀδελφόν μου], I will never eat meat, lest I cause my brother to fall [τὸν ἀδελφόν μου σκανδαλίσω]' (RSV). In more general terms, at the conclusion of his argument in this section, Paul says: 'I try to please everyone in everything I do, not seeking my own advantage but that of many, so that they may be saved' (10.33). Whatever else it may be, this is a statement with strong political connotations. The use of autobiography as an example to imitate is well known in ancient political and philosophical literature.[18] The question of whether it is possible to 'please [ἀρέσκειν] everyone' was the subject of political debate as well, and it was held that 'pleasing everyone' was a positive thing if done for good motives. Most importantly, the idea of 'pleasing' people was a political *topos* in discussions of how to maintain peace and stability.[19] In the context of Paul's argument, it is an explicitly anti-factionalist position, for it is part of his admonition to the strong to seek the common good rather than their own personal advantage (σύμφορον, 10.33).

But the most complete and rhetorically crafted expression of this autobiographical testimony to being one who 'pleases everyone' for the sake of the majority comes in 9.19–23. In 9.3–18, Paul engages in an ironic ἀπολογία (9.3) in which he piles argument upon argument in support of his apostolic εξουσία to make his living by preaching the gospel, only to show that, by virtue of divine 'necessity' (ἀνάγκη) and God-given 'commission' (οἰκονομία) (9.16,17), he refrains from exercising this 'right' in order to make the gospel

---

[17] See further, Margaret M. Mitchell, *Paul*, 128–130.

[18] For an earlier example of the same strategy of appealing to apostolic autobiography in order to combat factionalism, see 1 Cor. 4.6–13. A recent analysis of the phenomenon which focuses on Galatians and 1 Thessalonians is George Lyons, *Pauline Autobiography. Toward a New Understanding* (Atlanta: Scholars Press, 1985).

[19] See further, Margaret M. Mitchell, *Paul*, 147–149.

'free of charge' (ἀδάπανος) (9.18). The political point is clear. Where the strong interpret freedom in terms of the advancement of their own interests, with consequences disastrous for the unity and growth of the body, Paul illustrates from his own practice the imperative of compromising and restricting one's freedom for the sake of the common good. Nothing, not even that prized possession ἐλευθερία, should be allowed to get in the way of the proclamation and reception by as many people as possible of 'the gospel of Christ' (9.12,16,18,23).

Paul epitomizes his argument in the rhetorically powerful *chiasmus* of vv. 19–23.[20] The main thrust comes at the beginning and the end, in vv. 19 and 22b–23: 'For though I am free with respect to all, I have made myself a slave to all, so that I might win more of them. ... I have become all things to all people, that I might by all means save some. I do it all for the sake of the gospel, so that I may share in its blessings.' The following two considerations are especially important. On the one hand, there is the striking repetition of words for 'all': for example, the artful sequence πᾶσιν – πάντα – πάντως in v. 22b. Seen in political terms, Paul is claiming to be something of a populist. Certainly, he represents himself as striving to be as inclusive as possible. For Paul, true freedom shows itself in what brings benefit to the greatest number, rather than in what separates off the few who are privileged.

On the other hand, there is the language of self-limitation and self-humiliation for the common good: πᾶσιν ἐμαυτὸν ἐδούλωσα (v. 19). Paul's freedom is such that he can forego it by enslaving himself to others. By so doing he expresses what is in any case his own self-understanding – namely that he is a δοῦλος Χριστοῦ (Gal. 1.10; Rom. 1.1; Phil. 1.1; cf. 1 Cor. 7.22; 2 Cor. 4.5). This self-understanding is doubtless rooted in the biblical concept of the 'servant of the Lord' or the 'servant of God'.[21] But the studies of Marshall, Martin and Mitchell have shown us, in addition, that this language of humility, compromise and accommodation is well known in political and philosophical treatises which address the problem of the political chameleon and the demagogue who seeks power by ingratiating himself with the masses.[22] This explains why Paul is careful to explain that the goal of his enslavement to all is *not* to increase either his own popularity or that of any one faction in the church, but to 'gain' (κερδαίνω) or to 'save' (σώζω) as many as possible to the gospel of Christ. He does not deny that his self-enslavement brings a personal reward.

---

[20] Cf. Barbara Hall, 'All Things To All People: A Study of 1 Corinthians 9:19–23', in R.T. Fortna and B.R. Gaventa, eds., *The Conversation Continues. Studies in Paul & John* (Nashville: Abingdon, 1990), 137–157, at p. 139, where the chiasmus is restricted to 9.19–22.

[21] K.H. Rengstorf, 'δοῦλος, κτλ', *TDNT*, II (1964), esp. 273ff.

[22] Peter Marshall, *Enmity in Corinth;* Dale B. Martin, *Slavery as Salvation. The Metaphor of Slavery in Pauline Christianity* (New Haven: Yale University Press, 1990); also, Margaret M. Mitchell, *Paul*, 130–138, 243–250.

But the 'payment' (μισθός) he receives is not financial (9.3–18), and the reward he refers to is eschatological (9.23, 27), being achieved by feats of the kind of 'self-control' (ἐγκράτεια) required of athletes (9.24–27). For Paul, the important 'partnership' (συγκοινωνός) is partnership in the gospel, not in competing interest groups (9.23).

In the intermediate verses (9.20–22), Paul expands on what he means by becoming 'a slave to all'. Since a detailed exegesis is beyond the scope of the present essay, I would make the following general claims for the interpretation of these verses. First, as we have seen, the literary and rhetorical context is Paul's appeal to the strong to accommodate to the weak over the practice of eating εἰδωλόθυτα (8.1–11.1). This helps us to explain why reference is made in vv. 20–22 to Jews, Greeks ('those outside the law') and 'the weak', for these are the parties for whom meat-eating and issues of commensality were so potentially threatening and divisive (cf. 10.31–32).[23] It also helps to explain why the series of groups Paul identifies culminates with 'the weak', and why Paul does not say, 'To the strong, I became strong'. Paul is addressing the strong and, rather than wanting to reinforce their privileged sense of identity as 'the strong', is trying to persuade them to imitate him by becoming weak in order to avoid placing a πρόσκομμα in the way of the gospel. Another implication of the rhetorical context is that 'all things to all people' is by no means only a 'missionary' principle, as is often assumed.[24] Indeed, its primary connotation here is a pastoral-political principle to do with compromise and self-denial for the sake of church unity. It is noteworthy, therefore, that in Paul's summing up along the same lines later on he says: 'Give no offense to Jews or to Greeks or to *the church of God*' (10.32). Here we have the same basic sequence as in 9.20–22 ('the Jews' – 'those outside the law' – 'the weak') and the same culminating reference to the community of faith.[25]

Second, in the face of the extreme difficulty both of correlating what Paul says here with specific episodes in his own life and of identifying the groups he lists here–whether, for example, the ones who are 'under the law' are the same as or different from 'the Jews', or whether 'the weak' listed last are intended by the chiastic structure to refer back to 'the Jews' listed first – I find attractive Wendell Willis's suggestion that the rhetorical style of these verses

---

[23] See in general, Wendell Willis, *Idol Meat in Corinth* (Chico: Scholars Press, 1985); also, the earlier study by C.K. Barrett, 'Things Sacrificed to Idols', *NTS*, 11 (1965), 138–153.

[24] E.g. G. Bornkamm, 'The Missionary Stance of Paul in I Corinthians and in Acts', in L.E. Keck and J.L. Martyn, eds., *Studies in Luke-Acts* (London: SPCK, 1968), 194–207; also, D. Daube, 'Missionary Maxims in Paul', in his *The New Testament and Rabbinic Judaism* (London: SPCK, 1956), 336–351.

[25] This parallel is why it is probably a mistake to identify 'the weak' as '*non-Christians, whether Jewish or Gentile, who are powerless (ἀσθενεῖς) to work out any righteousness for themselves*', as does David A. Black, in *Paul Apostle of Weakness* (New York: Peter Lang, 1984), 118 (author's emphasis).

is the key.[26] In other words, Paul is not refering to particular occasions, nor is he responding to accusations about specific actions. Rather, he is using broad *categories of difference* which are directly relevant to the mixed make-up of the Corinthian church and its environment (cf. 1.22–24; 7.18–19; 10.32; 12.13). In relation to these categories of difference, Paul asserts that he has used his freedom for the common good by a practice of accommodation designed to 'gain' people of every kind. The fact that he can sum up these broad categories by saying τοῖς πᾶσιν γέγονα πάντα (9.22) – noting with C.K. Barrett the definite article implying, 'to all the lot of them'[27] – reinforces the suggestion that Paul's main point here is not about his behaviour in relation to the law on specific occasions, as is often assumed. Rather, he is arguing in a rhetorically powerful manner that the strong should imitate his example of self-denial in order to stave off harmful division and faction and unite in Christ's body as many people as possible.

This is not to deny that 9.20–22 contains autobiographical testimony which is relevant is some way to the question of 'Paul and the law'. It is to suggest, nevertheless, that the moral-theological questions surrounding 'the law' elsewhere in Paul's letters, especially in Galatians and Romans, are not the main focus of attention here. The focus here is Paul's political-rhetorical attempt to combat factionalism by redefining freedom[28] in terms of the apparently paradoxical notion of enslavement to others for the sake of the common good.

3. The sociological context

In response to Wayne Meeks's call for a 'hermeneutics of social embodiment',[29] it is important to introduce yet another dimension to the interpretation of our text: namely, observations of a social-historical and sociological kind to do with class and social status in particular. For the interpretation of 1 Cor. 9, we can do no better for a starting-point than to refer to Dale Martin's study, *Slavery as Salvation*, mentioned in passing already. For our purposes, I would draw attention to two major conclusions from his study.

First, Paul's self-understanding as a 'slave of Christ' (implicit in 9.16–18 and explicit in other letters), is not an acceptance of personal and social self-

---

[26] Wendell Willis, 'An Apostolic Apologia?', 37.

[27] C.K. Barrett, *The First Epistle to the Corinthians* (London: A. & C. Black, 1971, 2nd ed.), 215.

[28] Another scholar who recognizes the political dimension of Paul's doctrine of freedom is H.D. Betz, in his essay, 'Paul's Concept of Freedom in the Context of Hellenistic Discussions about Possibilities of Human Freedom', *Colloquy 26 of the Center for Hermeneutical Studies in Hellenistic and Modern Culture*, ed. W. Wuellner (Berkeley, 1977), 13pp. Note the comment on p. 7 n. 43: 'Paul's political ideas have not been explained to any satisfactory degree. New Testament scholars still doubt whether the apostle had any political theory.'

[29] Wayne A. Meeks, 'A Hermeneutics of Social Embodiment', *HTR*, 79 (1986), 176–186.

immolation. On the basis of a detailed study of the institution of slavery in antiquity, Martin shows that slavery meant different things to different people and by no means had purely negative connotations, as it does for us today. Instead, 'in Paul's society it mattered less that one was a slave than whose slave one was'.[30] By linking his personal and social identity to Christ as *his* slave, Paul is claiming high social status as a leader, but is doing so in christocentric terms, not in terms of normal status criteria like birth, education, wealth and social class.

Second, Paul's claim to have made himself a 'slave to all' is usefully amplified by setting it in the context of ancient politics – and here, Martin's argument complements that of Mitchell well. In these terms, leadership could be practised either along aristocratic lines from the top down, as a benevolent patriarch whose position was one of social superiority, or it could be exercised on populist, demagogic lines, a practice which entailed stepping down the social scale in order to accommodate to those at the bottom ('the weak') and thereby win over or benefit as many people as possible.[31] At considerable cost to himself, Paul chooses what most closely resembles the latter course and becomes a 'slave to all'. Hence the store he places on doing manual work to support himself and his refusal to accept financial support from wealthy Corinthian patrons.[32] Hence also the enmity Paul generates from his high status social peers ('the strong') when he calls upon them to imitate him.[33]

The Paul who emerges from this analysis is a leader who is politically aware and who does not eschew the exercise of power, but does so from a deliberate position of low social status when it is appropriate to do so. This is his policy and practice as an apostle, a policy and practice which corresponds closely with, and is grounded in, his theology of the cross (cf. esp. Phil. 2.1–11).[34] So Paul's idea of leadership and his Christian theology are mutually reinforcing. Furthermore, his aim in adopting this stance is not social revolution: it is the unity and upbuilding of a church made up of people from a disconcertingly wide range of social backgrounds.[35]

---

[30] Dale B. Martin, *Slavery*, 85.

[31] On the proximity of Paul's practice of accommodation to the Cynic Antisthenes' idealization of Odysseus, who was famous (or notorious) in antiquity for his opportunism, cunning and adaptability, see Abraham J. Malherbe, 'Antisthenes and Odysseus, and Paul at War', *HTR*, 76 (1983), 143–173.

[32] On the likely influence of patron-client social patterns on the Corinthian church, see now John K. Chow, *Patronage and Power. A Study of Social Networks in Corinth* (Sheffield: JSOT, 1992).

[33] The theme of social enmity is explored thoroughly in Peter Marshall, *Enmity in Corinth*.

[34] See further, Stephen C. Barton, 'Paul and the Cross: A Sociological Approach', *Theology*, 85 (1982), 13–19; also, Dale Martin's own comments in *Slavery*, 135.

[35] Dale B. Martin, *Slavery*, 148.

On this reading, the main focus of Paul's enslavement to all in 9.19–23 is 'the weak' and, along with Gerd Theissen, Ronald Hock and others, Martin argues both that they are the majority of church members and that they are people of low social status (cf. 1.26–29).[36] To such people, Paul becomes 'weak to the weak' by stepping firmly down the social ladder and working with his hands to support himself, in so doing making the gospel 'free of charge' (9.18). Now Paul expects the social élite in the church to follow his example in relation to the analogous matter of εἰδωλόθυτα. Just as he avoids allowing his 'right' of support from becoming an ἐγκοπή, so the strong are to do likewise in relation to their 'right' to eat idol meat. Drawing out the implications of all this for understanding Paul's approach to power, Martin says this: 'Paul's self-enslavement to all, therefore, advocates not general self-denial or the relinquishment of authoritative leadership; rather, it argues for a certain kind of authoritative leadership: one from a social status position among the lower class. In 9:19–23, the issue is not giving up power but lowering status. The power is shifted, not lost.'[37]

For at least some interpreters of Paul, the kind of position advocated by Martin and others will doubtless evoke a suspicion that what Paul says in 1 Corinthians is being skewed: that Paul's sacrificial giving of himself for others in imitation of Christ is being misrepresented as the manipulative behaviour of a demagogue. Such reservations need to be taken seriously, for it would be a pity if the substantial rewards to be had from Martin's socio-historical reading were to be dismissed as the thin end of a reductionist, secularizing wedge in the interpretation of Paul. It may be the case, then, that Martin does not guard sufficiently against this kind of possibility.[38] Nor is it difficult to see how he might do so. For one thing, he might explore much more fully the extent to which Paul's practice is influenced by models of authority and servanthood which he has inherited from the Scriptures, for this inheritance is part of Paul's context also.[39] For another, he might ask more searchingly about the extent to which Paul's faith in Christ crucified-and-risen may have led him to adopt a 'political' stance which was neither oligarchic nor demagogic, but something significantly different altogether – a transformation, perhaps, of every available model, political or otherwise.

---

[36] Dale B. Martin, *Slavery*, 118–124; Gerd Theissen, 'The Strong and the Weak in Corinth: A Sociological Analysis of a Theological Quarrel', in his *The Social Setting of Pauline Christianity* (Edinburgh: T. & T. Clark, 1982), 121–143; Ronald F. Hock, *The Social Context of Paul's Ministry, Tentmaking and Apostleship* (Philadelphia: Fortress, 1980), esp. 59–62.

[37] Dale B. Martin, *Slavery*, 134.

[38] Cf. Graham Shaw, *The Cost of Authority. Manipulation and Freedom in the New Testament* (London: SCM, 1983) for an example of what can happen along these lines.

[39] In Dale B. Martin, *Slavery*, 62, the relevant Old Testament usage is touched upon only very briefly.

III. 'Paul and the law' in the light of 1 Cor. 9.19–23

Having attempted to set our text within a literary, rhetorical and sociological context, we are now in a better position to ask about its implications for our theme of 'Paul and the law'. In the interests of prompting further debate, I offer the following suggestions.

First, the fact that Paul enunciates his principle of accommodation – not once, but twice (i.e. 9.19–23 and 10.31–11.1)! – in the context of a response to factionalism in Corinth, suggests that Paul's attitude to the law is governed, at least in part, by political considerations. By 'political' I mean (as I hope is clear by now) considerations which are closely analogous to the common *topoi* of contemporary rhetoric about leadership, public affairs, and the exercise of power for the building up of the social body. Certainly, the law is also, for Paul, part of his soteriology and christology. But what Paul's act of 'deliberative rhetoric'[40] in 1 Corinthians helps us to see, more clearly perhaps than in Galatians or Romans, is that the complexity, subtlety and downright 'inconsistency' of Paul's attitude to the law is a function of his strenuous and heroic attempt to nurture to maturity a *new kind of polity*, the eschatology polity of 'the body of Christ', born out of separate polities – Jews and Greeks – which are (ideologically and historically) estranged and at loggerheads.

This helps to explain the tightrope character of Paul's statements in 9.20–22. When he refers to his identification with 'those under the law', he qualifies his statement immediately by saying, μὴ ὢν αὐτὸς ὑπὸ νόμον. In so doing he guards against the accusation from the 'strong' that he has sold out. On the other hand, when he refers to his identification with 'those outside the law', he qualifies that statement also, lest he be accused from another quarter of antinomianism: μὴ ὢν ἄνομος θεοῦ ἀλλ᾿ ἔννομος Χριστοῦ. It is clear from this that the law separates two social worlds, two communities. What Paul the apostle is trying to do, however, is to build one single, eschatological community *on the boundary* (as it were) between the two, a boundary radically redefined in terms of 'the gospel of Christ' and reflected in the relational phrase, ἔννομος Χριστοῦ.[41]

---

[40] The term represents Margaret Mitchell's conclusion about the kind of communication 1 Corinthians is, in her *Paul*.

[41] For the inadequacy of C.H. Dodd's attempt, available in *More New Testament Studies* (Manchester: Manchester U.P., 1968), 134–148, to define ἔννομος Χριστοῦ and 'the law of Christ' (Gal. 6.2) in terms of traditions of the sayings of Jesus, see V.P. Furnish, *Theology and Ethics in Paul* (Nashville: Abingdon, 1968), 59–65. H. Conzelmann, *1 Corinthians* (Philadelphia: Fortress, 1975), 179–180, makes the noteworthy point that in 11.1, Paul does not speak of himself as imitator of Jesus, but as imitator of Christ. For a revival of Dodd's view, see most recently, J.D.G. Dunn, *The Epistle to the Galatians* (Peabody, Mass.: Hendrickson, 1993), 322–324.

Because this new, eschatological community is made up of people so different that they can be polarized in stark binary terms – Jew/Greek, 'under the
law'/'lawless', 'strong'/'weak', circumcised/uncircumcised, slave/free, male/
female, and so on – the task of forming them into a single body involves a
constant process whereby the differences within the body are *mediated and
transformed* into something new.[42] Paul's principle of 'all things to all people'
encapsulates that principle of mediation for the sake of transformation (ἵνα
πάντως τινὰς σώσω, 9.22b; μὴ ζητῶν τὸ ἐμαυτοῦ σύμφορον ἀλλὰ τὸ τῶν
πολλῶν, ἵνα σωθῶσιν, 10.33b).

Second, the question is worth asking: how adequate is it to designate 1 Cor.
9.19–23 as a 'missionary maxim' (so David Daube) or as an expression of
Paul's 'missionary stance' (so Günther Bornkamm)?[43] Certainly, Paul's
preaching of the gospel 'free of charge' is not for away (9.18). Certainly also,
'Jews' and 'Greeks' are distinguished (as outsiders) from 'the church of God'
(as insiders), in 10.32. But does the 'missionary' designation have a distract-
ing or narrowing effect, lifting what Paul says out of the context of his attempt
as 'father' of the church in Corinth to counteract factionalism into the realm of
something more appealing religiously or theologically – namely, Paul 'the
missionary'? To put it sharply, my point is that Paul was not a missionary, but
ἀπόστολος Χριστοῦ Ἰησοῦ (1.1; cf. 4.9; 9.1,2; 15.9), a calling that meant being God's 'master builder' in laying the foundations of the eschatological temple of God's people in Corinth and elsewhere (cf. 3.10–17).[44]

This socio-political dimension of Paul's work[45] easily becomes submerged
under the assumption-laden word 'missionary'. A corollary of this is that 'winning' Jews, 'those under the law' and so on (9.20–22) is interpreted in largely
anachronistic terms as gaining converts to a new religion. What Paul is in fact
talking about is how Jews and Greeks, law-observant and law-free, strong and
weak, slave and free can together be the one, united body of Christ – something he makes explicit in 12.12–13. Differences, including differences over
the Jewish law, are not here being disregarded or annihilated. Rather, they
become the stuff out of which, through the practice of ἀγάπη, life together in
the body of Christ is fashioned (cf. 1 Cor. 13). As Alan Segal, in a comment on
our text, says of Paul: 'If Paul's call for unity is taken seriously, he did not

---

[42] For a similar argument with respect to Galatians, see J. Louis Martyn, 'Apocalyptic
Antinomies in Paul's Letter to the Galatians', *NTS*, 31 (1985), 410–425. Cf. also, Wayne A.
Meeks, 'Social Functions of Apocalyptic Language in Pauline Christianity', in D. Hellholm,
ed., *Apocalypticism in the Mediterranean World and the Near East* (Tübingen: J.C.B. Mohr,
1983), 687–705.

[43] See D. Daube, 'Missionary Maxims' and G. Bornkamm, 'Missionary Stance', cited
above.

[44] For a similar argument, see Krister Stendahl, *Paul Among Jews and Gentiles* (London:
SCM, 1977), 1–77.

[45] On which see, Margaret M. Mitchell, *Paul*, 99–111.

merely want to be the apostle to the gentiles. He wanted to be an apostle of all the church, for his vision was for a new community formed of all gentiles and Jews (I Cor. 9:22).'[46]

Finally, this vision and the practice of self-enslavement which it entailed was, for Paul, a costly business. The cost is intimated perhaps by the linguistic fact that, when Paul comes to 'the weak' at the rhetorical climax of his state-ment (9.22a), he omits the ὡς: simply, 'to the weak I became weak'.[47] Paul has stepped down in the social scale. He works with his hands to support himself in order to make the gospel ἀδάπανος to the *hoi polloi*. It is not coincidental that, when in chapter 4 he gives a catalogue of apostolic hardships, he says, 'We are weak [ἡμεῖς ἀσθενεῖς], but you are strong' (4.10b), and then in the catalogue of weaknesses which follows, a prominent place is given to the apos-tle's manual labour (καὶ κοπιῶμεν ἐργαζόμενοι ταῖς ἰδίαις χερσίν, 4.12a).

Another, not unrelated, intimation of the cost to Paul is the suggestion of Anthony Harvey that Paul's ironic 'boast' in 2 Cor. 11.24 of having received from the Jews the forty lashes less one on no less than five occasions, shows that Paul continued to maintain his ties with synagogue communities while at the same time fulfilling his vocation as apostle to the Gentiles.[48] In other words, Paul's practice of becoming 'as one outside the law' to the Gentiles repeatedly brought upon himself the severe corporal discipline of the Jewish synagogue courts. Nevertheless, for the sake of becoming 'as a Jew to the Jews' so as to 'gain' them also, this was a price Paul was prepared to pay. No wonder Paul is able to testify, at the conclusion of the Epistle to the Galatians: 'I bear on my body the marks [τὰ στίγματα] of Jesus' (Gal. 6.17b). Harvey concludes: 'Had he remained ... content with a mission to the Jews, his being 'under the law' might have been a painless constraint. But to combine this with being 'as not under the law to those not under the law' – that is with adopting Gentile customs in open breach of the legal requirements of Jewish society – was to incur the virtual necessity of regular punishment in order to maintain his Jewish connections. It was a heroic course, of a piece with all those other ordeals which Paul underwent for the sake of the gospel.'[49]

---

[46] Alan F. Segal, *Paul the Convert. The Apostolate and Apostasy of Saul the Pharisee* (New Haven: Yale U.P., 1990), 265.

[47] So too, Barbara Hall, 'All Things To All People', 146ff.

[48] A.E. Harvey, 'Forty Strokes Save One: Social Aspects of Judaizing and Apostasy', in *idem*, ed., *Alternative Approaches to New Testament Study* (London: SPCK, 1985), 79–96.

[49] A.E. Harvey, 'Forty Strokes Save One', 93.

'Do we undermine the Law?'

A Study of Romans 14.1–15.6

by

JOHN M.G. BARCLAY

In the history of scholarship on 'Paul and the Law' by far the greatest attention has been paid to Paul's theoretical statements on our topic, with numerous attempts to plot the location of the law in relation to faith, Christ, grace and works on the complex map of Pauline theology. How Paul's thoughts on this matter were translated into practice, what he actually observed of the law's regulations and what he expected others to observe are matters which have been comparatively neglected or else relegated to an appendix on 'ethics'. Such an imbalence is not, in itself, surprising: most of the passages where the term νόμος appears are couched in abstract theological language, and as readers of his letters we, of course, encounter Paul only in his word, not his practice. Yet there is a strong case to be made that an historical understanding of Paul requires much greater attention to the social functions of his theological views, and that *for his contemporaries* what he did or encouraged others to do counted for much more than what he said. It is an important feature of some recent scholarship that the practical ramifications of Paul's theology of the law have begun to attract serious investigation, enabling Paul in his actual life-choices to come much clearer into focus.[1]

In line with this determination not just to *hear* but to *see* Paul in relation to the law, I have chosen to discuss a passage whose significance for our topic has not been sufficiently exploited. I will argue that in Romans 14.1–15.6 we are given a valuable insight into the practical effects of Paul's stance on the law, even though the term νόμος does not appear in this passage. Paul's discussion of law-observance in relation to food and sabbath is to be discussed in the context of their social significance for Jews in Rome, and by examining

---

[1] The social implications of observance or non-observance of the law have been consistently emphasized by J.D.G. Dunn, for instance in his *Jesus, Paul and the Law*, London: SPCK, 1990. The practical options in some aspects of the food laws have been discussed recently by, e.g., P.J. Tomson, *Paul and the Jewish Law*, Compendia Rerum Iudaicarum ad Novum Testamentum III.1, Assen / Maastricht: Van Gorcum, 1990 and A.F. Segal, *Paul the Convert*, New Haven / London: Yale University Press, 1990.

how Paul directs the Roman Christians to behave we will be able to measure the practical (and paradoxical) effects of his instructions. In answer to our title question νόμον οὖν καταργοῦμεν διὰ τῆς πίστεως; Paul had responded μὴ γένοιτο· ἀλλὰ νόμον ἱστάνομεν (Rom 3.31). From Romans 14.1–15.6 we may assess to what extent Paul lives up to that claim in practice.

1. The Situation Addressed in Romans 14.1–15.6

Two presuppositions undergird this study and here require some clarification:

1. I take it as probable that here, perhaps more than anywhere else in this letter, Paul has in view live issues in the Roman churches. The motivations for the writing of Romans are complex and multiple, but I support what is now the dominant opinion that Paul's composition of the letter is at least partly related to the prevailing conditions in the Roman churches.[2] While the degree of relevance to issues in Rome might vary through the letter, there is good reason to believe that in our passage Paul had Roman conditions in mind. There are, of course, some similarities with 1 Corinthians 8–10 in vocabulary, theme and general stance, but these should not lead us to conclude that Romans 14–15 is merely a generalized reprise of a common paraenetic theme.[3] Our passage differs from 1 Corinthians 8–10 not just in omitting certain items specific to Corinth (such as reference to εἰδωλόθυτα) but in adding certain specifics, such as the eating of vegetables (Rom 14.2) and the observance of days (14.5), which limit rather than widen the applicability of the instruction. Moreover, the space which Paul devotes to this theme, his careful description of opposing positions and the prominence of this passage at the end of the paraenesis all suggest its immediate applicability in Rome.[4] The fact that Paul can confidently number himself among 'the strong' (15.1) also indicates that he knows the issues involved. If he can predict his allegiance with one of the two groups

---

[2] The question is well discussed in K.P. Donfried (ed.), *The Romans Debate*, revised edition, Edinburgh: T & T Clark, 1991 and A.J.M. Wedderburn, *The Reasons for Romans*, Edinburgh: T & T Clark, 1988. Among recent commentators Wilckens, Dunn and Stuhlmacher have all found Roman relevance in some aspects of the letter.

[3] As was argued by R.J. Karris, 'Romans 14:1–15:13 and the Occasion of Romans', reprinted in *The Romans Debate*, 65–84. W. Meeks regards this passage as a 'paradigmatic address to the scrupulous and the enlightened', 'Judgment and the Brother: Romans 14:1–15:13', in *Tradition and Interpretation in the New Testament. Essays in Honor of E. Earle Ellis*, ed. G.F. Hawthorne and O. Betz, Grand Rapids: Eerdmans, 1987, 290–300, here at 293.

[4] So, for instance, E. Käsemann, *An die Römer*, Handbuch zum Neuen Testament 8a, 4th edition; Tübingen: J.C.B. Mohr (Paul Siebeck), 1980, 353; U. Wilckens, *Der Brief an die Römer*, Evangelisch-Katholischer Kommentar zum Neuen Testament VI/3; Zürich/Einsiedeln/Köln: Benziger Verlag and Neukirchen-Vluyn: Neukirchener Verlag, 1982, 79–80, 109–115.

in the debate, he must know where they stand: he would hardly donate his authority as a blank cheque cashable by any Pauline group claiming to be 'the strong'.

To be sure, the theme is discussed with a degree of generality and obliqueness (e.g. 14.5, 15, 21), but this is easily explained on rhetorical grounds. In relation to a church he has neither founded nor visited, and in which his reputation is mixed, Paul has to proceed with tact. It would be presumptuous to write with instructions so specific as to give the appearance that he thought himself entitled to regulate their affairs in detail. The same diplomacy that requires Paul to insist that all he has written was only a reminder (15.15) demands that his instructions are couched in terms of apparent generality. Like a visiting preacher who knows the problems of a congregation but dares not presume to pronounce directly upon them, Paul frames his advice in generalized terms, yet with enough specific detail to hint to whom his advice applies.[5] Thus there is good reason to believe that Paul aims his words at actual disputes in the Roman churches. Any knowledge of local conditions in Rome could help illuminate those disputes and clarify the options open to the parties involved.

2. My second presupposition is that the issues Paul addresses in this passage concern the observance or non-observance of the Jewish law. The obliqueness of the passage and the variety of interpretations it has spawned have led some investigators to doubt that it is possible to discover its referents.[6] But there are good reasons to take the Jewish law as the central issue, as in fact most recent analysts do. The two topics directly referred to are the restriction of diet to vegetables (as opposed to eating 'everything', i.e. meat as well, Rom 14.2; cf.14.21) and the observance of certain days in preference to others (14.5). A third, the drinking of wine (14.21; cf. 14.17), may be a purely hypothetical addition (since 'drinking' is naturally combined with 'eating'), but our case will be stronger if it is possible to incorporate this as well. In common with many others, I take these verses to refer to Jewish scruples (which could be held by Jews or Gentiles) concerning the consumption of meat considered unclean and the observance of the sabbath and other Jewish feasts or fasts; the wine, if it is relevant, is also a matter of Jewish concern, relating to its use in 'idolatrous' worship. There are four strong arguments to support this interpretation: [7]

---

[5] The illustration derives from a class discussion on the reasons for Romans in Glasgow University, in particular from a remark by my student Rolf Billes.

[6] Karris declares 'History of Religions' investigation of the passage to be 'bankrupt' (in *The Romans Debate*, 66–70). More positively, Wilckens carefully lists the problems of reconstruction, but presents a strong thesis of his own, *Der Brief an die Römer*, 3.109–15.

[7] Cf., among others, P.S. Minear, *The Obedience of Faith*, London: SCM, 1971; W. Schmithals, *Der Römerbrief als historischer Problem*, Gütersloh: Gütersloher Verlagshaus Gerd Mohn, 1975, 95–107; O. Michel, *Der Brief an die Römer*, Kritisch-Exegetischer

i) *Paul describes the issue as concerning 'purity' and 'impurity'*. At the heart of the passage is Paul's affirmation of his conviction that 'nothing is impure of itself' (οὐδὲν κοινὸν δι' ἑαυτοῦ, 14.14), or conversely, that 'all things are pure' (πάντα καθαρά, 14.20). These terms are characteristic of Jewish purity concerns, and κοινός is used here in this specialized Jewish sense unattested in non-Jewish Greek (where it means 'common' in the sense of 'shared', not 'common' in the sense of 'impure'). Paul takes this term to express not only his own perception of the issues, but also the perception of those he calls the weak (τῷ λογιζομένῳ τι κοινὸν εἶναι, ἐκείνῳ κοινόν, 14.14). While abstention from meat might be considered 'purifying' in non-Jewish asceticism, the peculiarly Jewish use of κοινός and the parallel use of such vocabulary in other NT passages (e.g. Mark 7.15–23; Acts 10.9–15; 11.5–9) strongly suggest that both the Roman Christians and Paul have Jewish purity issues in mind.[8]

ii) *The literary context of Romans 14.1–15.6 suggests that Jewish issues are under discussion*. It is now generally recognized that the theme of Romans is the 'righteousness of God' with specific reference to 'both the Jew, first, and the Greek' (1.16). The impartiality of God in relation to Jew and Gentile is a theme which permeates the letter, in which Paul both affirms and relativizes the priority of the Jew in relation to law, circumcision, promise and election (Rom 2–3, 9–11). It is therefore natural to interpret the paraenesis as related to such ethnic and cultural issues, which were indeed central to Paul's mission. Since some other aspects of the paraenesis cohere with the earlier chapters, and since a leading motif in our passage is the same term, πίστις, which has dominated earlier chapters, we are entitled to expect some connection with Paul's intercultural ecclesiology, unless the evidence points decisively in another direction.[9] The fact that 15.7–13 returns to the topic of Jew and Gentile united in Christ gives further support to our position, though this is not in itself as decisive as some interpreters have made out.[10]

Kommentar über das Neue Testament IV, 14th edition, Göttingen: Vandenhoeck & Ruprecht, 1978, 419–21; C.E.B. Cranfield, *The Epistle to the Romans*, International Critical Commentary, Edinburgh: T & T Clark, 1979, 2.690–98; Wilckens, *Der Brief an die Römer*, 3.109–15; F. Watson, *Paul, Judaism and the Gentiles*, SNTSMS 56, Cambridge: Cambridge University Press, 1986, 88–98; Wedderburn, *The Reasons for Romans*, 30–35; J.D.G. Dunn, *Romans 9–16*, Word Biblical Commentary 38B, Dallas: Word Books, 1988, 795–806.

[8] Dunn, *Romans 9–16*, 818–20; Wilckens, *Der Brief an die Römer*, 3.112–13.

[9] Dunn, *Romans 9–16*, 704–5, 800.

[10] E.g. Watson, *Paul, Judaism and the Gentiles*, 96–97 and Wilckens, *Der Brief an die Römer*, 3.113. It is possible to hold that 15.7–13 constitutes a summary of the whole epistle which illustrates the principle of mutual welcome urged in 14.1–15.6 (15.7 obviously mirrors 14.1) but does not identify precisely the parties involved; see Schmithals, *Römerbrief*, 95–96. For this reason I will refrain from employing 15.7–13 in the exegesis of 14.1–15.6, but will draw it in to the wider conclusions.

iii) *The controversies reflected here are easily imagined among Christians with differing perceptions of the Jewish law.* The main objection to our thesis that Paul here refers to Jewish concerns is that a general abstinence from meat and wine is not characteristic of Judaism.[11] But this objection can be met if it is recognized that Paul is discussing here not the general practices of the Christians concerned but their specific behaviour when they meet and eat together. The disputes arise when they do (or do not) welcome one another to meals (14.1–3), and their debates are given urgency not as general discussions of lifestyle but as specific arguments about the food set before them on such occasions. It is hard to see why the strong should despise the weak or the weak judge the strong with such strength of feeling unless their different behaviour made immediate impact on their lives, and this would occur, of course, when they attempted to share common meals.

One does not therefore have to speculate about the general ease or difficulty in acquiring kosher meat in Rome:[12] the question is simply whether or not the meat on the table in a Christian's house was considered pure by those observing the Jewish law on this matter.[13] There is no reason to take this passage as referring to principled vegetarianism or dietary asceticism, or a specially stringent form of Jewish practice as found, for instance, among the Therapeutae.[14] The issue that arises here is a typical problem of commensality – how observant Jews (and perhaps law-observant Gentiles) can participate in a meal hosted by those who do not scruple to observe the law. As has often been pointed out, there were well-known precedents in which faithful Jews like Daniel and Esther restricted their diet to vegetables and water when eating meals prepared by Gentiles, and there are first-century parallels to this solution in the behaviour of priests in captivity in Rome.[15] Here we have simply to imagine some Christians, who were influenced by the prohibitions of the law, refusing to eat the meat (or, perhaps, drink the wine) which had been provided by those whose law-observance they had reason to doubt. Whether the meat was from an impure animal, or an animal incorrectly slaughtered, or was sus-

---

[11] E.g. Käsemann, *An die Römer*, 355: 'Provenienz aus jüdischer Orthodoxie ist ausgeschlossen ... Generelle Enthaltsamkeit von Fleisch und Wein gab es dort nicht.'

[12] *Pace* Dunn, *Romans 9–16*, 801 (exaggerating the significance of Claudius' expulsion of Jews in 49 CE in dialogue with C.K. Barrett, *A Commentary on the Epistle to the Romans*, London: A & C Black, 1971, 256); cf. Watson, *Paul, Judaism and the Gentiles*, 95, who suggests that Jewish Christians would be unwelcome customers in Jewish shops.

[13] This is rightly perceived by Schmithals, *Römerbrief*, 103–4 and Cranfield, *Romans* 2.695; cf. Minear, *The Obedience of Faith*, 10.

[14] Philo, *Vita Contemplativa* 37, 73. The references to the asceticism of Ebionites and of James (see Schmithals, *Römerbrief*, 98 n16 and Wilckens, *Der Brief an die Römer* 3.114) are intriguing but historically questionable and difficult to interpret.

[15] Daniel 1.8–16; Esther 14.17 LXX; Josephus, *Vita* 13–14; cf. 4 Macc 5.2–3; Judith 12.1–4; Josephus, *Ant* 4.137.

pected of idolatrous connections, it was to such people in such circumstances χοινόν; the wine (if it is relevant) could also have been suspected of association with idolatry through its use in libation.[16]

It is natural to take the observance of days (14.5) as arising from the same set of scruples. It is easy to imagine the awkwardness in arranging Christian meetings if some did, and others did not, observe the Jewish sabbath. While Jewish feasts and fasts may enter the equation as well, that 'days' are the subject of significant controversy suggests that they are a *regular* problem, which the sabbath could most obviously become.

iv) *All the alternative reconstructions are highly implausible.* We have already seen that this passage is unlikely to be a generalized instruction unrelated to particular issues. Nor can its reference be restricted to the issue of 'food offered to idols',[17] though, as we have seen, the question of idolatry may be part of the wider Jewish concern with impure food (and wine). The most frequently canvassed alternative is that Paul is referring here to Christians who have adopted (or continued from their pre-Christian past) ascetic habits related to (neo-) Pythagorean or even Gnostic sensibilities. This thesis in its pure form was first advocated by Rauer,[18] but it has been partially adopted by Schlier, Barrett, and Käsemann who all suggest some form of Jewish-Pythagorean syncretism, possibly paralleled in Colossae (Col 2.16–23).[19]

I find this thesis implausible for three reasons: a) Paul's argument presupposes that 'the weak' consider their vegetarian practices and observance of days central to their Christian faith: their lifestyle is 'in honour of the Lord' (14.6) and if they are pressurized to drop such practices, Paul fears that they will lose their faith altogether (Rom 14.20). It is hard to imagine Pythagorean vegetarianism being so closely wedded to Christian faith as to be an issue on which believers could feel their loyalty to God depended. b) Secondly, if those who ate only vegetables *judged* (i.e. condemned) the meat-eaters (14.2), they must have considered their abstinence a universal requirement: for them, to eat the meat constituted a serious Christian sin. However, asceticism in the ancient world was a matter of personal choice; I know no parallels for vegetarians making their lifestyle a standard by which to convict all others of sin.

---

[16] On the problems (and possibilities) of commensality between Jews and Gentiles see E.P. Sanders, *Jewish Law from Jesus to the Mishnah. Five Studies*, London: SCM Press, 1990, 272–83, and *idem*, 'Jewish Association with Gentiles and Galatians 2.11–14', in R.T. Fortna and B.R. Gaventa (ed.), *The Conversation Continues. Studies in Paul and John in Honor of J. Louis Martyn*, Nashville: Abingdon, 1990, 170–88.

[17] *Pace*, e.g., J. Ziesler, *Paul's Letter to the Romans*, TPI New Testament Commentaries, London: SCM, 1989, 322–27.

[18] M. Rauer, *Die „Schwachen" in Korinth und Rom nach den Paulusbriefen*, Freiburg: Herder, 1923, 76–186.

[19] H. Schlier, *Der Römerbrief*, Herders Theologischer Kommentar zum Neuen Testament VI, Freiburg: Herder, 1977, 403–6; Barrett, *The Epistle to the Romans*, 257–58; Käsemann, *An die Römer*, 355–56.

c) Thirdly, it is inconceivable that Paul should be so accommodating to scruples which derived from Pythagorean, Gnostic or other Gentile convictions. In our passage he urges the strong (including himself) to 'bear the weaknesses of the weak' (15.1) and cautions them severely against putting a 'stumbling-block' in their way (14.13, 21). Can we imagine him being so considerate of those who thought animal meat clogged the brain, or who observed 'pagan' fast days or considered certain days unpropitious? The author of Colossians, whether Paul or his disciple, is certainly less accommodating than this! Here in Romans Paul writes with a real sympathy for the views of the weak, as one who understands and appreciates their point of view, while personally differing from them. It is hard to imagine that he would do so if the basis of their viewpoint were some Gentile scruple or superstition.

However, all these characteristics – the centrality of the issue for the faith of the weak, their insistence that they stand for righteousness against sin and the accommodations required by Paul – make excellent sense on the hypothesis that Jewish scruples are at stake. We have no difficulty imagining in Rome the existence of those who continued their Jewish commitments after their adoption of Christian faith and who therefore judged Christian law-breakers as sinners. It is also easy to understand Paul's special concern here not to intimidate or antagonize such law-observant Christians. He knows very well how deeply rooted their convictions could be and what Scriptural support they could claim. He has just urged Gentile Christians not to boast over Jews (11.17–18) and he naturally turns that anxiety into a practical concern that Jewish (and any other) law-observant Christians should not feel intimidated or despised by their more aggressive brothers.

Thus we may conclude that the issue addressed in Romans 14–15 concerns the observance or non-observance of certain key aspects of the Jewish law. The 'weak' maintain Jewish kosher laws and observe the sabbath; the 'strong' do not. I have been careful not to describe the one party as Jewish Christians and the other as Gentile Christians, as we might be inclined to do. Although some of the 'weak' were probably Jewish, Paul, of course, is a Jew on the side of the 'strong' (15.1) and some of his Jewish Christian friends in Rome (e.g. Prisca and Aquila) may have agreed with him on these issues. Conversely, there may have been Gentile Christians among the 'weak' who found Jewish laws in this matter attractive. The letter itself indicates that the Roman Christians were of mixed ethnicity (11.13; cf. those listed in Romans 16) but the proportions, inclinations and relative power of Jews and Gentiles in the church are notoriously hard to discern. Fortunately for our purposes all that is necessary to know is that the issues Paul discusses here concern the observance or non-observance of Jewish law. We may therefore proceed to enquire into some practical aspects of the Jewish food and sabbath laws in Rome (2), before examining Paul's treatment of these issues (3) and assessing its effects (4).

2. Jewish Food and Sabbath Laws in Rome

If, as I have argued, Paul discusses real issues of dispute among Roman Christians concerning Jewish law-observance, it is worth gaining as full a picture as possible of the social context in which such disputes took place. Fortunately we are reasonably well informed from both Jewish and Roman sources about the practices and reputations of Jews in Rome concerning food and sabbath. Much of what we discuss here may also have been true elsewhere, but there are some unique features in the Roman environment which need to be taken into account.

A. Jewish Food Laws

It is evident from a number of sources that the Jews in Rome were particularly well known for their abstinence from pork. Macrobius (*Sat* 2.4.11) records a quip by Augustus that he would rather be Herod's pig than Herod's son,[20] a remark which suggests that Jews even at the highest social level were known to be faithful to the Jewish law on this point. The notoriety of Jews in abstaining from one of the most popular meats in Rome is evident from the comments of another emperor, Gaius, who is said to have challenged Philo's delegation to explain why they wouldn't eat pork (Philo, *Legatio* 361). According to Philo the question elicited laughter from Gaius' entourage; Jewish practice on this matter was a quirk which simply baffled the Romans and led to ill-informed discussions as to whether they abstained out of reverence or loathing for the pig.[21] The former theory made good sense on the analogy of the Egyptian animal cults and is entertained by Petronius (fragment 37 = *GLAJJ* #195: *porcinum numen*). Other Roman authors simply amuse their readers by reference to the Jewish *clementia* which allows pigs to live to an old age (Juvenal, *Sat* 6.160), and their equal abhorrence at eating human or swine's flesh (Juvenal, *Sat* 14.98–99). Tacitus' suggestion that the Jews abhorred the pig having once being plagued by its scabies (*Hist* 5.4.2) also suggests that some of the venom of Egyptian anti-Jewish sentiment influenced Roman perspectives on this issue.

It is clear, then, that Jews in Rome were expected to abstain from pork. For that reason, among others, they were regarded as pernickety in their eating habits, the kind of people who would abstain from certain foods or decline to share a meal with non-Jews altogether. Seneca recounts a time when, under

---

[20] See M. Stern, *Greek and Latin Authors on Jews and Judaism* (Jerusalem: The Israel Academy of Sciences and Humanities, 1974, 1980) (= *GLAJJ* #543, with notes supporting its historical accuracy; the joke of course is a play on the Greek υἱός and ὗς.

[21] See e.g. Plutarch, *Quaestiones Conviviales* 4.5–5.3 (669e–671b; *GLAJJ* #258), included in this discussion since the author had spent much time in Rome.

the influence of Pythagoreanism, he abstained from meat, but was persuaded to revert to a normal diet by his father since 'certain foreign rites' were becoming controversial, which required abstinence from some animal meats (*Epistulae Morales* 108.22). He dates this incident to the early years of Tiberius' rule, and it is very likely that the 'foreign rites' concerned were those of Judaism, which just at this time (19 CE) became the subject of public concern, issuing in the exile or conscription of many thousand Roman Jews (Josephus, *Ant* 18.65–84; Tacitus, *Ann* 2.85.4; Suetonius, *Tiberius* 36; Cassius Dio 57.18.5a). Seneca's anecdote confirms that Judaism was widely associated with eating peculiarities and that Jews were known as the sort of people who would decline to partake of certain meats when these were on offer. How Jews in Rome handled their distinction we do not know, but the tendency of such 'peculiarity' to lead to separatism at meals is clear from Tacitus' observation that the Jews were *separati epulis* (*Hist* 5.5.2).

Seneca's testimony also indicates that it was not only Jews in Rome who had unusual eating habits. Some Romans (chiefly philosophers) became vegetarian under Pythagorean influence and other ethnic groups (e.g. Egyptians) had their own taboos concerning animal meats (Philo, *Legatio* 361–62; Erotianus, fragment = *GLAJJ* #196). Josephus' comment about non-Jews observing 'our food prohibitions' (*Contra Apionem* 2.282) *may* indicate that some Jewish food practices were imitated by Gentiles, but his vagueness perhaps indicates that others' practices were merely similar to Judaism, not copied from it. However, Juvenal indicates that Gentiles sympathetic to Judaism were known to abstain from pork (as well as resting on the sabbath, *Sat* 14.96–99), though in his eyes they would thereby be tarred with the same brush as the Jews themselves. Considering the mixed reputation of Jews in Rome in the first century CE, this is a factor which we will have to bear in mind when we consider what Paul requires of the 'strong' Roman Christians in their accommodation to the 'weak'.

In any case, we may safely conclude from this evidence that:

1. Jews in Rome of all social classes were generally careful to preserve their food laws (most noticeably, abstention from pork). These laws were indeed one of the chief means by which they were publicly identified as Jews.

2. Any Jews in Rome who did not observe the Jewish law on this point (who ate pork, for instance) would constitute a serious affront to the Jewish community. They would also cause confusion among non-Jews if they still claimed to belong to the Jewish community.

3. Any Gentiles who observed Jewish food laws (or what appeared to be such) were likely to be identified with Jews, for good or ill.

B. Jewish Sabbath Laws

Jews were well known in Rome for their observance of the sabbath and for their gatherings on that day in their synagogues. The Jewish community in Rome was sufficiently well organized already in Cicero's day to constitute a political caucus and to send regular contributions to the Jerusalem temple (*Pro Flacco* 28.66–69). The basis of their organization seems to have been the regular meeting in 'associations' which Julius Caesar exempted from his general ban on *collegia* (cf. Suetonius, *Divus Julius* 42.3). According to a slightly dubious text (Josephus, *Ant* 14.213–16), the Jews in Rome were given permission to meet, to collect contributions of money and to share common meals.[22] Such license seems to have been preserved by Augustus (Philo, *Legatio* 155–57) who also gave special permission that those Jews who were Roman citizens could collect their corn handout on the following day if the distribution happened to fall on the sabbath (*Legatio* 158). This is in many respects a striking concession. Clearly a significant number of Jews were entitled to such corn handouts but were also scrupulous enough in their observance of the sabbath not even to collect their dole on that day. It would be hard to find clearer testimony to the significance of the sabbath and its faithful observance in Rome. Nor could such a measure have gone unnoticed by the general public in Rome.[23]

Synagogue meetings and sabbath observance were of course closely integrated in Jewish community life. Philo talks of the Roman Jews' προσευχαί and their meetings in them 'especially on the sabbaths, when they receive as a body their education in the ancestral philosophy' (καὶ μάλιστα ταῖς ἱεραῖς ἑβδόμαις, ὅτε δημοσίᾳ τὴν πάτριον παιδεύονται φιλοσοφίαν, *Legatio* 156). A key function of the sabbath, therefore, was communal: it not only publicly identified the Jews as Jews, it also enabled them to gather and to reaffirm their communal identity in recommitment to their ancestral customs. It also reinforced their link with the Jerusalem temple, for it was probably at such gatherings that the collections of 'holy money' were made for Jerusalem (*Legatio* 156).

Among Roman writers, impartial observers note the 'sabbath rites' of the Jews (*cultaque Iudaeo septima sacra Syro*, Ovid, *Ars Amatoria* 1.76). More hostile voices, however, regard the Jews' well-known sabbath rest as a sign of their laziness; Seneca, for instance, complains that Jews lose a seventh of their lives by idleness (*apud* Augustine, *De Civitate Dei* 6.11 = *GLAJJ* #186), while

---

[22] There are textual and historical oddities in this text, but its general thrust is plausible (and explains the Jews' special grief at Caesar's death, Suetonius, *Divus Julius* 84.5); see Z. Yavetz, *Julius Caesar and his Public Image*, London: Thames and Hudson, 1983, 85–96.

[23] It is possible that the Jews' refusal to collect their dole on the sabbath contributed to the impression that Jews fasted on the sabbath (e.g. Suetonius, *Divus Augustus* 76.2; Pompeius Trogus, epitome 36.2.14; Martial 4.4).

Juvenal and Tacitus, those jaundiced commentators on Roman life, complain about the Jewish custom of dedicating each sabbath to sloth (Juvenal, *Sat* 14.105–6; Tacitus, *Hist* 5.4.3–4). The Roman spirit of duty and hard work, as expressed by these upper-class representatives, was clearly incompatible with such regular cessation of activity.

In fact, however, there is evidence that many ordinary Romans were inclined to observe Jewish sabbaths, at least to the degree of ceasing work. Horace, for one, indicates the influence of the Jewish custom in the Augustan era (*Sermones* 1.9.60–78). Here his friend Fuscus declines to rescue him from a bore, claiming his inability to converse on the grounds that 'today is the thirtieth sabbath; do you want me to insult the circumcised Jews?'.[24] When Horace replies that he has no such scruples, Fuscus teases by responding that he, however, has, since he is 'somewhat weaker, one of the many' (*sum paulo infirmior, unus/multorum*, 69–72). Fuscus is being mischievous, of course, but the joke would fail if there were not some general perception that the sabbath was a superstition observed by many ordinary and less educated Romans. (We shall return to the link between Horace's *infirmior* and Paul's ἀσθενῶν).

That this was indeed the case is confirmed by several references to the sabbath in Ovid (cf. *Remedia Amoris* 219–20). Particularly fascinating is the assumption underlying *Ars Amatoria* 1.413–16. Here Ovid is discussing good days on which to court a girl and, in a fine inversion of tradition, recommends the Allia (a mournful commemoration of Roman defeat by the Gauls) and the sabbath. The reason for noting such days is that the shops will be shut and one will therefore avoid impoverishment by the girl's demands for presents! Ovid considers the sabbath to have such general effect as to cause a significant closure of shops and businesses on that day (*quaque die redeunt rebus minus apta gerendis*, 415), presumably Gentile as well as Jewish.[25]

It is probable that the observance of such sabbath rest was more common among the lower social ranks, as Horace's *infirmior* and *unus multorum* suggest. The phenomenon may in fact be linked to the unofficial observance of the seven-day planetary week, which was coming into vogue at just this time. For the Jewish sabbath coincided with Saturn's day, known to be specially inauspicious. The two systems of counting, the planetary week and the sabbath week, thus reinforced each other and it is likely that, as Colson comments,

---

[24] The reference to the *thirtieth* sabbath remains obscure; see Stern ad loc. (=*GLAJJ* #129).

[25] The implication is noted by A.S. Hollis, *Ovid: Ars Amatoria Book One*, Oxford: Clarendon Press, 1977, 108, who remarks on the impact of Judaism on the social and economic life of Rome.

the existence of the planetary week and the fact that the day on which the Jew abstained from work coincided with the day of the planet most adverse to enterprise promoted Sabbatarianism, and served to confirm many outsiders in the belief that it and Judaism in general deserved their respect and imitation.[26]

We may add further evidence of Roman imitation of the Jewish sabbath. Both Seneca (*Epistulae Morales* 95.47) and Persius (*Sat* 5.180–84) rue the fact that some Romans light lamps on the Jewish sabbath, a custom which from his side Josephus is proud to mention, alongside abstention from work (*Contra Apionem* 2.282). It thus seems that many non-Jews observed the sabbath in Rome, at least to the extent of lighting lamps and shutting up shop. Their legal entitlement to cease work was another matter (the dole and any other legal concessions were extended only to Jews) and the Jews' complete rest from labour must have been impractical for most non-Jews.[27] It was also another question whether any of these 'sabbatarian' Gentiles attended Roman synagogues. For the Jews, synagogue and sabbath were closely connected, but it was probably only a minority of Gentiles who used their opportunity of rest in the same way as the Jews (cf. Juvenal, *Sat* 14.105–6). It is in this light that we will have to consider the varying practices of the Roman Christians and the options open to them and suggested (or ignored) by Paul.

Again we may draw three conclusions:

1. The observance of the sabbath was, in general, carefully maintained by Jews in Rome, for whom abstention from work and attendance at synagogue was an essential element of their Jewish identity.

2. Any Jews in Rome who regularly ignored the sabbath would not only undermine the Jewish stance on this matter (over which they had won official recognition) but also forfeit an important means of maintaining their position in the Jewish community. To forego the social and educational opportunities of the synagogue meetings was to jeopardize the maintenance of one's Jewish identity.

3. Many Gentiles in Rome, especially in the lower social classes, appear to have observed Jewish sabbaths to the extent of ceasing work on that day. But in most cases the influence of Judaism seems to have been minimal (Saturn's day being at least as significant). Sabbath observance and attendance at a synagogue did not necessarily go together for such sabbatarian Romans.

---

[26] F.H. Colson, *The Week*, Cambridge: CUP, 1926, 41; cf. J.P.V.D. Balsdon, *Life and Leisure in Ancient Rome*, London: The Bodley Head, 1969, 59–65. Cf. the connection between the sabbath and Saturn suggested by Tacitus, *Hist* 5.4.4 and firmly asserted by Dio (37.16–19), by whose day (2nd–3rd century CE) the 7-day cycle had become traditional among Romans.

[27] Decrees from some Asian cities indicate the difficulties Jews themselves sometimes had in defending their legal rights on this matter (e.g. Josephus, *Ant* 14.262–64; 16.45); a Gentile would not be able to appeal to 'ancestral custom'.

We have now gained a clearer conception of the social realities of Jewish food and sabbath laws in Rome and the options open to the members of the Roman churches. Precisely what influenced the Roman Christians to take differing stances on these matters it is hard to assess. Our fragmentary evidence suggests that Jewish Christians in Rome had already been at the centre of controversy in certain Roman synagogues, if we may match Suetonius' famous *impulsore Chresto* (*Claudius* 25.4) with the reference in Acts 18.2 to the expulsion of Aquila and Priscilla.[28] The extent of this expulsion should not be exaggerated: Luke's 'all the Jews' is a manifest exaggeration, and the event does not merit mention either in Tacitus or in Josephus.[29] Thus it is hard to assess precisely how serious were the difficulties for Jewish Christians in Rome in their relations with the synagogue communities. We need to bear in mind the possibility of tensions here, while recognizing that the situation may have varied in different synagogues. We should also note that, if the example of Paul is anything to go by, Jewish Christians may have been anxious to maintain their place in the Jewish community even if they met opposition in that context.[30] How Gentile Christians viewed Jewish customs in relation to food and sabbath must have varied according to their previous contact with Jews and their personal convictions; as we have seen, there may have been Gentiles on both sides of the dispute between weak and strong in the Roman churches.

Having explored the relevant social context of Romans 14.1–15.6, we may turn now to examine Paul's advice in these verses.

3. The Key Elements of Paul's Instruction

Paul's response to these disputes concerning law-observance is composed of three main elements:

---

[28] Suetonius probably indicates a Christian element in the Roman Jewish troubles, but not certainly so; see S. Benko, 'The Edict of Claudius of A.D. 49 and the Instigator Chrestus' *TZ* 25 (1969) 406–18.

[29] Tacitus' account of affairs in 41 CE is missing, so if the 'expulsion' is to be dated in that year, his silence is easily explained. However, it is more likely that Claudius' attempts to repress Jews in 41 CE (Cassius Dio 60.6.6) were not followed up with expulsion until 49 CE. Such at least is the 'harmonizing' solution of our conflicting evidence advanced by, e.g., A. Momigliano, *The Emperor Claudius and His Achievement*, revised edition, Oxford: OUP, 1961, 31–38 and E.M. Smallwood, *The Jews Under Roman Rule: From Pompey to Diocletian*, second edition, Leiden: Brill, 1981, 210–16.

[30] Observance of 'days' does not alone prove synagogue attendance, but it is likely that Roman Christians who observed sabbaths did attend synagogues given a) the importance of the sabbath as the opportunity for synagogue meetings, b) the example of Paul (and Matthean and Johannine Christians) in remaining in synagogue communities until forced out, and c) Paul's respect for their observance of the sabbath as 'in honour of the Lord' (14.6).

A. Paul counts himself among the strong (15.1) and shares with them the conviction that the Christian believer may eat 'anything' (14.2). Although there was no particular need in this context to declare his own position in the debate, he is in fact quite unashamed to declare that 'I know and am persuaded in the Lord Jesus that nothing is unclean of itself' (οἶδα καὶ πέπεισμαι ἐν κυρίῳ Ἰησοῦ ὅτι οὐδὲν κοινὸν δι' ἑαυτοῦ, 14.14). A few verses later he echoes this with the summary statement that 'all things are clean' (πάντα καθαρά, 14.20). This constitutes nothing less than a fundamental rejection of the Jewish law in one of its most sensitive dimensions. One may hesitate to join Käsemann in reckoning that Paul here 'removes for Christians the basic distinction of all antiquity, which is still influential today, between the cultic sphere and the profane';[31] the context here only concerns food, and Paul can still use purity language in other contexts (e.g. 1 Cor 5.6–8). But this strong denial of the Scriptural distinction between 'clean' and 'unclean' food should not be watered down.[32]

It is important to observe that Paul does not base his judgment here on an appeal to a 'higher principle' in the law or on an allegorical interpretation of the law. The law's regulations on this matter and the long history of interpretation of those regulations are here so summarily dismissed as not even to receive mention. Earlier in this letter Paul relativizes the significance of circumcision by appeal to the Scriptural tradition of 'circumcision of the heart' (Rom 2.25–29), but no reference is made here to an 'inner purity' which renders unnecessary the 'visible purity' of abstention from foods. Nor does Paul attempt an allegorical explanation of the law (cf. 1 Cor 9.8–11). Hellenized Jews from at least the time of Aristeas (2nd century BCE) had developed sophisticated means of interpreting the Jewish food laws in line with the Greek virtues (*Aristeas* 128–71), and Paul might have appealed to the exercise of such virtues (through the Spirit) as the proper 'fulfilment' of the law. But in fact he makes no such effort to explain or excuse himself, as if the relationship between his convictions and the law is no longer of central concern. The basis of his judgment is unashamedly non-legal: simply a 'knowledge' and 'conviction' in the Lord Jesus (14.14), or, as he puts it elsewhere, 'faith' (14.2, 22–23). It is possible that there lies behind the assertion of 14.14 some awareness of a saying of Jesus (later interpreted in Mark 7.15–19);[33] but Paul makes no at-

---

[31] *An die Römer*, 362, as translated by G. Bromiley in *Commentary on Romans*, London: SCM, 1980, 375.

[32] Tomson, *Paul and the Law*, 247–48 considers such radicalism 'very unlikely', but is unable, in my view, to provide a satisfactory alternative interpretation. Thus some differences remain between this essay and his own in this volume, despite our fruitful discussion at and since the Symposium. If the total effect of Paul's advice is a relativization of the food laws, that still entails a denial of the absolute value they are accorded in the Scriptures, even for Jews like Paul himself. That denial is what is articulated here.

[33] See, e.g., Dunn, *Romans 9–16*, 819–20.

tempt here to present Jesus as an interpreter of the law. He here expresses views which indicate that he is no longer ὑπὸ νόμον (Rom 6.14–15; 7.1–6), but he makes no attempt to 'legalize' his position by a claim to be ἔννομος Χριστοῦ (cf. 1 Cor 9.19–21).

The certainty and candour with which Paul here expresses his freedom from the law is thus quite breathtaking. In principle, it appears, he could see no objection to eating shellfish, hare or pork. Do we have reason to doubt that his diet was sometimes as scandalously 'free' as his principles? As regards the allied topic of sabbath observance, his own convictions and practices are less clear. He recognizes (14.5–6) that different believers have different practices in this regard, but he does not declare his own hand. His identification with the strong would suggest that here too he had no objection to the principle that the special observance of days (i.e. sabbaths) was unnecessary. But it may be that he declined to make so explicit his own convictions on this matter since it was known that he often in fact attended synagogues (i.e. observed sabbath days).

B. While holding his own opinion, Paul accepts an element of subjectivity in the definition of proper conduct relating to diet and calendar. As soon as he has expressed his own opinion in 14.14a, he adds that food is unclean to any-one who considers it such (εἰ μὴ τῷ λογιζομένῳ τι κοινὸν εἶναι, ἐκείνῳ κοινόν, 14.14b).[34] This allowance for individual perception is also strikingly portrayed in 14.5–6 where the issues of days and food are paralleled. On the matter of days, each individual is to act according to his/her own individual conviction: ἕκαστος ἐν τῷ ἰδίῳ νοῖ πληροφορείσθω (14.5). Thus each Christian can act, even if with opposite effect, 'in honour of the Lord': 'he who eats, eats to the Lord, for he gives thanks to God; he who abstains from eating, abstains to the Lord and gives thanks to God' (14.6). The individual definition of morality could hardly be more plainly stated, and is further reinforced to-wards the end of the discussion: 'the faith that you have, keep to yourself be-fore God' (14.22). Paul refuses to allow matters of diet or sabbath to function as part of the defining structure of the Christian community. Within this sphere, which he is bold enough to claim for 'the kingdom of God', food and drink cannot define the legitimate bounds of the community: what counts rather is 'righteousness, peace and joy in the Holy Spirit' (cf. Rom 5.1–5). Precisely by refusing to allow food and drink (or sabbath observance) to enter into the definition of 'righteousness' (δικαιοσύνη), Paul indicates that the norms of the Christian churches will be decisively different from the defining values of the Jewish community.

---

[34] The same point may be made after the πάντα καθαρά statement in 14.20, ἀλλὰ κακὸν τῷ ἀνθρώπῳ τῷ διὰ προσκόμματος ἐσθίοντι. But it is difficult to know whether the 'man' mentioned here is a representative of the weak or the strong. Wilckens, *Der Brief an die Römer*, 3.95 sees a reference to the weak; Dunn, *Romans 9–16*, 826 regards the phrase as ambiguous, but probably referring to the strong.

This does not mean, of course, a lack of moral seriousness in Paul's depiction of Christian conduct. Each individual is to conduct his/her life as the household slave (οἰκέτης) of the κύριος (14.4) and in anticipation of the final judgment, in which a personal account will be rendered to God (14.10–12). In this sense a Christian morality outside the law is no less rigorous than one operating according to its structures (cf. Rom 6.1–15). But the shift in values requires that what was the basis of social unity and persuasion in the Jewish community could not operate as such in the church. Law-abiding members of the synagogue would be entitled to 'judge' (i.e. condemn) other members of the synagogue who failed to observe sabbath or food laws. As members of the church, however, they are instructed to 'welcome' and tolerate fellow believers even if they do not observe such rules. The mutual tolerance demanded by Paul in the Roman churches requires that neither side allow their strongly-held convictions to determine the contours of Christian commitment. We shall consider below the effects of this requirement on those with a double loyalty to synagogue and church.

C. Having stated the basic principle of mutual toleration (14.1–12, summed up in 14.13a: μηκέτι οὖν ἀλλήλους κρίνωμεν), Paul goes on to require of the strong that they refrain from activity which would cause the weaker Christians to stumble or fall. Applying the same principle he had employed in 1 Cor 8–10, Paul warns the strong against putting a stumbling-block in the path of the weak (14.13), which could result in their injury (14.15a) or even destruction (14.15b). Whatever was the numerical balance between the weak and strong, it appears that the power relations between the two groups were such that the weak were considerably more vulnerable than the strong. It is implied that the strong, through 'despising' (ἐξουθενεῖν, 14.3) the weak, were liable to pressurize them to act contrary to their own convictions and thus undermine their Christian commitment. Such social disparities are also implicit in the labels 'weak' and 'strong': Horace's *infirmior* (see above) suggests that they could represent differential social locations.[35] Thus within the Roman churches the law-observant Christians were socially vulnerable and more easily induced to adopt the practices of the strong than vice versa. Paul's instruction here requires that they be protected in their law observance, both for their own sakes and for the sake of Christ who redeemed them (14.15; cf. 14.20).

Paul requires such accommodation to the practices of the weak specifically in relation to food (14.15, 20). His instruction seems to imply that to avoid the 'disputes' (14.1) liable to lead to the overpowering of the weak, the strong should refrain from offering food at the communal meals which the weak were unable to consume: hence the advice that 'it is good not to eat meat or

---

[35] Compare Paul's use of such labels in Corinth, as discussed by G. Theissen, *The Social Setting of Pauline Christianity*, Edinburgh: T & T Clark, 1982, 121–43.

drink wine or do anything by which your brother is made to stumble' (14.21). This suggests that, in this context, the communal meal should consist only of food (and drink) concerning which the weak could have no scruples, either limited to vegetables or, if meat, perhaps what they themselves provided. There is no good reason to take this advice as applying outside the particular context of the Christian communal meals. In 1 Cor 8–10 Paul talks of the strong eating meals in various public contexts, but here the specific context is the occasion when they 'welcome one another' (14.1), i.e. the community meals. In other words, Paul is requiring the strong to allow for Jewish scruples at their common meals, but not necessarily suggesting a complete change in their dietary habits.

It is intriguing that, although he mentions the parallel case of 'days' in his appeal for tolerance (14.5–6), Paul does not return to this issue when urging accommodation to the scruples of the weak. He does not require the strong to observe the sabbath. Presumably this matter was less immediately threatening to the convictions of the weak: if the church gathered on another day of the week, that did not prevent them observing the sabbath or attending synagogue, and if their meeting was on a sabbath, it could presumably be arranged not to clash with the synagogue meetings. Thus Paul leaves the matter of sabbath-observance as a standing difference between the different groups in the Roman churches and makes no attempt to 'judaize' those who did not observe the law in this respect.

4. The Social Effects of Paul's Advice

We may now assess the social effects of Paul's advice concerning these aspects of law-observance, bearing in mind the social and cultural realities in Rome. We may summarize our conclusions here under three heads:

1. *Paul protects Law-observance and Jewish Christianity*. By insisting that the strong should neither despise the weak nor pressurize them to change their convictions, Paul is careful to preserve the legitimacy of law-observance among Roman Christians. His requirement that the strong adapt their diet at the communal meals is a measure of how seriously he takes this matter. This certainly means that those Jewish Christians in Rome who wished to retain their links with the Jewish community in Rome were enabled to do so. As we have seen, a Jew in Rome who was found eating pork or otherwise infringing well-known Jewish food laws would destroy his Jewish identity in the eyes of both Jews and non-Jews. The effect of Paul's advice is to protect Jewish Christians from this danger. Similarly the acceptance that some in good conscience honour sabbath days grants permission to such Jewish Christians (and

any Gentile sympathizers of Judaism) to attend the all-important synagogue gatherings and thus maintain their place in the Jewish community. On these two sensitive issues, Paul allows Jewish Christians to maintain their social base in the Jewish community and to preserve their Jewish identity. There is no reason why they should not also circumcise their sons, pay their temple dues and otherwise continue their Jewish life-style.[36]

To be sure, the tone in which Paul grants this permission is somewhat condescending. By employing the terms 'weak' and 'strong' and by openly declaring his position on the side of the 'strong', Paul endorses the perspective of the strong. 'Weak in faith' (14.1) is not the most complimentary phrase Paul could have used (cf. Rom 4.19)! It is only of the strong that he requires the application of love (14.15) and only to them that he applies the example of Christ (15.2–3). In all these ways Paul patronizes the weak and tips the theological balance in favour of the strong, even while attempting to make the scales even. Nonetheless, his genuine concern to protect the legitimacy of the weak cannot be overlooked, nor its social effects in enabling them to maintain their Jewish (or Jewish-sympathetic) identity and their honour within whatever Roman synagogue they attended. Just as Christ was a διάκονος of the circumcised (Rom 15.8), so Paul attempts to serve the social and cultural needs of the Jewish-oriented members of the churches in Rome.[37]

2. *Paul allows Law-neglect and a Gentilized Christianity*. As we have seen, Paul makes clear his own conviction 'in the Lord Jesus' that the Jewish food laws may be abandoned, even by Jewish Christians like himself. In principle he supports the strong, though he here requires from them accommodation in certain practical respects with the scruples of the weak. In their common meals – though probably, as we have suggested, only there – the strong are to observe Jewish laws in relation to food and drink. It is not entirely clear how this limited adaptation of their behaviour would affect their reputations in Roman society. It may be that the Christian meals were sufficiently private for this accommodation to be of no social significance, though it is possible that

---

[36] Compare Justin's stance in *Dialogue with Trypho* 46–47, where, unlike some other Christians, he accepts that Jewish Christians may practise circumcision, keep the sabbath and observe other Jewish laws. But he considers such 'ceremonies' as instituted only because of the Jews' 'hardness of heart', and he strongly opposes any attempt to persuade Gentile Christians to follow suit. I am grateful to Graham Stanton for drawing this passage to my attention.

[37] To this extent I would take issue with the thesis of Watson, *Paul, Judaism and the Gentiles* that 'Paul's purpose in writing Romans was to defend and explain his view of freedom from the law (i.e. separation from the Jewish community and its way of life), with the aim of converting Jewish Christians to his point of view so as to create a single 'Pauline' congregation in Rome' (98). Watson's thesis has been criticized by W.S. Campbell, *Paul's Gospel in an Intercultural Context*, Frankfurt am Main: Peter Lang, 1992.

Paul subtly acknowledges here the potential damage to their social standing. We may recall how, in some circles at least, Romans who gave the impression of 'judaizing' in their diet were subject to criticism: Seneca's anecdote certainly indicates sensitivity on this point and Juvenal lashes out in criticism of the pork-abstaining Gentile. When Paul talks of the strong bearing the weaknesses of the weak and not pleasing themselves (15.1–2), he appeals to the example of Christ and cites from Psalm 68.10 LXX: οἱ ὀνειδισμοὶ τῶν ὀνειδιζόντων σε ἐπέπεσαν ἐπ' ἐμέ (15.3). Beyond the general appeal to the self-sacrifice of Christ, why should this particular verse be cited here? Perhaps Paul intended to indicate a quite specific application to the case in point: the slanders and reproaches levelled at Jews in Rome would be shared by the strong to the extent that they were willing to adopt Jewish eating habits in their common Christian meals.[38]

As we saw above, Paul does not require of the strong similar accommodation in relation to sabbath-observance. At first sight, this is surprising. As we have seen, even among the non-Jewish population in Rome the Jewish sabbath was in part imitated and it would not have been culturally inappropriate for Paul to request the Gentiles in the Roman churches to make some gestures towards sabbath-observance. But further reflection suggests why he did not advocate this compromise. Paul's Jewish heritage indicated that the purpose of the sabbath was not just to rest from work but to gather in worship, prayer and communal education in the synagogues. If anyone honoured this day, it had to be 'to the Lord' (14.6). Paul cannot encourage Gentile Christians to enter the ambit of the synagogue and he cannot encourage the celebration of the sabbath except in this social and liturgical context. Thus the alternative to sabbath-and-synagogue has to be not some partial sabbath of lighting lamps or shutting up shop, but treating every day alike.

Thus, despite the partial 'judaizing' of the common Christian meals, Paul does not require Law-observance of the Roman Christians in these crucial respects. He permits the Roman Christian community to welcome and retain members who, in general, pay no heed to the Jewish law in relation to food and sabbaths.

3. *Paul effectively undermines the social and cultural integrity of the Law-observant Christians in Rome.* This final point is crucial and is stated in full

---

[38] The psalm would thus be refracted through a double lens: it applies in the first instance to Christ absorbing the blasphemies directed against God, and by transference to the strong in Rome sharing the anti-Jewish sentiment which was suffered by Torah-observers. This is perhaps a clearer reading of the relevance of the quotation than that offered by Dunn, *Romans 9–16*, 839. The following reference to the teaching of the Scriptures and their encouragment of 'endurance' (ὑπομονή, 15.4; cf. Rom 5.3–4) seems to underline the specific applicability of the quotation.

awareness of the paradox it creates in juxtaposition with Conclusion 1 above. For it seems to me that while, *on the surface* and *in the short term*, Paul protects the Law-observant Christians, in the long term and at a deeper level he seriously undermines their social and cultural integrity. This conclusion deserves a fuller explication than is possible here, but it may be presented in outline under two heads.[39]

a) *Social Integrity*. While permitting Law-observant Christians to keep the food laws, observe sabbaths and thus maintain their social base in the Jewish community, Paul *also* requires of them that they associate regularly and at the deepest inter-personal level with 'brothers and sisters in Christ' who are not bound by the regulations of the Jewish law. The weak Roman Christians have to accept that non-kosher and non-sabbatarian Christians are nonetheless living 'in honour of the Lord', and they are requested to associate with them intimately, on the basis of their common faith in Jesus as Lord. In prayer and worship (15.7–13), in common meals (14.1ff.), in the sharing of prophecy and teaching (12.6–7), financial resources (12.8) and the common kiss (16.16), they are required to express a deep bond of unity with people fundamentally neglectful of the law. They are even expected to welcome Paul and to pool their spiritual gifts with his (1.11–12), just as they are now asked to pray for his visit to Jerusalem (15.30–32). In all these ways, while accepting their right to remain attached to the Jewish community, Paul requires from the weak a deep social commitment to their fellow Christians, even if they do not respect the Jewish law in their conduct.

The question is whether such dual loyalties can be maintained in the long term. Some comments of Josephus are relevant at this point. While rebutting charges of 'anti-social' behaviour in *Contra Apionem* book 2, Josephus is concerned to insist that Judaism is not an exclusive code, but he admits that there are limits to the associations allowed to Jews. 'He [Moses] graciously accepts all those who desire to come and live under the same laws with us, considering that relatedness is not a matter of race alone, but of choices taken in one's way of life. But he did not admit casual visitors (τοὺς ἐκ παρέργου προσιόντας) to

---

[39] The fundamental issues here have been addressed from a wider perspective by D. Boyarin, *A Radical Jew. Paul and the Politics of Identity*, Berkeley / London: University of California Press, 1994. Boyarin's claim that Paul 'erases' or 'annuls' cultural difference, in a universalizing drive towards 'sameness', does not, in my view, accurately represent Paul's theology. But he is right to detect that in (as I would say) relativizing the Jewish cultural tradition Paul challenges certain claims which lie *at the core of Jewish identity*. Thus there is an important measure of truth in Boyarin's statement (p.32) that 'what will appear from the Christian perspective as tolerance, namely Paul's willingness – indeed insistence – that within the Christian community all cultural practice is equally to be tolerated, from the rabbinic Jewish perspective is simply an eradication of the entire value system which insists that our cultural practice is our task and calling in the world and must not be abandoned or reduced to a matter of taste' (cf. pp.9–10, 290 n10).

join in our common life (ἀναμίγνυσθαι τῇ συνηθείᾳ)' (*Contra Apionem*
2.210). Later in the same work Josephus admits the charge of Apollonius
Molon that Jews 'do not wish to associate with those who choose to live according to a different mode of life' (μηδὲ κοινωνεῖν ἐθέλομεν τοῖς καθ᾽
ἑτέραν συνήθειαν βίου ζῆν προαιρουμένοις, *Contra Apionem* 2.258).[40] Yet
Paul here requires of Christian members of the Jewish community a very significant depth of 'association' with those declining to live according to the
same mode of life. Is this transcultural Christian φιλαδελφία (Rom 12.10)
and κοινωνία (Rom 12.13; cf. 15.26–27) compatible with continued membership in a Jewish community, which is naturally concerned to preserve its social integrity? Can a law-observant synagogue member associate at the deepest level with a law-neglectful 'brother' or 'sister'? Paul's instructions, though
palliative in the short term, created tensions which were likely to grow to the
point when a difficult social choice would have to be made between the Jewish and Christian community.

b) *Cultural Integrity.* As we have seen, Paul accepts that law-observant
Christians may continue to observe Jewish food and sabbath regulations and
protects their rights to do so. But the way he discusses the matter makes it
clear that, within his frame of reference, such conduct is not a foundational
but merely an optional aspect of a life lived in honour of God.[41] By refusing to
allow that the weak condemn the strong, Paul requires of them the acceptance
of an alternative, non-observant lifestyle as *equally valid* in the sight of God.
He who eats (even pork!), eats in honour of the Lord, serving God as worthily
as he who abstains in honour of the Lord (14.6). Sabbath and food are removed from the sphere of 'righteousness' and made peripheral to 'the kingdom of God' (14.17). Thus the Jewish cultural heritage in these matters is no
longer regarded as the divinely sanctioned norm, but as merely one option,
one preference among others. In other words, while allowing the expression
of the Jewish cultural tradition, Paul relativizes its significance and undermines key aspects of its theological and intellectual foundation.

The weak Roman Christian who observed the sabbath and attended his/her
synagogue, would receive instruction there in the Jews' 'ancestral philosophy'
(πάτριος φιλοσοφία, Philo, *Legatio* 156). The religious basis of that philosophy lay in the conviction that the law was uniquely God-given and therefore
sacrosanct. Its intellectual claim was that the Jewish way of life represented

---

[40] The application of this principle in Rome is attested from another angle by Juvenal and
Tacitus, although their evidence is biased by hostility. Juvenal remarks that the Gentiles in-
corporated into the Jewish community flout the laws of Rome and decline to indicate the
way to any 'not worshipping the same rites' (*nisi sacra colenti*, *Sat* 14.103). Tacitus complains that the Jews *separati epulis, discreti cubilibus … alienarum concubitu abstinent*;
those who 'cross over to their ways' reject the gods, their homeland and their families, *Hist*
5.5.2.

[41] Cf. Watson, *Paul, Judaism and the Gentiles*, 97.

the most pious and the most virtuous mode of conduct ever conceived. Such is the claim, explicit or implicit, of all Jewish literature from this period, not least of Josephus' apology, *Contra Apionem*, which therefore properly claims that Jews are utterly committed to the observance of the law. What Paul demands of these weak Christians is their commitment to a church in which the Jewish mode of life is tolerated but not required, in which credence is given to the claim that men and women can honour God as effectively by ignoring the sabbath as by observing it. Such toleration of each individual's conviction would surely have been castigated by Josephus as a crude example of τὸ αὐτεξούσιον, that self-defined liberty which he considered the root of apostasy (*Ant* 4.145–49). In demanding this toleration, Paul subverts the basis on which Jewish law-observance is founded and precipitates a crisis of cultural integrity among the very believers whose law-observance he is careful to protect. Such is the fundamental paradox of the passage we are studying.

It is important to observe that the laws here discussed cannot be dismissed, from the Jewish perspective, as merely 'ceremonial' or 'ritual'.[42] As we have seen from the evidence of Jewish life in Rome, they are of central significance in defining the social and cultural identity of the Jewish community.[43] However Paul may extol the law as 'holy, righteous and good' (Rom 7.12, 14), law-observant Christians in Rome would want to know more precisely whether he actually observed it and encouraged others to do so. His claim that those who walked in the Spirit would fulfil the law (Rom 8.4; 13.8–10) would inevitably be subject to the litmus test of praxis. Josephus, in common with other Jews, was not impressed by words alone: it was his special boast that Judaism combined words and deeds (ἔργα) to a degree unparalleled in other cultural traditions (*Contra Apionem* 2.171–78).

As we have seen, on the surface Paul supports the weak Christians in their right to observe the Jewish food and sabbath laws. In response to our title question, Paul had insisted that he upheld the law (Rom 3.31) and in this passage he fulfils his claim in the limited sense that he protects the right of others to uphold it. But he himself regards key aspects of the law as wholly dispensable for Christian believers and, more subtly, his theology introduces into the Roman Christian community a Trojan horse which threatens the integrity of those who sought to live according to the law. In this respect, Jewish Christians were right to fear Paul *et dona ferentem*.

---

[42] *Pace* Cranfield, *Romans* 2.697; Käsemann, *An die Römer*, 362 and many others.

[43] The point is rightly emphasized by Dunn, *Romans 9–16*, 800–2, 805–6.

In Search of Common Ground

by

JAMES D.G. DUNN

1. Introduction

The issues confronting the Symposium, both the agreements and the disagreements, can perhaps best be focused in the question of continuity and discontinuity. The very terms in which the question is posed indicate the extent of the problem and the range of agreement/disagreement. Do we mean continuity/discontinuity between the OT and the NT, or between Israel and the Church, or between the gospel and the law? The first formulation would presumably attract a strong measure of agreement in such a gathering, since the Christian tradition counts the Jewish scriptures as part of the Christian Bible, a claim in effect dependent on maximising the measure of continuity between the Testaments. Whereas the last evokes the classic Reformation antithesis between law and gospel, where the greater light focused on the latter seems inevitably to cast the former into deeper shadow. And yet the tension between gospel and law in Paul can hardly be understood except against the background of the other two continuities/discontinuities, especially since Torah (law) overlaps to such an extent with scripture (OT) and has been so constitutive of the identity of Israel.

It is this fact, however, which gives us some hope of finding a greater degree of common ground on the issue of Paul and the law. For the issue for us as Neutestamentlers focuses on points of exegesis, and that inevitably means an exegesis which takes historical and social factors of Paul's time as fully into consideration as possible. This was indeed the task the Symposium set itself, as indicated in the programme and in the subjects of the papers. *The common ground we seek, therefore, is not first and foremost agreement among ourselves, but some measure of consensus on what was the common ground between Paul and his fellow Christian Jews with whom he was in dispute.* Or in our present terms, what was the continuity/discontinuity between Paul and his Gentile converts (won by Paul's gospel) on the one hand, and those Jews who, like Paul, had believed in Jesus as the Messiah of Israel on the other? The more clarity we can gain on this point, the greater we may find the common ground to be among ourselves.

Two preliminary points should be made which reflect some of the methodological agreement among the participants in the Symposium. The first has already been alluded to: that Paul's principal treatment of the law in his letters
was formulated in dialogue and dispute not with non-Christian Jews, but with
fellow Christian Jews. This at once cuts the nerve of much of the charge of
anti-Judaism laid against Paul, an issue which, somewhat surprisingly, hardly
arose within the Symposium. At the same time, it is important to realise that
the protests against Paul's gospel in reference to the law arose because so
many of Paul's fellow Jewish believers felt their own identity as children of
Abraham and their heritage as the people of Israel to be under question or even
threat from the success of Paul's mission.

The other is the problem of terminology. At several points in the Symposium we found ourselves stumbling across the problem of language, in particular the unclarity of some key words. On the one hand, there were words
used which evidently have (very) different overtones in German and English –
for example, 'legalism', 'self-righteousness', 'covenant' and 'political'. Some
of the discussions began to run aground because there are what might be called
hidden reefs within our different traditions of which those from other traditions were not sufficiently aware. On the other hand, there were key terms
within the text on whose scope we were unable to achieve full agreement – for
example, 'sin', 'works of the law', 'life' and 'salvation', and their relation to
the Torah. Other terms like 'narrative' provoked unexpected responses. Not
least of the value of the Symposium was that by spending so much time in each
other's company we began to open up these deeper issues and to penetrate
below the surface of disputes. We began to appreciate not only the dimensions
of the dispute (the 'what'), but also the reasons why alternative views could be
held with such conviction and passion (the 'why'). In such circumstances any
common ground which can be realised is likely to be the more significant and,
hopefully, enable a greater degree of genuine rapprochement than can ever be
achieved by a single seminar or a few emollient slogans.[1]

2. The character of the continuity

2.1   It can hardly be disputed that Paul understood his gospel to be thoroughly
consistent with and continuous from his heritage as a Jew, the teaching, that is,
in Christian terms, of the OT. As hardly needs to be documented or argued (I
refer particularly to Romans and Galatians), he draws his understanding of his

---

[1] In what follows I limit footnotes to a minimum, since the primary reference points are
the papers presented to the Symposium (but now revised) and the discussion which they
evoked. However, to avoid the paper becoming merely an in-house dialogue, I have added a
number of explanatory notes with a wider readership in mind.

Hauptmotif, 'the righteousness of God', directly from the Psalms and Second Isaiah.[2] His key texts in the exposition of his gospel are Gen. 15.6 and Hab. 2.4. Abraham is his principal model of the person who has faith, who believes (Gal. 3; Rom. 4). He is desperately concerned to show that the gospel preached to the Gentiles does not contradict God's faithfulness to Israel (Rom. 3.1–8.21–26; 9–11). Gal. 3.8 in effect sums up the difficult case he had to make in face of Christian Jewish objections: the promise given to Abraham was in fact the *gospel*, precisely because it spoke of the blessing which would come to the *Gentiles*.

The disputes, however, begin when we ask whether the continuity is in effect only between Paul and the OT itself, jumping over, as it were, the intervening period of Second Temple Judaism. So far as righteousness and the law is concened, do we have to distinguish the biblical treatment from that more characteristic from the Maccabees (or the Exile) onwards? Did the context of Second Temple Judaism for Paul's own training in the law differ decisively from the biblical context? After all, the continuity could hardly be complete or obvious, since so few of Paul's fellow Jews became Christians. And, as we shall remind ourselves more fully later, Paul's critique of the law seems to be more radical than a simple hypothesis of continuity can bear.

In many ways this was the key question confronting the Symposium: how to explain and elucidate Paul's treatment of the law in the light of the understanding of the Torah prevalent in Second Temple Judaism. It was an issue which was unavoidable since it had been posed by 'the new perspective' on Paul,[3] albeit from the opposite side: that the view of God's righteousness in Second Temple Judaism was not as 'legalistic' nor as conducive to 'self-righteousness' as had traditionally been maintained in NT exegesis. From whatever perspective, therefore, whether that of squaring Paul's treatment of the law with his own claims to continuity, or that of reaction against a certain Christian tendency to denigrate the Judaism of Paul's day on this subject, it was essential that the Symposium begin with an attempt to clarify the understanding of the Torah within Judaism at the time of Paul.

2.2   Lichtenberger's paper therefore had particular importance as establishing the historical context within Second Temple Judaism for Paul's teaching on the law with reference to which the Symposium's discussion would proceed. His findings could be summed up thus: Although some elements of legalism in Second Temple Judaism cannot be denied, we also cannot conclude that Second Temple Judaism as a whole is to be branded as 'legalistic' (that is, that salvation or life in the world to come is earned by obedience to the Torah). The diversity of Second Temple Judaism's teaching on the law can

---

[2]   See e.g. my *Romans* (WBC 38, Dallas: Word, 1988) 41 (with bibliography), and P. Stuhlmacher, *Der Brief an die Römer* (NTD; Göttingen: Vandenhoeck, 1989) 31.

[3]   See Introduction n. 2.

also be summed up in such phrases as: obedience to the Torah is the presupposition of membership of the covenant; or in Lichtenberger's own helpful phrase, 'Weisung zum Leben und Lebens-Weise', that is, not one or other, but both together. The resulting discussion also provided some agreement that while we can speak of salvation in individual and corporate terms in Second Temple Judaism, the question of the individual's status is derivative from membership of the covenant people. Important also was the fact that no one seemed to want to maintain that Second Temple Judaism taught the need for 'perfection' in law-keeping.[4]

Integral to the view of Torah which emerges is the two-fold assertion: (1) That membership of the covenant people is a presupposition (Deuteronomy is addressed to those who are already the people of Israel). Consequently the function of the law (again as archetypically expressed in Deuteronomy) is not to enable 'getting in' to the covenant people nor to make it possible to earn God's acceptance.[5] (2) Obedience to the Torah is a requirement for continuing membership of the covenant, for life within the people, and for gaining a portion in the life of the world to come.[6]

If this is the case, then the question naturally arises: which of these two emphases was Paul reacting against? Or rather, which of these two emphases was Paul's gospel thought to come into conflict with, occasioning the opposition to Paul's gospel from fellow Christian Jews, which is reflected in several of his letters? It could be the first, since a gospel for Gentiles raises the question of whether and how non-Jews, 'get in' to the covenant people. It could be the second, since the question of Gentile Christian non-fulfilment of the law raises the question whether and how far obedience to the Torah is still necessary for Christian Jew as well as for (or as distinct from) Christian Gentile. In fact, however, the two emphases would not be easily separable in Jewish self-understanding. It is this fact which causes the confusion in NT exegesis in the first place, since the importance of obedience to the Torah for life (2) can easily be heard as making final acceptance by God conditional on that obedience.

The issue of Paul's attitude to the Torah cannot be resolved, of course, solely by reference to the understanding of the function of the Torah in Second Tem-

---

[4] This misunderstanding, however, continues to bedevil the discussion elsewhere, as we see in T.R. Schreiner, *The Law and its Fulfilment: A Pauline Theology of the Law* (Grand Rapids: Baker, 1993) e.g. 71, 181.

[5] The 'getting in' language is drawn from E.P. Sanders, *Paul, the Law, and the Jewish People* (Philadelphia: Fortress, 1983): 'Much of what Paul wrote falls within a framework which I call "getting in and staying in"' (6).

[6] The Symposium needed to give more discussion to the character of this double affirmation. Of particular importance is the obviously deliberate echo of Lev. 18.5 in Ezek. 20.11, 13,21 – בָהֶם וְחַי הָאָדָם אֹתָם יַעֲשֶׂה אֲשֶׁר. As the בָהֶם makes clear, and also the reverse formula in Ezek. 20.25 (בָהֶם יִהְיוּ לֹא), what is in view is *a way of living* ('he shall live by them'), not life as the reward ('he shall gain life as a result of his obedience').

ple Judaism. That can only be gleaned from Paul's own writings, and to these the Symposium quickly turned. But it was (and is) important that the debates on the interpretation of Paul's letters remain informed by and in touch with these initial findings.

2.3 Equally if not more crucial for our enterprise was clarification of Paul's attitude to the law in the period covering his conversion up to and including the incident at Antioch (Gal. 1–2). Hengel's paper and the resulting discussion produced a general agreement that Paul's understanding of the law as a Christian was rooted in the Damascus road encounter, that it changed Paul's attitude to the law, and that faith in Jesus was decisive for Paul's gospel and theology from the first. There was significant disagreement, however, over what the change in Paul's attitude amounted to, and on whether and how his attitude to the law developed.

For my own part, the issue of Paul's conversion, of what he was converted from and to, is central, and no clearer answer can be found than that provided by Paul himself in Gal. 1.13–16.[7] (a) What Paul was converted *from* was 'Judaism' (Gal. 1.13–14). Not 'Judaism' as we now define it in contemporary sociological description of Second Temple Judaism. But 'Judaism' as it had been defined in the only other literary uses of the term current at the time of Paul (2 Macc. 2.21; 8.1; 14.38; 4 Macc. 4.26), that is, as the label coined or used to identify the national religion trying to define and defend itself over against the influences of Hellenism (2 Macc. 4.13). That is, 'Judaism' as marked out by loyalty to the laws of God and of their fathers, where the test cases of that loyalty were sabbath and feasts, circumcision, and refusal to eat forbidden flesh (2 Macc. 6). (b) Again, what Paul converted *from* was 'zeal', zeal for these traditions (Gal. 1.14), the zeal that caused him to 'persecute the church of God' (Phil. 3.6; cf. 1 Cor. 15.9),[8] in the tradition of Phinehas and the Maccabees (1 Macc. 2.19–28, 49–64), that is, as the human reflection of the 'jealousy of God' (Exod. 20.4–5; 34.14; Deut. 5.8–9; 6.14–15), in a violent attempt to maintain Israel's set-apartness from Gentiles and their corrupting ways. (c) And again, what Paul was converted *to* was the recognition that the gospel of Jesus had to be taken to the Gentiles (Gal. 1.15–16); that is, he was converted to the beliefs (of the Hellenists) which he had persecuted.

If this is so, then the change in Paul's understanding of the law, occasioned by his conversion, must be related to his conversion as he understood it. The change in his attitude to the law therefore probably focused on the role of the

---

[7] For what follows see more fully my 'Paul's Conversion – A Light to Twentieth Century Disputes', in *Evangelium – Schriftauslegung – Kirche*, hrsg. O. Hofius (Göttingen: Vandenhoeck, 1996).

[8] The repetition of the phrase shows how deeply rooted it was in Paul's memory. That it probably goes back to the period of Paul's conversion is confirmed by Gal. 1.23 – ὁ διώκων ἡμᾶς.

law as crystallized and reinforced by the Maccabean crisis and as fundamental to the 'Judaism' of the middle Second Temple period thereafter. That is, the law in its role as hedging Israel around and protecting it from outsiders, the law understood as requiring Israel's set-apartness from the Gentiles, the law as consisting of 'pallisades and iron walls to prevent (their) mixing with any of the other peoples in any matter' (in the terms used by the *Letter of Aristeas* 139–42). The issue, in other words, was nothing to do with earning or achieving God's favour, and not even so much about Gentiles 'getting in' to the covenant people. If anything, it would be more accurate to say that the issue was about Jews (Hellenist Christians) breaking down the 'walls' that separated Jew from Gentile. And not necessarily by wholesale abandoning of the law (after all, it was the Hellenist Jewish Christians at Antioch who later sided with Peter in withdrawing from table fellowship with Gentile Christians – Gal. 2.11–14), but by virtue of taking the good news of the (Jewish) Messiah Jesus to the Gentiles in the first place (Acts 11.20).

As for the question of development in Paul's attitude to the law, the issue may be unresolvable. Did Paul see things so clearly from the first, as his account in Gal. 1 indicates? For Paul, as he looked back, the conclusions embodied in Gal. 1 were probably always obvious. But was this hindsight, the product of 'biographical reconstruction'?[9] Was there actual development in his view, or only an unfolding of what was implicit, or not (yet) fully stated at the first? If the above reconstruction of Paul's conversion (drawn from Gal. 1.13–16) is any guide, then the conclusion 'to the Gentiles' seems to have been the immediate reaction to the earlier motivation of the persecutor ('*not* to the Gentiles'). Which would suggest that indeed the reconstruction of Paul's view of the law, at least in respect to its boundary role of separating Jew from Gentile, was formed in Paul's mind as an immediate outcome of his conversion experience.[10]

On the other hand, all the puzzles of the unknown years between Damascus and Antioch remain:[11] When was it that Paul began to engage in extensive missionary work (Gal. 1.17?), and was it directly to Gentiles or only after preaching to his own people (cf. Gal. 5.11), and was it usually (in the first instance at least) directed to the God-fearing and proselyte penumbra round the diaspora synagogue (as Acts indicates)? What actually was achieved at the consultation in Jerusalem so far as the acceptability and Torah obligations of Gentile converts within the church of God were concerned (Gal. 2.1–10)?

---

[9] As argued by N. Taylor, *Paul, Antioch and Jerusalem: A Study in Relationships and Authority in Earliest Christianity* (JSNTS 77; Sheffield: JSOT, 1992).

[10] Cf. H. Räisänen, 'Paul's Call Experience and his Later View of the Law', *Jesus, Paul and Torah. Collected Essays* (JSNTS 43; Sheffield: Sheffield Academic, 1992) ch. 1.

[11] For my own views I may refer to my *The Epistle to the Galatians* (Black's NT Commentaries: London: A. & C. Black/Peabody, Mass.: Hendrickson, 1993).

Why did Peter and the other Christian Jews, including Barnabas, withdraw from table-fellowship with the Gentile Christians in Antioch (Gal. 2.11–14)? Was there an increasing nationalistic pressure upon James and coming from James in Jerusalem? And to what extent, if at all, should we discount Paul's language as rhetoric?

What is clear is that Paul and Peter at Antioch did not share the same understanding of the continuing function of the law; the fact and seriousness of the dispute between the two is no mere rhetorical flourish. The corollaries drawn by each from the Jerusalem agreement were decisively different when the question of continuing table-fellowship between Christian Jew and Christian Gentile arose. Here the issue of continuity is posed as sharply as anywhere. For Peter and all the other Christian Jews evidently concluded that the practice at Antioch prior to the coming of the group from James constituted a breach of continuity, and in the event, an unacceptable breach. The continuity of divine purpose, attested by the grace of God through the ministry of Paul and Barnabas to Gentiles, which had proved decisive in the earlier confrontation (Gal. 2.7–9), was no longer evident or determinative for Peter (contrast Acts 11.2–17), or Barnabas! (contrast Acts 11.23), in the disputed practice at Antioch. And thus we come to a further phase of our discussion.

2.4 The confrontation at Antioch caused Paul to formulate his theological position afresh – Gal. 2.15–16. Had he so formulated it before? If so, had Peter (and Barnabas!) rejected it before? Or did he now so formulate it for the first time, a formulation provoked and shaped by the incident at Antioch itself? The latter would seem to make better sense of the narrative.

As to the meaning of the text itself, what does it tell us of the basic conflict (whether with Peter in particular, or now more generally) over the law as seen by Paul? Here the issues were complicated in the Symposium's discussion, since there was sharp disagreement on the significance of ἁμαρτωλός in 2.15 and 2.17, and on the meaning of πίστις Χριστοῦ in 2.16 and 20. For my own part, it seems most unlikely that ἁμαρτωλός in 2.17 should be read differently from the same word two verses earlier (2.15), where (*pace* Lambrecht) it clearly expresses the factional, nationalistic view which we find elsewhere in Second Temple Judaism (e.g. 1 Macc. 2.44, 48; Pss.Sol. 2.1–2).[12] And I remain unpersuaded by the renewedly popular view that πίστις Χριστοῦ refers to the 'faith(fulness) of Christ' rather than to 'faith in Christ',[13] though we had insufficient time to enter into that debate at the Symposium itself.

---

[12] See my 'Echoes of Intra-Jewish Polemic in Paul's Letter to the Galatians', *JBL* 112 (1993) 459–77, here 462–5; full discussion in E. Kok, '*The Truth of the Gospel*': *A Study in Galatians 2.15–21* (Durham PhD, 1993) 207–12.

[13] See my 'Once More, *PISTIS CHRISTOU*, *Society of Biblical Literature 1991 Seminar Papers*, ed. E.H. Lovering (Atlanta: Scholars Press, 1991) 730–442; and further below § 3.1. However, I retain the Greek phrase in the text in order that my formulation should facilitate

What can be said with more confidence of agreement is that 2.15–16 does reflect, at least in some measure, Paul's arguments at or conclusions from the Antioch incident. In which case the disagreement over the relation between gospel and law as it comes to expression in Gal. 2.15–16 boils down to the question, whether πίστις Χριστοῦ is sufficient in and of itself to secure the full Christian standing of the one who believes and complete acceptability (table-fellowship) between believers. Paul had no doubt that the answer was and should be Yes. Peter and the other Jewish Christians (including Barnabas) were pushed to the conclusion that, for them at any rate, other conditions had to be met – presumably at least the sort of dietary rules which allowed observant Jews elsewhere in the diaspora to share in at least some table-fellowship with Gentile business associates and friends.[14] In 2.16 Paul expresses this policy in terms of πίστις Χριστοῦ plus works of the law, where the 'works of the law' particularly in mind must at minimum have included the rules by which Peter and the others expected the practice of fellowship between Christian Jews and Christian Gentiles to be governed, following the arrival of the group from James.

In other words, the dispute at Antioch and the resulting formulation in Gal. 2.15–16 was occasioned by the 'both-and' outlined above in the description of Second Temple Judaism's understanding of the law (§ 2.2). The 'law-for-life' attitude described there is just the one which Peter and the other Christian Jews were persuaded to return to in Antioch. But for Paul a more fundamental principle had supervened and relativised the other. For Paul πίστις Χριστοῦ had now to be seen as not only a necessary but also the *sufficient* condition for acceptability within the Christian gatherings.

2.5   Which brings us back to the crunch issue. For Peter and the other Christian Jews, πίστις Χριστοῦ was no doubt also an essential prerequisite for those seeking to join the band of Christians in Antioch (as indeed Gal. 2.15–16 indicates – 'we know that …'). But for them πίστις Χριστοῦ was also wholly consistent with living as a devout Jew, observing the works of the law (the deeds required by the law).[15] That is to say, Peter and the others were acting on

---

as much consensus as possible, since the issue of how to understand and translate πίστις Χριστοῦ for the most part bears only tangentially on the issues of Paul and the Law.

[14] See particularly S.J.D. Cohen, 'Crossing the Boundary and Becoming a Jew', *HTR* 82 (1989) 13–33; E.P. Sanders, 'Jewish Association with Gentiles and Galatians 2.11–14', in *Studies in Paul and John*. J.L. Martyn FS, ed. R.T. Fortna & B.R. Gavena (Nashville: Abingdon. 1990) 170–88; Dunn, *Galatians* 119–21. P.F. Esler, 'Sectarianism and the Conflict at Antioch', *The First Christians in their Social World* (London: Routledge, 1994) 52–69, simply dismisses the evidence there cited, attempts to define the ambiguous ἰουδαΐζειν solely from Galatians in complete disregard for its usage elsewhere, and insists that the issue at Antioch must have been precisely the same as that in Galatia.

[15] F.G. Martinez, *The Dead Sea Scrolls Translated* (Leiden: Brill. 1994) 79, 84 translates the now famous מקצת מעשי התורה from 4QMMT 113 (= 4Q398 fr. 2,2.3) as 'some of the precepts of the Torah' (as also *Discoveries in the Judean Desert Vol. X: Qumran Cave 4 Vol. V:*

the assumption of continuity between their own religious heritage and the gospel of Christ. It was that continuity which required them to continue to live as good Jews, that is, separated from Gentiles (even Gentile Christians) in table-fellowship at least. The πίστις Χριστοῦ, (and) their believing in Christ, evidently made no difference to that. On the contrary, for them πίστις Χριστοῦ was part of the continuity between Second Temple Judaism and the new movement focused in Jesus the Christ.

Are we then being forced to the conclusion that it was Peter and the other Christian Jews who were much the stronger proponents of continuity between the common Jewish heritage and the new believing in Christ? that they saw no conflict between the gospel and the law? And that Paul in pressing for πίστις Χριστοῦ as the sole determinant of the Christian status of Gentile believers was in fact undermining that continuity? that he saw a much deeper theological issue behind the gospel/works of the law conflict which erupted at Antioch? Evidently it is time to turn to the other side of the continuity-discontinuity motif which we have made the Leitmotif in this attempt to search out as much common ground as possible from the Symposium.

3. The problem of discontinuity

3.1   If the problem of discontinuity weakened as some of the older stereotypes of 'late Judaism' and 'legalistic Judaism' dropped away, it seemed to re-emerge again with varied force as the discussion of the Symposium papers progressed.

For example, if πίστις Χριστοῦ does denote 'the faith(fulness) of Christ' (Longenecker), then that itself would strike a strong note of continuity: at the centre of Paul's gospel would be the claim that Jesus himself was faithful, presumably as Abraham had been found faithful in his readiness to offer up Isaac (1 Macc. 2.52; Jas. 2.21–23). My problem with such an exposition is that it would make the πίστις Χριστοῦ phrase in effect continuous and consistent with Jewish faithfulness in doing what the law requires ('the works of the law'). And yet Paul seems to set the two concepts in antithesis, not least in Gal. 2.16. Moreover, quite how this faithfulness of Christ would count as decisive in exempting Gentile Christians from showing an equivalent faithfulness is a logic which proponents of the πίστις Χριστοῦ = 'the faith of Christ' thesis need to explain. It seems more likely that πίστις Χριστοῦ should be reckoned on the side of *dis*continuity (cf. Gal. 3.23–24).

Miqsat Ma'ase Ha-Torah, ed. E. Qimron & J. Strugnell [Oxford: Clarendon, 1994]). However, at the SBL meeting in Chicago in November 1994, Martinez accepted that his translation was unsatisfactory, and that the phrase should be rendered 'some of the *works* of the Torah'; see further my '4QMMT and Galatians' (forthcoming in *NTS*).

Perhaps we could even say that a πίστις Χριστοῦ = 'the faith of Christ' thesis makes better sense of *Peter's* position in the Antioch confrontation, a Christ whose faithfulness warranted the faithful in maintaining their separateness from Gentiles, and thus confirmed Jewish believers in their refusal to eat with Gentile believers. Whereas Paul's position makes better sense if πίστις Χριστοῦ denotes the faith *in* Christ which calls in question the need for the faithfulness practised by Peter and the other Jewish Christians. Again we have to conclude that πίστις Χριστοῦ, as an expression of Paul's own convictions belongs more to the side of *dis*continuity than of continuity.

A similar issue comes to the fore in the other disagreement already alluded to, over the significance of ἁμαρτωλός in Gal. 2.17. For if it was primarily an issue of factional usage, as seems to be the case in 2.15, of those who counted themselves 'righteous' denying acceptability before God of the 'sinner' who belonged to another faction, or of 'Gentiles sinners' generally, then it is primarily an issue of human relationships, and the debate stays within the factional debates which characterise the literature of Second Temple Judaism.[16] A greater degree of continuity can then be postulated, if not with all factions within Second Temple Judaism, at least with the factional spirit of Second Temple Judaism, and particularly in the case of Peter and the other Christian Jews. But if, as Lambrecht argues, the issue in 2.17 is the deeper one of sin as accounted such by God, then the issue is one of relationship between God and human beings, and the dispute has been moved on to a different level. In which case Paul's shift in usage marks a shift from a more containable continuity to a more serious discontinuity.

3.2   Galatians, of course, poses the question of discontinuity in very sharp terms, as recent debate on the letter has underscored. It is not simply a matter of the way the term 'law' itself is used within the letter. In the discussion of Stanton's paper there was general agreement on the negative force attributed to the law in Gal. 3–4, and that the audiences/churches to whom the letter was read could hardly fail to hear the sustained antithesis between law and faith. The strength and force of the negative was disputed, but no one could deny that 'under the law' was linked with 'under sin' (3.22–23) and was equated with a slave-like status, indeed with slavery under 'the weak and beggarly elemental forces' (4.3,8–10).

Even more important for the question of continuity/discontinuity, however, is the apocalyptic context within which the question of the law is raised in

---

[16] See further my 'Pharisees, Sinners and Jesus', in *The Social World of Formative Christianity and Judaism*, H.C. Kee FS, ed. J. Neusner et al. (Philadelphia: Fortress, 1988) 264–89, reprinted in my *Jesus, Paul and the Law: Studies in Mark and Galatians* (London: SPCK/Louisville: Westminster, 1990) 61–86, here 71–7; and again my 'Echoes of Intra-Jewish Polemic' 462–5.

Galatians.[17] The note is struck at both beginning and end of the letter: references to 'the present evil age' (1.4) from which believers are delivered, and to
the world crucified to Paul and Paul to it (6.14), indicate that 'the revelation of
Jesus Christ' (1.12, 16) involved a still more radical shift in Paul's perspective
– not simply a passing from 'Judaism' to faith in Messiah Jesus, but from one
age to another. And in this schema the law seems to belong to the age now past
(Gal. 3.23–26). Hence the sharpness of the antithesis in the allegory of the two
wives of Abraham, the two covenants: the law stands with Sinai/Hagar in the
opposite/opposed column to Sarah/'the Jerusalem above' (4.22–27), resulting
in the very radical command that those of present Jerusalem are to be cast out
of their inheritance like Hagar and Ishmael of old (4.28–30). The antithesis
between law and Spirit (particularly 3.1–5 and 5.16–23) also reflects a similar
eschatological perspective, the Spirit as the power of the age to come over
against the law as the power of the age past.

The question which this emphasis poses to the continuity/discontinuity debate is nicely highlighted by reference to the word 'covenant'.[18] For while it is
an attractive line of interpretation to argue that Paul saw faith (in Christ) and
the Spirit as the fulfilment of the promise to Abraham, and therefore to describe Paul's theology as 'covenant theology', that is not a conclusion which
Paul's further argument seems to support. Despite it being an inviting corollary to the argument of 3.15–18, Paul himself does not put 'covenant' and 'law'
in antithesis. On the contrary, in the allegory of chapter 4 he speaks of 'two
covenants' (4.24); both Sinai/Torah and the promise of a son in accordance
with the Spirit are designated as 'covenants', and not as old and new covenant
either. 'Covenant' here functions as a neutral term, able to express discontinuity as much as continuity. Despite first appearances, then, Galatians does not
validate the designation of Paul's theology of continuity as 'covenant theology'.[19]

3.3   The same issues were reinforced by Kertelge's paper and the subsequent discussion on 2 Cor. 3. There can be little question that Spirit and law are
being set in opposition: 3.3,7 – 'Spirit'/'tablets of stone' (Ex. 32.16; 34.1); 3.6
– Spirit/γράμμα. Or that Paul had in view two covenants, with the contrast
between new and old this time being quite explicit (3.6,14). Or indeed that the

---

[17] In recent scholarship the issue has been posed particularly by J.L. Martyn, 'Apocalyptic Antinomies in Paul's Letter to the Galatians', *NTS* 31 (1985) 410–24; also 'Events in
Galatia', in *Pauline Theology Volume I*, ed. J.M. Bassler (Minneapolis: Fortress, 1991) 160–
79; for my own debate with Martyn see my *The Theology of Paul's Letter to the Galatians*
(Cambridge University, 1993) ch. 3.

[18] I have been influenced here by the thesis of E. Christiansen, *The Covenant in Judaism
and Paul: A Study of Ritual Boundaries as Identity Markers* (AGAJU 27; Leiden: Bill, 1995)
232–49; similarly Martyn, in *Pauline Theology Volume I* 179.

[19] To that extent, therefore, N.T. Wright's title, *The Climax of the Covenant* (Edinburgh:
T. & T. Clark, 1991), may be misleading as an indication of the Hauptmotif of Galatians.

contrast is extended in very radical terms, as between a ministry of death and a ministry of life (Spirit), and again between a ministry of condemnation and a ministry of justification (3.7–9). At the same time, the point was generally taken that the primary discussion in the chapter was focused on ministry and determined by the contrast between Moses and Paul.

Here the issue was particularly highlighted by Paul's use of the word 'glory' – in fact, the key term in the chapter, where it occurs no less than 10 times. Did it soften the contrast otherwise drawn so sharply? After all, Paul ascribes glory also to the ministry of Moses (3.7,9). It is true that he speaks of it as a glory which faded, was transitory and is now nullified/set aside (3.7, 11, 13, 14 – but how should the force of καταργέω be rendered?). But it was nevertheless also the glory of God; in the comparison (3.9–11 – 'how much more', 'the ὑπερβάλλουσα glory') the same heavenly reality stands on both sides. So much so that Paul is able to use the account of Moses going in to the Lord (Ex. 34.34) with unveiled face, as a result of which his face reflected the divine glory (Ex. 34.35), as a type of the Jew (or Gentile) of his own day who turned to the Lord, the Spirit, and who thus beheld the glory of the Lord and likewise began to reflect that glory (3.16–18).

There was thus marked disagreement in the Symposium on the extent to which Paul could be said to speak of the Torah in 2 Cor. with any degree whatsoever of approbation. Not only was the question unresolved as to whether Paul attributed glory to it and of the significance of that attribution. But the question of the correlation between Spirit and Torah in 3.3 and 6 became entrapped within a sequence of interlinked and disputed issues. Was an echo of Jer. 31.31–33 intended in 3.3 and 6?[20] If so, did Paul think of the 'new covenant' as a writing of the law upon the heart (Jer. 31.33), and therefore identify the Spirit's writing upon the human heart (3.3) with the law thus internalised, the circumcision of the heart (Deut. 30.6; Phil. 3.3)? And how to correlate the concept 'Torah/law', which Paul nowhere uses in 2 Cor., and the term actually used here, γράμμα? Which led in turn to questions of the relation between Torah and γραφή, and between Torah and the νόμος Χριστοῦ of Gal. 6.2. The problem of getting the right balance between continuity and discontinuity in Paul's thought seemed to be as intractable here as anywhere in Paul, if not more so.

3.4   The papers and discussions on Romans naturally posed many of the same issues. Out of the session on Rom. 2 (Wright) there emerged substantial agreement that the indictment of the 'Jew' (2.17) came within and as part of Paul's indictment of humanity at large (Rom. 2 as following on from Rom. 1.18–32, and leading into 3.1–20); that Paul's indictment embraced both the

---

[20] For a positive response and other bibliography see e.g. V.P. Furnish, *II Corinthians* (AB 32A; New York: Doubleday, 1984) 181, 183–4, 196–7; F. Thielman, *Paul and the Law* (Downers Grove, Ill: InterVarsity (1994) 110–1 and n. 32.

sense of privilege (2.4, 9–11, 13–16, 17–20, 25) and the actual law-breaking of 'the Jew' (2.1–3, 9, 12–13, 21–27); and that the idea of justification includes both the decisive act of the 'already', but also the still final judgment (2.12–13). But unclarity remains on the degree to which 2.16 (gospel judgment) qualifies or merely restates in another form the judgment spoken of in 2.12–15 (law judgment).[21] And discussion became stuck on the unresolved issue of whether the law-doing Gentile of 2.14, 26–27 was a real or hypothetical figure and whether he was or could (in Paul's view) only be a Christian Gentile.[22]

3.5 With the paper and discussion on Rom. 3–4 (Hays) came agreement that we have to speak of several functions of the law, including that of defining Israel as God's people and the importance of works of the law within this framework. There was also agreement on the richness of the concept of the law; it is a unity, not a chameleon; νόμος is also γραφή. But on the continuity/discontinuity question the same issues could not be resolved: how to relate the positive affirmation of Torah/γραφή as a witness to God's way of 'righteousing' (3.21; 4) with a 'righteousing apart from the law' introduced as a new/eschatological development (νυνὶ δέ – 3.21), and how to correlate the νόμος πίστεως of 3.27 with the faith-establishing-law/Torah of 3.31 (a question to which we must return).[23]

Not least of the Symposium's unattained goals was the unresolved question of how to relate the crucial text, 4.4–5,[24] to Paul's on-going argument and particularly to what he says about the law, both the negative and the positive thrust of the preceding verses just alluded to. Fundamental to Paul's gospel of justification is obviously his understanding of God as 'he who justifies the ungodly', including 'him who does not work but believes in' God so understood. But would this come as a total shock and as an unacceptable theological proposition to Christian Jews, or Jews at large? How would they or Paul relate it to his understanding of 'the righteousness of God', so completely based as it was on the theological affirmations of the Psalms and Second Isaiah in particular?[25] There was an interesting debate on the significance of narrative at this point, and on the degree to which we should speak of correspondence more than of continuity (a synchronic or a diachronic reading of the whole chapter). But the questions with which the Symposium began remained on the table.

---

[21] See the helpful discussion by Stuhlmacher, *Römer* 44–6.

[22] In recent years the issue was posed must sharply by C.E.B. Cranfield, *Romans* (ICC: Edinburgh: T. & T. Clark, 1975) 156–7.

[23] See below § 3.7.

[24] Were it necessary to underline the centrality of this text to the debate on Paul and the law, S. Westerholm would have done so firmly enough in his *Israel's Law and the Church's Faith* (Grand Rapids: Eerdmans, 1988); see also Schreiner 51–5, 97–8.

[25] See above n. 2.

3.6   The paper by Hofius on Rom. 5 posed the issue of discontinuity with his customary forcefulness. For in the sharp antithesis between Adam and Christ, the law/Torah seems to belong wholly on the side of Adam, on the side of sin and death. The law makes sin accountable and binds the sinner more firmly to death (5.13–14). Most incriminating of all, 'the law came in to increase the trespass', establishing all the more firmly sin's reign in death (5.20–21). Here again we have an apocalyptic or eschatological antithesis: two ages/epochs different in character and effect, the one characterised by law increasing sin reinforcing death, and the other characterised by Christ embodying grace producing life. And for Paul the new age/epoch of Christ has superceded the old age of law. Hence Rom. 10.4: 'Christ is the end of the law as a means to righteousness for all who believe' (10.4).

The discussion here was hampered by failure to achieve agreement on the relation between 'sin' as power and 'sin' as sinful action, and therefore on the relation between sin and death. As ever the precise force of ἐφ' ᾧ in 5.12 remains obscure. More important for the objectives of the Symposium, crucial questions had to be left hanging. In particular, how far one can generalise from the rhetorically impressed antitheses of Rom. 5 and apply the generalisation as an overarching principle elsewhere in Romans.[26] Putting the same point another way, does Rom. 5.12–21 provide a rounded statement of Paul's view of the law? Is it only one aspect of the law which Paul had in mind at this point or what might be described as the essence of the law? How should one relate the shocking assertion of 5.20 to the positive affirmations elsewhere in the letter, not least 3.31, 7.12–13 and 8.4?

3.7   The multiplicity of questions posed by Rom. 7 (Hübner) prevented a full discussion of the passage. It was agreed that Rom. 7 was intended by Paul as a defence of the law, but the Symposium was unable to develop that point of consensus very far. There was an interesting debate on the question of reading Rom. 7 in context, that is, both in reference to the flow of thought from chapters 5 to 8, and in reference to a Jewish and/or philosophical background. The former has clearly to be acknowledged: if Rom. 7 is a defence of the law, it must function as such in relation not least to the negative portrayal of the law which has built up in the preceding chapters and verses. But surprisingly, 7.1–6, with its clear implication of discontinuity between old epoch and new, was not really brought into the discussion, and the relation of 5.20 to 7.7–8.4 was not really followed through. At the same time, setting Rom. 7 within a wider philosophical discussion is a reminder that the issue of continuity/discontinuity of Paul's gospel with his Jewish heritage is itself part of a wider and deeper appreciation of the anthropological tension between willing and doing. The discussion, however, became caught up in the old dispute over the extent to

---

[26] See further below § 4.5.

which the chapter was retrospective – Paul's Christian view of (his old) life under sin (again implying greater discontinuity), or also of his own life still as a believer (implying greater continuity).[27]

For my own part, two crucial issues do emerge. First, the question cannot be avoided, whether the defence of the law in Rom. 7 functions also as a defence against the charge Paul himself brought against the law in 5.20 (and implicitly in 7.6). The argument from 7.7 through to and climaxing in 8.4 surely attempts to get the law 'off the hook' as being not a willing ally of sin but rather sin's (unwitting) tool. Despite all that Paul has said, the law still remains 'the law of God', 'holy and just and good', unveiling the deceitfulness and sinfulness of sin even when being abused by sin (7.7–13), still a delight to the inner self and a proper aspiration for the willing 'I' (7.22, 25). And above all, according to 8.3–4, the purpose of God in sending his Son was 'in order that the requirement of the law might be fulfilled in us who walk ... in accordance with the Spirit' – an astonishing assertion if the law belonged so exclusively to the age of Adam and to the power of sin and death.

The other issue is again the question posed in reference to 3.27 – the meaning of νόμος πίστεως. Here the question becomes the meaning of the similar phrase in 8.2, 'the νόμος of the Spirit of life'. On my view, this phrase shows that Paul can use νόμος very positively – 'the law of the Spirit of life' (8.2) being a summary way of speaking of the law fulfilled in those who walk in accordance with the Spirit (8.4), 8.3–4 functioning, as the γάρ indicates, to explain the logic and force of 8.2. There is for Paul a function of the law apart from its function as the tool of sin and death ('the law of sin and death'). On Räisänen's view, in contrast, νόμος in the phrase 'the νόμος of the Spirit of life' cannot be understood as attributing such a positive role to the law, and so has to be understood as meaning 'rule' or 'principle', or, (Räisänen's preference) '(saving) order'.[28] Either way, however, the flexibility of the concept νόμος is considerable, and that must have important implications for Paul's theology of νόμος which the posing of 'law' and 'principle' as *alternatives* may not adequately reflect.

3.8   The discussion of Rom. 9–11, initiated by Westerholm's paper, ran into similar problems. It was helpful to be reminded that the question of the law was part of a much larger issue, though it meant that most of the discussion was on the larger issue rather than on the law![29] A salutary question drew atten-

---

[27] The most recent full treatment is by J. Lambrecht, *The Wretched "I" and its Liberation: Paul in Romans 7 and 8* (Louvain: Peeters, 1992).

[28] H. Räisänen, 'The "Law" of Faith and the Spirit', *Jesus, Paul and Torah. Collected Essays* (JSNTS 43; Sheffield: Sheffield Academic, 1992) ch. 2; see also Schreiner 35–6; Thielman 183 with 293 n. 71, and 200 with 297 n. 24 (with further bibliography).

[29] In view of its importance in the gospel/law antithesis, more, attention should have been given to 10.4 than time or the run of discussion permitted.

tion to the horizon of Paul's thought: the focal point may be *Israel*, but is not the *horizon* the larger question of the character of God's mercy? Is the issue in Rom. 9–11 Israel, or God? Certainly it would appear that this was where the issue of continuity/discontinuity 'bit' most deeply for Paul himself. The implication of continuity in 9.4–5 seems to be decisively countered or qualified by the thematic affirmation of discontinuity of 9.6 ('Not all those descended from Israel are "Israel"'), and by the growing recognition through the three chapters that those now caught in the dark shadow of God's electing purpose seem to be Paul's own Israelite contemporaries. And yet Paul can still conclude that 'all Israel shall be saved' (11.26), in a strong reassertion of continuity in the divine purpose (11.29).

The tensions within and between the chapters were clearly highlighted by Räisänen's response in particular. How typical is the idea of election in Paul's thought? Is it quite the same as his teaching on justification by faith (where does faith come in in the final denouement of 11.26, 31–32)? Do Rom. 9–11 contain special pleading? In short, do these chapters reveal the impossibility of Paul holding together both the integrity of his gospel and his despairing belief in the faithfulness of God to Israel? My own answer, that for Paul 'Israel' is *defined* by grace, by divine call (Rom. 9.6–13),[30] is presumably at least a partial answer, but did not succeed in convincing the Symposium as a whole.

But again the Symposium was unable to bring further clarity to the role of the law within this complex area of debate. Does the law belong on the side of the discontinuity, or on the side of continuity? And if Paul's exposition is caught up in irreconcilable inconsistency, is the same true of his understanding of the law within the whole process? Discontinuity seems to be asserted with all vigour in the famous 10.4, though had Paul wished to denigrate the law as he did in 5.20, one might have expected that he would tie the law in to the process of Israel's hardening, the law as part of their entrapment (11.7–10). In contrast, however, Paul had also affirmed that the law is one of Israel's great privileges (9.4). Moreover, to the surprise of many translators and commentators, Paul can talk of the 'νόμος of righteousness' as a proper goal for Israel to have pursued and which they failed to attain only because they pursued it in the wrong way (9.31–32).[31] And it can hardly be coincidence that his exposition of 'the righteousness which is from faith' used a passage which had affirmed the ease of doing the law (Deut. 30.11–14) and which had already been interpreted of the heavenly wisdom embodied in the Torah (Bar. 3.29–30, 4.1).[32]

---

[30] See my *Romans* 539–40.

[31] RSV/NRSV typify the surprise felt by many commentators when they translate νόμον δικαιοσύνης as 'the righteousness which/that is based on (the) law'.

[32] See further my *Romans* 603–5; Thielman 208–10.

We still have the final sessions of the Symposium to review, but the reflections on the discussion of Rom. 9–11 provide a particularly appropriate place to make the transition to the final section of this paper, since the passage expresses so clearly the problems and tensions with which the commentator on Paul's theology has to wrestle.

4. Towards common ground?

4.1   The search for common ground in such a controversial area is rendered difficult, some might say impossible, by two factors which came up at different points in the discussions of the Symposium.

The first is whether Paul in fact managed to achieve complete consistency in what is, in effect, his own plea for continuity. The question was posed particulary in the discussions of Rom. 2 and (as we have just noted) Rom. 9–11. It is partly a problem of how we today 'hear' a text like Rom. 2. Should our exegetical assumption necessarily be that Paul's thinking in this chapter was and can be shown today to be consistent with what he wrote elsewhere? One side of that is the problem of recognizing the rhetorical character of what Paul wrote: how to allow most judiciously for an argument slanted to catch the attention of a particular group, for what we might call loud- or soft-peddling in the replaying of a particular theme, for dramatic or stylistic effect in tightly worded passages, and so on? The other side is that our questions may be so much the more determined by issues subsequent to Paul's writing that they are not actually resolvable from what Paul actually says, and may in fact be misleading if it is Paul's theology we wish to uncover. Does our constant search for new analytical or synthetic categories, like 'covenantal nomism' and 'narrative', simply pull the threads of Paul's thought into another pattern of our own designing?

A second problem which emerged with force towards the end of the Symposium is the distinction between Paul's *intention* in his theology and the actual *effect* of his mission. Here the papers and discussion on 1 Cor. 9 (Barton) and Rom. 14–15 (Barclay) were of particular interest. Not only because they highlighted afresh the importance of the social context and its dynamic for our own understanding of Paul's theology in these passages. But also because they posed the issue of whether Paul's strategy inevitably provoked a *social instability* which was bound to work against his *theological ideal*. Would not Paul's policy as stated in 1 Cor. 9.19–23 inevitably have seemed to lack integrity and to have caused confusion to those whose identity was constituted by their being 'under the law'? And in Rom. 14 the appearance of even-handedness is similarly misleading. Paul seemed to be asking more of Gentile believers (who had already shifted from a Gentile frame of reference), but was in fact asking more of Jewish believers (who had not yet shifted from their traditional frame of reference). How could Paul claim both that the law is holy and that nothing is unclean? No doubt he saw behind the two claims a higher logic, but the social reality was that his teaching undermined the social and cultural integrity of the observant Jewish believer.[33]

More fundamental still, by putting circumcision and uncircumcision on the same level of irrelevance (1 Cor. 7.19a, etc.) Paul cut at the root of the identity of those whom he himself called simply 'the circumcision'. Was this the only way for the Christian Jew to go? Could the continuity be maintained only by those who followed Paul's example? In the event, the restructuring of Jewish identity which Paul's gospel called for proved totally unacceptable to the great bulk of his fellow Jews. In other words, the theological question posed by Paul's gospel cannot be resolved solely at the level of ideas and doctrines. And if the social reality of Jewish identity proved an effective stumbling block even among sympathetic Jewish believers, how much less realistic were Paul's hopes regarding Israel as a whole?

The search for common ground, therefore, whether as common ground among present-day interpreters of Paul's writings, or as common ground between Paul himself and his fellow Christian Jews, may be a search for an ideal which Paul himself was unable to achieve and which we today are unable fully to appreciate. Nevertheless, if only out of respect for Paul and for the greatness of his vision, something can and should be said.

4.2   Let us begin with what has usually been regarded as a major expression of Paul's gospel, namely, justification by faith.[34] Although its centrality in Paul's thought has been periodically questioned, it is certainly the teaching of Paul which made the law a problem for Paul's theology, if questions like those posed in Rom. 3.31 ('Do we make the law invalid through faith?') and 7.7 ('Is the law sin?') signal more than 'mere rhetoric'. And it is the doctrine of justification by faith which continues to pose that problem most sharply for contemporary interpreters of Paul. From the Symposium's discussions several threads of agreement can be brought together.

a) The question of justification arises as an issue in Paul's letters within the context of his mission to the Gentiles.[35] The question as posed, particularly in Galatians and Romans, is whether, and if so how, Gentiles may be accounted

---

[33] However, the argument is pushed much too far by F. Watson, *Paul, Judaism and the Gentiles: A Sociological Approach* (SNTSMS 56; Cambridge University, 1986).

[34] We need only recall how Luther, and in this century Bultmann and Käsemann, regarded 'justification by faith' as the fundamental principle of the gospel; see particularly J. Reumann, *Righteousness in the New Testament* (Philadelphia: Fortress/New York: Paulist. 1982).

[35] Here we may say that the arguments of W. Wrede, *Paul* (London: Philip Green, 1907) 122–8, and K. Stendahl, *Paul Among Jews and Gentiles* (Philadelphia: Fortress, 1976/London: SCM, 1977) particularly 1–7, have carried the day.

acceptable to God, whether, and if so how, they may come to share in the blessings of Abraham and of the chosen people. To be noted is the fact that the issue as discussed by Paul is not about whether and how Gentiles might be deemed acceptable to God without reference to father Abraham and his seed – a possible reading of Rom. 2 but only if taken in isolation from the rest of the letter. Nor does it matter at this point who first raised the issue of Gentile believers sharing in Abraham's seed and inheritance (Paul himself or other Christian Jewish missionaries in Galatia).[36] The crucial point for us is that this issue is the context in which Paul's major expositions of justification take place.

b) Underlying this specific contingent issue (whether and how Gentiles may be accounted acceptable to God) is the more fundamental theological assertion of divine initiative and human helplessness. This is implicit in the apocalyptic perspective from which Paul views the whole process of God's purpose of salvation; it is not simply a healing and a cleansing which is necessary, but a whole new act of creation, a giving of life to the dead and a calling into existence what had no existence (Rom. 4.17). And it is explicit in the universal indictment of Rom. 1–3, as crystallised not least in Rom. 4.4–5.

c) Both aspects are reflected in the term 'sinner'. Partly as a question of Jews regarding Gentiles as outside the people of God ('sinners' – Gal. 2.15); and partly also as the question of actual sin with the consequent liability to condemnation. The way in which the issue is posed in Eph. 2.11-12 may well express a genuinely Pauline synthesis of both aspects: uncircumcised Gentiles were by definition *both* aliens from the commonwealth of Israel, strangers to the covenants of promise, *and* separated from Christ, having no hope and without God in the world.

4.3   The degree of continuity between Paul's gospel of justification and central emphases not only in the OT but also within Second Temple Judaism can also be sketched in a broad outline which commands a fair degree of consensus.

a) Characteristic of both Paul and his Jewish heritage is the common recognition that standing with God depends on the initiative of divine grace. Israel's identity was determined from the first by divine election and call. Deuteronomy as the classic expression of 'covenantal nomism' starts from the recognition of Israel's slave status, without any claim on God, at the time of God's choice (Deut. 5.6; 6.21; 7.6–8; etc.). As noted already, Paul's understanding of the διχιαοσύνη Θεοῦ is derived directly from the fundamental theological assertions on the theme in Israel's scriptures (above n. 2).

b) Equally characteristic of both Paul and his Jewish heritage is the other side of covenantal nomism – that is, the insistence that certain obligations fol-

---

[36] This in response to J.L. Martyn, 'A Law-Observant Mission to Gentiles: The Background of Galatians', *SJT* 38 (1985) 307–24.

low for those who have been recipients of this grace. Paul insists on the ethical corollary and consequences of God's choice and acceptance as strongly as the Deuteronomist, with the equal recognition on the part of both that the necessary obedience has to be from the heart. For Paul as much as Deuteronomy 'righteousness' in effect sums up both sides of covenantal nomism, both the saving action of God and the obligation of obedience to that righteousness (e.g. Rom. 6.18–19).[37]

c) And Paul would certainly insist that his own commission to preach the gospel to the Gentiles was in fulfilment of Israel's own obligation to be a light to the Gentiles. He implies as much in Gal. 1.15–16 with its clear echo of Isa. 49.1–6 and Jer. 1.5, his conversion being understood by him to be wholly in the tradition of the call and commissioning of Israel's prophets.[38] As Gal. 3.8 also indicates, he focuses the apologia for his gospel in the third strand of the promise to Abraham: the promise not only of seed and of land, but also of blessing to the nations (Gen. 12.3 etc.). What Israel had not yet fully delivered Paul saw to be his task, but precisely as the fulfilment of Israel's task.

It is within this continuity that the issue of discontinuity is posed. For what separates and marks out Paul's theology of grace from that of his Jewish contemporaries is, of course, his sense (in common with other Christian voices of the NT) that the decisive eschatological climax has already come in the death and resurrection of Jesus. I say 'within this continuity', since Paul hardly sees the coming of Christ as a disruption or abandoning of the divine purpose as expressed through Abraham and Israel. If the apocalyptic perspective signals discontinuity it also signals climax. Nevertheless, for all Paul's assertions of continuity here too, the practical effect was that the terms of grace, the basis of acceptance before God, had in his view shifted with the coming of Israel's Messiah. However much the faith called for was like the faith of Abraham, it was now faith focused in and through Christ Jesus, a cause of stumbling for the bulk of Israel (Rom. 9.32–33). And the theological/christological discontinuity was mirrored in the sociological discontinuity reflected in Rom. 14–15, despite Paul's continuing ideal (15.7–12).

4.4   It is within this larger theological picture, with its measure of common ground opened up, and with full recognition of the tensions it contains, that the question of Paul and the law must be resolved if at all.

We may start with the least controversial point: that there is a spectrum in Paul's references to the law, a spectrum running from what sounds a highly positive approbation to what sounds a highly negative condemnation. On the one hand, in his defence of the law, Paul does not hesitate to describe it as

---

[37] Thielman 238–41 is part of the growing consensus on these first two points; contrast Schreiner 114–21.

[38] The point is only partially grasped by K.O. Sandnes, *Paul – One of the Prophets?* (WUNT 2.43; Tübingen: Mohr, 1991) 56–69.

'holy, just and good' (Rom. 7.12), a very positive gift of God (Rom. 9.4); the recognition of such a positive affirmation does not depend, it should be noted, on the disputed interpretation of the phrase, 'the νόμος of the Spirit of life' later on in the same section (Rom. 8.2). On the other hand, he clearly speaks of the law as an enslaving power, increasing the trespass and used by sin to bring about death (Gal. 4.1–10; Rom. 5.20; 7.5; 1 Cor. 15.56).[39]

Coordinated with this is the further recognition that for Paul the law has a variety of functions. Three of these call for comment.

The first is the role of the law in disclosure of the will of God, with consequent awareness or consciousness of sin. Somewhat surprisingly Paul says nothing of this function in Galatians. And when in Romans he refers to it repeatedly (Rom. 3.20; 4.15; 5.13; 7.13), he does so as to an established axiom which no one would question and which he therefore did not have to argue for. This function is obviously related to that of condemning sin, as indicated in 4.15, and is thus also the function referred to in 2.12–13.

This might seem to be the most negative feature of the law – its function in bringing about divine wrath, in condemning transgression, in cursing the one who fails to do all that is written in the book of the law (Gal. 3.10). But this is simply part of its God-given purpose, which Paul takes for granted. Certainly at the heart of Paul's gospel is the claim that Christ brings deliverance from the coming wrath (Rom. 5.9), that there is no condemnation for those in Christ (Rom. 8.1), and that Christ has redeemed from the curse of the law (Gal. 3.13). But that is not entirely a point of discontinuity. The law itself also provided for forgiveness and atonement as David attested (Rom. 4.7–8); Abraham was justified by faith long before the coming of Christ. There is continuity here too.

Does this taken-for-grantedness of the law's function in bringing sin to conscious transgression and condemnation give us a clue? Here is a function which the law had from the beginning (5.13; 7.13), and which, for Paul, it evidently still has (3.20; 4.15) and will have in the final judgment, or so the argument of Rom. 2.12–16 seems to indicate. Paul continues to affirm, or rather to assume this function of the law, even in the midst of his more negative comments about the law. However, because this function is part of the common ground which he shared with his fellow (Christian) Jews he saw no need to elaborate it. Whereas, it was the more controversial negative comments for which he had to argue, and as a result of which he had to mount an elaborate (but for us confusing) defence of the law.

The question thus arises whether we have been misled by this imbalance of Paul's exposition. That is to say, has our attention been distracted by the greater emphasis given to the negative function of the law, and have we failed to give sufficient weight to the continuing function of the law in making con-

---

[39] See e.g. Schreiner ch. 3.

scious of and condemning sin, simply because the latter is alluded to so briefly in the midst of other argumentation? In classic treatments the law's role in making conscious of sin and condemning sin leads directly into its role in inciting sin (Rom. 5.20; 7.7–11);[40] but it is only the latter on which Paul mounts his defence of the law (7.7–8.4). Ought not the two functions to be held more distinct in Paul's thought – one affirmed by Paul without question, the other seen by him as an issue calling for a defence of the law?

4.5   A second function of the law, which was generally recognized in the Symposium's discussion, was its role in marking out the people of God. This is indicated for example in Paul's distinction between those who have and 'those who do not have the law' (Rom. 2.12–14), and by this talk of Israel as 'under the law' (as in Gal. 3.23–24)[41] and of the 'Jew' as marked out by his boasting in the law (Rom. 2.23). Paul is obviously critical of this role of the law, a fact which gives rise to several important questions.

a) First, how negative is his criticism of this function of the law? The imagery he uses in Gal. 3.23–4.2 is essentially positive: a protective garrison, the custodian-tutor (παιδαγωγός), the heir under guardians and stewards.[42] The imagery is not far from that used in the Letter of Aristeas 139–42 already referred to (§ 2.3).

b) Second, Paul clearly sees this function of the law as essentially *temporary*, until the coming of Christ and the possibility of faith in him (Gal. 3.22–25; 4.3–7). How much of Paul's negative assessment of the law is focused on this temporary function of the law? And does his criticism amount to a criticism of his fellow Jews for wanting to preserve this function and to remain within the law's protective custody as minors, no better than slaves, when the eschatological moment has come for the transition to full sonship, for the heir to enter his heritage?

Here it needs to be observed that it is when the question shifts to what such an attitude says about Gentile participation in Israel's heritage that the issue of works of the law comes to the fore, as Gal. 2.15–16, Rom. 3.27–30 and Rom. 9.30–32 all indicate: Gal. 2.15–16 – the statement provoked by Christian Jews who will not eat with Christian Gentiles; Rom. 3.27–30 – boasting in works of the law as tantamount to affirming that God is God of Jews only; Rom. 9.30–32 – Gentiles attained raighteousness from faith, but Israel failed to attain the law of righteousness because they pursued it as if it was a matter of works. Is this the primary reason why Paul opposes justification by faith against justifi-

---

[40] I am thinking of R. Bultmann, *Theology of the New Testament* Vol. 1 (London: SCM, 1952) 261–8; Cranfield, *Romans* 846–8.

[41] The suggestion of L. Gaston, 'Paul and the Torah', *Paul and the Torah* (Vancouver: University of British Columbia, 1987) 29–30, that Paul used the phrase, 'under the law' 'to designate the Gentile situation' is simply incredible.

[42] For detailed exposition I may refer simply to my *Galatians, ad loc.*

cation by works? – because justification by works of the law is another way of
saying Israel has clung too long to the protective status of the law which set
Israel apart from the other nations? Even if that is not the whole answer, it
surely must be a significant part of the answer.[43]

Rom. 5.20 also needs to be correlated under this head. For on the one hand
it has in view the entry of the law within the processes of human history, that
is to Israel's history through Moses (5.13). Its function within the age of Adam
is not distinct from its role in relation to Israel (cf. 7.7–13).[44] And on the other
hand, as already observed, the defence of the law in 7.7–8.4 must have the
charge of 5.20 in view as well, and must therefore serve as Paul's own answer
to that charge (above § 3.7). The law in its role as the (unwitting) agent of sin
and death is also not distinct from its role in relation to Israel.

c) Third, underlying this more specific issue which so absorbed Paul is the
more fundamental issue of human dependence wholly on divine grace. Here
the crucial text Rom. 4.4–5 comes centre stage. The issue is of sufficient importance to warrant a separate section.

4.6   With Rom. 4.4–5 the question has to be posed: however much the preceding exposition (3.27–31) was focused on the relation of Jew and Gentile
within the justifying purposes of God, does the issue here not clearly become
the impossibility of human endeavour to achieve God's favour and the fundamentally flawed character of the theology which claims otherwise?[45]

The answer is probably Yes! The question is, however, whether such a conclusion runs counter to the theology of the law built up in the preceding paragraphs. Do we have in Rom. 4.4–5 a concept of 'works of the law' at odds with
the correlation between 'works of the law' and the issue of Gentile acceptability
just noted? Not necessarily so. Here the earlier question, already asked above,
also comes into play: would this statement (Rom. 4.4–5) come as a total shock
and as an unacceptable theological proposition to Christian Jews, or Jews at
large? For my own part, the more probable answer has to be No! And the degree
of agreement noted above (§§ 4.2b and 4.3a) points to the same conclusion.

In other words, the proposition of Rom. 4.4–5 was probably *not* at issue
between Paul and his fellow Christian Jews (or Jews in general). This was in

---

[43] At this point, of course, I am drawing on my own thesis regarding 'works of the law' in
Paul, though at this point in a noncontroversial way, I hope. See e.g. my 'Yet Once More –
"The Works of the Law": A Response', *JSNT* 46 (1992) 99–117; also '4QMMT and Galatians', forthcoming in *NTS*. That the thesis can be fruitful for Jewish reassessment of Paul is
indicated by A.F. Segal, *Paul the Convert: The Apostolate and Apostasy of Saul the Pharisee*
(New Haven: Yale University, 1990) particularly 124, and D. Boyarin, *A Radical Jew: Paul
and the Politics of Identity* (Berkeley: University of California, 1994) e.g. 52–6.

[44] I am more open than I was in *Romans* 383 to the likelihood that Rom. 7.9–11 includes
an allusion to Israel's own fall into sin and death as well as that of humankind at large; see
e.g. Thielman 295 n. 15.

[45] See above n. 24.

fact part of the common ground that Paul could take for granted, like his understanding of 'the righteousness of God' (§§ 2.1, 4.3a). That, presumably, is
why Paul did not need to argue the point but could simply assert it without
argument – because he was confident it would not be disputed by any typically
Jewish reader. That is to say, Paul restates the theologoumenon in 4.4–5, not
(so much) because it was contested by his fellow (Christian) Jews, but more as
a reminder of what they themselves also regarded as fundamental in the establishment of a relationship between God and human beings.

Here we may see a parallel with the argument or repetition of the tactic used
a few verses earlier. In Rom. 3.27–30 Paul sets the problem of relating faith
and works at once into the context of the issue of Gentiles' acceptability to
God, and to resolve the question he appeals to a fundamental Jewish axiom:
that God is one (3.29–30). It was precisely because it was a Jewish axiom that
Paul appealed to it and could entertain good hope that this argument based on
it would have effect on Christian Jews. In like manner in 4.4–5 it makes best
sense to assume that Paul repeats the tactic by again appealing to a Jewish
axiom and drawing from it a deduction which his fellow Christian Jews could
be expected to acknowledge, even when applied to the more contentious question of 'works of the law' as it bore upon the Jew-Gentile issue.

In other words, it should be possible to hold together two conclusions which
have been set in contrast. One is that the issue of 'works of the law', like justification, arises in relation to the question whether and how Gentiles can be
reckoned acceptable to and by God, since (what Paul refers to as) 'works of the
law' served normally to reinforce the separateness of Israel from the other
nations. The second is that Rom. 4.4–5 exposes a more fundamental issue, as
Luther rightly saw – the error of thinking that God's acceptance of any person
was to be reckoned in terms of God's owing a debt to the latter rather than as
an act of divine grace. The only difference is that the latter was probably not in
dispute between Paul and other Christian Jews; it was more likely to be common ground, a reassertion as it was of another Jewish axiom. The real issue
between Paul and his opponents at this point was how the axiom works out in
the continuing Torah obligations of Christian Jews and in their relationships
with Gentile Christians. The fundamental theological axiom remains just that;
but it was not that which was at issue between Paul and his opponents.

The assertion of Rom. 4.4–5, in other words, is also like the assertion of the
first function of the law, as designed to bring about consciousness of sin (§
4.4). As the former point did not need to be argued, but merely stated as an
axiom (like the axiom of Jewish monotheism), so here the point does not need
to be argued but merely asserted, as one which no biblically based Jew would
wish to dispute. That point of basic agreement having been restated, the issue
of how Torah obedience relates to justification, given that God justifies by
faith, could be tackled. Or as we might say, the point of continuity having been

restated (the basic principle of God's righteousness as justifying grace), the issue of discontinuity could be confronted (what the new manifestation of God's life-giving power in the ressurection meant for Israel's special status before God and under the law).

4.7   Once the focus of Paul's negative critique of the law is thus clarified – as primarily directed against the prolongation or extension of its temporary function vis-a-vis Israel – it becomes easier to recognize a third function of the law which Paul sees as also continuing. This is its function of providing divine direction for life, now distinct from its function in keeping Israel separate from the other nations. That it still has a continuing function is clearly implicit in 1 Cor. 7.19b; 'neither circumcision is anything nor uncircumcision, but keeping the commandments of God'. The challenge of this text was pressed upon us by Tomson's paper. What are 'the commandments of God'? If they are not just the ten commandments, the Torah, then what are they? Did Paul have in mind a different kind of Halakah, or a different set of 'commandments' (of Christ)? The issue is posed equally by Rom. 13.9, and by the fact that Paul's own paraenesis (Halakah?) in a passage like Rom. 12.14–21 is so thoroughly impregnated with the paraenesis of Jewish wisdom.[46] And the assertions of such passages as Rom. 3.31, 8.4 and 13.8–10 surely cannot be discounted, or reduced to the love command, however much the love command informs and infuses the way the requirements of the law are to be fulfilled by the believer.[47]

And if this is so, then are we not back once again into a major point of continuity between the Testaments, and with the law itself, in this function at least, as the bridge? The fact is, as noted above (§§ 2.2, 4.3a, b), that Israel's covenantal nomism maintains a tension between divine grace and resulting human obligation, and that the tension is remarkably like the tension in Paul's own teaching, between justification by faith and 'faith working through love' (Gal. 5.6). The coming of Christ has changed the focus, but the balance of passages like Rom. 8.12–13 and Gal. 6.8, between *Gabe und Aufgabe*, is not so very different from the balance in Second Temple Judaism's Torah theology, characterised in § 2.2 as *Weisung zu Leben und Lebens-Weise*. A turn in the ages had indeed taken place for Paul, but the eschatological tension familiar in Pauline ethics, between the already and the not-yet, is not so very different from what we find in those prophets and writers who denounced superficial obedience and looked for obedience from the heart.[48]

---

[46]   For details see my *Romans* 738.

[47]   Compare and contrast the various wrestlings with the otherwise problematic character of Paul's conception of Christians 'fulfilling the law' – H. Hübner, *Das Gesetz bei Paulus* (Göttingen: Vandenhoeck, ²1980) 76–80; J.M.G. Barclay, *Obeying the Truth: A Study of Paul's Ethics in Galatians* (Edinburgh: T. & T. Clark, 1988) 135–42; Westerholm 201–5; Schreiner ch. 6.

[48]   More attention should be given to the observation of M.D. Hooker that 'in many ways, the pattern which Sanders insists is the basis of Palestinian Judaism fits exactly the Pauline

5. Conclusion

What can we conclude from all this? If the above lines of reflection are at all sound, then we do have to recognize a stronger line of continuity between the function of the law in OT and Second Temple Judaism and a continuing function for the law into the new age inaugurated by Christ. This is evident both in two of the law's functions as analysed above: (1) in making conscious of sin, in condemnation of transgression and in final judgment; (2) in providing continuing guidance for conduct and in expressing requirements of God which need to be fulfilled.

As to discontinuity, three things should be said. First, it follows from the discussion above that the gospel-law antithesis is only partially a feature of the continuity-discontinuity discussion. The law has always had the function of condemning transgression (a God-given function), and that function continues for believers. Forgiveness and atonement has always been a necessary desideratum in consequence of this function of the law, but forgiveness and atonement were available also before Christ. The discontinuity is the means by which that atonement has now been rendered effective (the death and resurrection of Christ) and the scope of that atonement enlarged (Gentiles as well as Jews). But that the Christ event counts as a denial or rebuke of this function of the law does not follow.

Second, the main thrust of Paul's negative attitude to the law seems to be directed against its function in separating Israel from the other nations. The irony here is that Paul's theological ideal ('Rejoice, O Gentiles, with his people' – Rom 15.9) seems to have run aground on the social reality of Israel's ethnic and religious identity.

Third, the primary theological issue in the continuity/discontinuity between OT and NT is thus not so much the law, but Christ. Or is even that quite accurate? Jesus is 'Christ' after all precisely as being Israel's Messiah. The problems arose, however, because his coming, and particularly his death and resurrection, seemed to raise the issue of the Gentiles in an unprecedented way, quickly establishing a logic which the Hellenists followed and which Paul first persecuted and then was converted to. Which, perhaps appropriately, brings us back to Paul's conversion, since it was there, in his own mind at least, that the intermingled ingredients of Christology, Israel and the Gentiles, and the law began to ferment in his mind, his mission and his theology.

---

pattern of Christian experience: God's saving grace evokes man's answering obedience' ('Paul and "Covenantal Nomism"', *From Adam to Christ: Essays on Paul* [Cambridge University, 1990] 157).

Bibliography

(1980–94)

ALETTI, J.-N., 'Rom 1.18–3.20: Incohérence ou cohérence de l'argumentation paulinienne?', *Biblica* 69 (1988) 47–62

BACHMANN, M., 'Rechtfertigung und Gesetzeswerke bei Paulus', *TZ* 49 (1993) 1–33

BADENAS, R., *Christ the End of the Law: Romans 10.4 in Pauline Perspective* (JSNTS 10; Sheffield: JSOT, 1985)

BANDSTRA, A.J., 'Paul and the Law: Some Recent Developments and an Extraordinary Book', *CTJ* 25 (1990) 249–61

BARCLAY, J.M.G., 'Paul and the Law: Observations on Some Recent Debates', *Themelios* 12 (1986–87) 5–15

–, *Obeying the Truth: A Study of Paul's Ethics in Galatians* (Edinburgh: T. & T. Clark, 1988)

BARRETT, C.K., 'Boasting (καυχᾶσθαι, κτλ.) in the Pauline Epistles', in *L'Apôtre Paul: Personnalité, Style et Conception du Ministère*, ed. A. Vanhoye (Leuven University, 1986) 363–8

BECHTLER, S.R., 'Christ, the Τέλος of the Law: The Goal of Romans 10:4' *CBQ* 56 (1994) 288–308

BEKER, J.C., *Paul the Apostle: The Triumph of God in Life and Thought* (Philadelphia: Fortress, 1980) 235–54

BELLEVILLE, L.L., '"Under Law": Structural Analysis and the Pauline Concept of Law in Galatians 3.21–4.11', *JSNT* 26 (1986) 53–78

BORGEN, P., 'Paul Preaches Circumcision and Pleases Men', in *Paul and Paulinism*, C.K. Barrett FS, ed. M.D. Hooker et al. (London: SPCK, 1982) 37–46

BOYARIN, D., *A Radical Jew: Paul and the Politics of Identity* (Berkeley: University of California, 1994)

BRASWELL, J.P., '"The Blessing of Abraham" versus "The Curse of the Law": Another Look at Gal. 3.10–13', *WTJ* 53 (1991) 73–91

BRUCE, F.F., 'The Curse of the Law', in *Paul and Paulinism*, C.K. Barrett FS, ed. M.D. Hooker et al. (London: SPCK, 1982) 27–36

–, 'Paul and the Law in Recent Research', in *Law and Religion: Essays on the Place of the Law in Israel and Early Christianity*, ed. B. Lindars (Cambridge: James Clarke, 1988) 115–25

CAMPBELL, W.S., *Paul's Gospel in an Intercultural Context: Jew and Gentile in the Letter to the Romans* (Frankfurt: Peter Lang, 1991)

CASSIRER, H.W., *Grace and Law: St Paul, Kant and the Hebrew Prophets* (Grand Rapids: Eerdmans, 1988)

COSGROVE, C.H., 'The Law has Given Sarah No Children (Gal. 4.21–30)', *NovT* 29 (1987) 219–35

–, 'The Mosaic Law Preaches Faith: A Study in Galatians 3', *WTJ* 41 (1987) 146–64
–, *The Cross and the Spirit: A Study in the Argument and Theology of Galatians* (Macon, Georgia: Mercer University, 1988)
CRANFIELD, C.E.B., *Romans* Vol. 2 (ICC; Edinburgh: T. & T. Clark, 1979) 845–62
–, 'Giving a Dog a Bad Name: A Note on H. Räisänen's *Paul and the Law*', *JSNT* 38 (1990) 77–85
–, '"The Works of the Law" in the Epistle to the Romans', *JSNT* 43 (1991) 89–101

DAVIES, G.N., *Faith and Obedience in Romans: A Study of Romans 1–4* (JSNTS 39; Sheffield: JSOT, 1990)
DAVIES, W.D., *Paul and Rabbinic Judaism* (Philadelphia: Fortress, [4]1981) Preface to Fourth Edition
DEIDUN, T.J., *New Covenant Morality in Paul* (AB 89; Rome: Biblical Institute, 1981)
–, 'E.P. Sanders: An Assessment of Two Recent Works: 1. 'Having His Cake and Eating It': Paul on the Law', *HeyJ* 27 (1986) 43–52
DONALDSON, T.L., 'The "Curse of the Law" and the Inclusion of the Gentiles: Galatians 3.13–14', *NTS* 32 (1986) 94–112
–, 'Zealot and Convert: The Origin of Paul's Christ-Torah Antithesis', *CBQ* 51 (1989) 655–82
DUNN, J.D.G., *Jesus, Paul and the Law: Studies in Mark and Galatians* (London: SPCK/Louisville: Westminster, 1990) – includes JD's essays on 'The Incident at Antioch (Gal. 2.11–18)', 'The New Perspective on Paul', 'Works of the Law and the Curse of the Law (Gal. 3.10–14)', and 'The Theology of Galatians'
–, 'What Was the Issue between Paul and "Those of the Circumcision"?', in *Paulus und das antike Judentum*, ed. M. Hengel & U. Heckel (WUNT 58; Tübingen: Mohr, 1991) 295–317
–, 'Yet Once More – ' "The Works of the Law": A Response', *JSNT* 46 (1992) 99–117
–, 'Echoes of Intra-Jewish Polemic in Paul's Letter to the Galatians', *JBL* 112 (1993) 459–77

ELLIOTT, N., *The Rhetoric of Romans: Argumentative Constraint and Strategy and Paul's Dialogue with Judaism* (JSNTS 45; Sheffield: JSOT, 1990)

FEUILLET, A., 'Loi de Dieu, Loi du Christ, et Loi de l'Esprit d'après les Épîtres pauliniennes', *NovT* 22 (1980) 29–65
FITZMYER, J.A., 'Paul and the Law', *To Advance the Gospel: New Testament Studies* (New York: Crossroad, 1981) 186–201
–, *Paul and His Theology: A Brief Sketch* (Englewood Cliffs, NJ: Prentice Hall, [2]1989) index 'law'
–, 'Paul's Jewish Background and the Deeds of the Law', *According to Paul: Studies in the Theology of the Apostle* (New York: Paulist, 1993) 18–35
–, *Romans* (AB 33: New York: Doubleday, 1993) 131–5

GARLINGTON, D.B., 'The Obedience of Faith in the Letter to the Romans' *WTJ* 52 (1990) 201–24 and 53 (1991) 47–72
–, *The Obedience of Faith: A Pauline Phrase in Historical Context* (WUNT 2.38; Tübingen: Mohr, 1991)
–, *Faith, Obedience and Perseverance: Aspects of Paul's Letter to the Romans* (WUNT 79; Tübingen: Mohr, 1994)

GASTON, L., *Paul and the Torah* (Vancouver: University of British Columbia, 1987) – includes LG's essays on 'Paul and the Torah', 'Paul and the Law in Galatians 2 and 3', 'Works of Law as a Subjective Genitive', 'For *All* Believers: The Inclusion of Gentiles as the Ultimate Goal of Torah in Romans', 'Israel's Misstep in the Eyes of Paul', and 'Paul and the Torah in 2 Corinthians 3'.

GORDON, T.D., 'Why Israel Did Not Obtain Torah-Righteousness: A Translation Note on Rom. 9.32', *WTJ* 54 (1992) 163–6

GUNDRY, R.H., 'Grace, Works, and Staying Saved in Paul', *Biblica* 66 (1985) 1–38

HALL, J., 'Paul, The Lawyer, on Law', *Journal of Law and Religion* 3.2 (1985) 1–49

HAMMERTON-KELLY, R.G., 'Sacred Violence and the Curse of the Law (Galatians 3.13): The Death of Christ as a Sacrificial Travesty', *NTS* 36 (1990) 98–118

–, 'Sacred Violence and "Works of Law": "Is Christ Then an Agent of Sin?" (Galatians 2.17)', *CBQ* 52 (1990) 55–75

HAYS, R.B., 'Christology and Ethics in Galatians: The Law of Christ', *CBQ* 49 (1987) 268–90

HEILIGENTHAL, R., *Werke als Zeichen: Untersuchungen zur Bedeutung der menschlichen Taten im Frühjudentum, Neuen Testament und Frühchristentum* (WUNT 2.9; Tübingen: Mohr, 1983)

HENGEL, M., 'Der vorchristliche Paulus', in *Paulus und das antike Judentum*, ed. M. Hengel & U. Heckel (WUNT 58; Tübingen: Mohr, 1991) 177–293 (particularly 283–9) = *The Pre-Christian Paul* (London: SCM/Philadelphia: TPI, 1991) particularly 79–84

HOFIUS, O., 'Das Gesetz des Mose und das Gesetz Christi', *ZTK* 80 (1983) 262–86

–, 'Gesetz und Evangelium nach 2. Korinther 3', *Paulusstudien* (WUNT 51; Tübingen: Mohr, 1989) 75–120

HOLLANDER, H.W. & HOLLEMANN, J., 'The Relationship of Death, Sin, and Law in 1 Cor. 15,56', *NovT* 35 (1993) 270–91

HONG, I.-G., *The Law in Galatians* (JSNTS 81; Sheffield: JSOT, 1993)

HOOKER, M.D., 'Paul and "Covenantal Nomism"', in *Paul and Paulinism*, C.K. Barrett FS, ed. M.D. Hooker et al. (London: SPCK, 1982) 47–56; reprinted in *From Adam to Christ: Essays on Paul* (Cambridge University, 1990) 155–64

HÜBNER, H., *Das Gesetz bei Paulus: Ein Beitrag zum Werden der paulinischen Theologie* (Göttingen: Vandenhoeck, [2]1980) = *Law in Paul's Thought* (Edinburgh: T. & T. Clark, 1984)

–, *Gottes Ich und Israel: Zum Schriftgebrauch des Paulus in Römer 9–11* (Göttingen: Vandenhoeck, 1984)

–, 'Was heißt bei Paulus "Werke des Gesetzes"?', in *Glaube und Eschatologie*, W.G. Kümmel FS, ed. E. Grasser et al. (Tübingen: Mohr, 1985) 123–33

–, *Biblische Theologie des Neuen Testaments. Band 2: Die Theologie des Paulus* (Göttingen: Vandenhoeck, 1993)

JEWETT, R., 'The Law and the Coexistence of Jews and Gentiles in Romans', *Interpretation* 39 (1985) 341–56

KALUSCHE, M., ' "Das Gesetz als Thema biblischer Theologie?" Anmerkungen zu einem Entwurf Peter Stuhlmachers', *ZNW* 77 (1986) 194–205

KERTELGE, K., *Grundthemen paulinischer Theologie* (Freiburg: Herder, 1991) – includes KK's essays on 'Autorität des Gesetzes und Autorität Jesu bei Paulus',

'Rechtfertigung aus Glauben und Gericht nach den Werken bei Paulus', 'Gesetz und Freiheit im Galaterbrief'

KERTELGE, K. ED., *Das Gesetz im Neuen Testament* (QD 108; Freiburg: Herder, 1986)

KIM, S., *The Origin of Paul's Gospel* (WUNT 2.4; Tübingen: Mohr, 1981) 269–311

KLEIN, G., 'Ein Sturmzentrum der Paulusforschung', *VuF* 33 (1988) 40–56

KLEIN, M.G., 'Gospel until the Law: Rom. 5.13–14 and the Old Covenant', *JETS* 34 (1991) 433–46

LAATO, T., *Paulus und das Judentum: Anthropologische Erwägungen* (Åbo: Åbo Academy, 1991)

LAMBRECHT, J., 'Why Is Boasting Excluded? A Note on Rom. 3.27 and 4.2', *ETL* 61 (1985) 365–9

–, 'Gesetzesverständnis bei Paulus', in *Das Gesetz im Neuen Testament*, ed. K. Kertelge (QD 108; Freiburg: Herder, 1986) 88–127

–, 'Transgressor by Nullifying God's Grace: A Study of Gal. 2.18–21', *Biblica* 72 (1991) 217–36

–, ED., *The Truth of the Gospel (Galatians 1.1–4.11)* (St. Paul's Abbey, Rome: Benedictina, 1993)

LARSSON, E., 'Paul: Law and Salvation', *NTS* 31 (1985) 425–36

LICHTENBERGER, H., 'Paulus und das Gesetz', in *Paulus und das antike Judentum*, ed. M. Hengel & U. Heckel (WUNT 58; Tübingen: Mohr, 1991) 361–78

LIEBERS, R., *Das Gesetz als Evangelium: Untersuchungen zur Gesetzeskritik des Paulus* (Zürich: Theologischer, 1989)

LINCOLN, A.T., 'Abraham Goes to Rome: Paul's Treatment of Abraham in Romans 4', in *Worship, Theology and Ministry in the Early Church*, R.P. Martin FS, ed. M.J. Wilkins & T. Paige (JSNTS 87; Sheffield: JSOT, 1992) 163–79

LINDARS, B., 'Paul and the Law in Romans 5–8: an Actantial Analysis', in *Law and Religion: Essays on the Place of the Law in Israel und Early Christianity*, ed. B. Lindars (Cambridge: James Clarke, 1988) 126–40

LINDEMANN, A., 'Die biblischen Toragebote und die paulinische Ethik', in *Studien zum Text und zur Ethik des Neuen Testaments*, ed. W. Schrage (Berlin: de Gruyter, 1986) 242–65

–, 'Die Gerechtigkeit aus dem Gesetz: Erwägungen zur Auslegung und zur Textgeschichte von Römer 10.5', *ZNW* 73 (1982) 231–50

LONGENECKER, B.L., *Eschatology and Covenant: A Comparison of 4 Ezra and Romans 1–11* (JSNTS 57; Sheffield: JSOT, 1991)

LÜDEMANN, G., *Paulus, der Heidenapostel. Band II: Antipaulinismus im frühen Christentum* (Göttingen: Vandenhoeck, 1983) = *Opposition to Paul in Jewish Christianity* (Minneapolis: Fortress, 1989)

–, *Paulus und das Judentum* (München: Kaiser, 1983)

LÜHRMANN, D., 'Paul and the Pharisaic Tradition', *JSNT* 36 (1989) 75–94

LULL, D.J., ' "The Law Was Our Pedagogue": A Study in Galatians 3.19–25', *JBL* 105 (1986) 481–98

MACCOBY, H., *Paul and Hellenism* (London: SCM/Philadelphia: TPI, 1991)

McHUGH, J., 'Galatians 2:11–14: Was Peter Right?', in *Paulus und das antike Judentum*, ed. M. Hengel & U. Heckel (WUNT 58; Tübingen: Mohr, 1991) 319–30

MARTENS, J.W., 'Romans 2.14–16: A Stoic Reading', *NTS* 40 (1994) 55–67

MARTIN, B.L., *Christ and the Law in Paul* (NovTSupp 62; Leiden: Brill, 1989)

MEEKS, W.A., 'Judgment and the Brother: Romans 14.1–15.13', in *Tradition and Interpretation in the New Testament*, E.E. Ellis FS, ed. G.F. Hawthorne & O. Betz (Grand Rapids: Eerdmans/Tübingen: Mohr, 1987) 290–300

MOO, D., ' "Law", "Works of the Law", and Legalism in Paul', *WTJ* 45 (1983) 73–100

–, 'Paul and the Law in the Last Ten Years', *SJT* 49 (1987) 287–307

MÜLLER, K., 'Gesetz und Gesetzeserfüllung im Frühjudentum', in *Das Gesetz im Neuen Testament*, ed. K. Kertelge (QD 108; Freiburg: Herder, 1986) 11–27

MUSSNER, F., *Die Kraft der Wurzel: Judentum – Jesus – Kirche* (Freiburg: Herder, 1989)

NIEBUHR, K.-W., *Heidenapostel aus Israel: die jüdische Identität des Paulus nach ihrer Darstellung in seinen Briefen* (Tübingen: Mohr, 1992)

OSTEN-SACKEN, P. VON DER, *Die Heiligkeit der Tora bei Paulus: Studien zum Gesetz bei Paulus* (München: Kaiser, 1989)

RÄISÄNEN, H., *Paul and the Law* (WUNT 29; Tübingen: Mohr, 1983)

–, 'Römer 9–11: Analyse eines geistigen Ringens', *ANRW* 2.25.4 (1987) 2891–939

–, *Jesus, Paul and the Torah: Collected Essays* (JSNTS 43; Sheffield: JSOT, 1992, largely overlapping with *The Torah and Christ* (Helsinki, 1986) – includes HR's 'Paul's Call Experience and his Later View of the Law', 'The "Law" of Faith and the Spirit', 'Paul's Word-play on *nomos*. A Linguistic Study', and 'Galatians 2.16 and Paul's Break with Judaism'.

REICKE, B., 'Pauls über das Gesetz', *TZ* 41 (1985) 237–57

REINBOLD, W., 'Paulus und das Gesetz: Zur Exegese von Röm 9.30–33', *BZ* 38 (1994) 253–64

REINMUTH, E., *Geist und Gesetz: Studien zu Voraussetzungen und Inhalt der paulinischen Paränese* (Berlin: Evangelische, 1985)

RHYNE, C.T., *Faith Establishes the Law* (SBLDS 55; Chico, CA: Scholars, 1981)

–, 'Nomos Dikaiosynes and the Meaning of Romans 10.4', *CBQ* 47 (1985) 486–99

RICHARDSON, P. & WESTERHOLM, S. EDS., *Law in Religious Communities in the Roman Period* (Waterloo, Ontario: Wilfrid Laurier University, 1991)

RIESNER, R., *Die Frühzeit des Apostels Paulus* (WUNT 71; Tübingen: Mohr, 1994)

SANDERS, E.P., *Paul, the Law, and the Jewish People* (Philadelphia: Westminster, 1983)

–, *Paul* (Oxford University, 1991) 84–100

SCHREINER, T.R., 'Is Perfect Obedience to the Law Possible? A Re-examination of Galatians 3.10', *JETS* 27 (1984) 151–60

–, 'Paul and Perfect Obedience to the Law: An Evaluation of the View of E.P. Sanders', *WTJ* 47 (1985) 245–78

–, 'The Abolition and Fulfilment of the Law in Paul', *JSNT* 35 (1989) 47–74

–, ' "Works of Law" in Paul', *NovT* 33 (1991) 214–44

–, *The Law and Its Fulfilment: A Pauline Theology of Law* (Grand Rapids: Baker, 1993)

SCOTT, J.M., ' "For as Many as Are of Works of the Law Are Under a Curse" (Galatians 3.10)', in *Paul and the Scripture of Israel*, ed. C.A. Evans & J.A. Sanders (JSNTS 83; Sheffield: JSOT, 1993) 187–221

SEGAL, A.F., 'Torah and *Nomos* in Recent Scholarly Discussion', *SR* 13 (1984) 19–27

–, *Paul the Convert: The Apostolate and Apostasy of Saul the Pharisee* (New Haven: Yale University, 1990) particularly chaps. 6 and 7

SEIFRID, M.A., *Justification by Faith: The Origin and Development of a Central Pauline Theme* (NovTSupp 68; Leiden: Brill, 1992)

SILVA, M., 'The Law and Christianity: Dunn's New Synthesis', *WTJ* 53 (1991) 339–53

SLOAN, R.B., 'Paul and the Law: Why the Law Cannot Save', *NovT* 33 (1991), 35–60

SMEND, R. & LUZ, U., *Gesetz* (Stuttgart: Kohlhammer, 1981) 89–112

SNODGRASS, K.R., 'Justification by Grace – to the Doers: An Analysis of the Place of Romans 2 in the Theology of Paul', *NTS* 32 (1986) 72–93

–, 'Spheres of Influence: A Possible Solution to the Problem of Paul and the Law', *JSNT* 32 (1988) 93–113

STANLEY, C.D., '"Under a Curse": A Fresh Reading of Galatians 3.10–14', *NTS* 36 (1990) 481–511

STEGEMANN, E.W., 'Die umgekehrte Tora: Zum Gesetzesverständnis des Paulus', *Judaica* 43 (1987) 4–20

STUHLMACHER, P., *Versöhnung, Gesetz und Gerechtigkeit: Aufsätze zur biblischen Theologie* (Göttingen: Vandenhoeck, 1981) = *Reconciliation, Law and Righteousness: Essays in Biblical Theology* (Philadelphia: Fortress, 1986) – includes PS's essays on 'Das Gesetz als Thema biblischer Theologie', and '"Das Ende des Gesetzes". Über Ursprung und Ansatz der paulinischen Theologie'.

–, 'Paul's Understanding of the Law in the Letter to the Romans', *SEA* 50 (1985) 87–104

–, *Biblische Theologie des Neuen Testaments. Band 1: Grundlegung von Jesus zu Paulus* (Göttingen: Vandenhoeck, 1992) .

THEISSEN, G., *Psychologische Aspekte paulinischer Theologie* (Göttingen: Vandenhoeck, 1983) = *Psychological Aspects of Pauline Theology* (Philadelphia: Fortress/ Edinburgh: T. & T. Clark, 1987) Parts 3 & 4

THIELMAN, F., *From Plight to Solution: A Jewish Framework for Understanding Paul's View of the Law in Galatians and Romans* (NovTSupp; Leiden: Brill, 1989)

–, 'The Coherence of Paul's View of the Law: The Evidence of First Corinthians', *NTS* 38 (1992) 235–53

–, *Paul and the Law: A Contextual Approach* (Downers Grove, IL.: InterVarsity, 1994)

THOMPSON, R.W., 'How Is the Law Fulfilled in Us? An Interpretation of Röm. 8.4', *LS* 11 (1986) 31–40

–, 'Paul's Double Critique of Jewish Boasting: A Study of Röm. 3.27 in its Context', *Biblica* 67 (1986) 520–31

TOMSON, P.J., *Paul and the Jewish Law: Halakha in the Letters of the Apostle to the Gentiles* (CRINT 3.1; Assen: Van Gorcum/Minneapolis: Fortress, 1990)

VOS, J.S., 'Die hermeneutische Antinomie bei Paulus (Galater 3.11–12; Römer 10.5–10)', *NTS* 38 (1992) 254–70

WALLACE, D.B., 'Galatians 3.19–20: A *Crux Interpretum* for Paul's View of the Law', *WTJ* 52 (1990) 225–45

WATSON, F., *Paul, Judaism and the Gentiles: A Sociological Approach* (SNTSMS 56; Cambridge University, 1986)

WATSON, N.M., 'Justified by Faith: Judged by Works – An Antinomy?', *NTS* 29 (1983) 202–21

WEDDERBURN, A.J.M., 'Paul and the Law', *SJT* 38 (1985) 613–22

WEIMA, J.A.D., 'The Function of the Law in Relation to Sin: An Evaluation of the View of H. Räisänen', *NovT* 32 (1990) 219–35

WELKER, M., 'Security of Expectations: Reformulating the Theology of Law and Gospel', *JR* 66 (1986) 237–60

WESTERHOLM, S., 'Letter and Spirit: The Foundation of Pauline Ethics', *NTS* 30 (1984) 229–48

–, *'Torah, nomos* and Law: A Question of "Meaning"', *SR* 15 (1986) 327–36

–, 'On Fulfilling the Whole Law (Gal. 5.14)', *SEA* 51–52 (1986–87) 229–37

–, *Israel's Law and the Church's Faith: Paul and His Recent Interpreters* (Grand Rapids: Eerdmans, 1988)

WILCKENS, U., 'Zur Entwicklung des paulinischen Gesetzesverständnis', *NTS* 28 (1982) 154–90

WINGER, M., *By What Law? The Meaning of Νόμος in the Letters of Paul* (SBLDS 128; Atlanta: Scholars, 1992)

WISCHMEYER, O., 'Das Gebot der Nächstenliebe bei Paulus: Eine traditionsgeschichtliche Untersuchung', *BZ* 30 (1986) 161–87

WRIGHT, N.T., *The Climax of the Covenant: Christ and the Law in Pauline Theology* (Edinburgh: T. & T. Clark, 1991)

YATES, R., 'Saint Paul and the Law in Galatians', *ITQ* 51 (1985) 105–24

YOUNG, N.H., 'Paidagogos: The Social Setting of a Pauline Metaphor', *NovT* 29 (1987) 150–76

ZELLER, D., 'Zur neueren Diskussion über das Gesetz bei Paulus', *TP* 62 (1987) 481–99

–, 'Tyrann oder Wegweiser? Zum paulinischen Verständnis des Gesetzes', *Bibel und Kirche* 48 (1993) 134–40

ZIESLER, J., *Pauline Christianity* (Oxford University, ²1990) ch. 6

List of Contributors

JOHN M. G. BARCLAY, Department of Biblical Studies, University of Glasgow, Great Britain

STEPHEN C. BARTON, Department of Theology, University of Durham, Great Britain

JAMES D. G. DUNN, Department of Theology, University of Durham, Great Britain

RICHARD B. HAYS, Divinity School, Duke University, Durham, USA

MARTIN HENGEL, Tübingen, Germany

OTFRIED HOFIUS, Evangelisch-theologisches Seminar, University of Tübingen, Germany

HANS HÜBNER, University of Göttingen, Germany

KARL KERTELGE, Seminar für Exegese des Neuen Testaments, University of Münster, Germany

JAN LAMBRECHT, Leuven, Belgium

HERMANN LICHTENBERGER, Institut für antikes Judentum und hellenistische Religionsgeschichte, University of Tübingen, Germany

BRUCE W. LONGENECKER, University of Cambridge, Great Britain

HEIKKI RÄISÄNEN, Vantaa, Finland

GRAHAM STANTON, Department of Theology, King's College, Strand, London, Great Britain

PETER J. TOMSON, Amsterdam, Netherlands

STEPHEN WESTERHOLM, Department of Religious Studies, McMaster University, Hamilton, Canada

N. TOM WRIGHT, Dean of Lichfield, Great Britain

Index of Biblical and Other Ancient Sources

Subject Index

Index of Modern Authors